PSYCHO BUSTERS

4

**Story by
Yuya Aoki**

**Manga by
Akinari Nao**

Translated and adapted by
Stephen Paul

Lettered by
North Market Street Graphics

DEL
REY

Ballantine Books ∗ New York

Psycho Busters volume 4 is a work of fiction. Names, characters, places, and incidents are the products of the author's imagination or are used fictitiously. Any resemblance to actual events, locales, or persons, living or dead, is entirely coincidental.

A Del Rey Manga/Kodansha Trade Paperback Original

Published in the United States by Del Rey, an imprint of The Random House Publishing Group, a division of Random House, Inc., New York.

DEY REY is a registered trademark and the Del Rey colophon is a trademark of Random House, Inc.

Publication rights arranged through Kodansha Ltd.

First published in Japan in 2007 by Kodansha Ltd., Tokyo

ISBN 978-0-345-50666-5

Printed in the United States of America

www.delreymanga.com

9 8 7 6 5 4 3 2 1

Translator/adapter: Stephen Paul
Lettering: North Market Street Graphics

Contents

Honorifics Explained v

Psycho Busters, Volume 4 1

Translation Notes 197

Honorifics Explained

Throughout the Del Rey Manga books, you will find Japanese honorifics left intact in the translations. For those not familiar with how the Japanese use honorifics and, more important, how they differ from American honorifics, we present this brief overview.

Politeness has always been a critical facet of Japanese culture. Ever since the feudal era, when Japan was a highly stratified society, use of honorifics—which can be defined as polite speech that indicates relationship or status—has played an essential role in the Japanese language. When addressing someone in Japanese, an honorific usually takes the form of a suffix attached to one's name (example: "Asuna-san"), is used as a title at the end of one's name, or appears in place of the name itself (example: "Negi-sensei," or simply "Sensei!").

Honorifics can be expressions of respect or endearment. In the context of manga and anime, honorifics give insight into the nature of the relationship between characters. Many English translations leave out these important honorifics and therefore distort the feel of the original Japanese. Because Japanese honorifics contain nuances that English honorifics lack, it is our policy at Del Rey not to translate them. Here, instead, is a guide to some of the honorifics you may encounter in Del Rey Manga.

-san: This is the most common honorific and is equivalent to Mr., Miss, Ms., or Mrs. It is the all-purpose honorific and can be used in any situation where politeness is required.

-sama: This is one level higher than "-san" and is used to confer great respect.

-dono: This comes from the word "tono," which means "lord." It is an even higher level than "-sama" and confers utmost respect.

-kun: This suffix is used at the end of boys' names to express familiarity or endearment. It is also sometimes used by men among friends, or when addressing someone younger or of a lower station.

-chan: This is used to express endearment, mostly toward girls. It is also used for little boys, pets, and even among lovers. It gives a sense of childish cuteness.

Bozu: This is an informal way to refer to a boy, similar to the English terms "kid" and "squirt."

Sempai/
Senpai: This title suggests that the addressee is one's senior in a group or organization. It is most often used in a school setting, where underclassmen refer to their upperclassmen as "sempai." It can also be used in the workplace, such as when a newer employee addresses an employee who has seniority in the company.

Kohai: This is the opposite of "sempai" and is used toward underclassmen in school or newcomers in the workplace. It connotes that the addressee is of a lower station.

Sensei: Literally meaning "one who has come before," this title is used for teachers, doctors, or masters of any profession or art.

[blank]: This is usually forgotten in these lists, but it is perhaps the most significant difference between Japanese and English. The lack of honorific means that the speaker has permission to address the person in a very intimate way. Usually, only family, spouses, or very close friends have this kind of permission. Known as *yobisute,* it can be gratifying when someone who has earned the intimacy starts to call one by one's name without an honorific. But when that intimacy hasn't been earned, it can be very insulting.

Psycho Busters

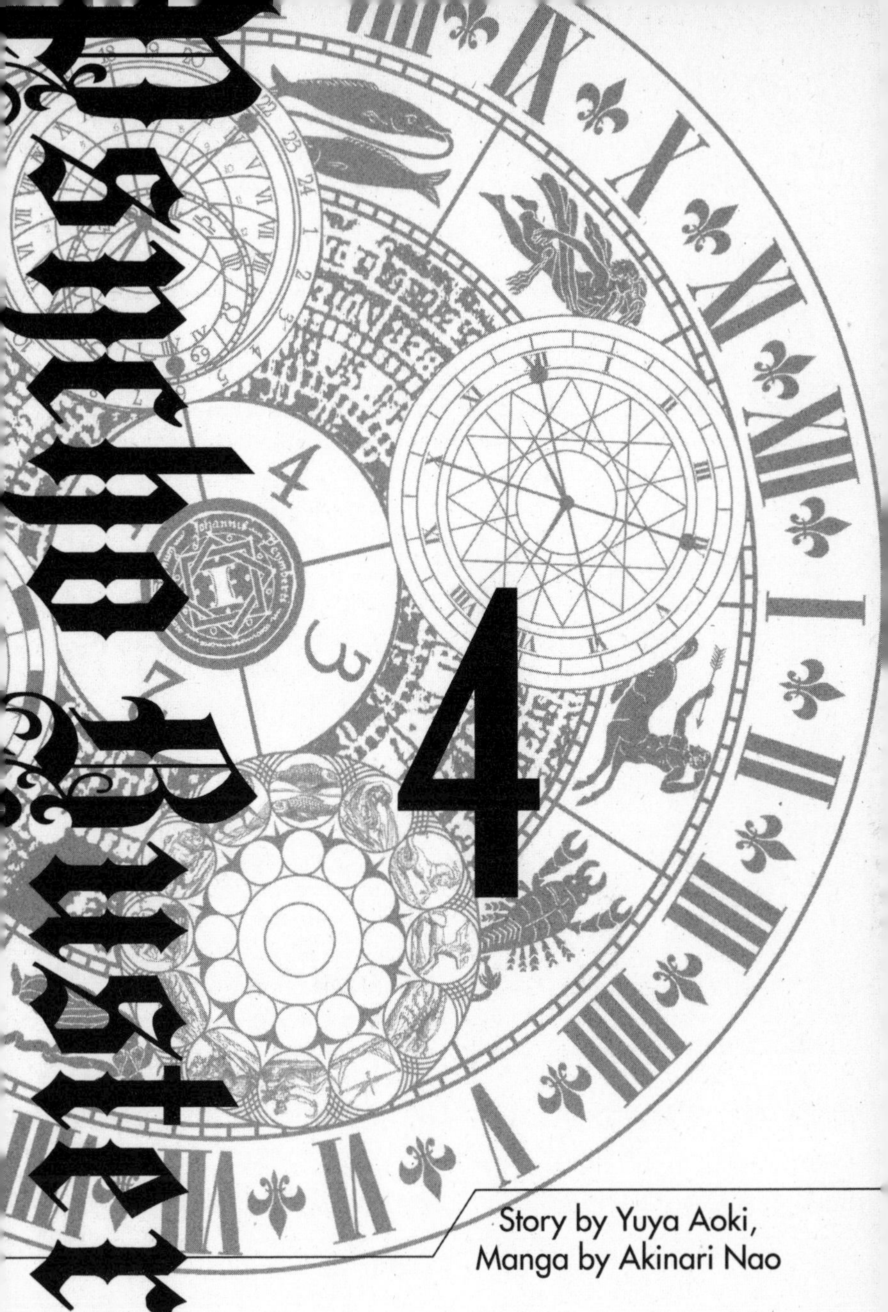

4

Story by Yuya Aoki,
Manga by Akinari Nao

Contents

Case 13   Love   003

Case 14   Jealousy   049

Case 15   Inhumanity   085

Case 16   Crack   121

Case 17   Progress   157

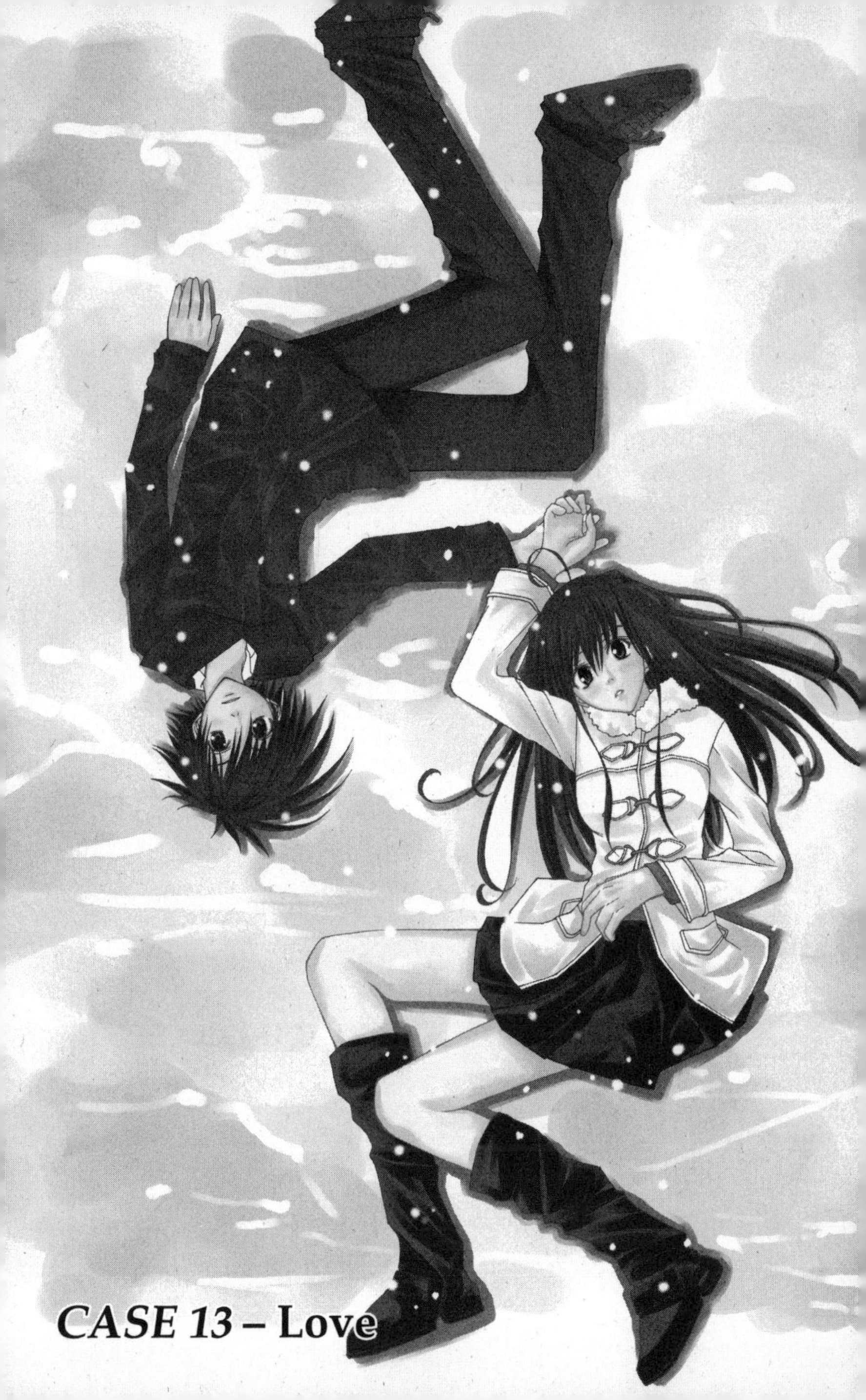

CASE 13 – Love

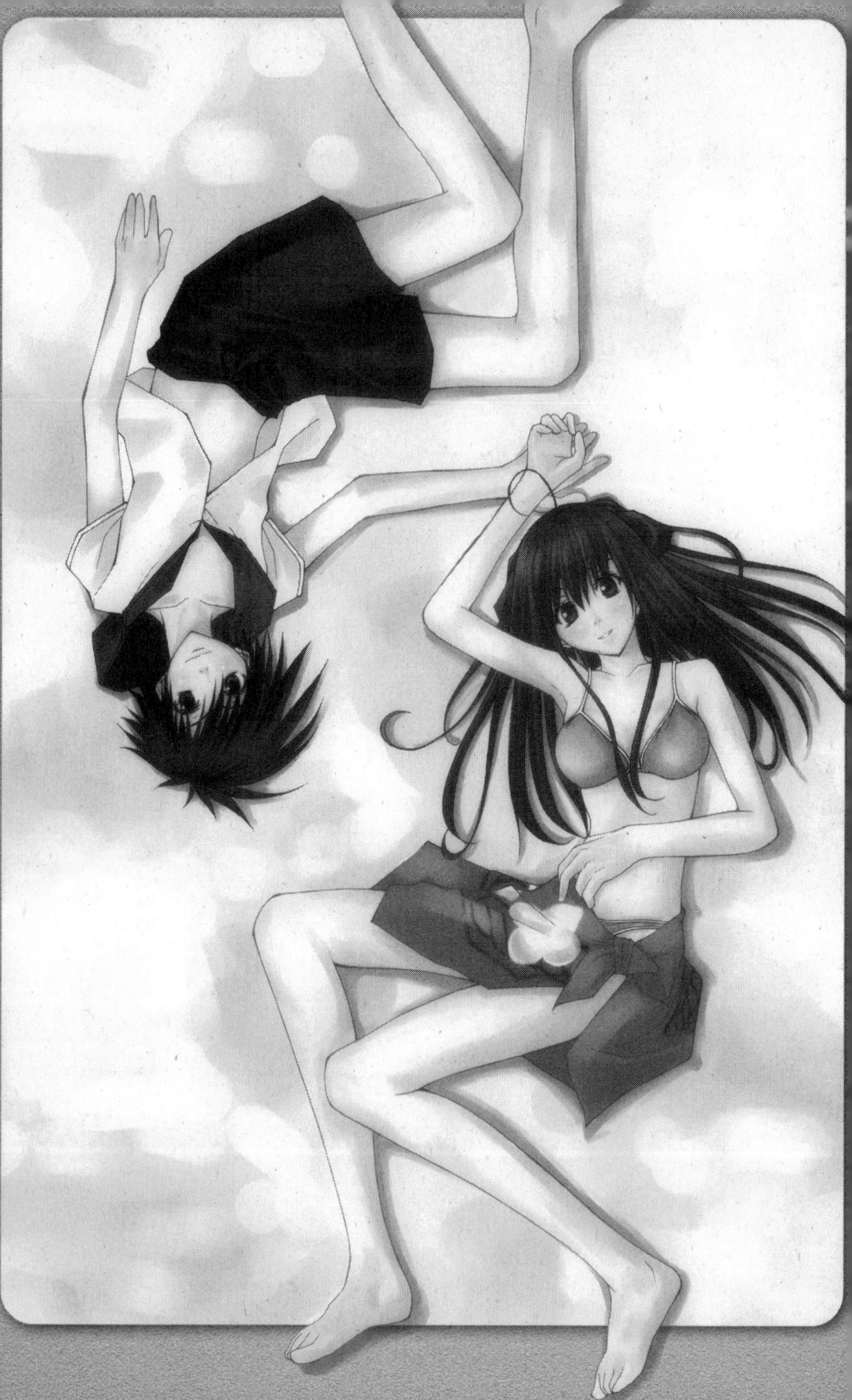

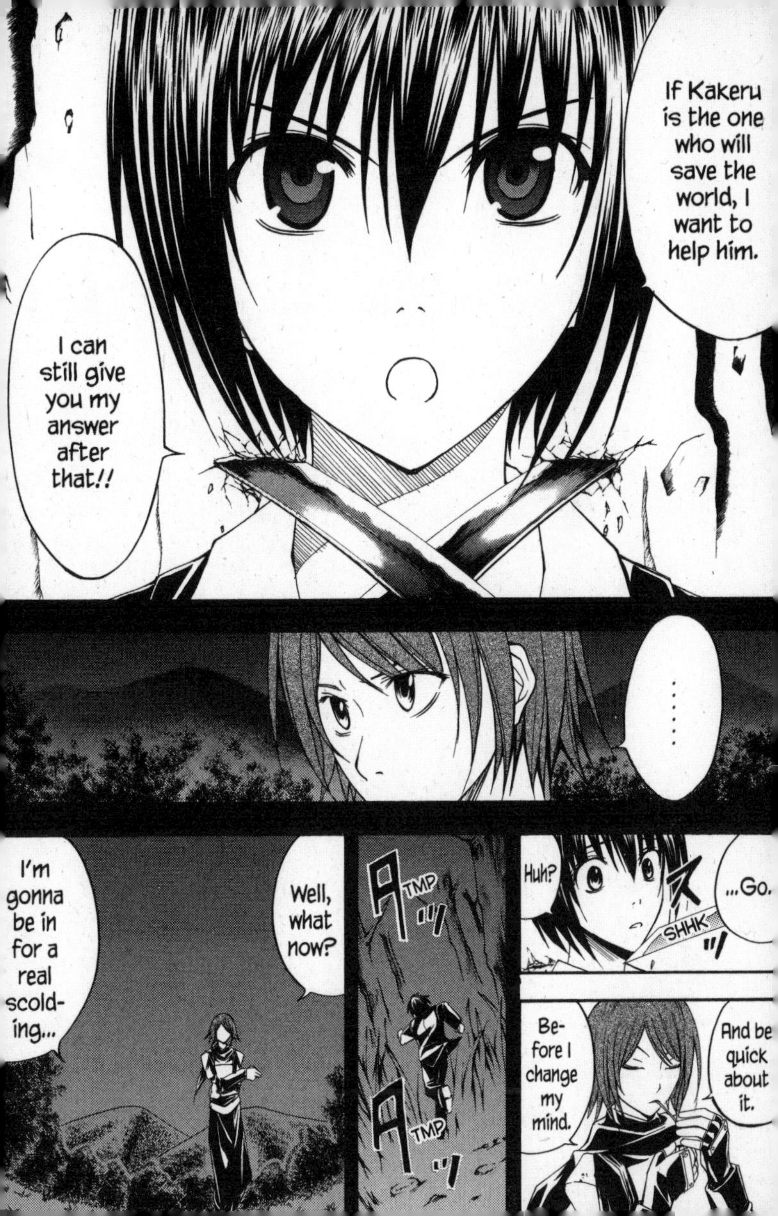
If Kakeru is the one who will save the world, I want to help him.
I can still give you my answer after that!!
......
...Go.
SHHK
Huh?
And be quick about it.
Be-fore I change my mind.
TMP
TMP
Well, what now?
I'm gonna be in for a real scold-ing...

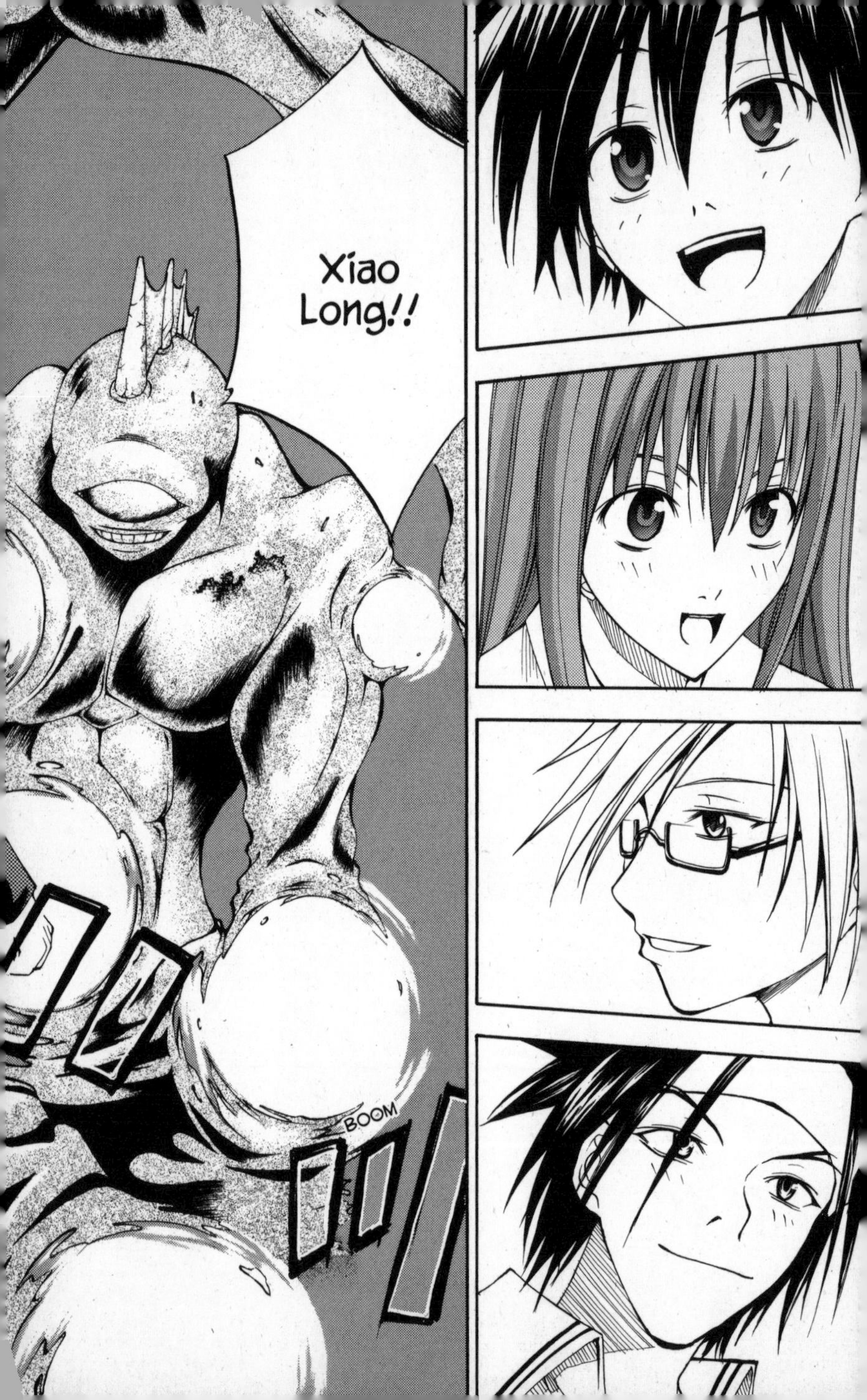
Xiao Long!!
BOOM

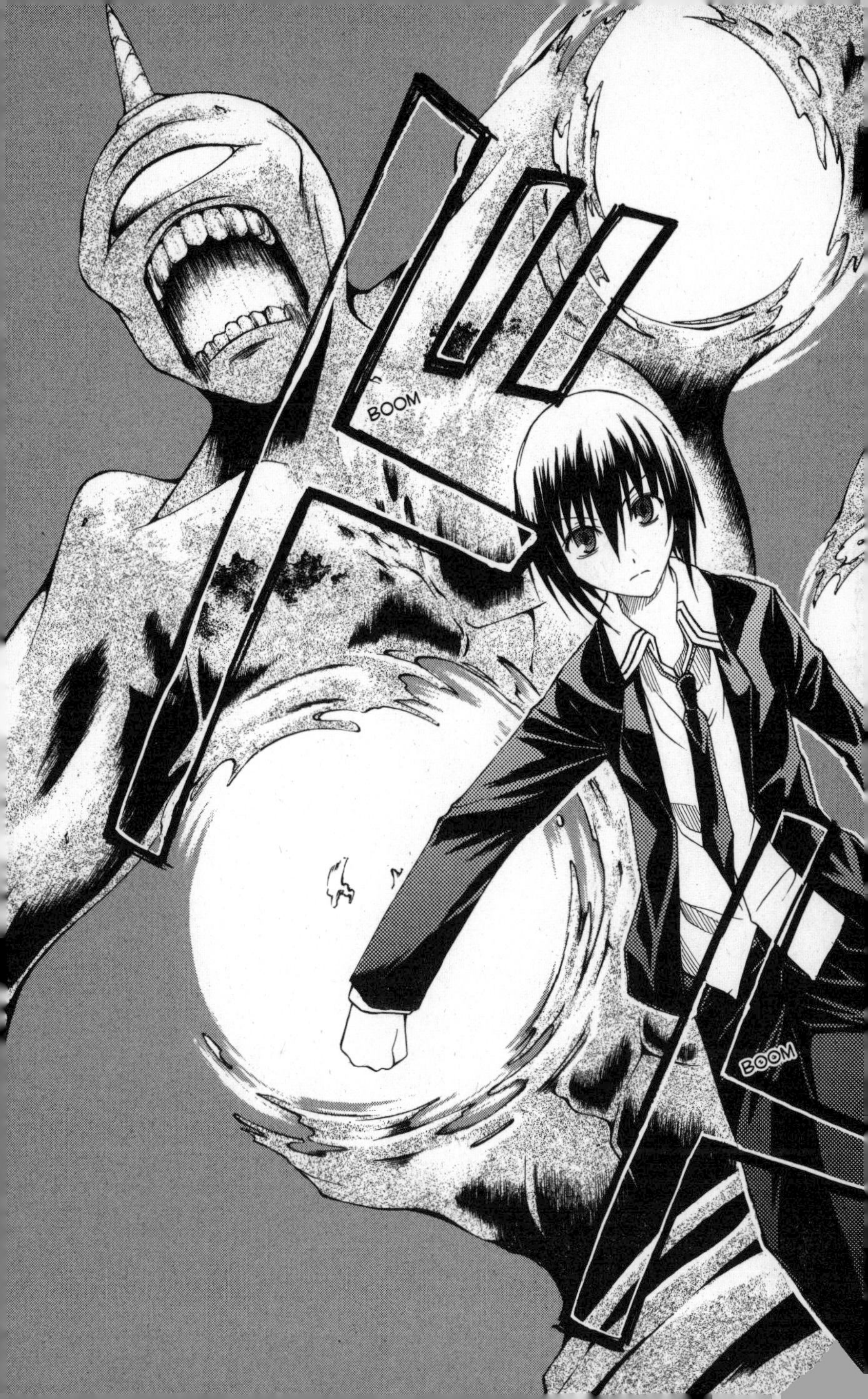
BOOM
BOOM

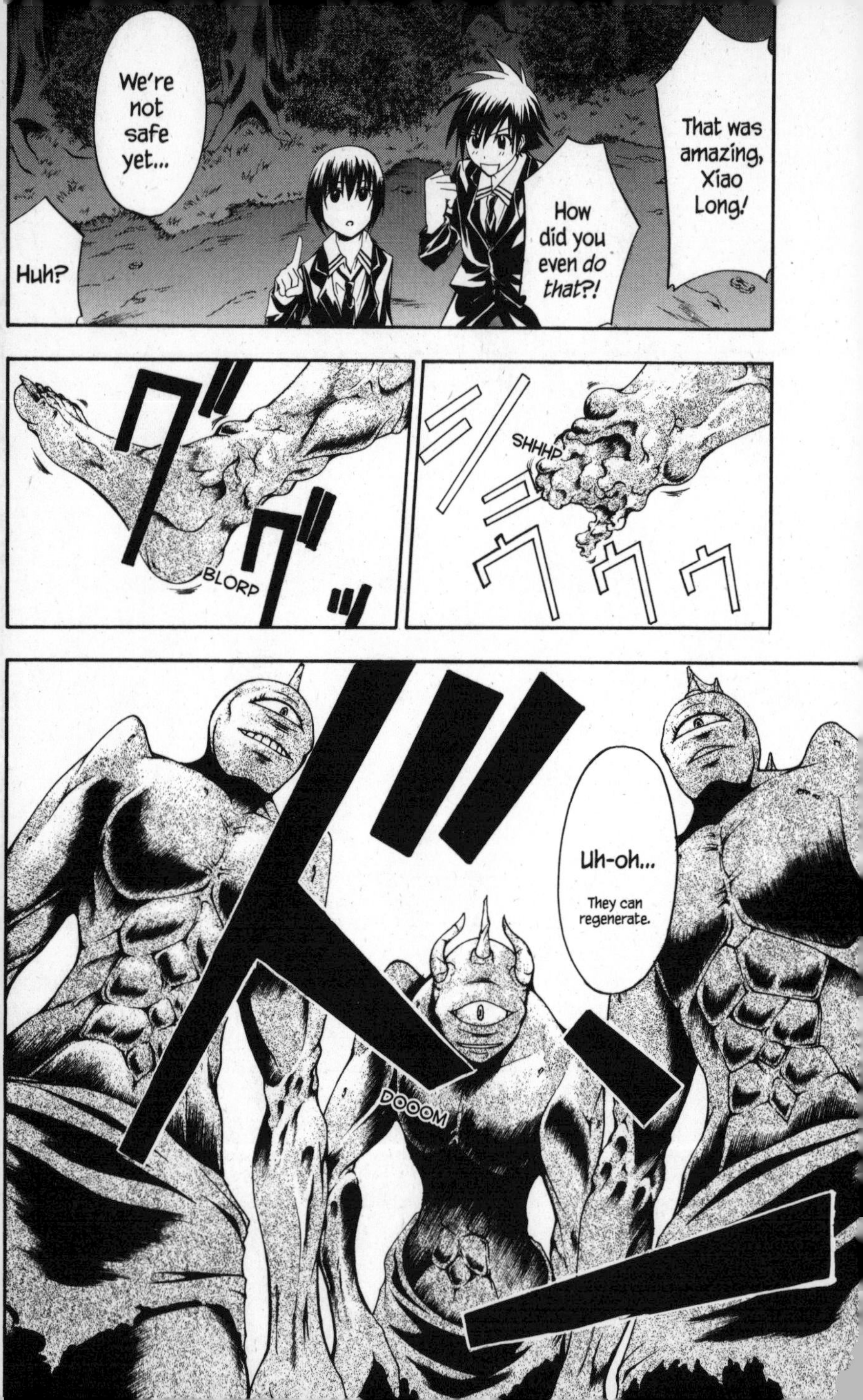
That was amazing, Xiao Long!
How did you even *do that*?!
We're not safe yet...
Huh?
SHHHP
BLORP
DOOOM
Uh-oh...
They can regenerate.

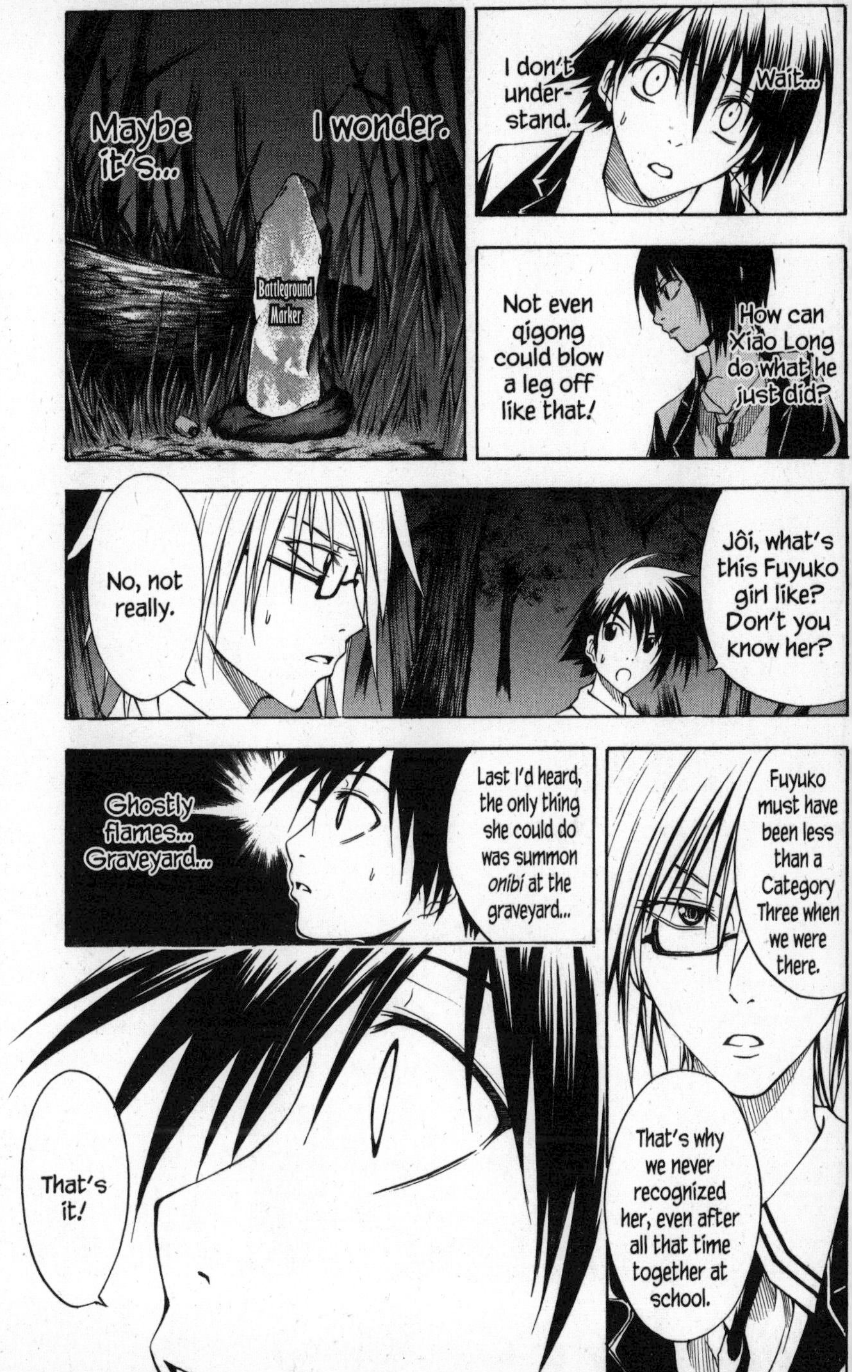
Wait...
I don't understand.
How can Xiao Long do what he just did?
Not even qigong could blow a leg off like that!
I wonder.
Maybe it's...
Battleground Marker
Jôi, what's this Fuyuko girl like? Don't you know her?
No, not really.
Fuyuko must have been less than a Category Three when we were there.
That's why we never recognized her, even after all that time together at school.
Last I'd heard, the only thing she could do was summon *onibi* at the graveyard...
Ghostly flames... Graveyard...
That's it!

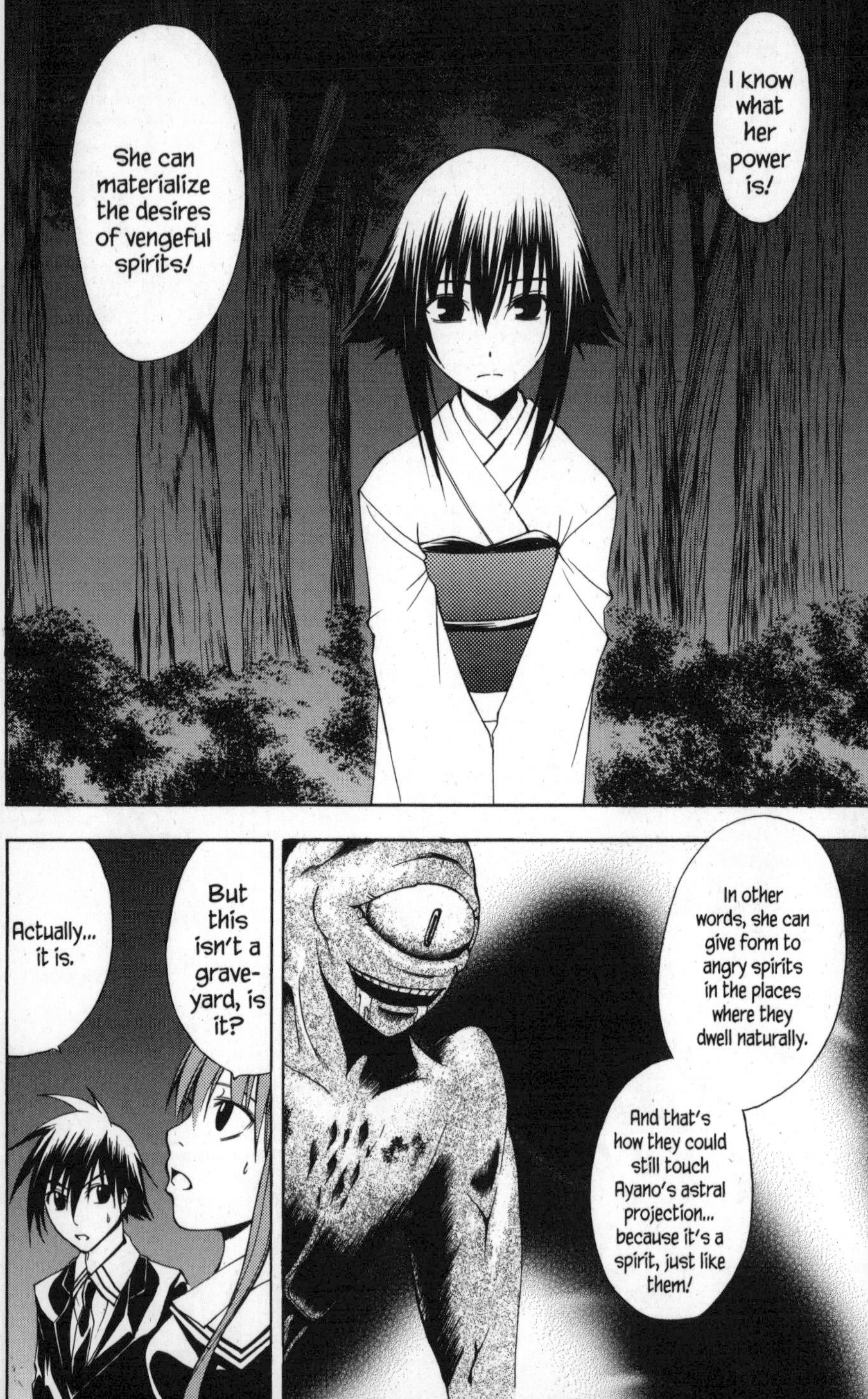
I know what her power is!
She can materialize the desires of vengeful spirits!
In other words, she can give form to angry spirits in the places where they dwell naturally.
And that's how they could still touch Ayano's astral projection... because it's a spirit, just like them!
But this isn't a graveyard, is it?
Actually... it is.

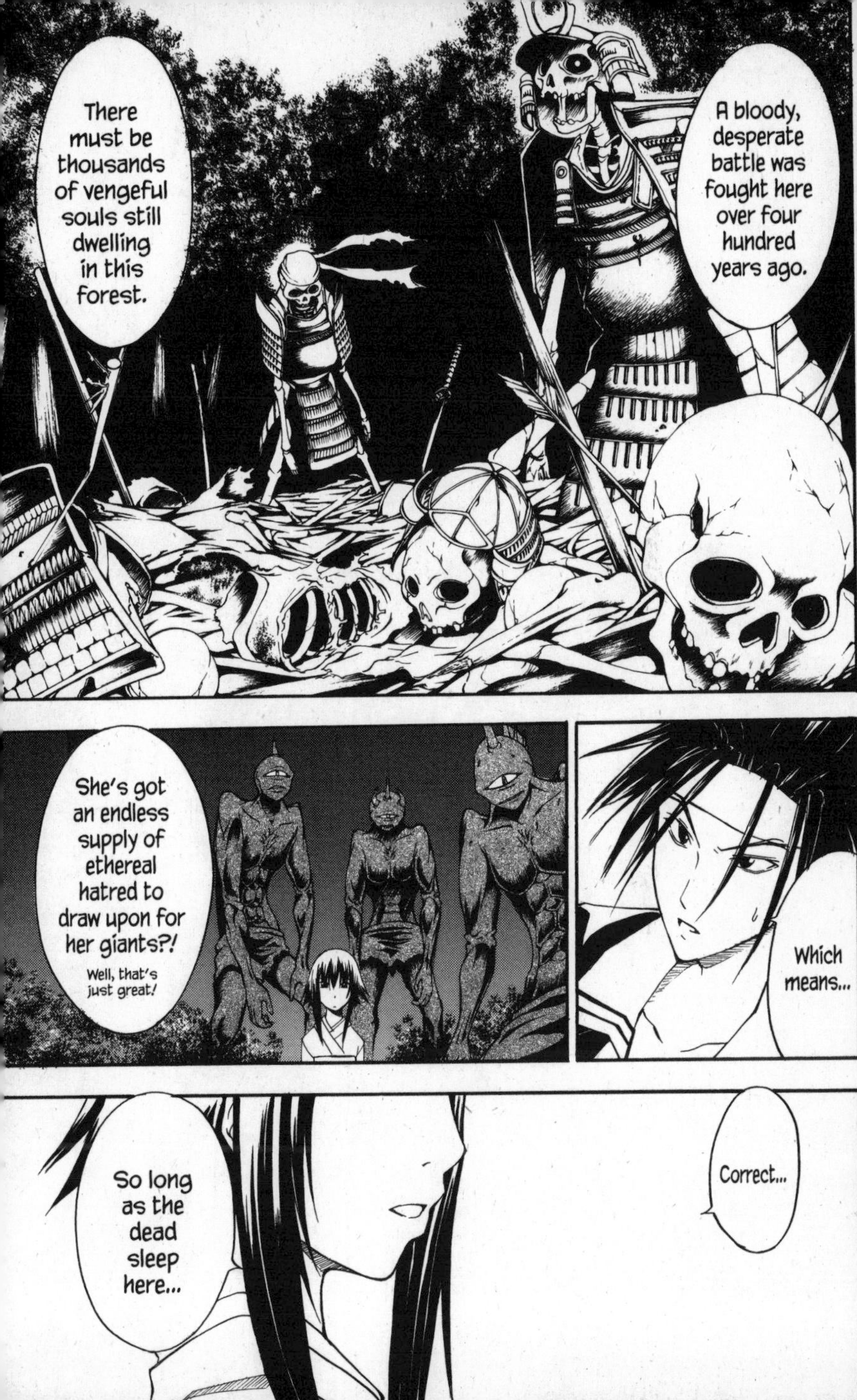
A bloody, desperate battle was fought here over four hundred years ago.
There must be thousands of vengeful souls still dwelling in this forest.
Which means...
She's got an endless supply of ethereal hatred to draw upon for her giants?!
Well, that's just great!
Correct...
So long as the dead sleep here...

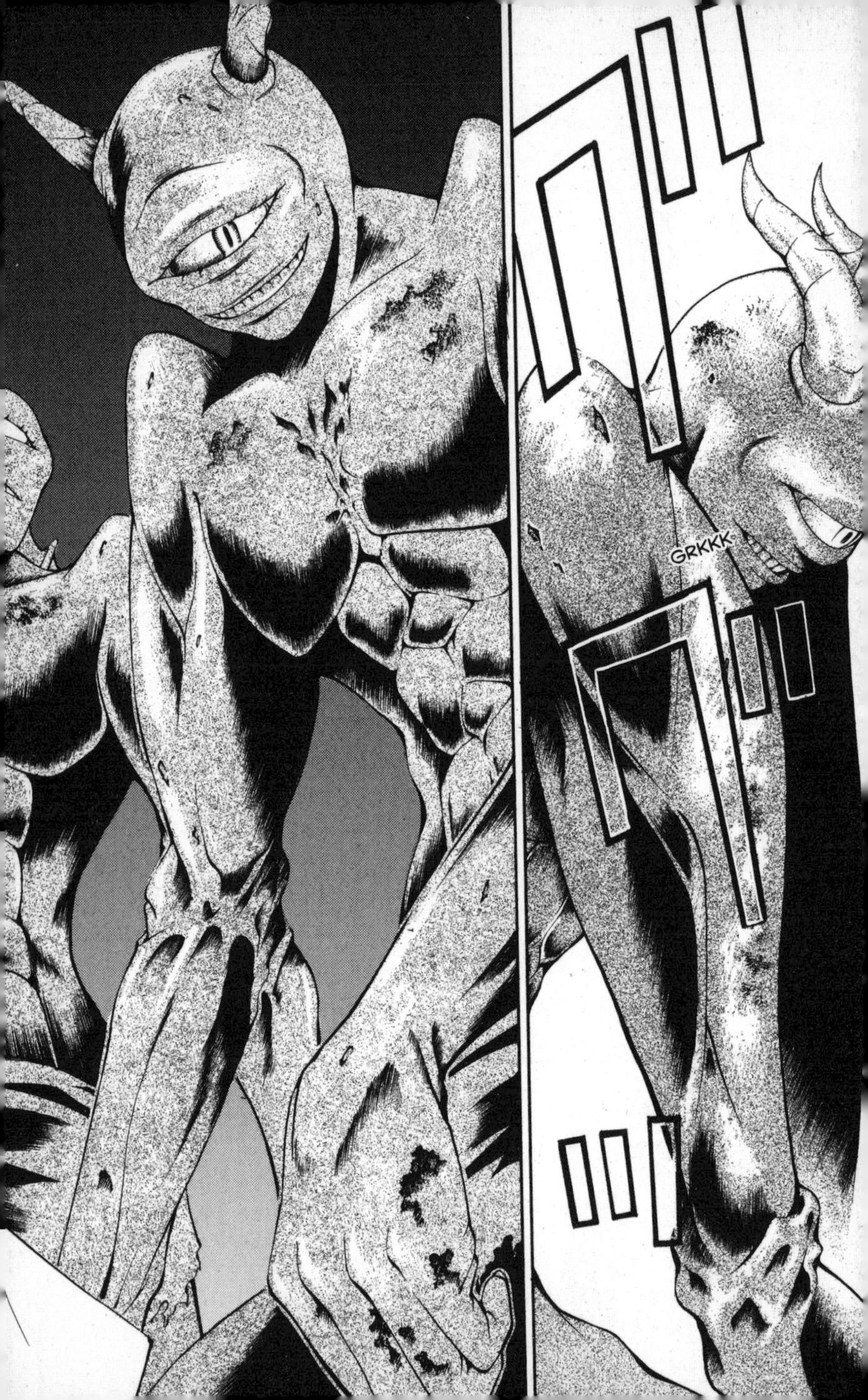
GRKKK

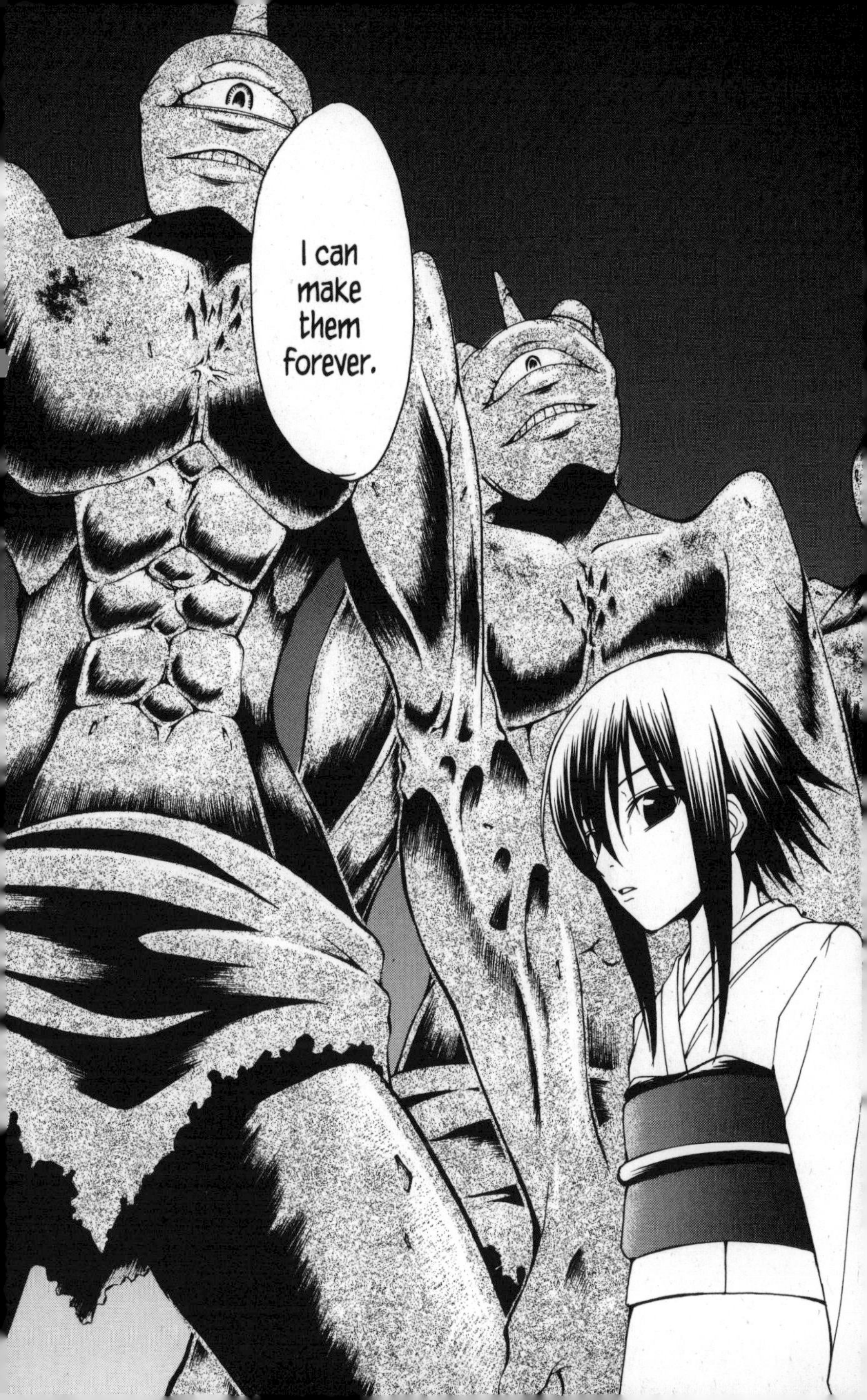
I can make them forever.

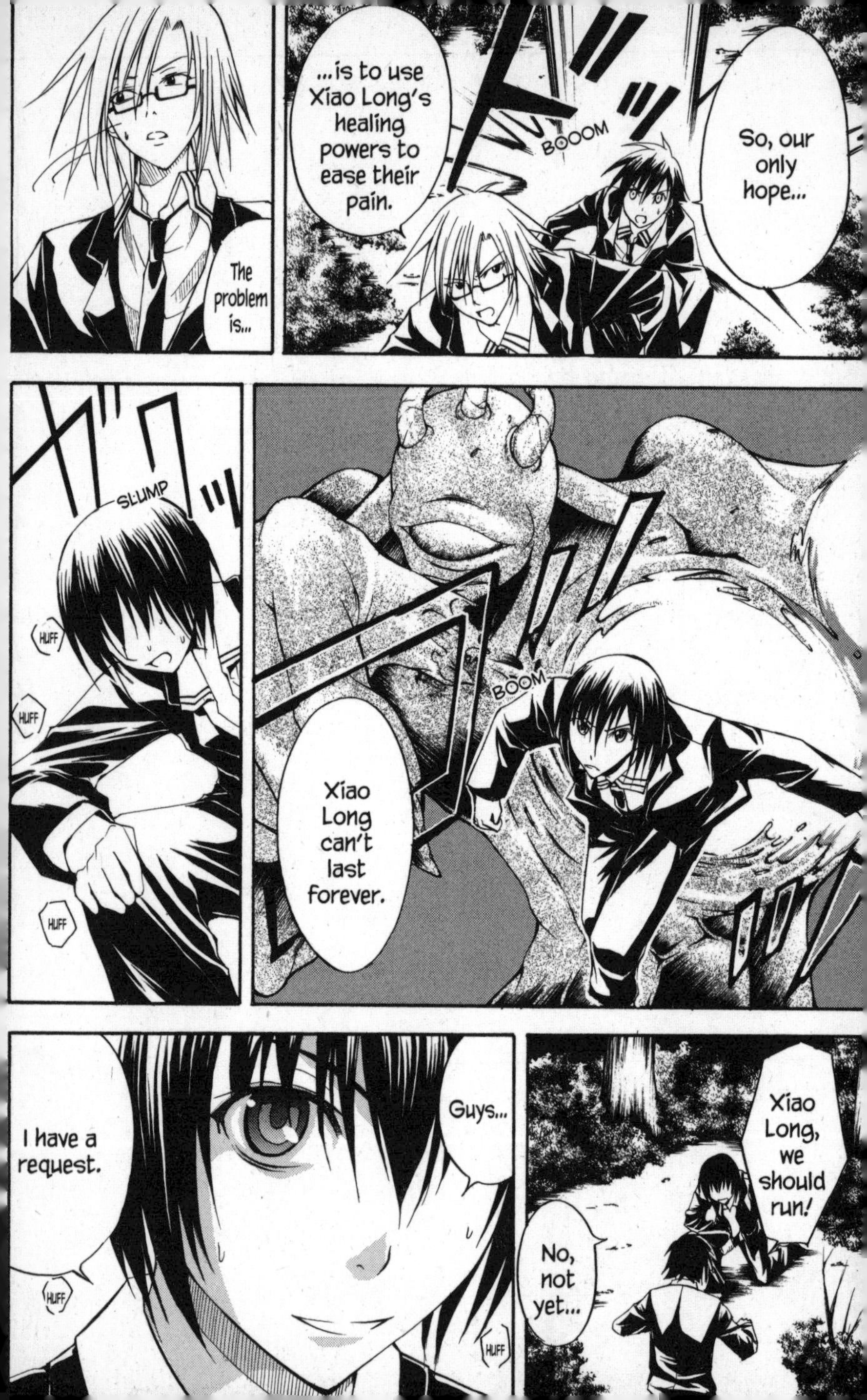
So, our only hope...
...is to use Xiao Long's healing powers to ease their pain.
BOOOM
The problem is...
BOOM
Xiao Long can't last forever.
SLUMP
HUFF
HUFF
HUFF
Xiao Long, we should run!
No, not yet...
Guys...
I have a request.
HUFF
HUFF

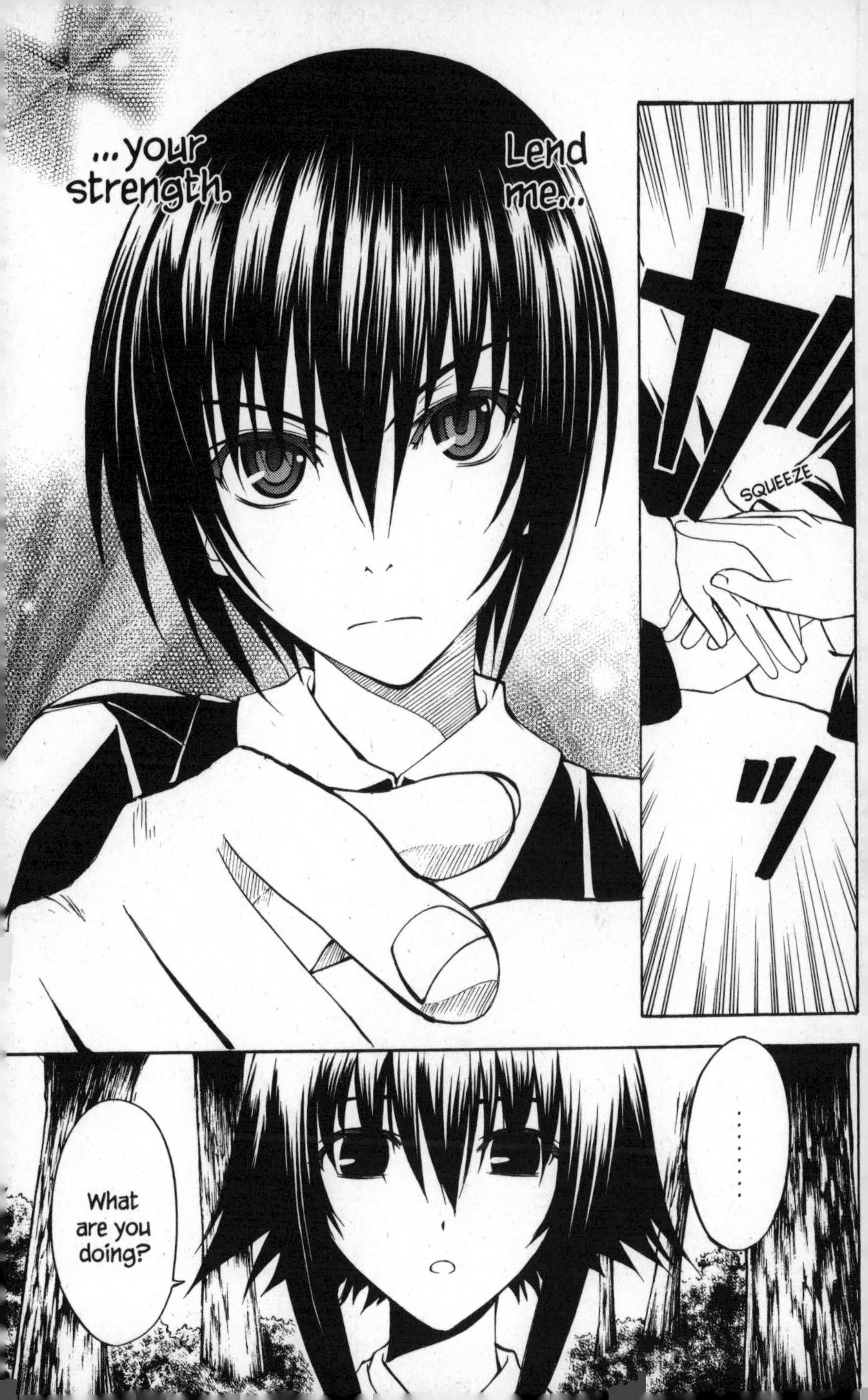
SQUEEZE
Lend me...
...your strength.
......
What are you doing?

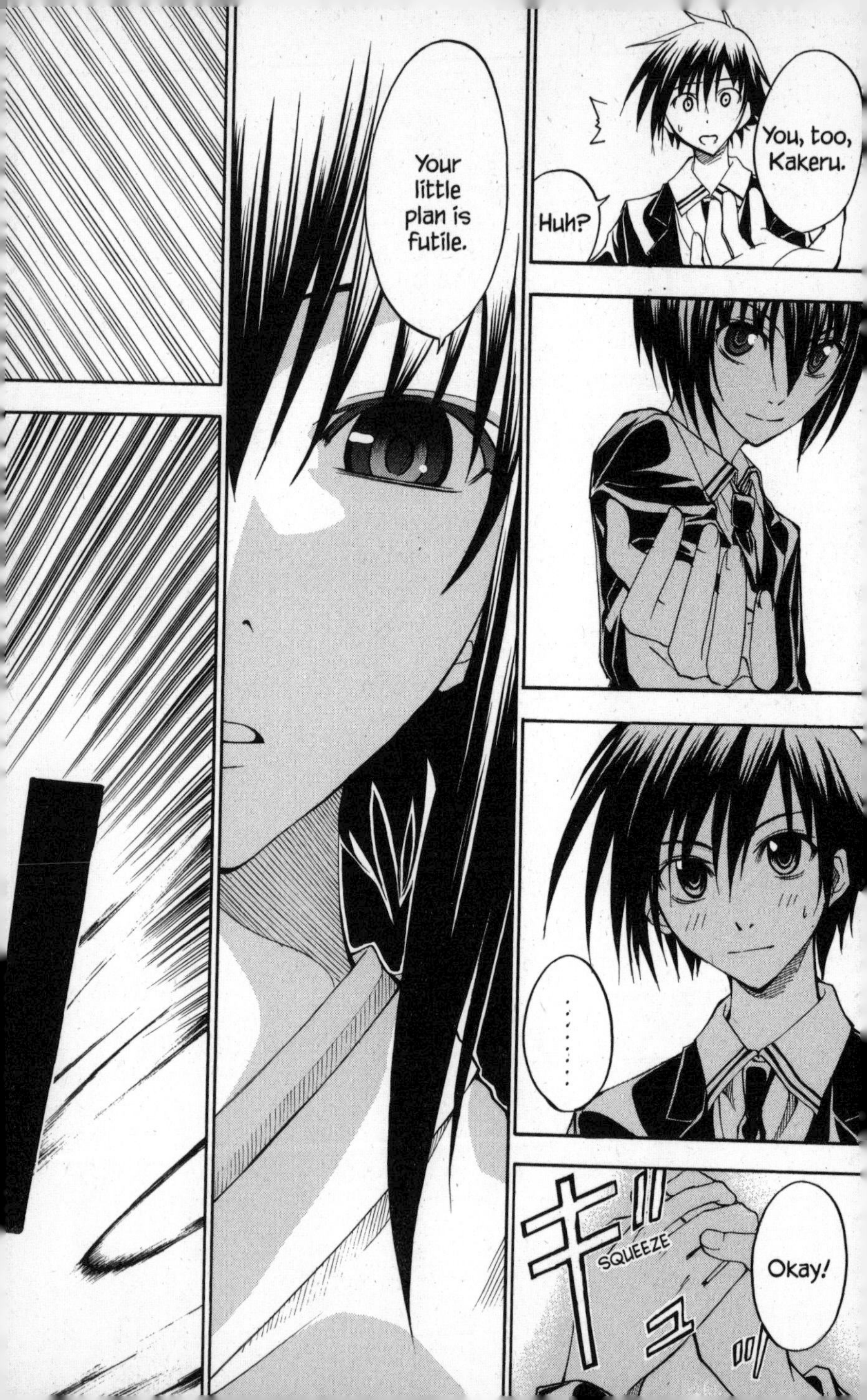
You, too, Kakeru.
Huh?
......
Okay!
SQUEEZE
Your little plan is futile.

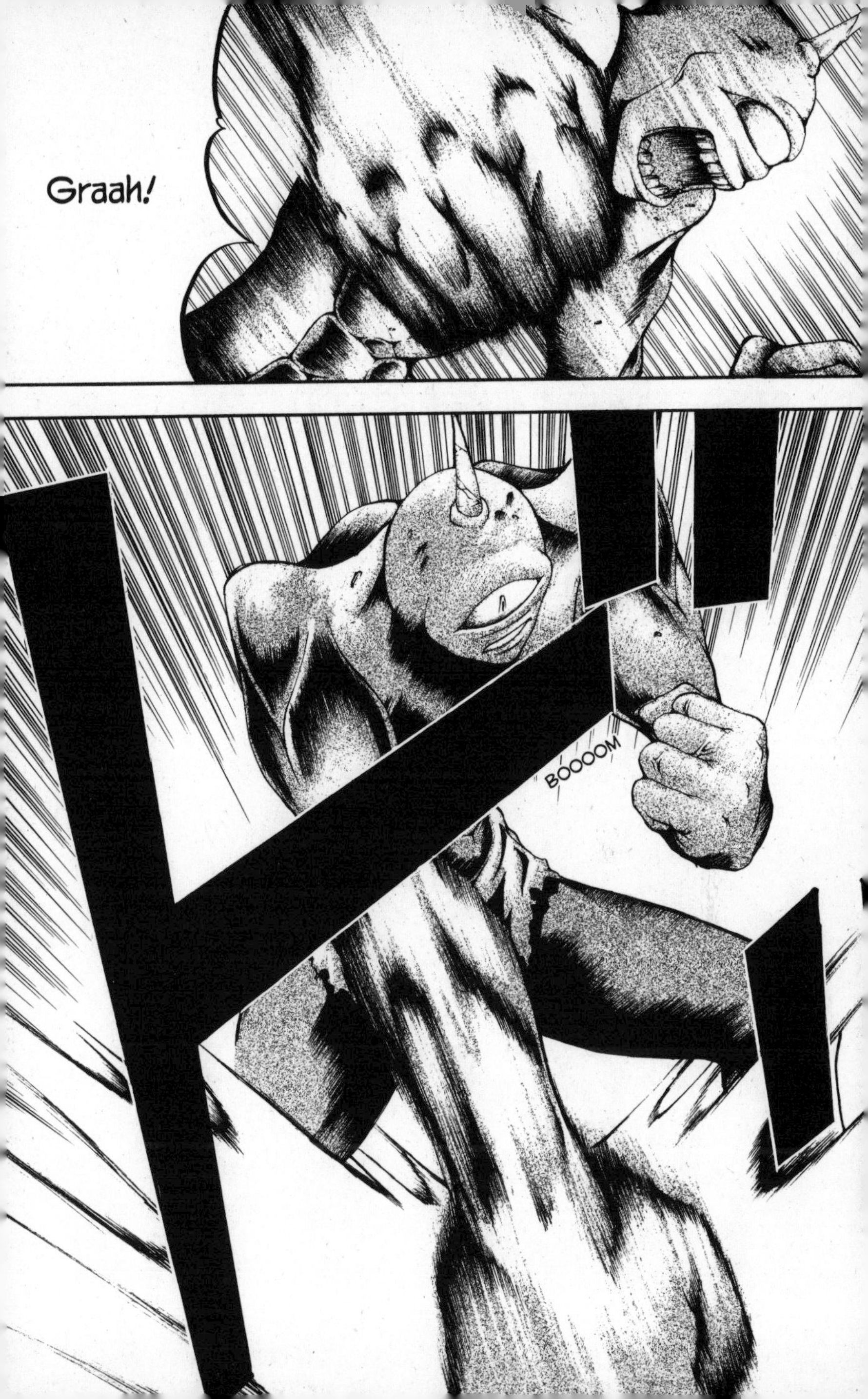
Graah!
BOOOOM

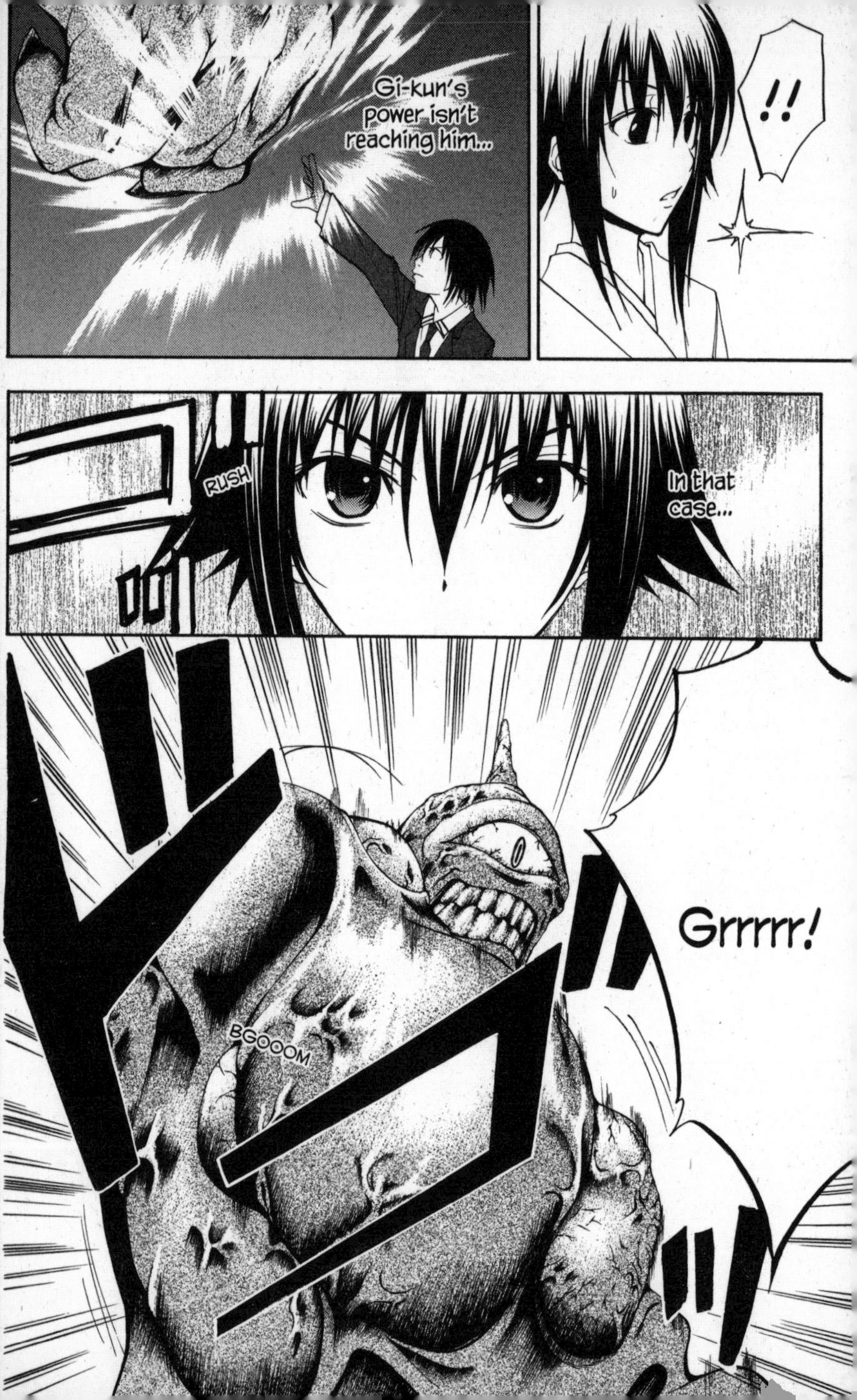
!!
Gi-kun's power isn't reaching him...
In that case...
RUSH
Grrrrr!
BGOOOM

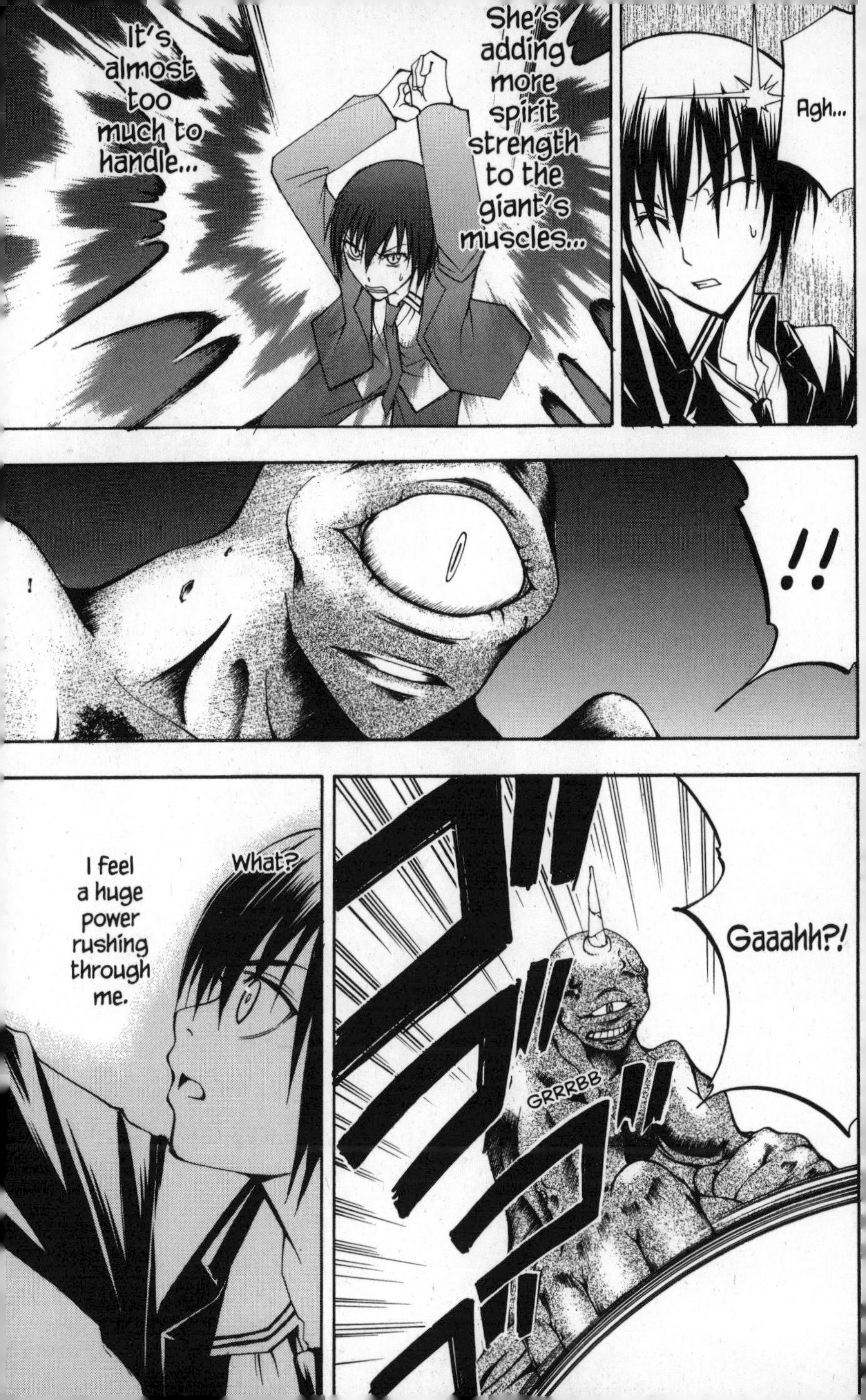
Agh...
She's adding more spirit strength to the giant's muscles...
It's almost too much to handle...
!!
Gaaahh?!
GRRRBB
What?
I feel a huge power rushing through me.

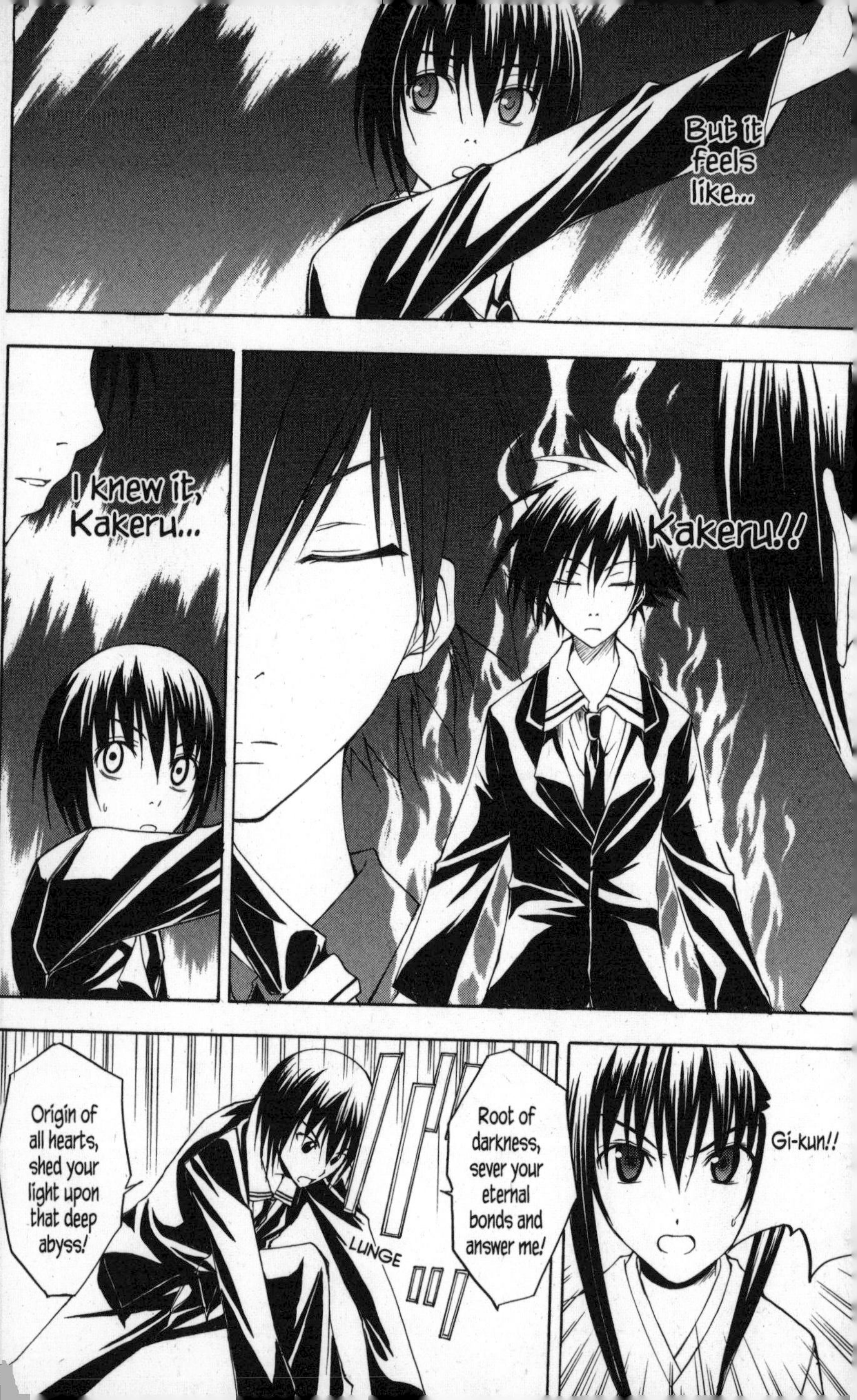
But it feels like...
Kakeru!!
I knew it, Kakeru...
Gi-kun!!
Root of darkness, sever your eternal bonds and answer me!
Origin of all hearts, shed your light upon that deep abyss!
LUNGE

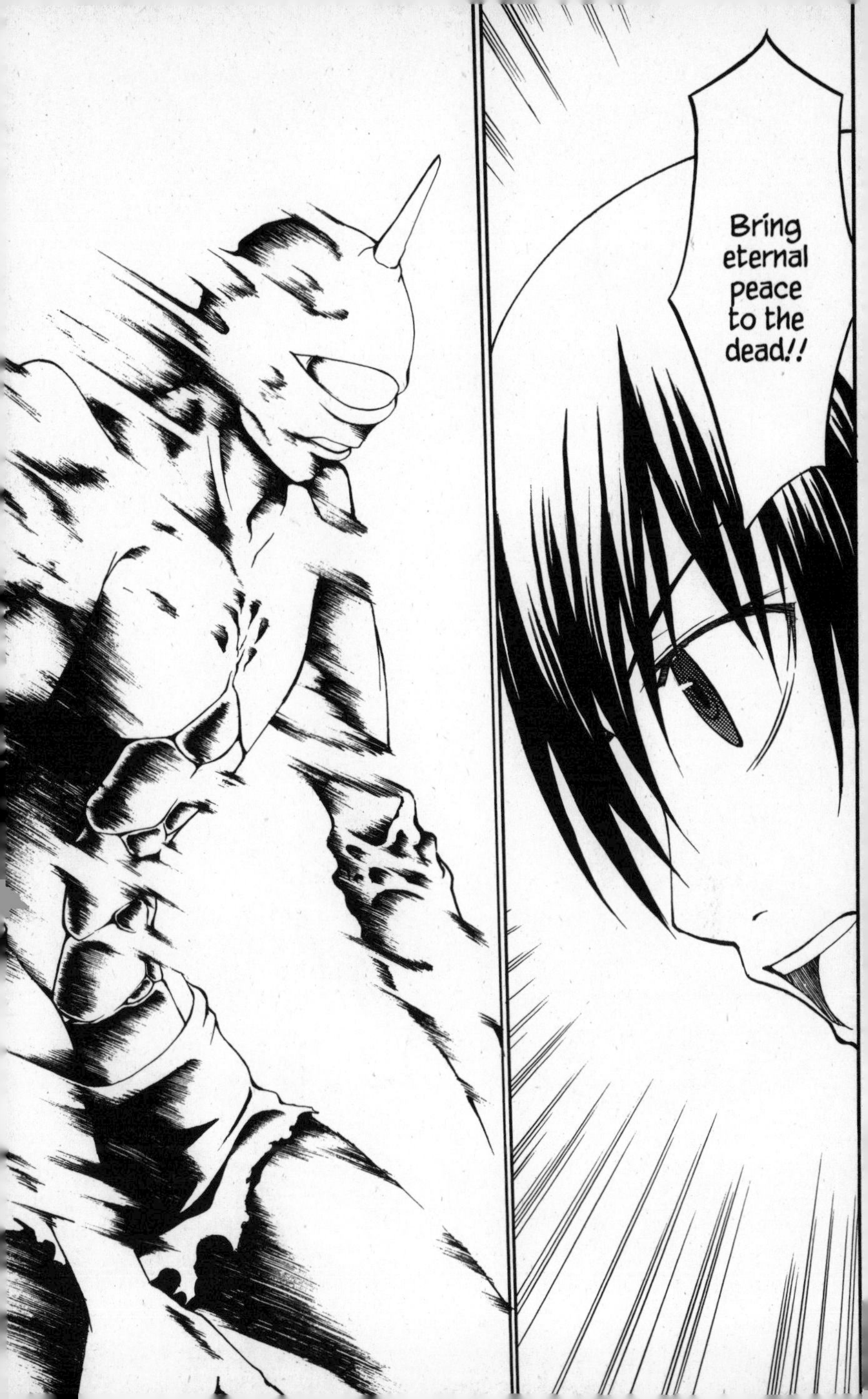
Bring eternal peace to the dead!!

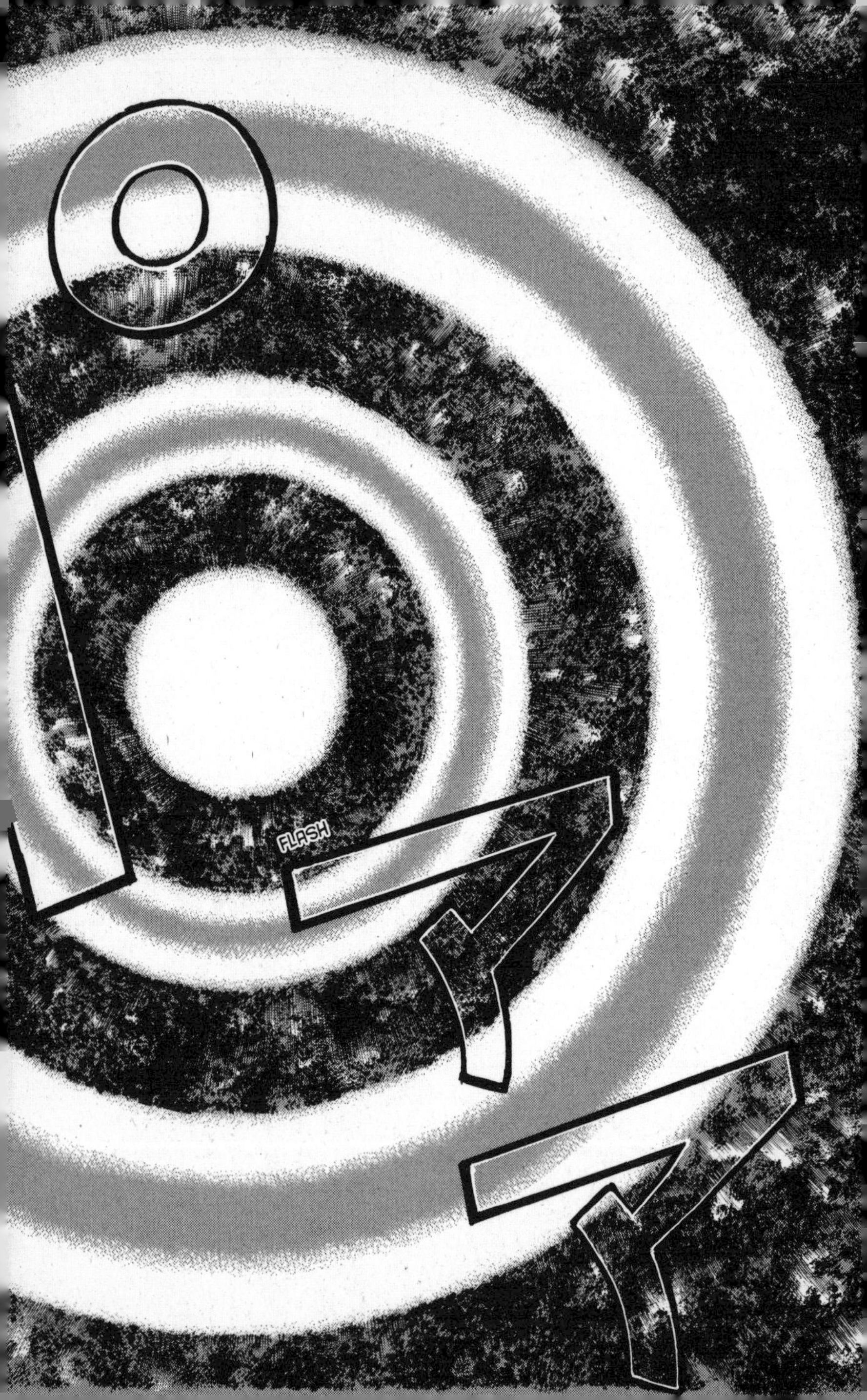
FLASH

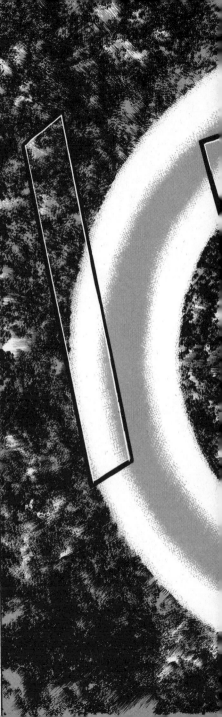

Incredible...!

BRRM

BRRM

GLOW

Even the plants are affected...

The giants...

...are vanishing.

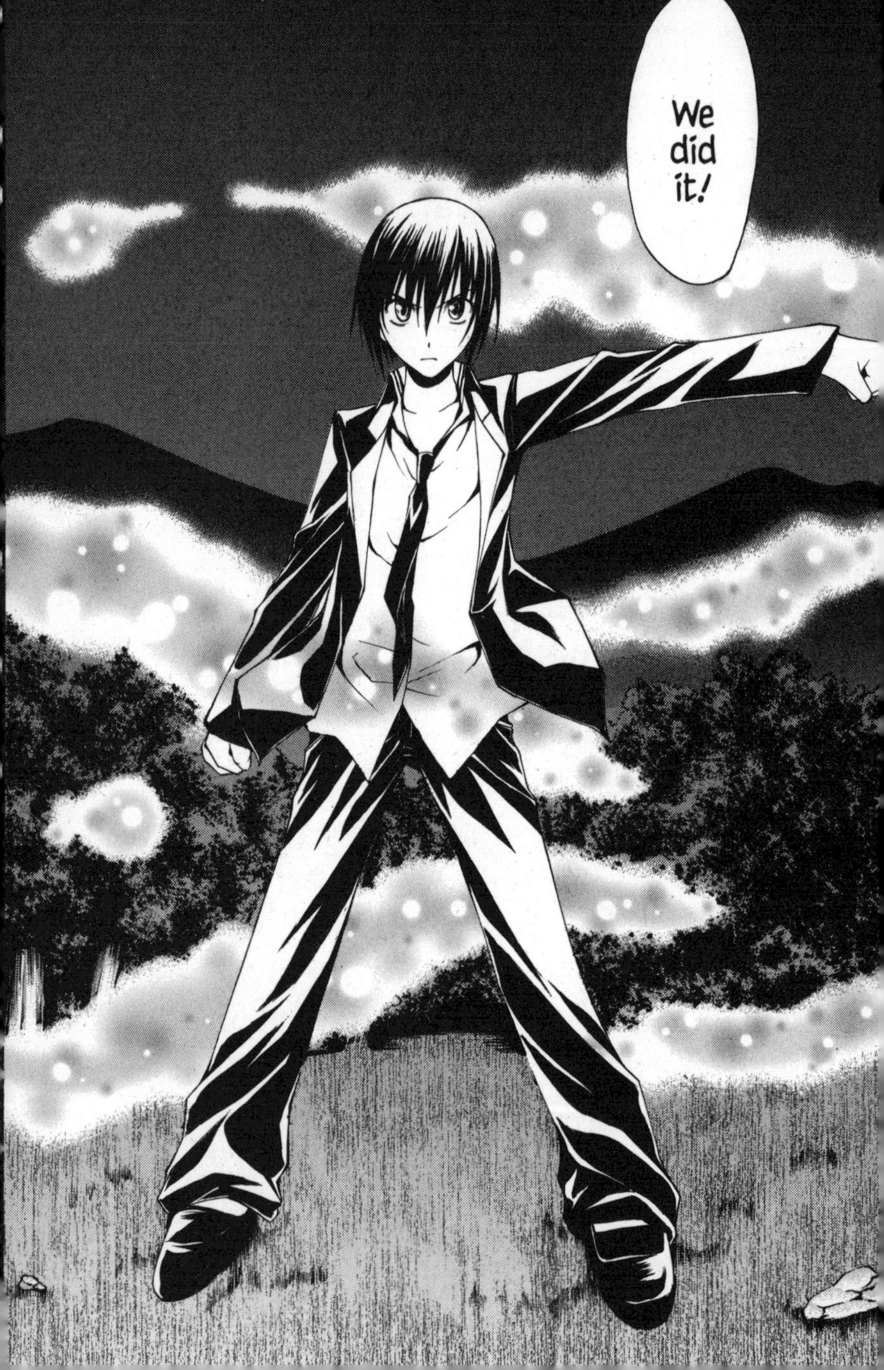
We did it!

You've gotta be kidding me!

No way...

CRUNCH

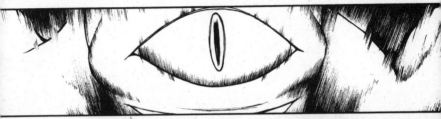

Giii.

It's... tiny!!

· · ·

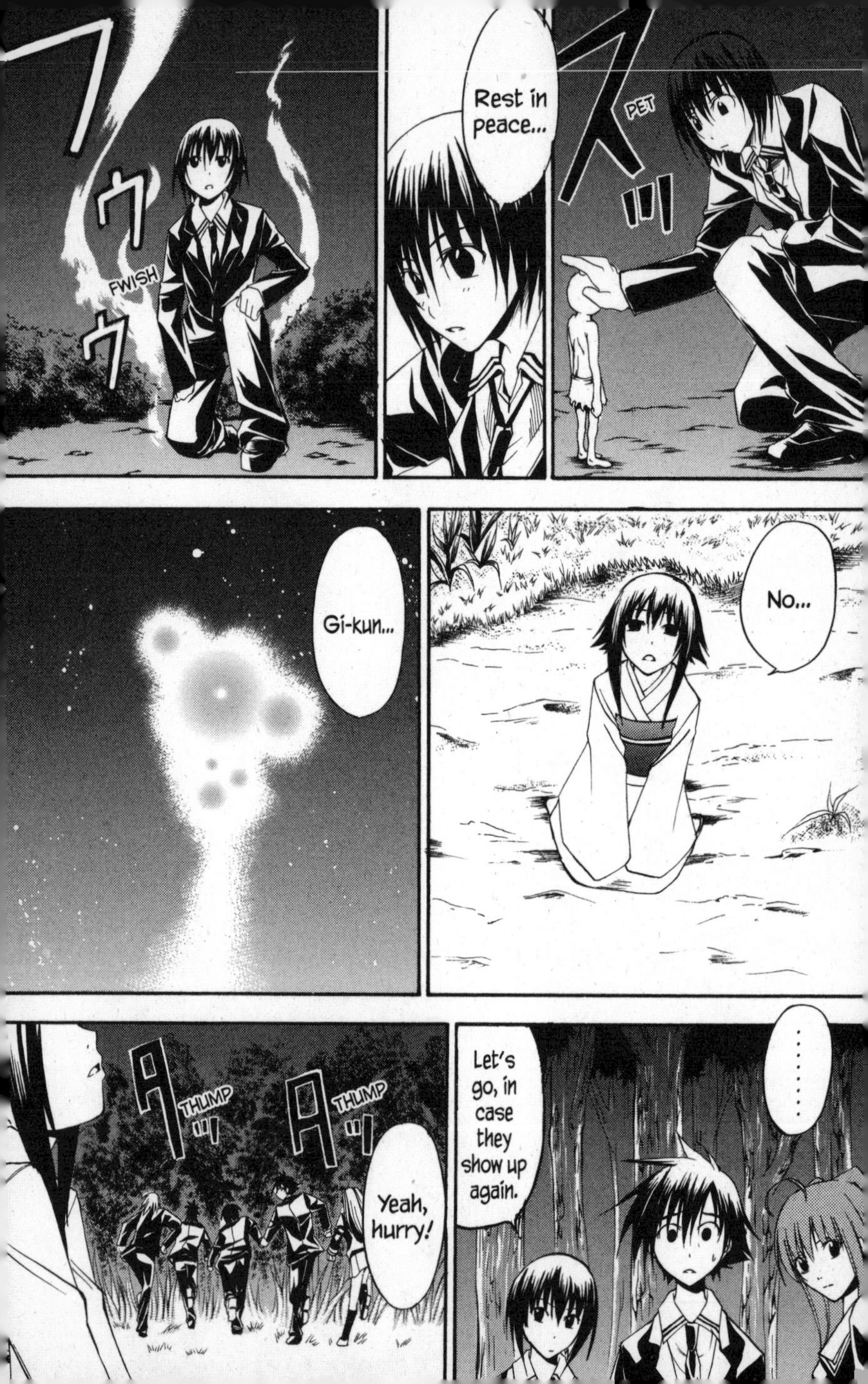
PET
Rest in peace...
FWISH
No...
Gi-kun...
......
Let's go, in case they show up again.
Yeah, hurry!
THUMP
THUMP

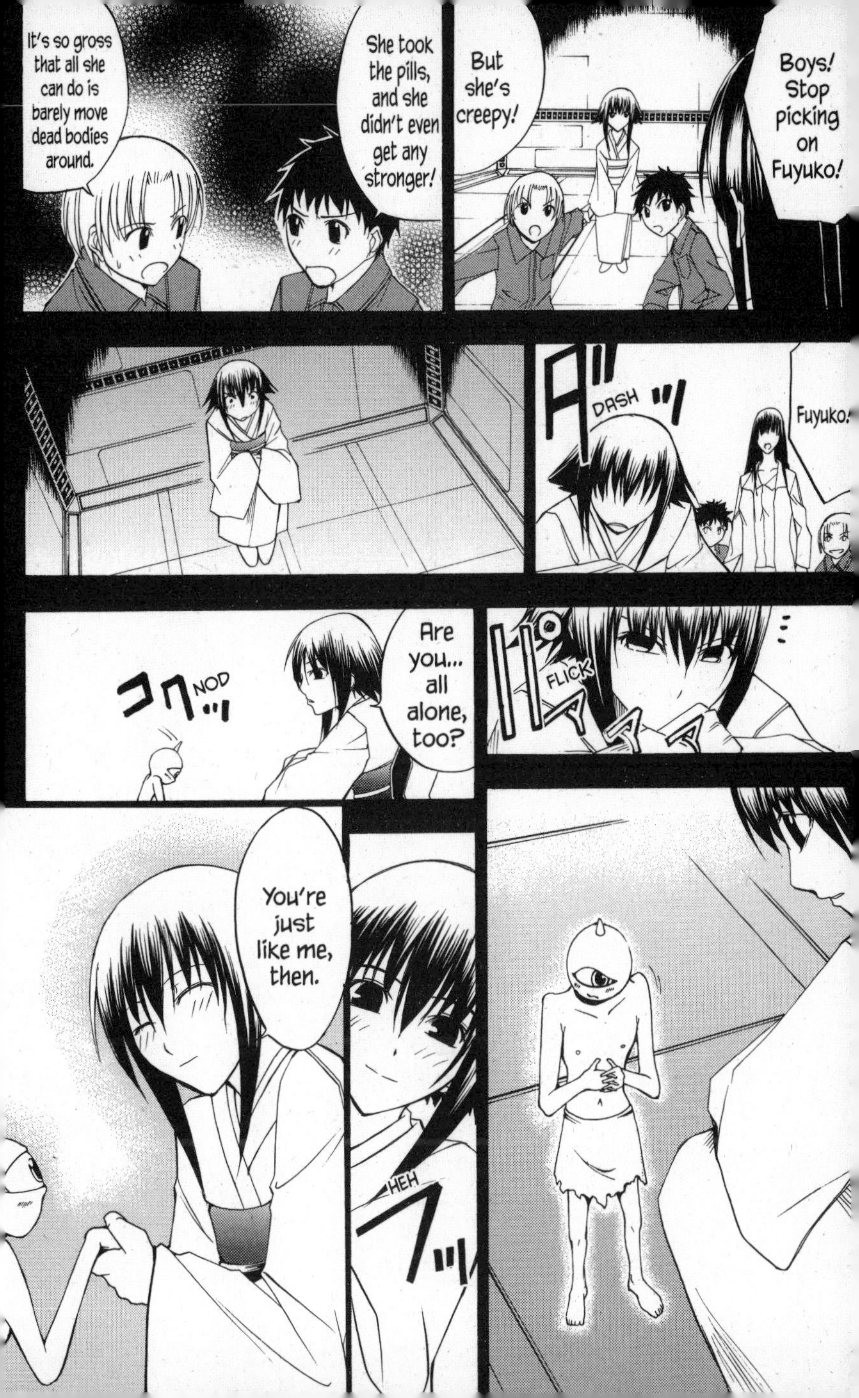
Boys! Stop picking on Fuyuko!
But she's creepy!
She took the pills, and she didn't even get any stronger!
It's so gross that all she can do is barely move dead bodies around.
Fuyuko!
DASH
FLICK
Are you... all alone, too?
NOD
You're just like me, then.
HEH

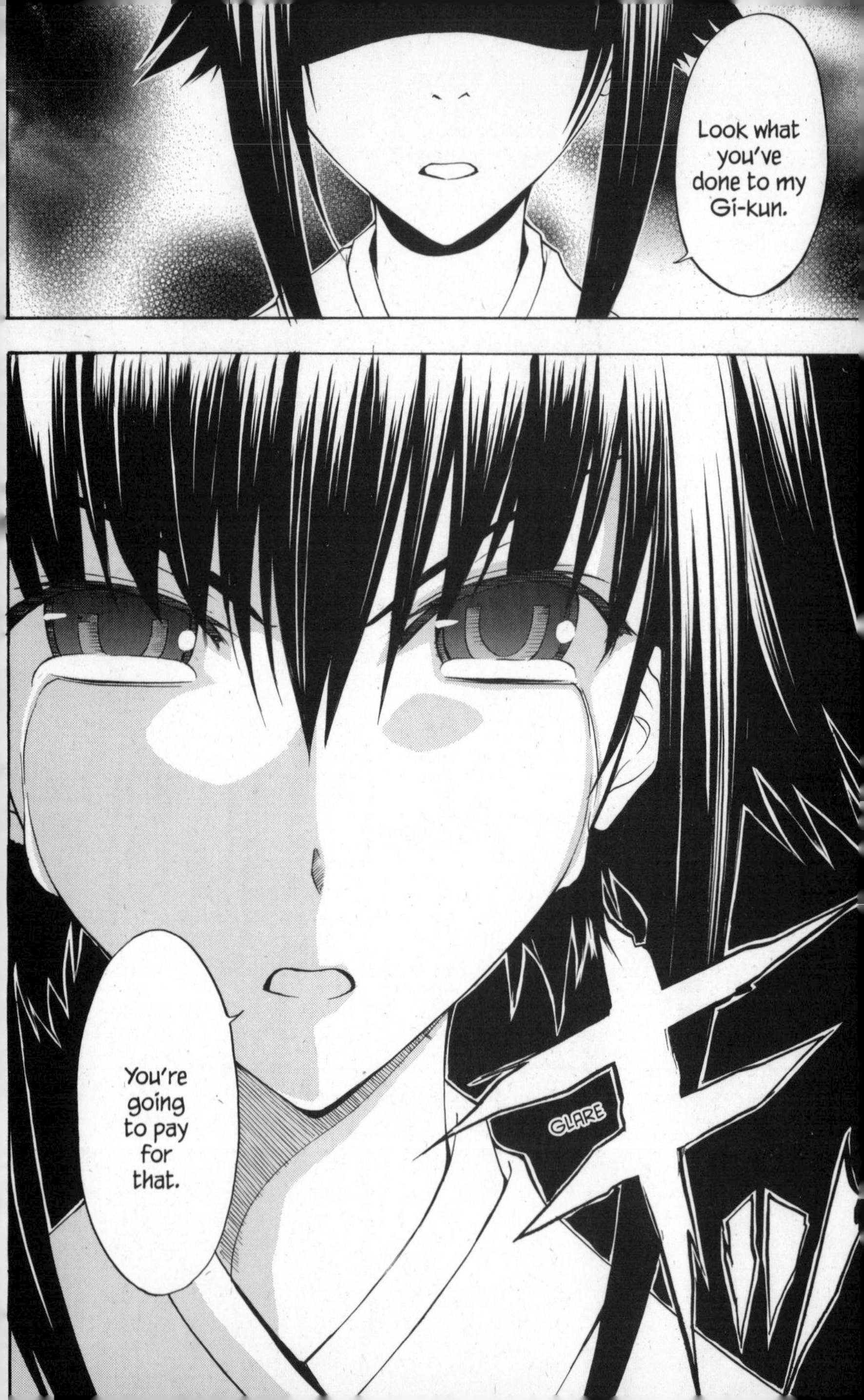
Look what you've done to my Gi-kun.
You're going to pay for that.
GLARE

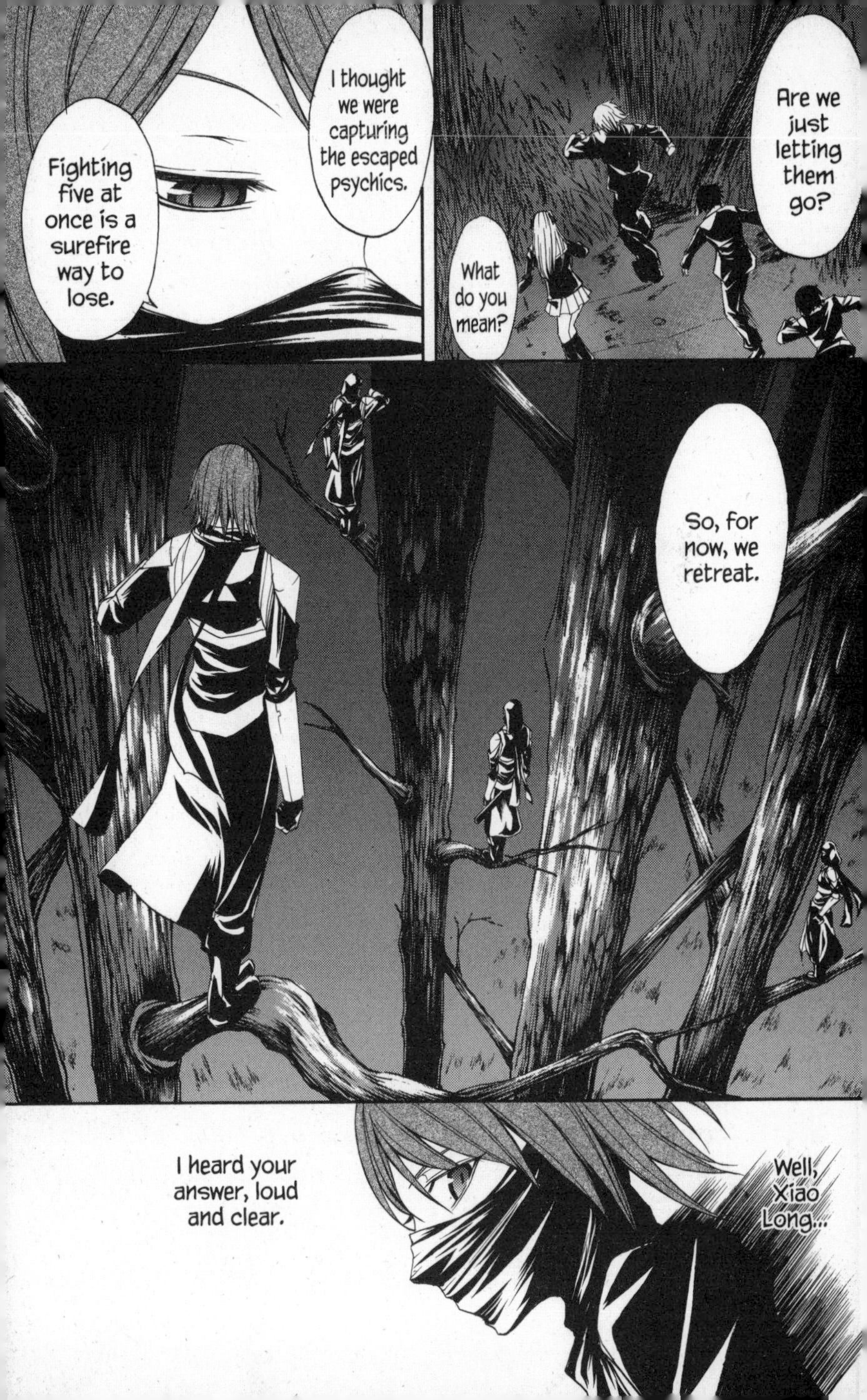
Are we just letting them go?
What do you mean?
I thought we were capturing the escaped psychics.
Fighting five at once is a surefire way to lose.
So, for now, we retreat.
Well, Xiao Long...
I heard your answer, loud and clear.

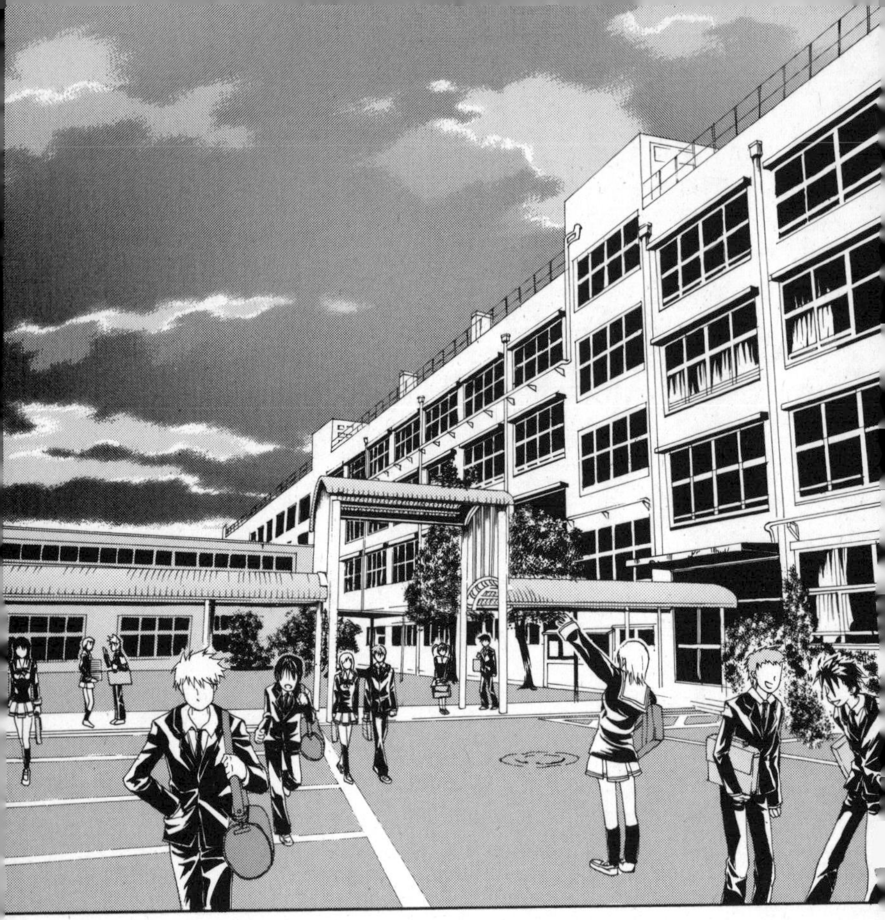

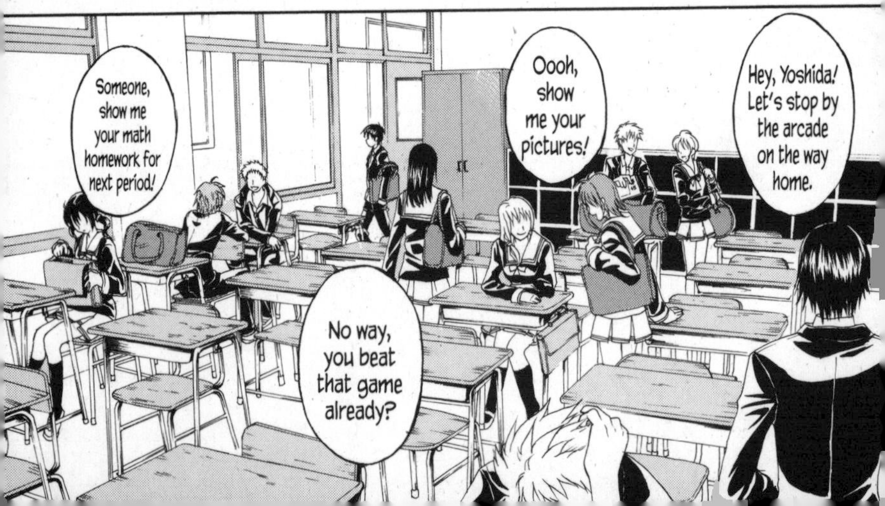
Hey, Yoshida! Let's stop by the arcade on the way home.
Oooh, show me your pictures!
Someone, show me your math homework for next period!
No way, you beat that game already?

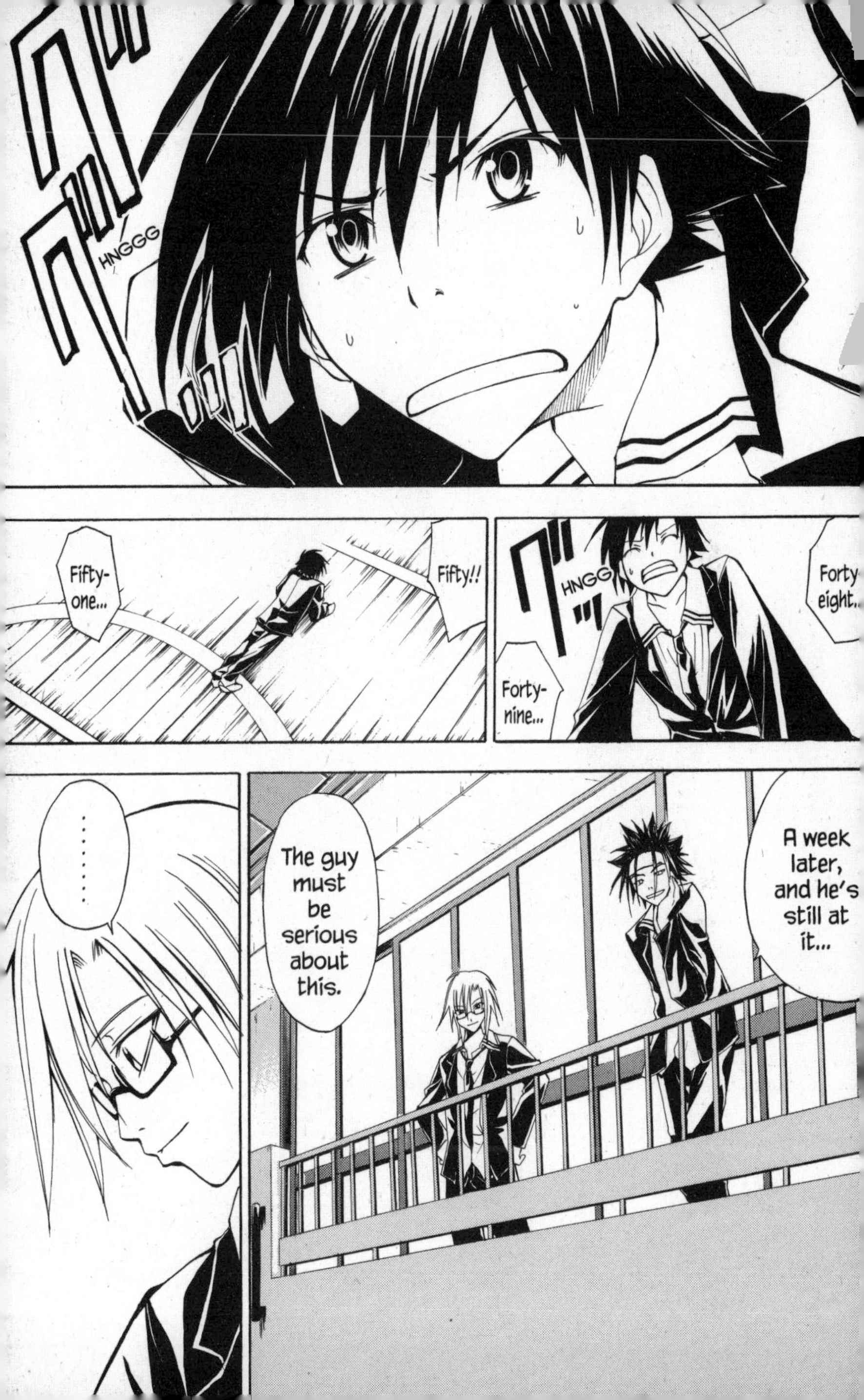
HNGGG
Forty eight..
HNGG
Forty-nine...
Fifty!!
Fifty-one...
A week later, and he's still at it...
The guy must be serious about this.
....

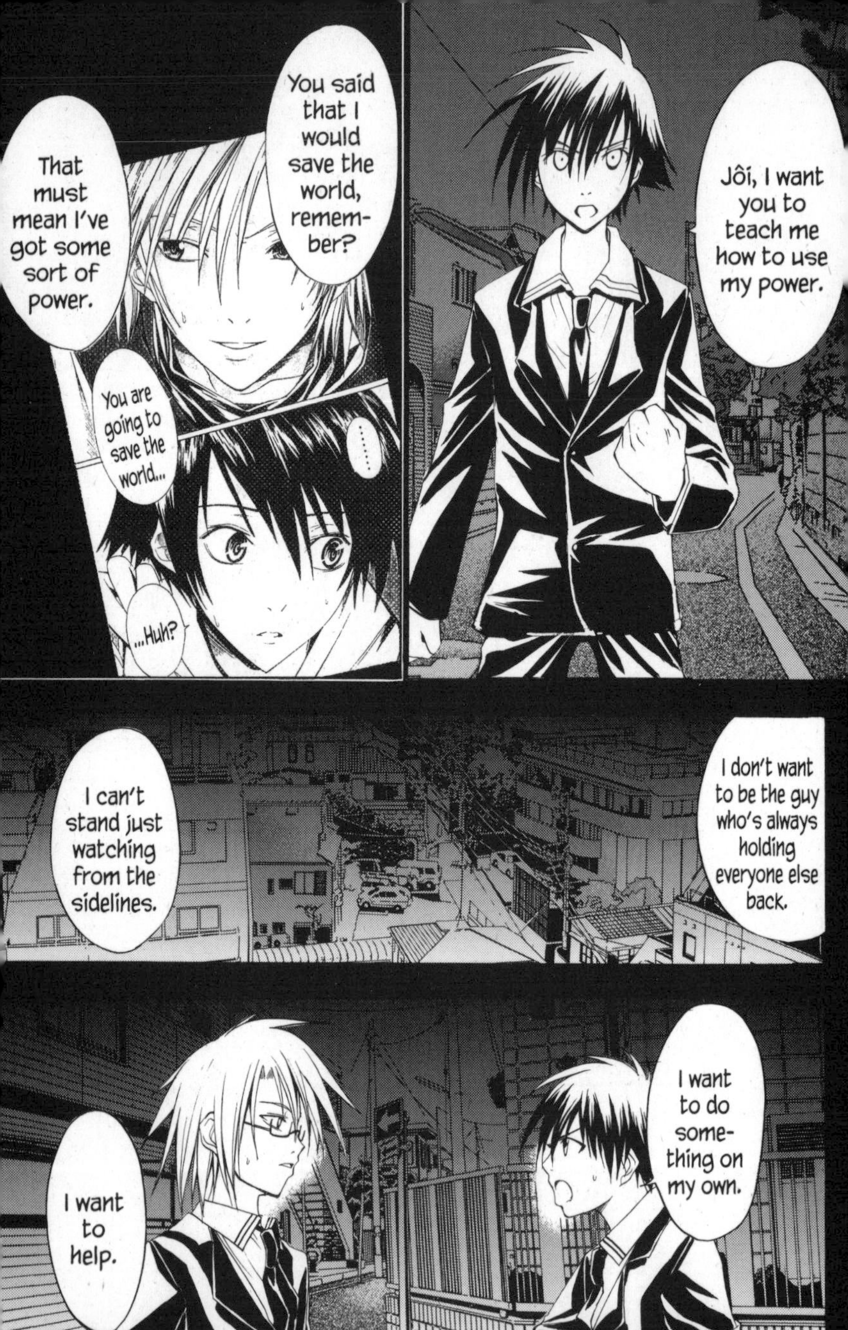
Jôi, I want you to teach me how to use my power.
You said that I would save the world, remember?
That must mean I've got some sort of power.
You are going to save the world...
......
...Huh?
I don't want to be the guy who's always holding everyone else back.
I can't stand just watching from the sidelines.
I want to do some-thing on my own.
I want to help.

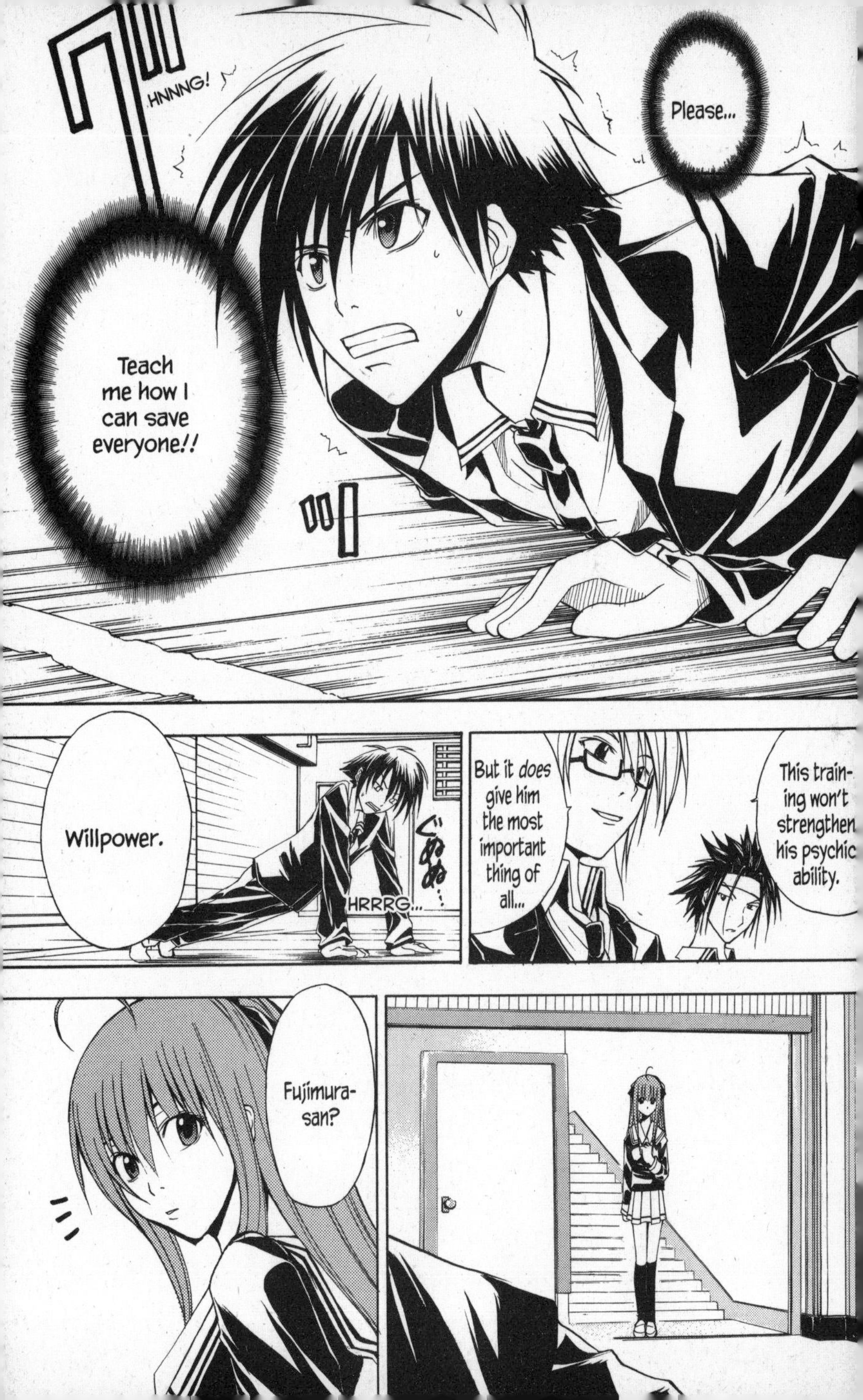
Please...
HNNNG!
Teach me how I can save everyone!!
This training won't strengthen his psychic ability.
But it *does* give him the most important thing of all...
Willpower.
ぐぬぬ...
HRRRG...
Fujimura-san?

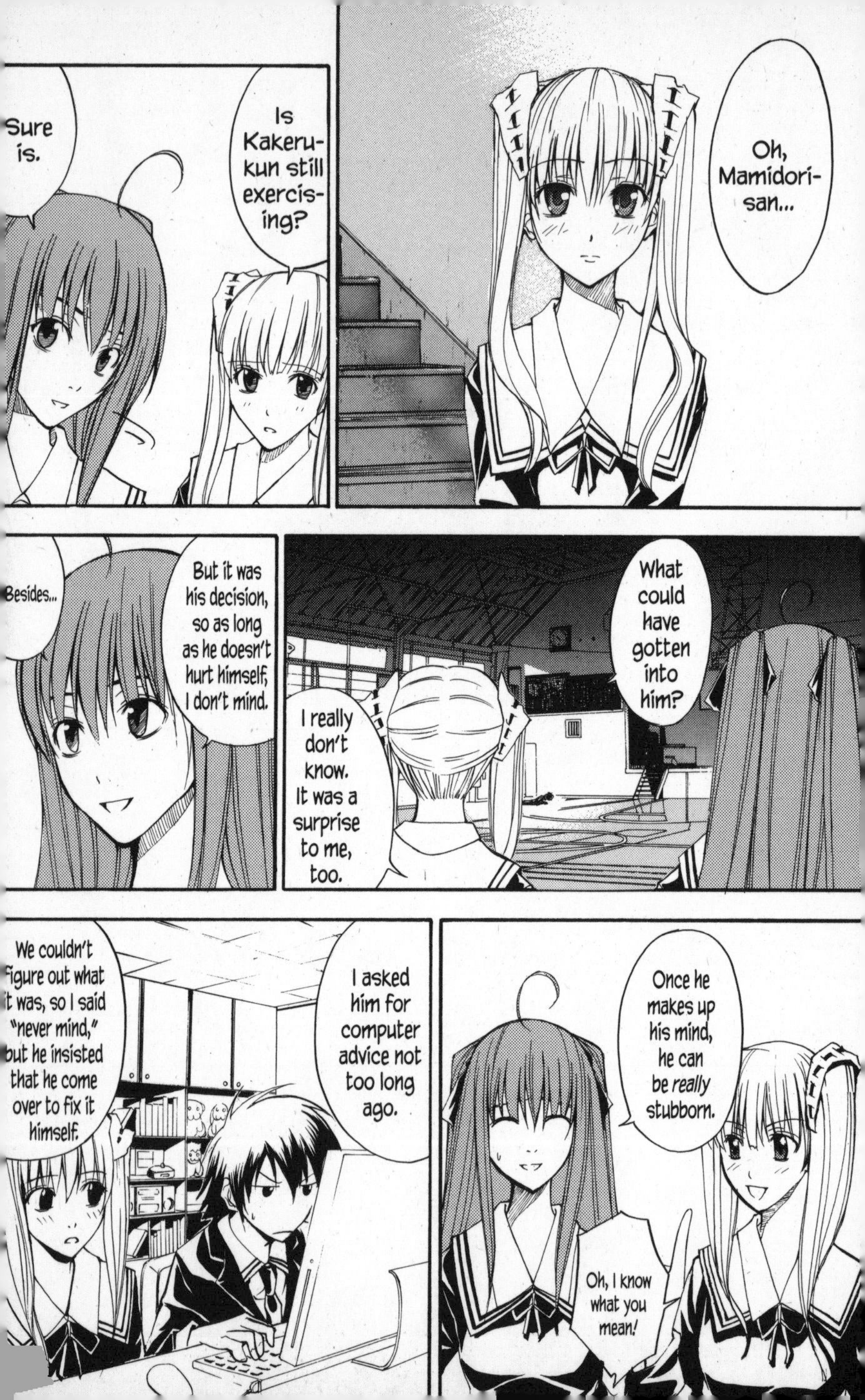
Oh, Mamidori-san...
Is Kakeru-kun still exercising?
Sure is.
What could have gotten into him?
I really don't know. It was a surprise to me, too.
But it was his decision, so as long as he doesn't hurt himself, I don't mind.
Besides...
Once he makes up his mind, he can be *really* stubborn.
Oh, I know what you mean!
I asked him for computer advice not too long ago.
We couldn't figure out what it was, so I said "never mind," but he insisted that he come over to fix it himself.

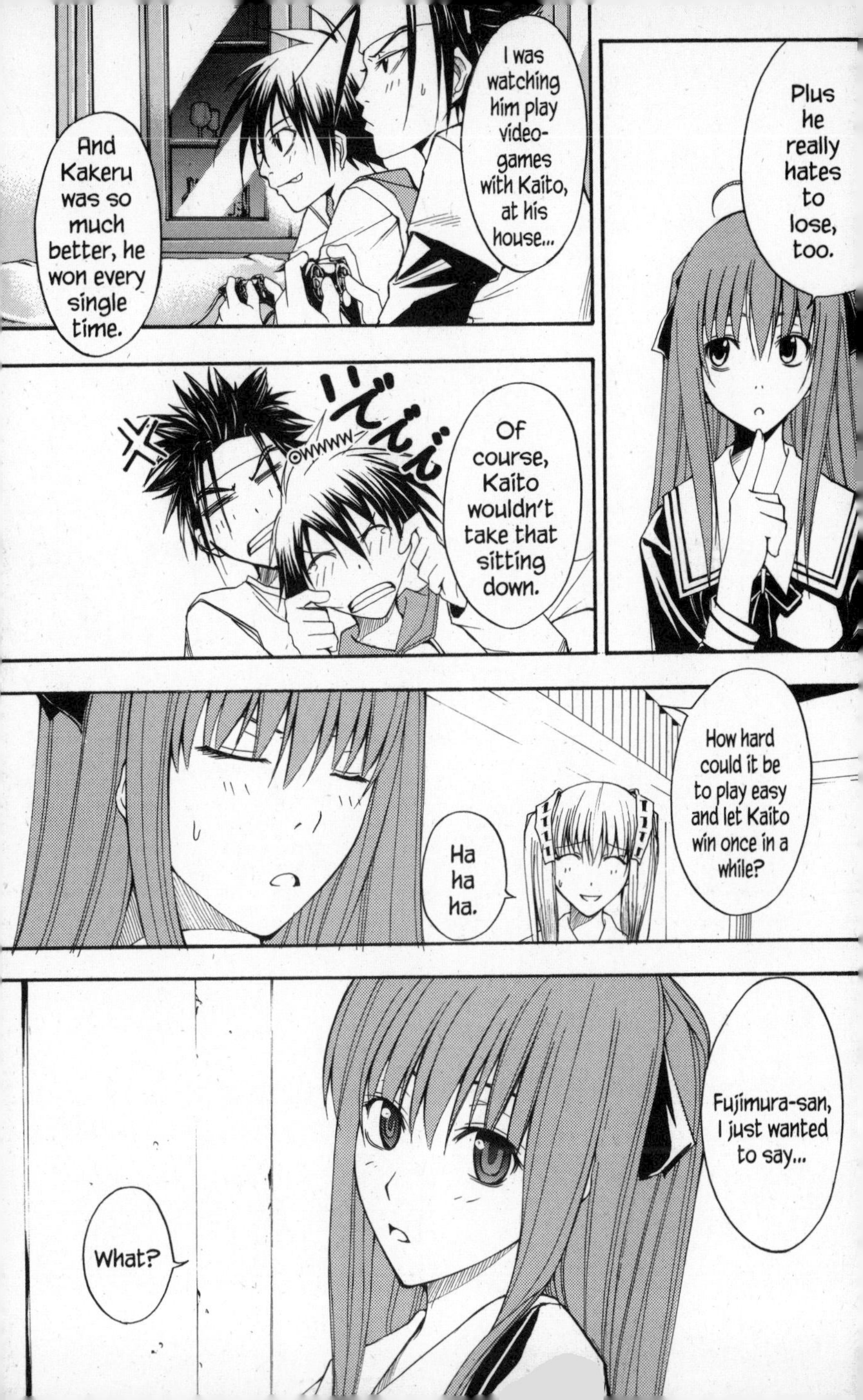
Plus he really hates to lose, too.
I was watching him play video-games with Kaito, at his house...
And Kakeru was so much better, he won every single time.
Of course, Kaito wouldn't take that sitting down.
OWWWW
How hard could it be to play easy and let Kaito win once in a while?
Ha ha ha.
Fujimura-san, I just wanted to say...
What?

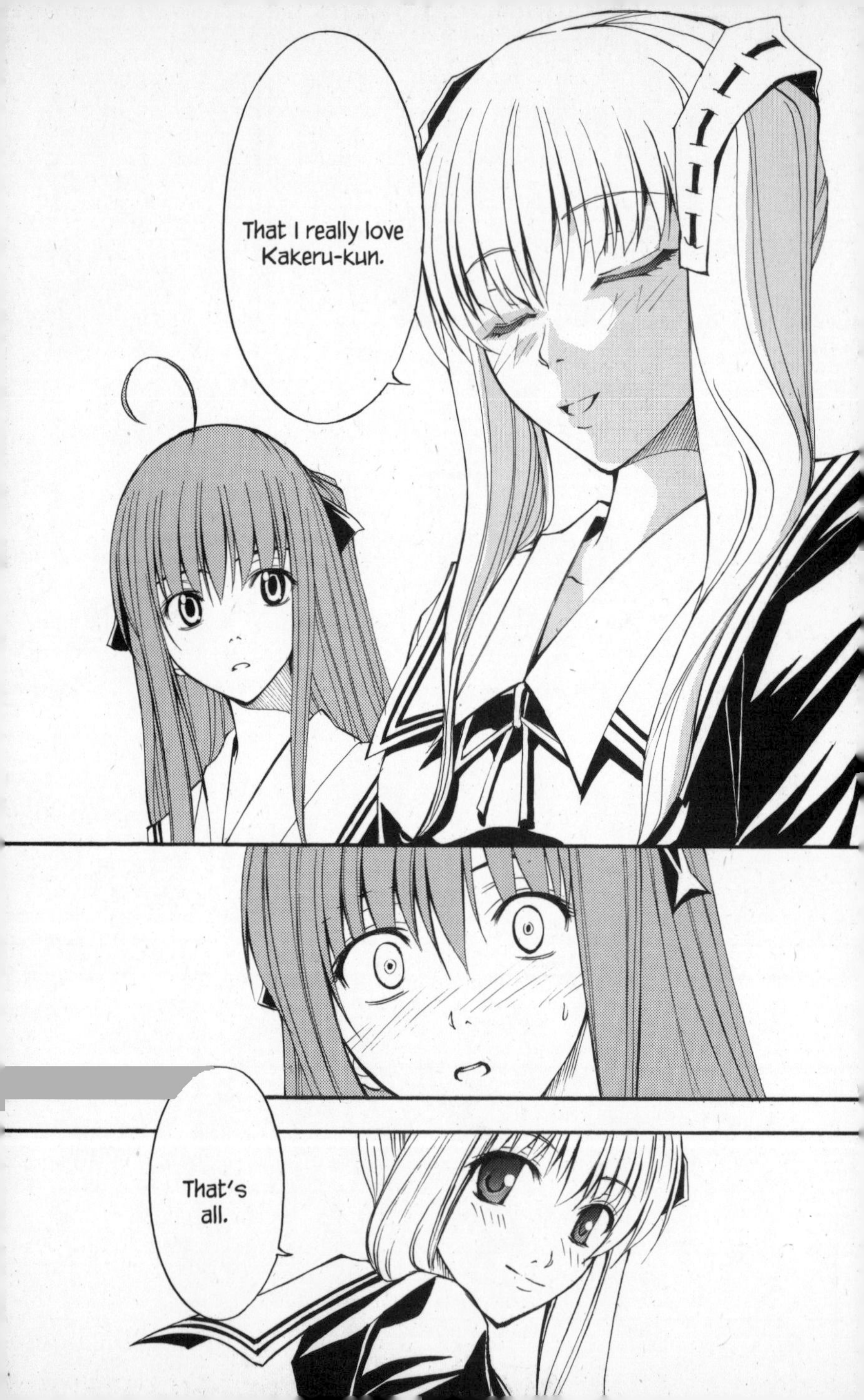
That I really love Kakeru-kun.
That's all.

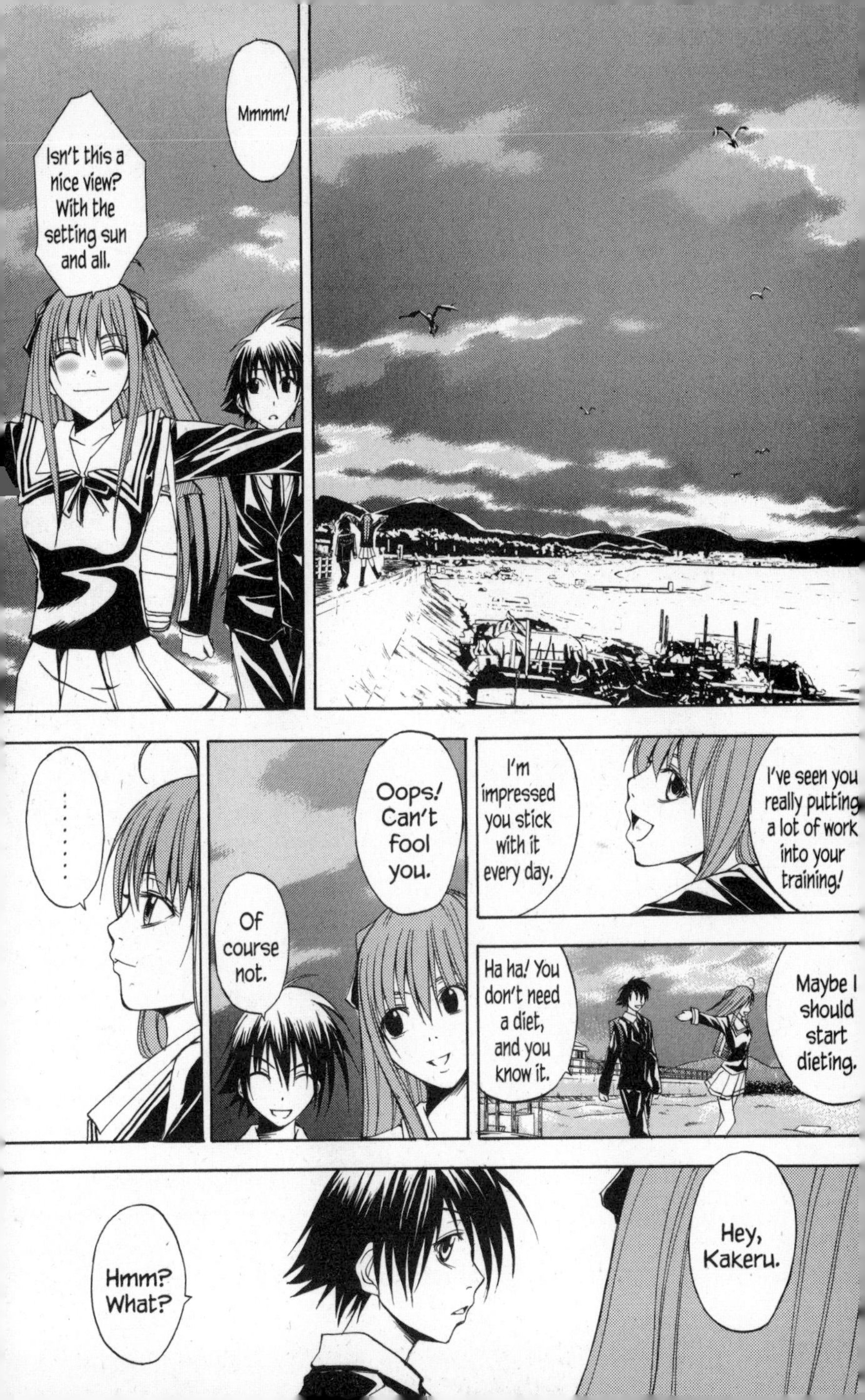
Mmmm!
Isn't this a nice view? With the setting sun and all.
I've seen you really putting a lot of work into your training!
I'm impressed you stick with it every day.
Maybe I should start dieting.
Ha ha! You don't need a diet, and you know it.
Oops! Can't fool you.
Of course not.
....
Hey, Kakeru.
Hmm? What?

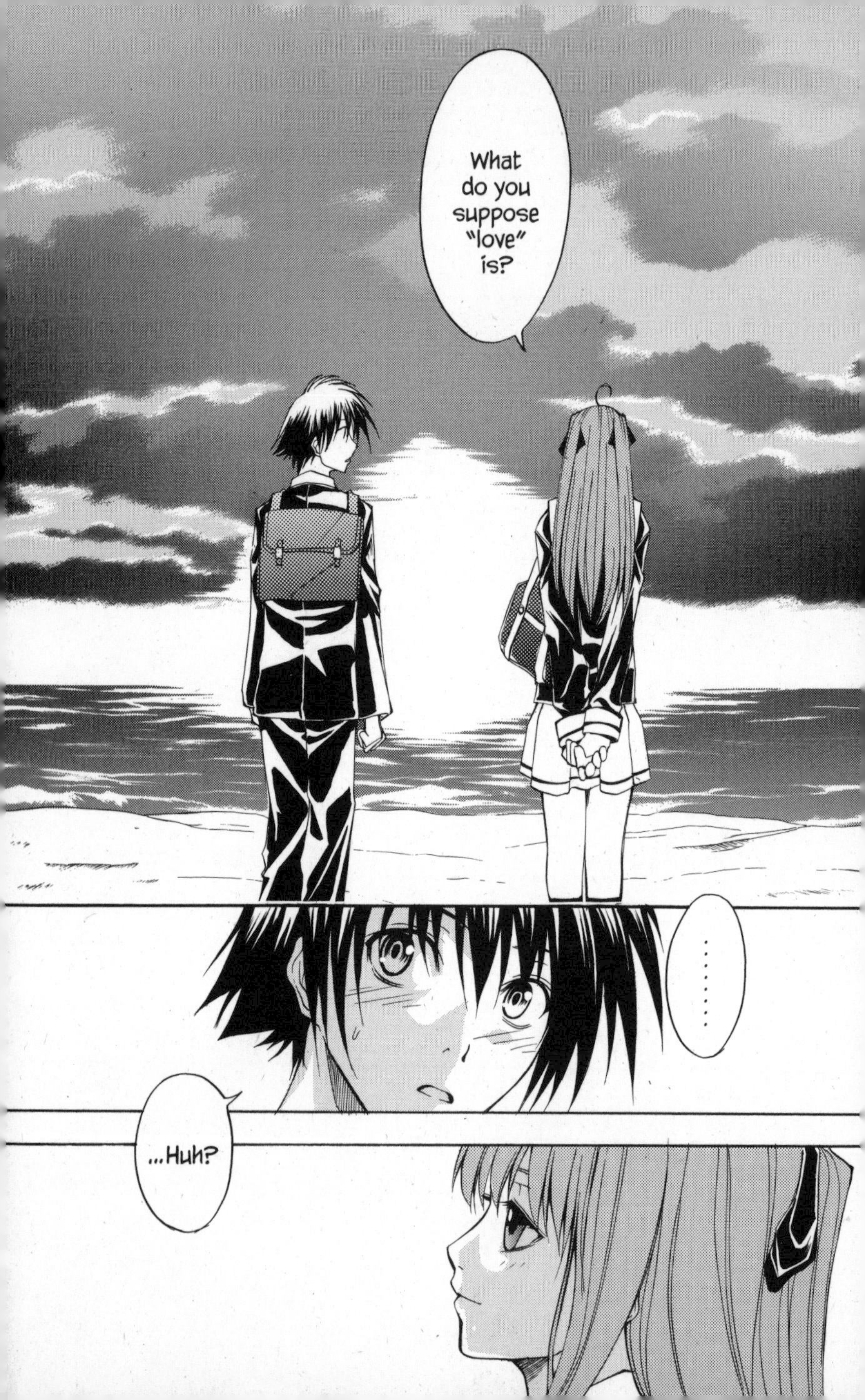
What do you suppose "love" is?
....
...Huh?

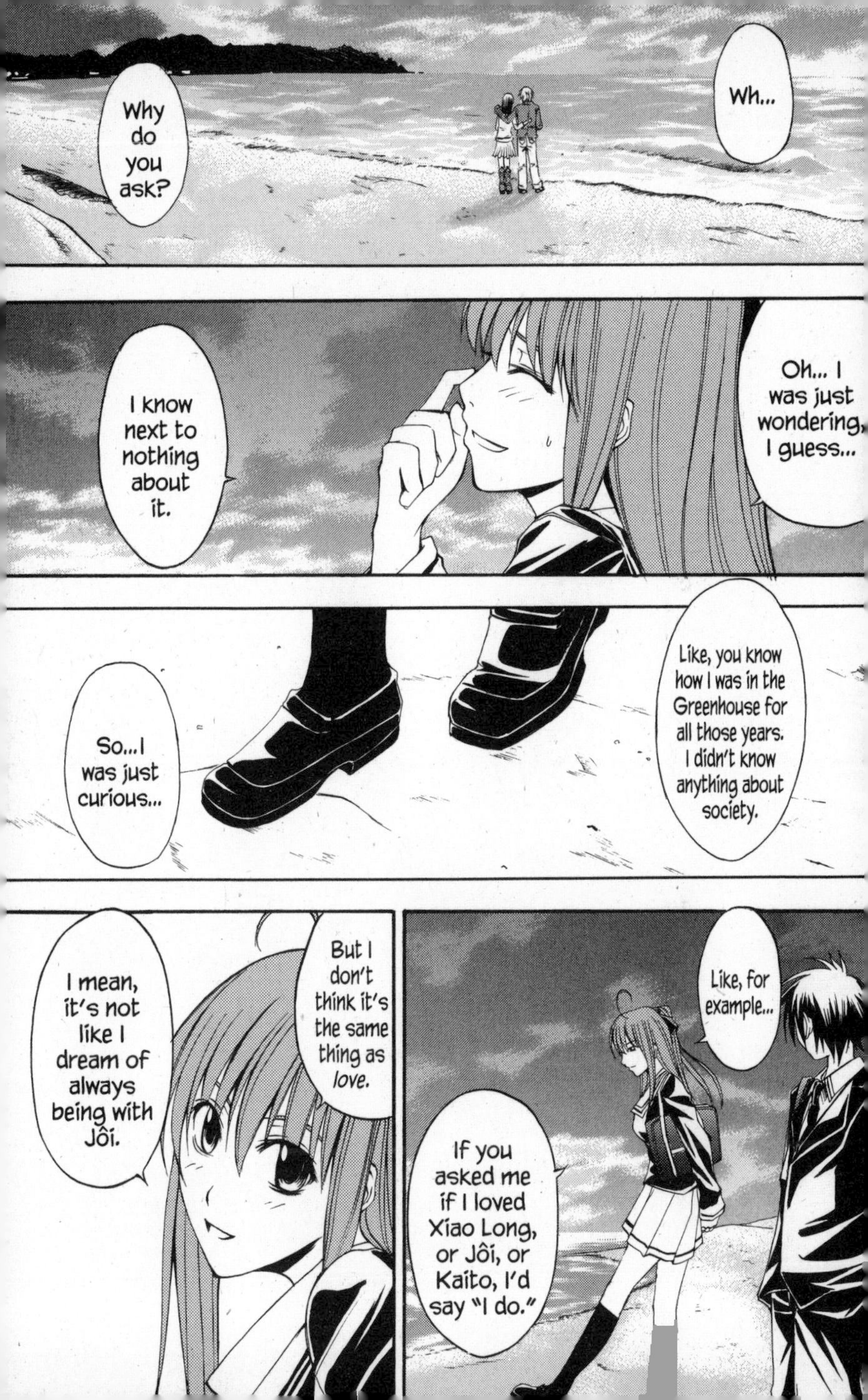
Wh...
Why do you ask?
Oh... I was just wondering, I guess...
I know next to nothing about it.
Like, you know how I was in the Greenhouse for all those years. I didn't know anything about society.
So...I was just curious...
Like, for example...
If you asked me if I loved Xiao Long, or Jôi, or Kaito, I'd say "I do."
But I don't think it's the same thing as *love*.
I mean, it's not like I dream of always being with Jôi.

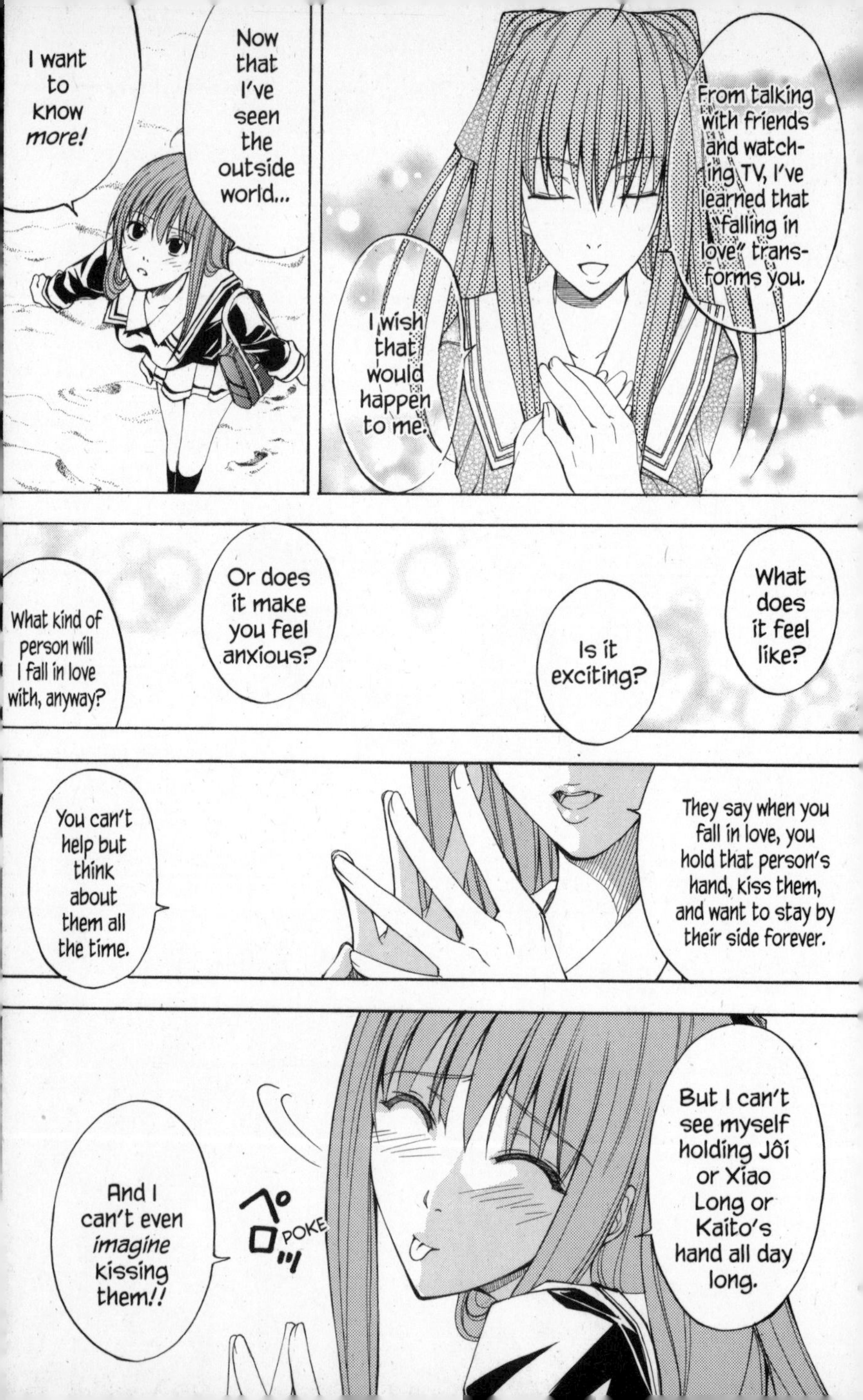
From talking with friends and watching TV, I've learned that "falling in love" transforms you.
I wish that would happen to me.
Now that I've seen the outside world...
I want to know *more!*
What does it feel like?
Is it exciting?
Or does it make you feel anxious?
What kind of person will I fall in love with, anyway?
They say when you fall in love, you hold that person's hand, kiss them, and want to stay by their side forever.
You can't help but think about them all the time.
But I can't see myself holding Jôi or Xiao Long or Kaito's hand all day long.
ペロッ
POKE
And I can't even *imagine* kissing them!!

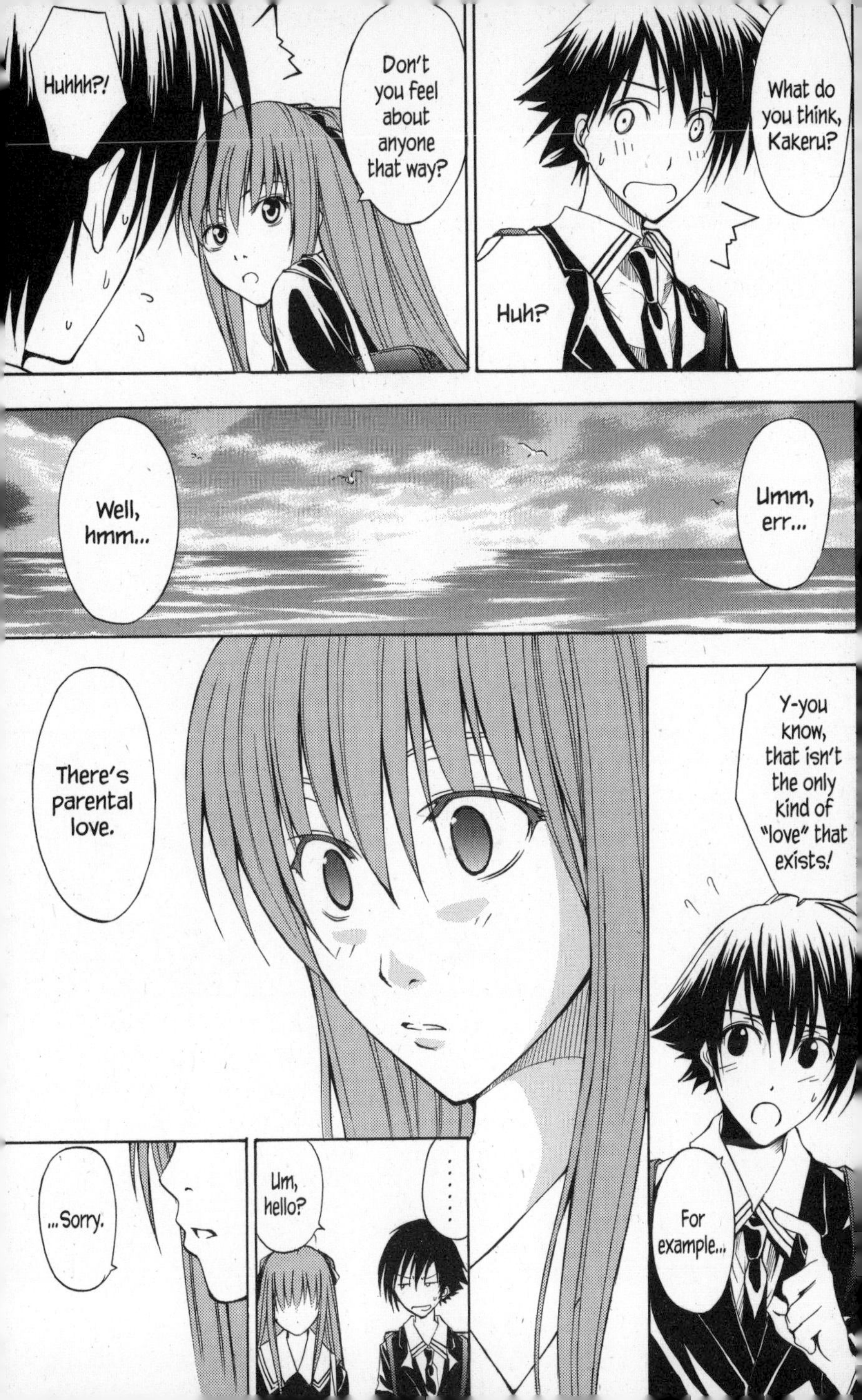

What do you think, Kakeru?
Huh?
Don't you feel about anyone that way?
Huhhh?!
Umm, err...
Well, hmm...
Y-you know, that isn't the only kind of "love" that exists!
For example...
There's parental love.
......
Um, hello?
...Sorry.

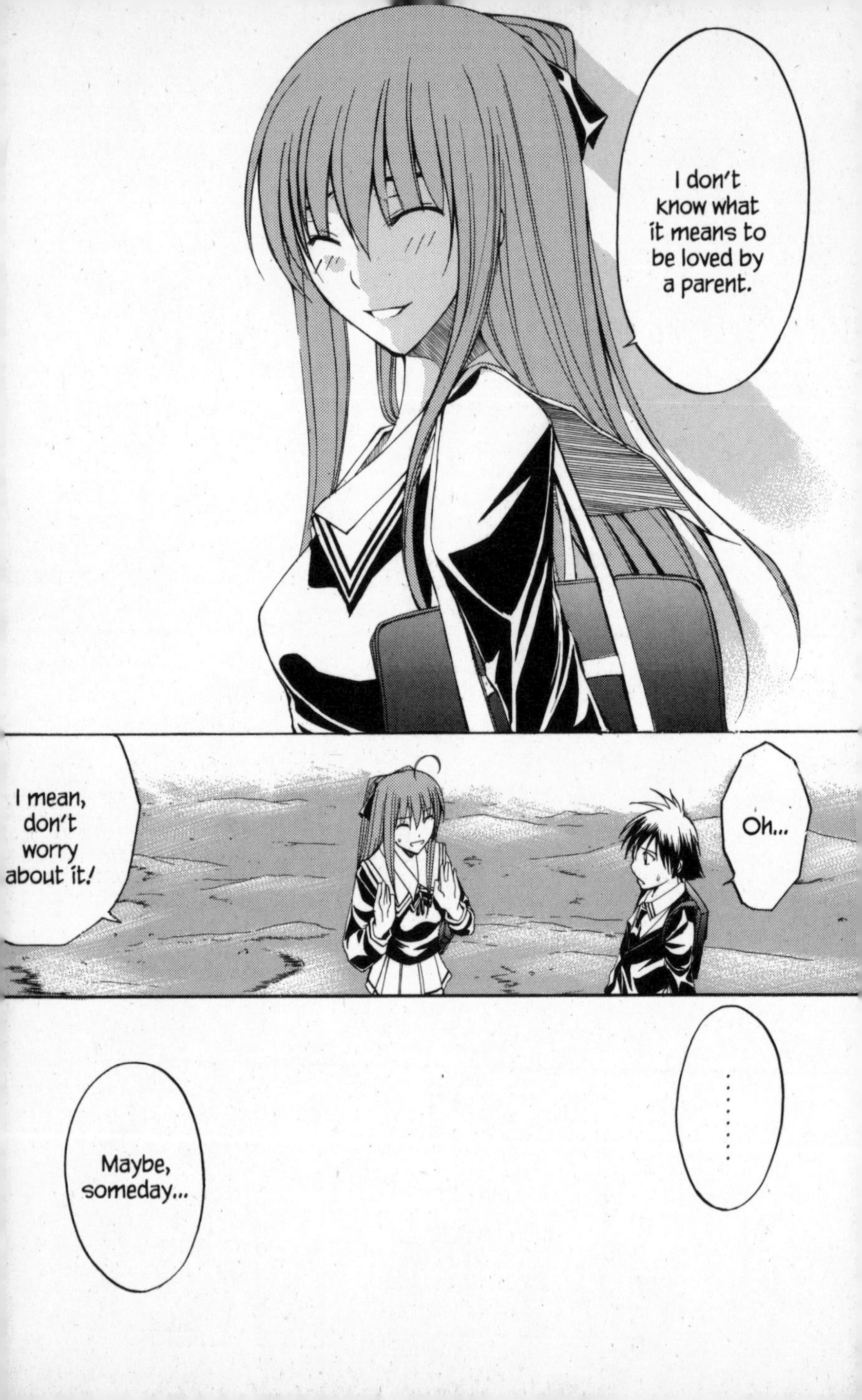
I don't know what it means to be loved by a parent.
Oh...
I mean, don't worry about it!
......
Maybe, someday...

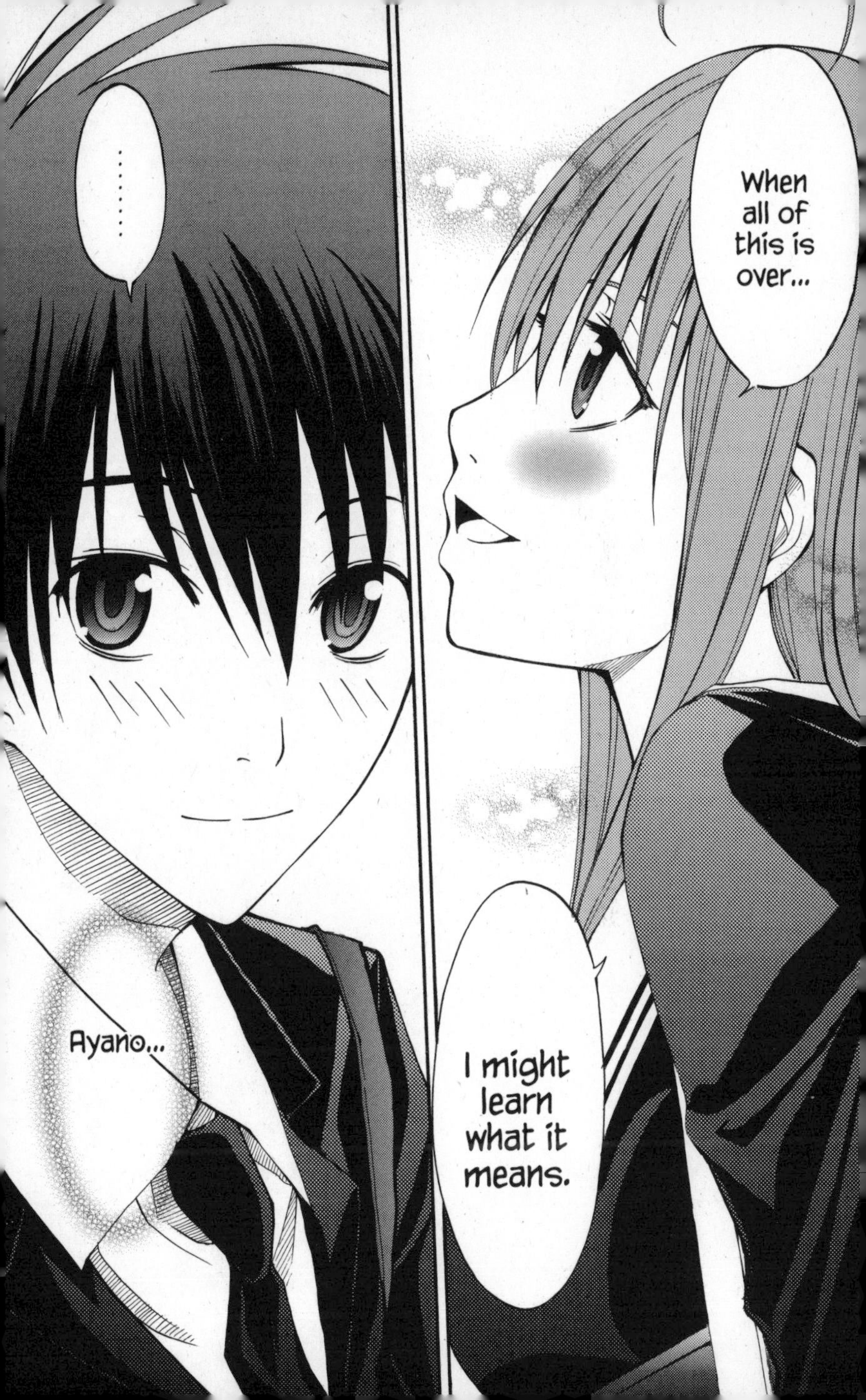
When all of this is over...
I might learn what it means.
......
Ayano...

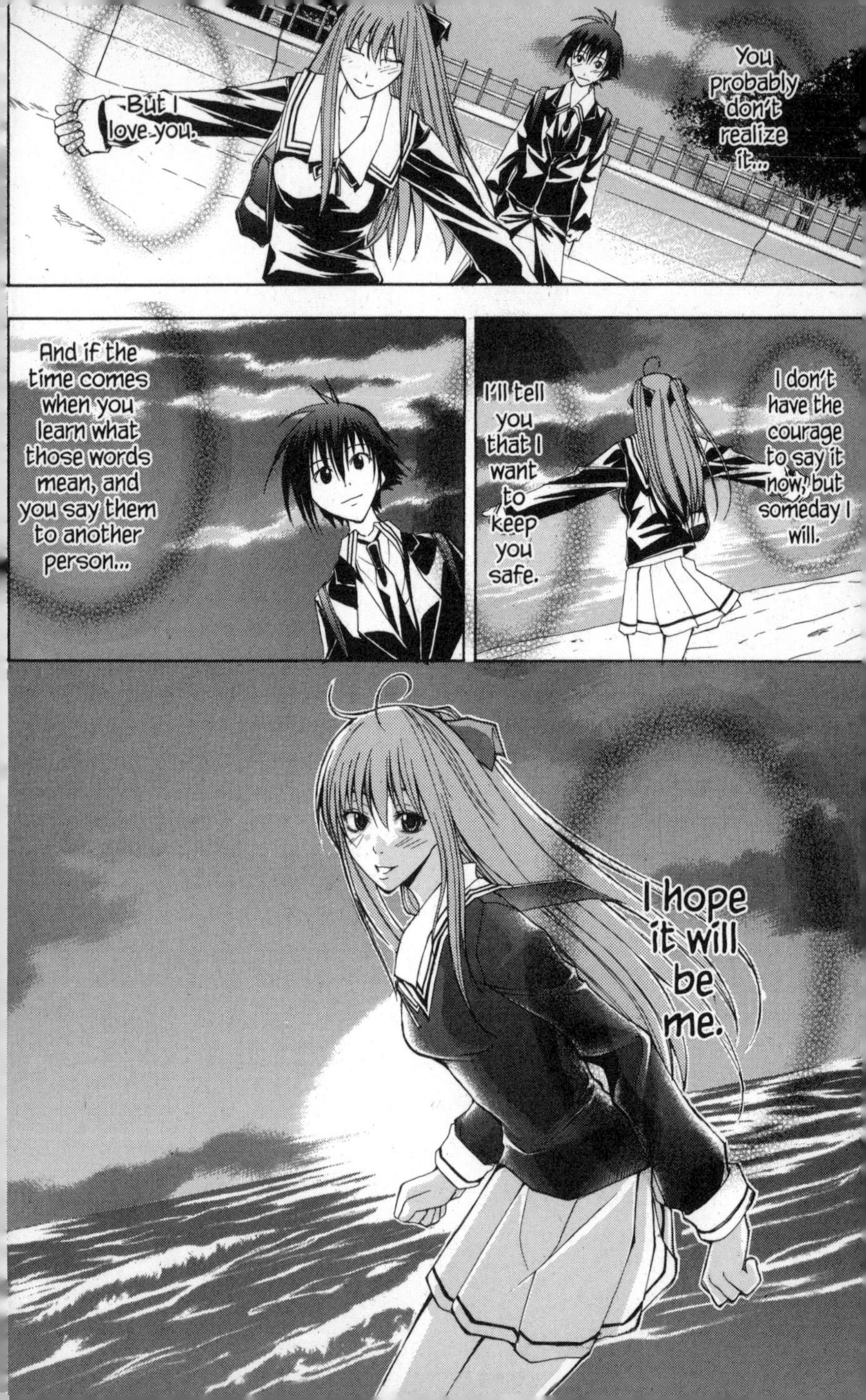
You probably don't realize it...
But I love you.
I don't have the courage to say it now, but someday I will.
I'll tell you that I want to keep you safe.
And if the time comes when you learn what those words mean, and you say them to another person...
I hope it will be me.

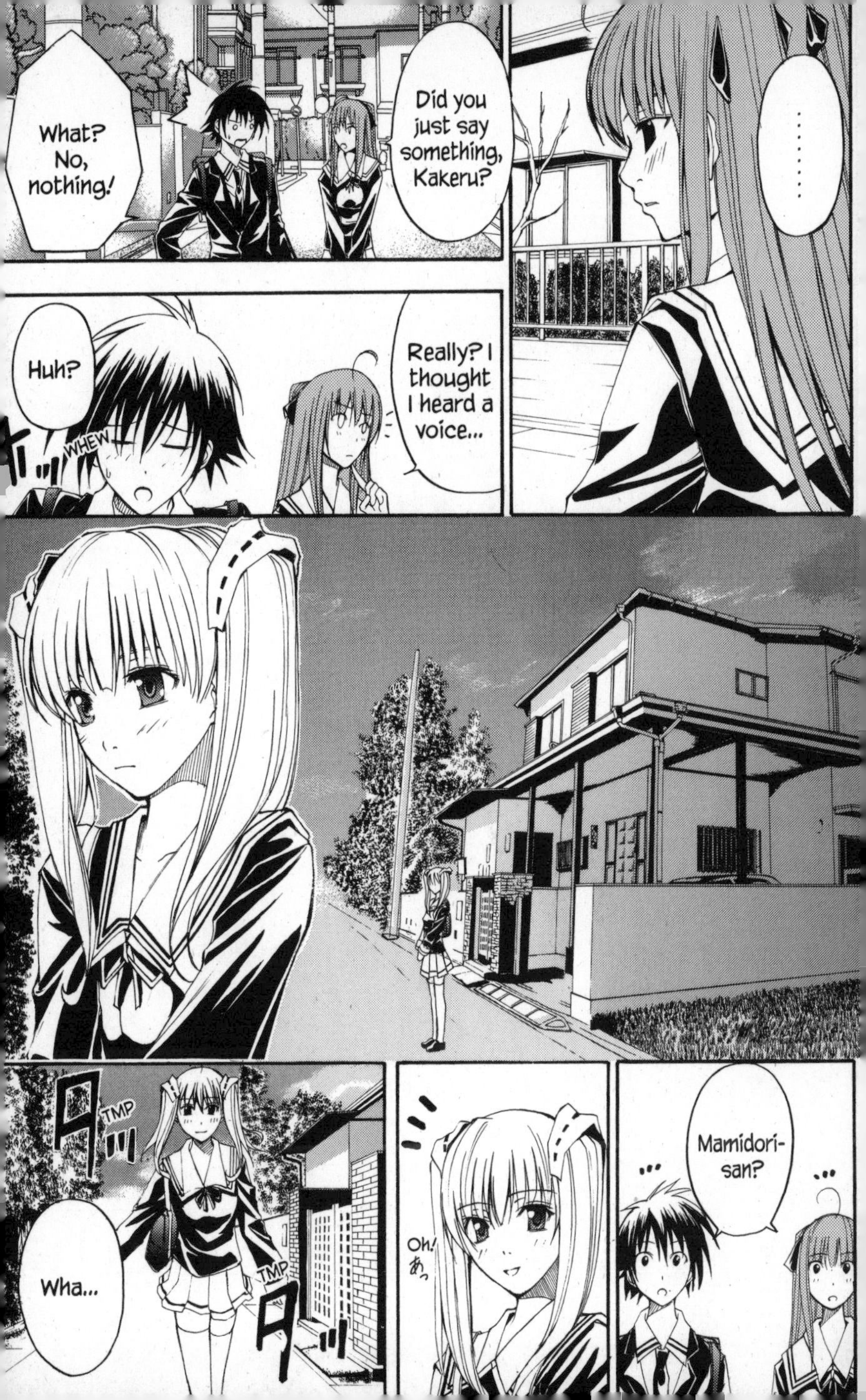
……
Did you just say something, Kakeru?
What? No, nothing!
Really? I thought I heard a voice...
Huh?
WHEW
...
...
Mamidori-san?
Oh! あっ
TMP
Wha...
TMP

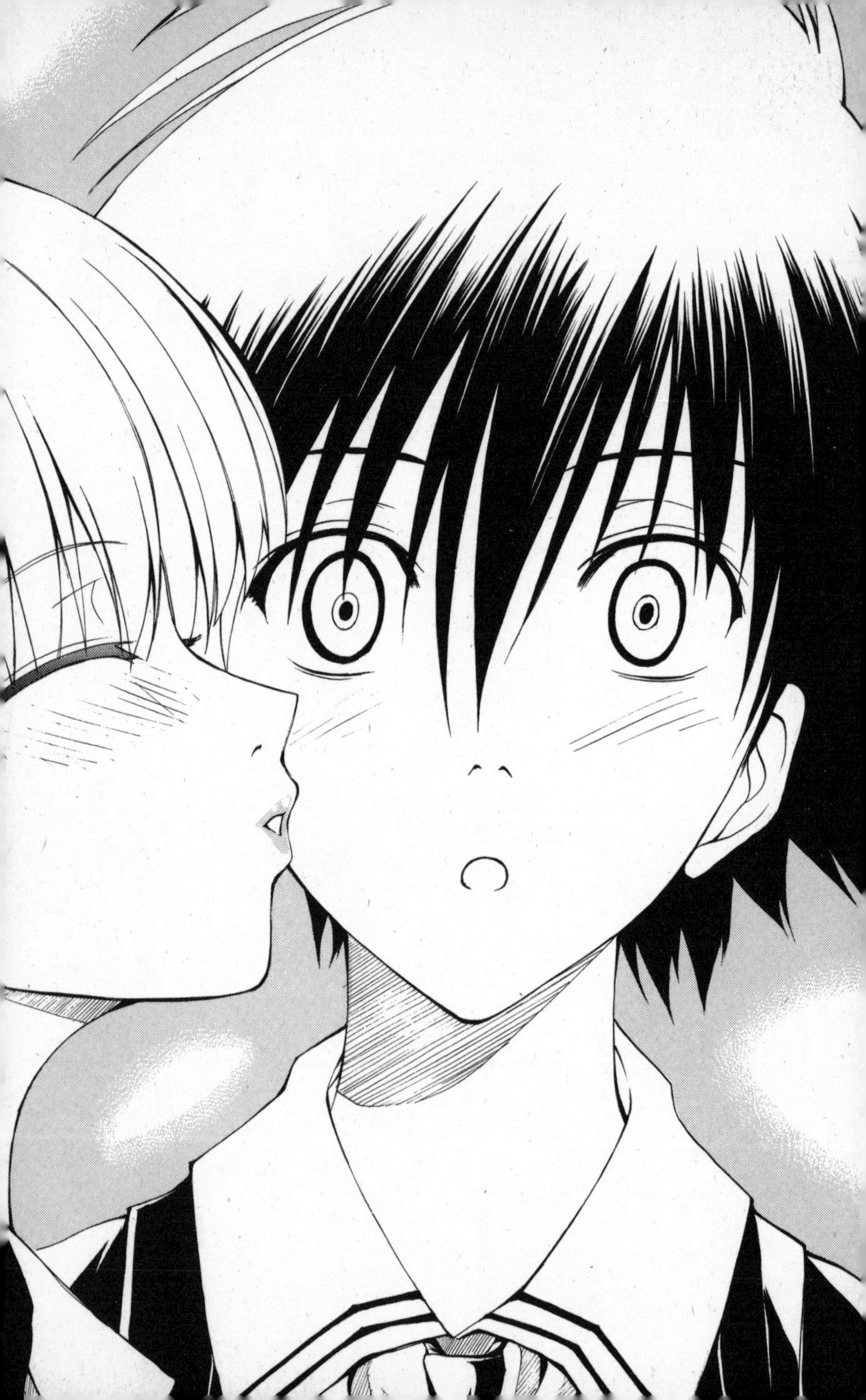

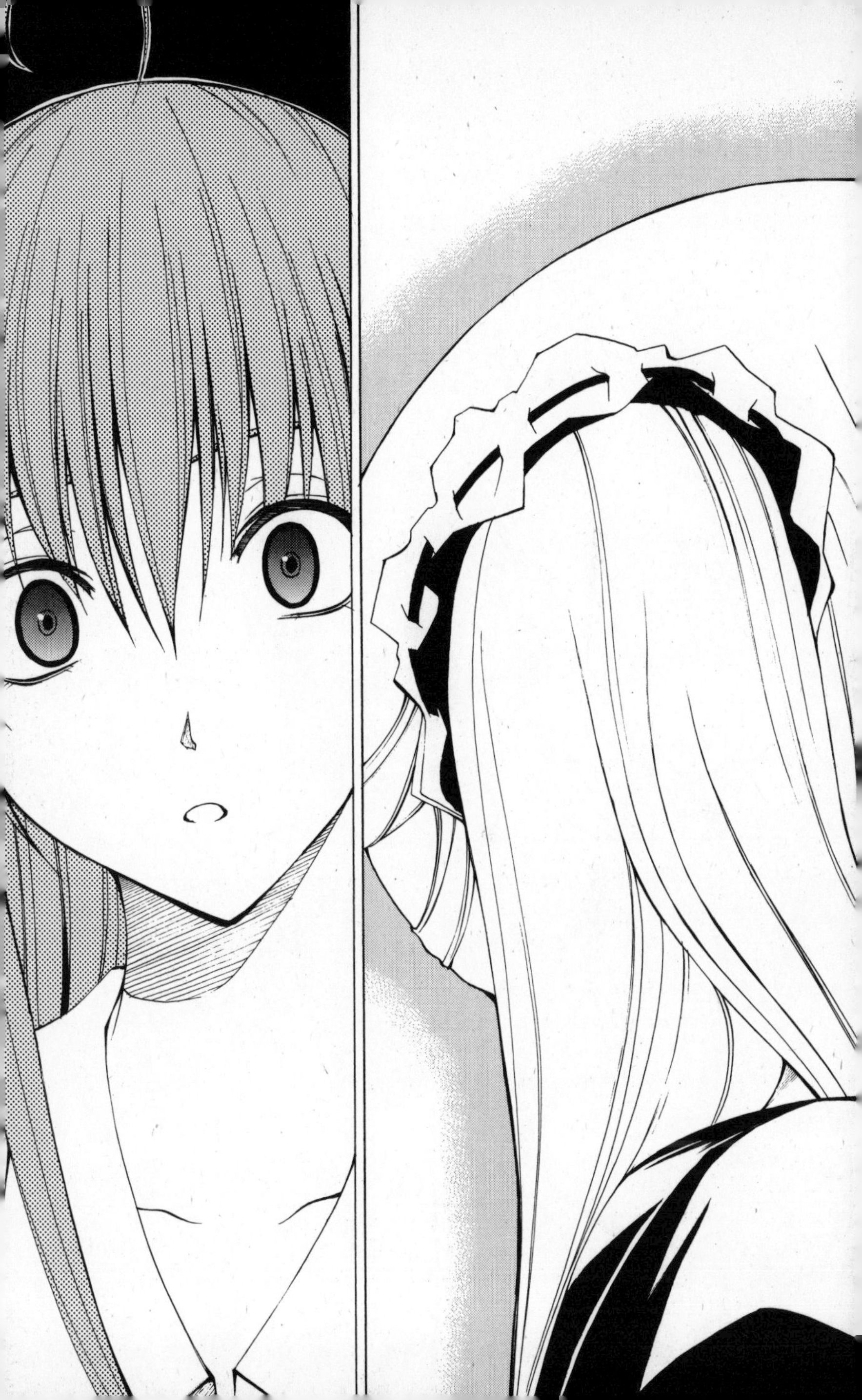

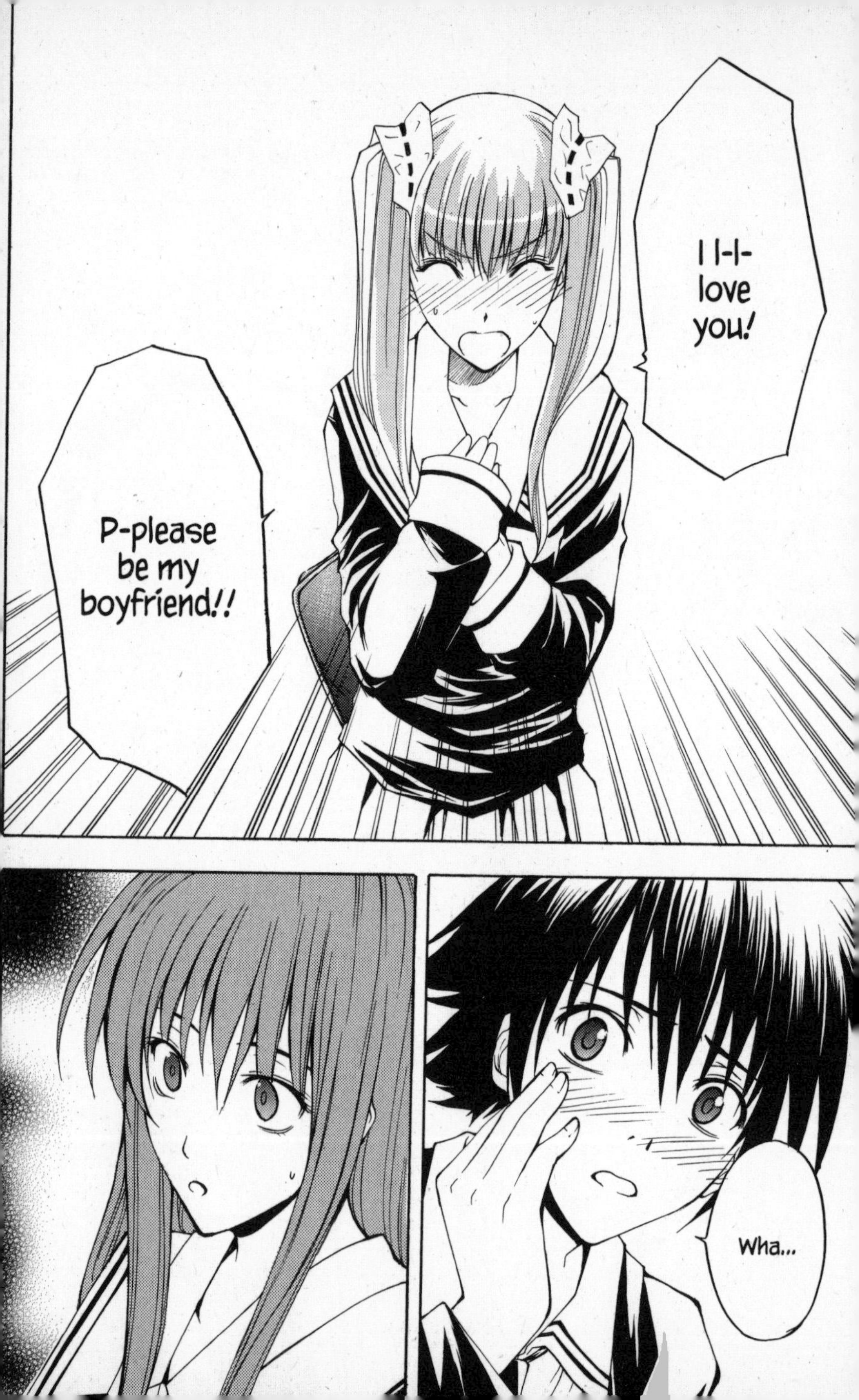
I I-I- love you!
P-please be my boyfriend!!
Wha...

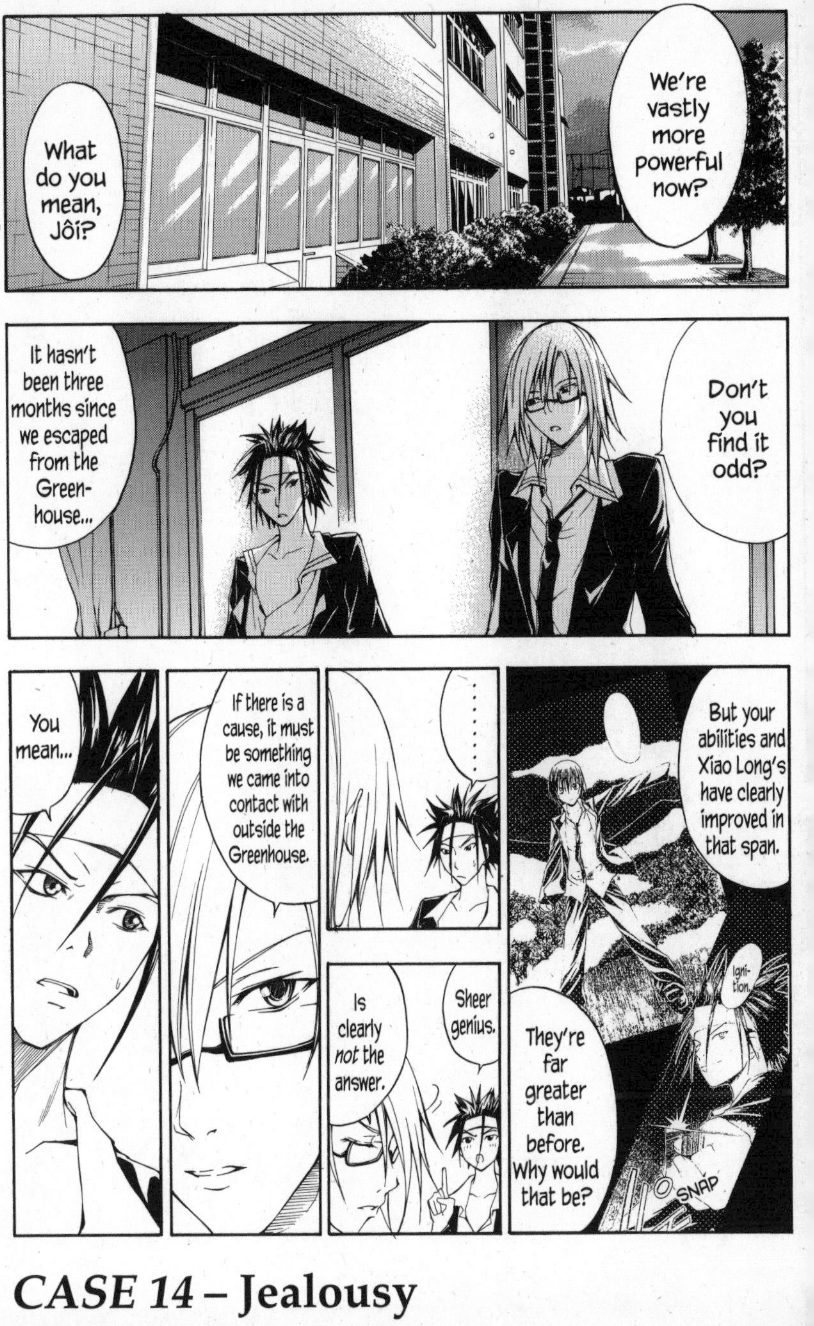
We're vastly more powerful now?
What do you mean, Jôi?
Don't you find it odd?
It hasn't been three months since we escaped from the Green-house...
But your abilities and Xiao Long's have clearly improved in that span.
Igni-tion.
SNAP
They're far greater than before. Why would that be?
......
Sheer genius.
Is clearly *not* the answer.
If there is a cause, it must be something we came into contact with outside the Greenhouse.
You mean...

CASE 14 – Jealousy

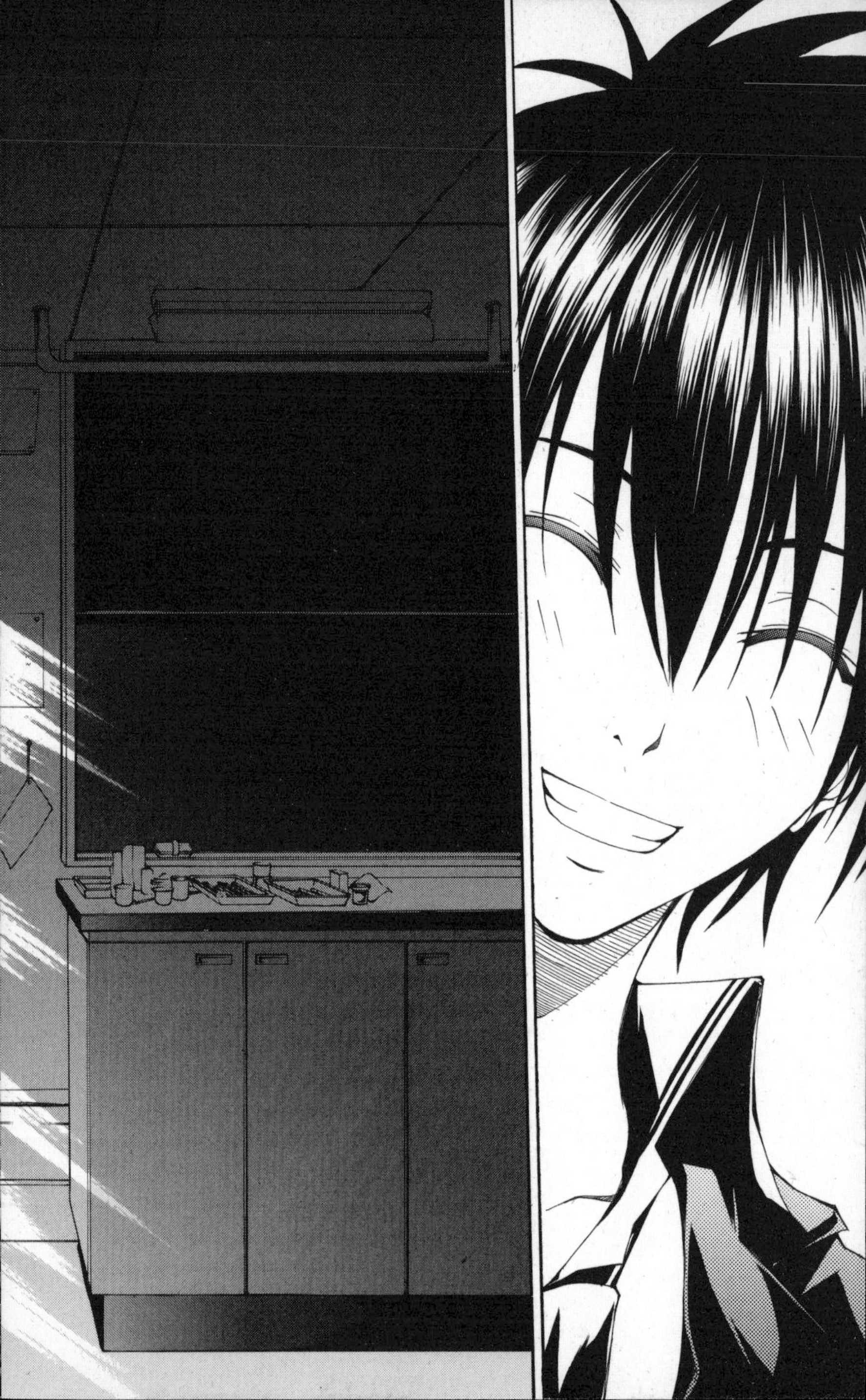

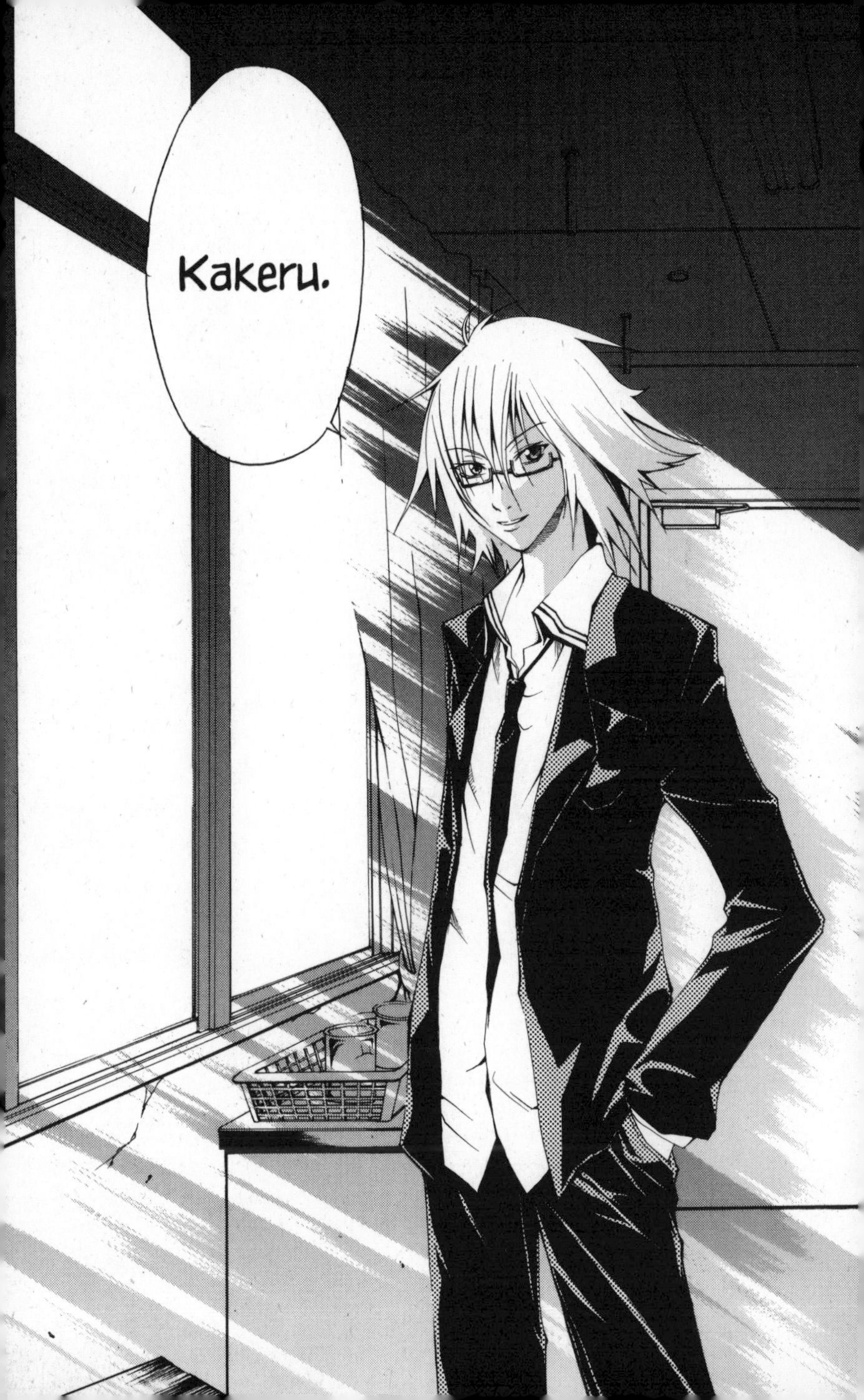
Kakeru.

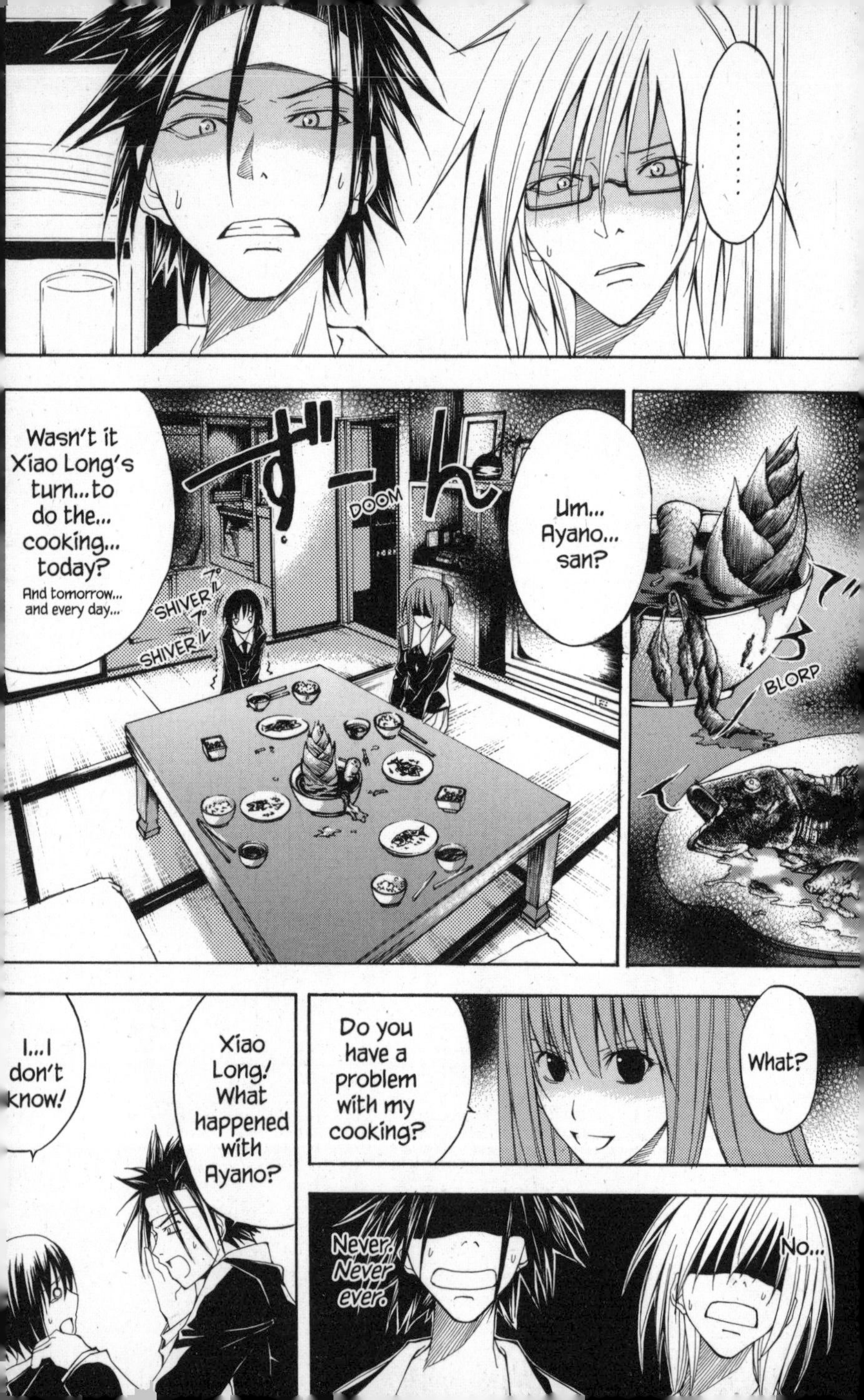

......
BLORP
Um... Ayano... san?
DOOM
Wasn't it Xiao Long's turn...to do the... cooking... today?
And tomorrow... and every day...
SHIVER
SHIVER
What?
Do you have a problem with my cooking?
No...
Never. Never ever.
Xiao Long! What happened with Ayano?
I...I don't know!

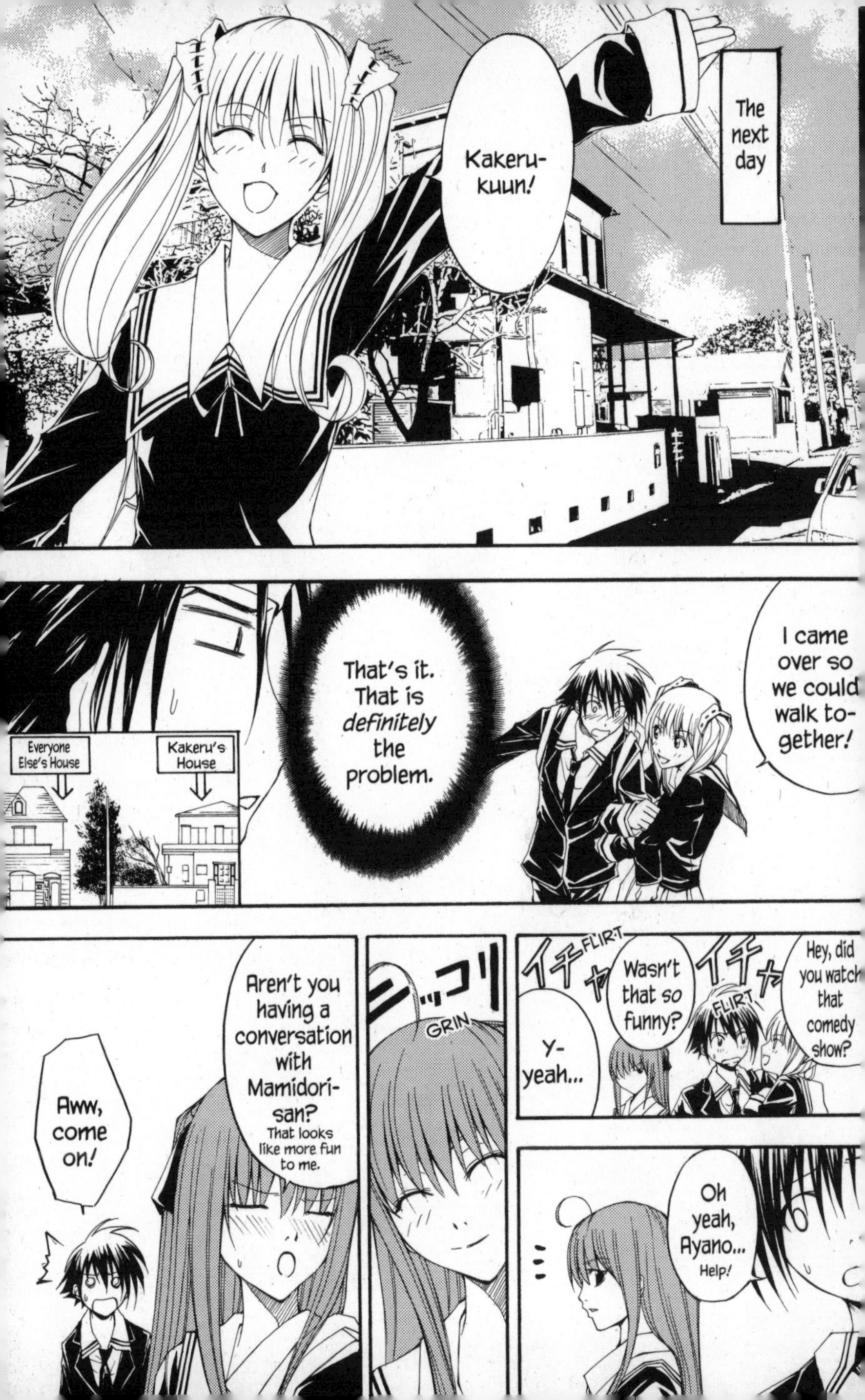

The next day
Kakeru-kuun!
I came over so we could walk together!
That's it. That is *definitely* the problem.
Kakeru's House
Everyone Else's House
Hey, did you watch that comedy show?
FLIRT
Wasn't that so funny?
FLIRT
Y-yeah...
Oh yeah, Ayano...
Help!
GRIN
Aren't you having a conversation with Mamidori-san?
That looks like more fun to me.
Aww, come on!

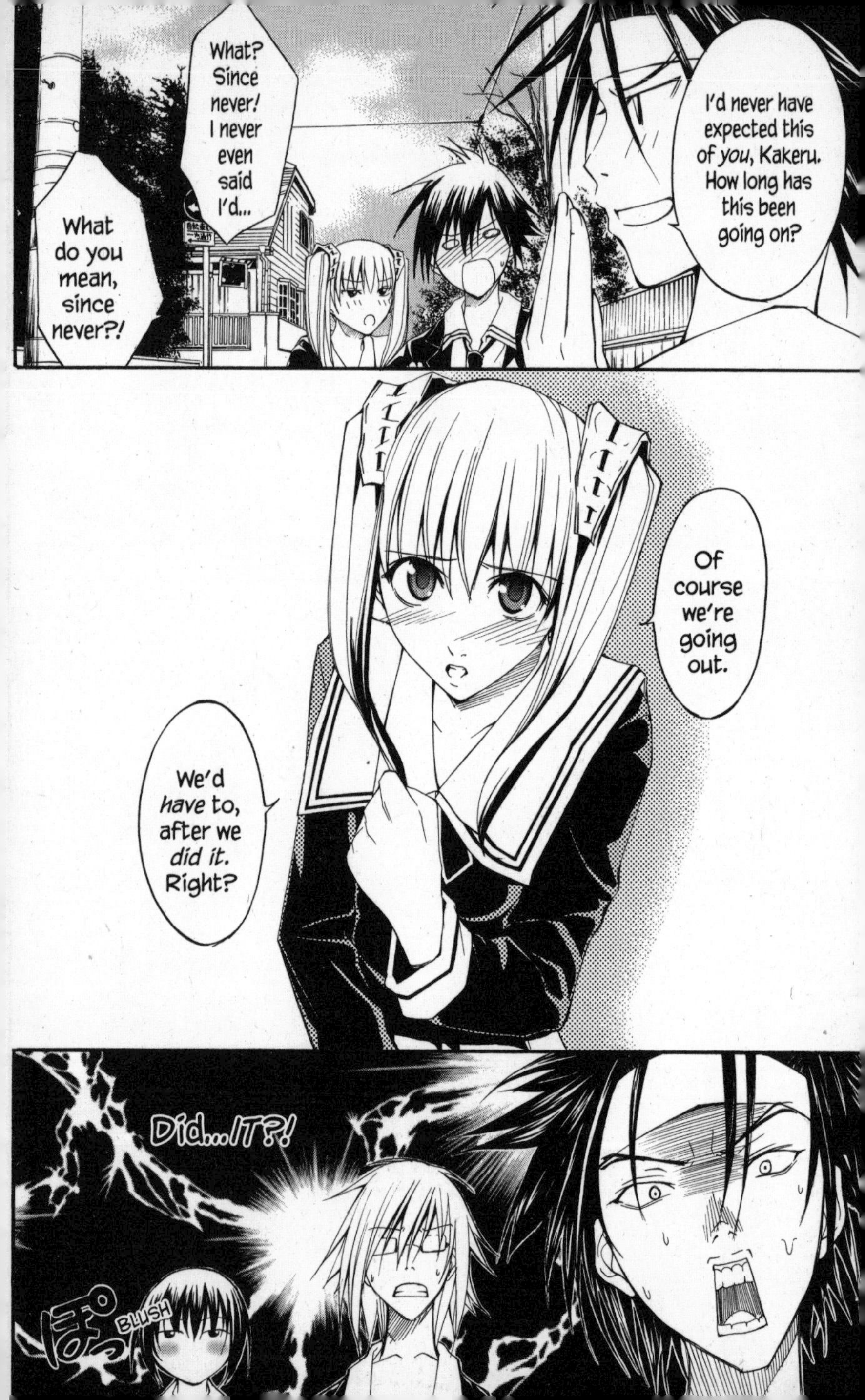
I'd never have expected this of *you*, Kakeru. How long has this been going on?
What? Since never! I never even said I'd...
What do you mean, since never?!
Of course we're going out.
We'd *have* to, after we *did it*. Right?
Did...IT?!
ぽっ
BLUSH

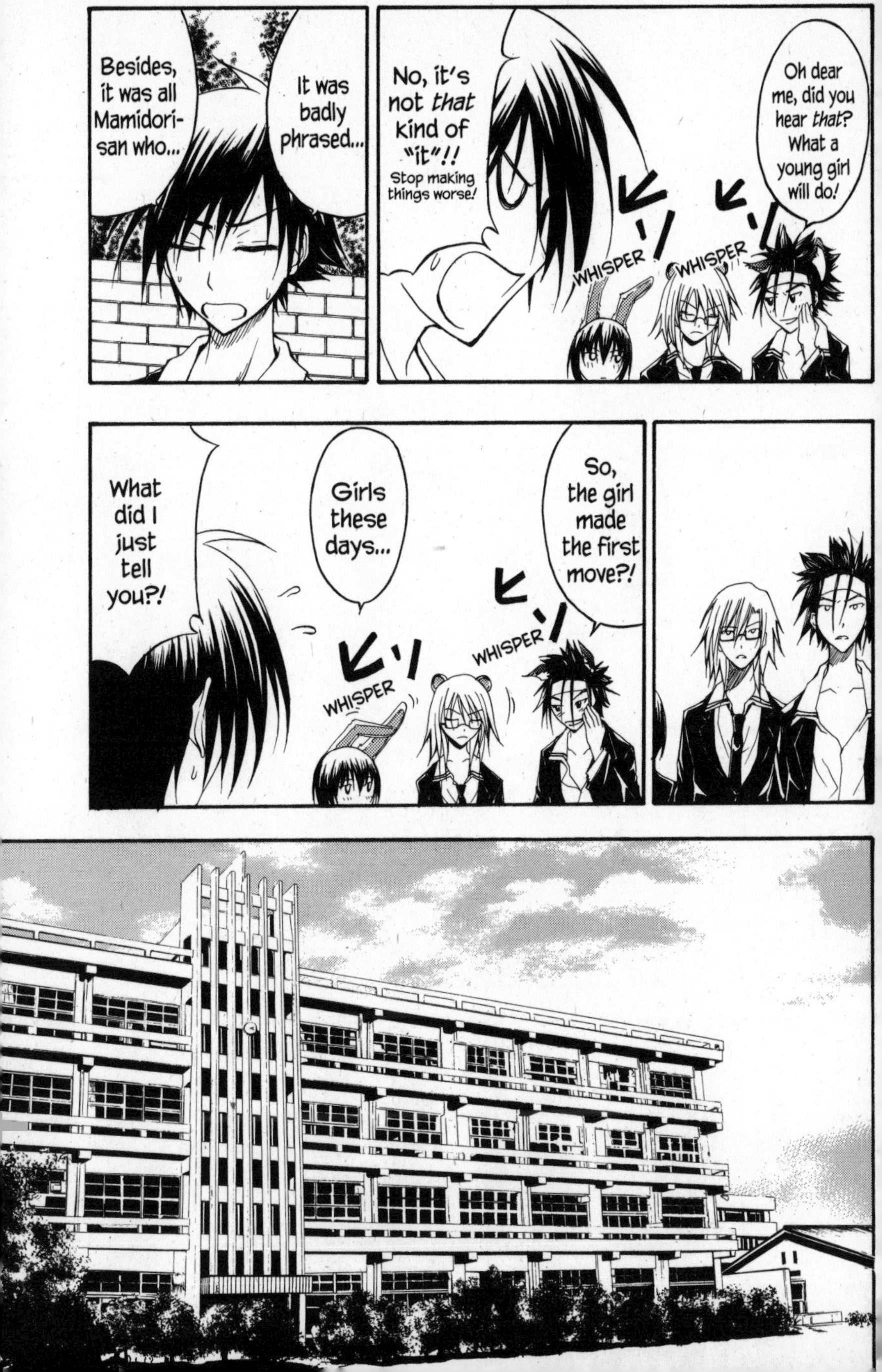
Oh dear me, did you hear *that*? What a young girl will do!
WHISPER
WHISPER
No, it's not *that* kind of "it"!!
Stop making things worse!
It was badly phrased...
Besides, it was all Mamidori-san who...
So, the girl made the first move?!
WHISPER
Girls these days...
WHISPER
What did I just tell you?!

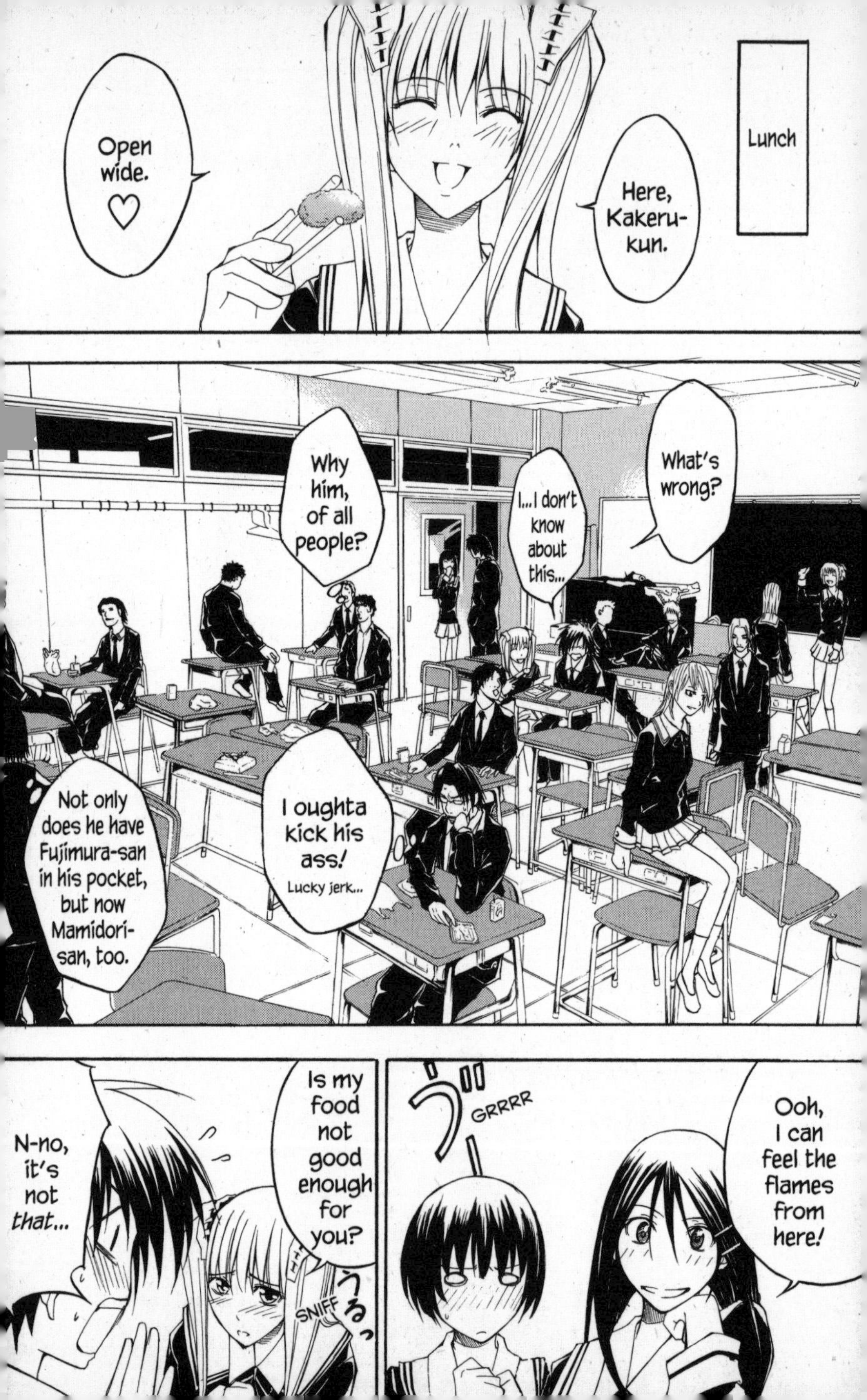
Lunch
Here, Kakeru-kun.
Open wide. ♡
What's wrong?
I...I don't know about this...
Why him, of all people?
I oughta kick his ass!
Lucky jerk...
Not only does he have Fujimura-san in his pocket, but now Mamidori-san, too.
Ooh, I can feel the flames from here!
GRRRR
Is my food not good enough for you?
SNIFF
N-no, it's not that...

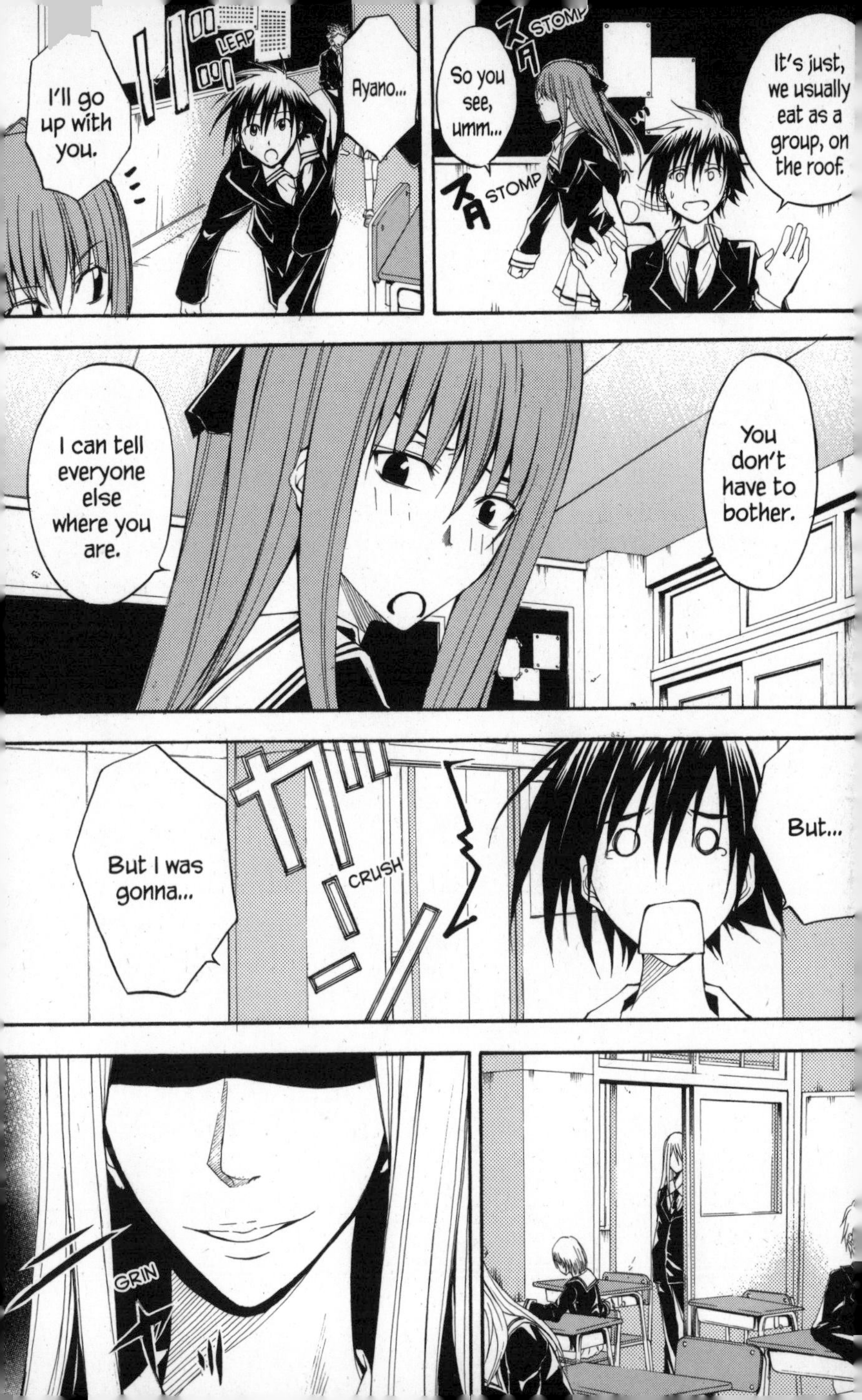
STOMP
It's just, we usually eat as a group, on the roof.
So you see, umm...
STOMP
Ayano...
LEAP
I'll go up with you.
You don't have to bother.
I can tell everyone else where you are.
But...
CRUSH
But I was gonna...
GRIN

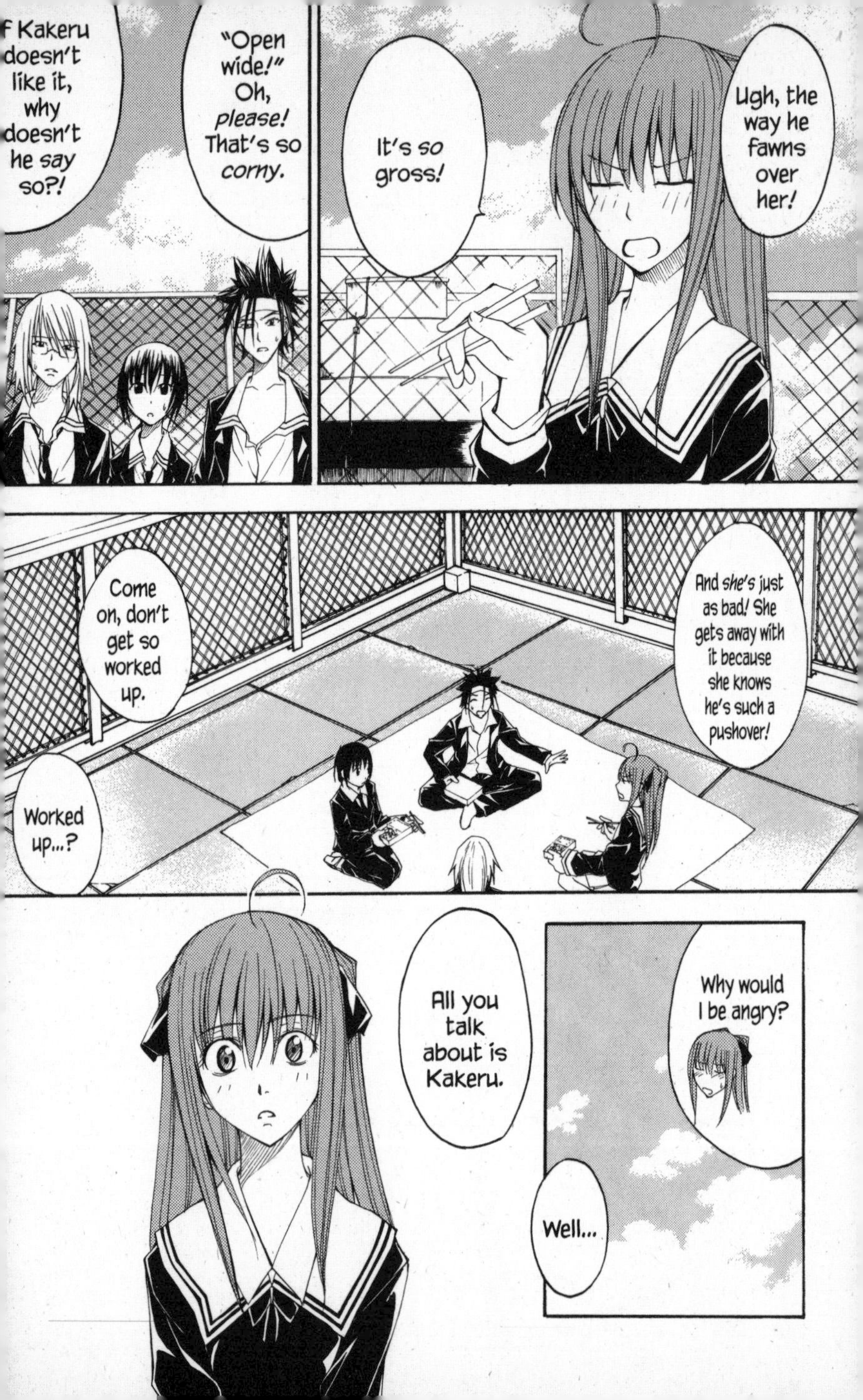
Ugh, the way he fawns over her!
It's so gross!
"Open wide!" Oh, *please!* That's so *corny.*
f Kakeru doesn't like it, why doesn't he *say* so?!
And *she's* just as bad! She gets away with it because she knows he's such a pushover!
Come on, don't get so worked up.
Worked up...?
Why would I be angry?
Well...
All you talk about is Kakeru.

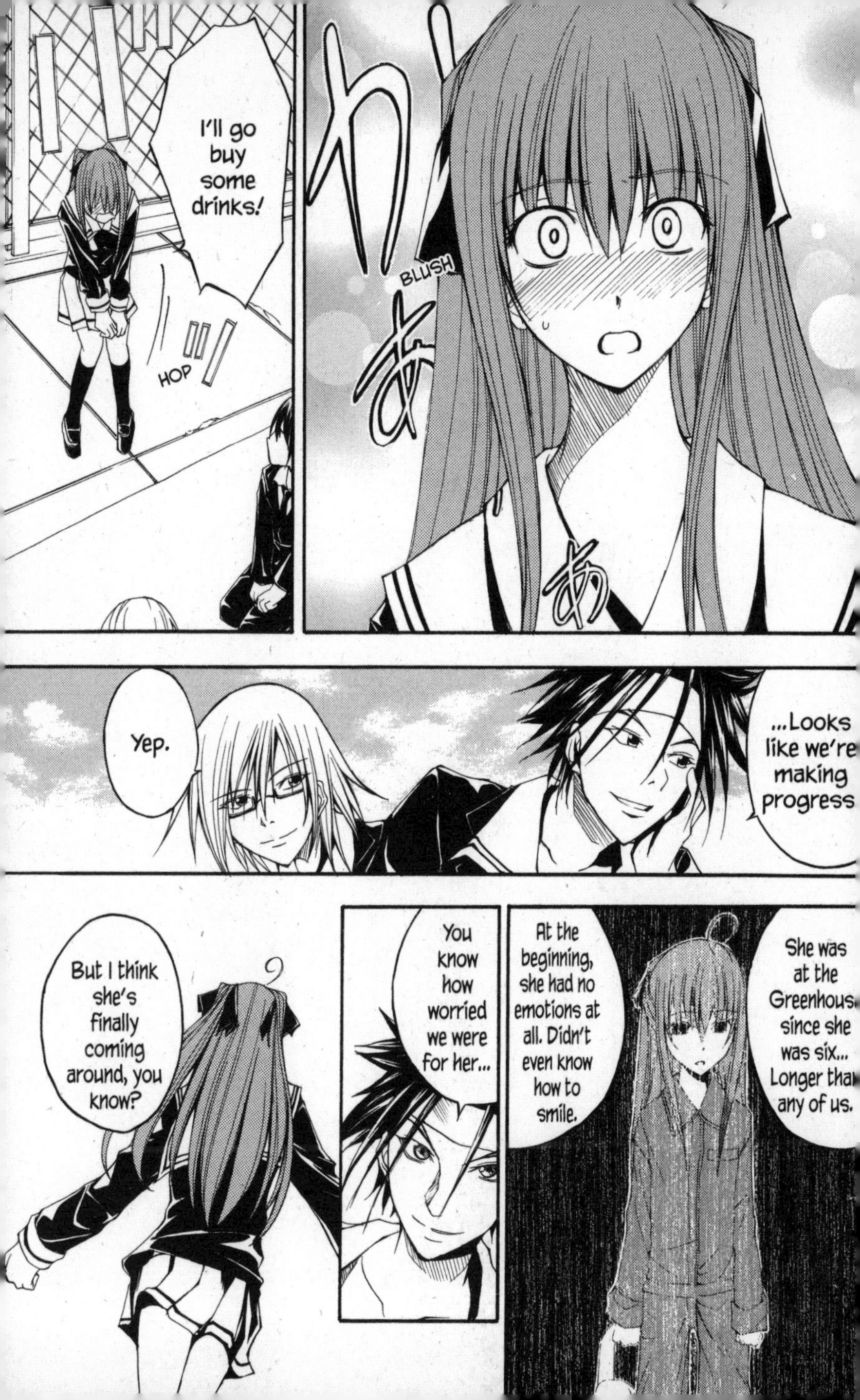
わ
BLUSH
あ
あ
I'll go buy some drinks!
HOP
...Looks like we're making progress
Yep.
She was at the Greenhous since she was six... Longer tha any of us.
At the beginning, she had no emotions at all. Didn't even know how to smile.
You know how worried we were for her...
But I think she's finally coming around, you know?

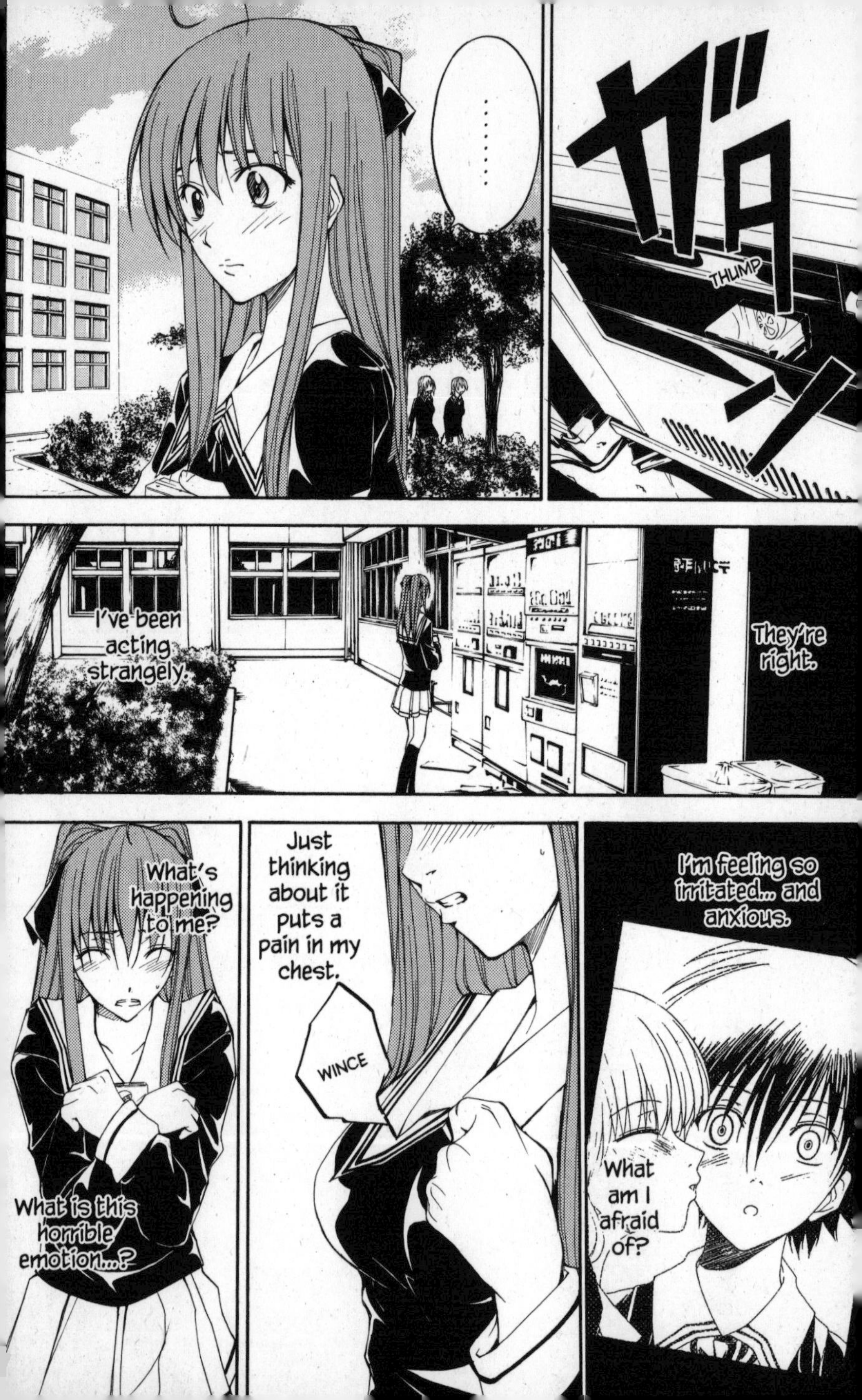
ガタン
THUMP
……
They're right.
I've been acting strangely.
I'm feeling so irritated... and anxious.
What am I afraid of?
Just thinking about it puts a pain in my chest.
WINCE
What's happening to me?
What is this horrible emotion...?

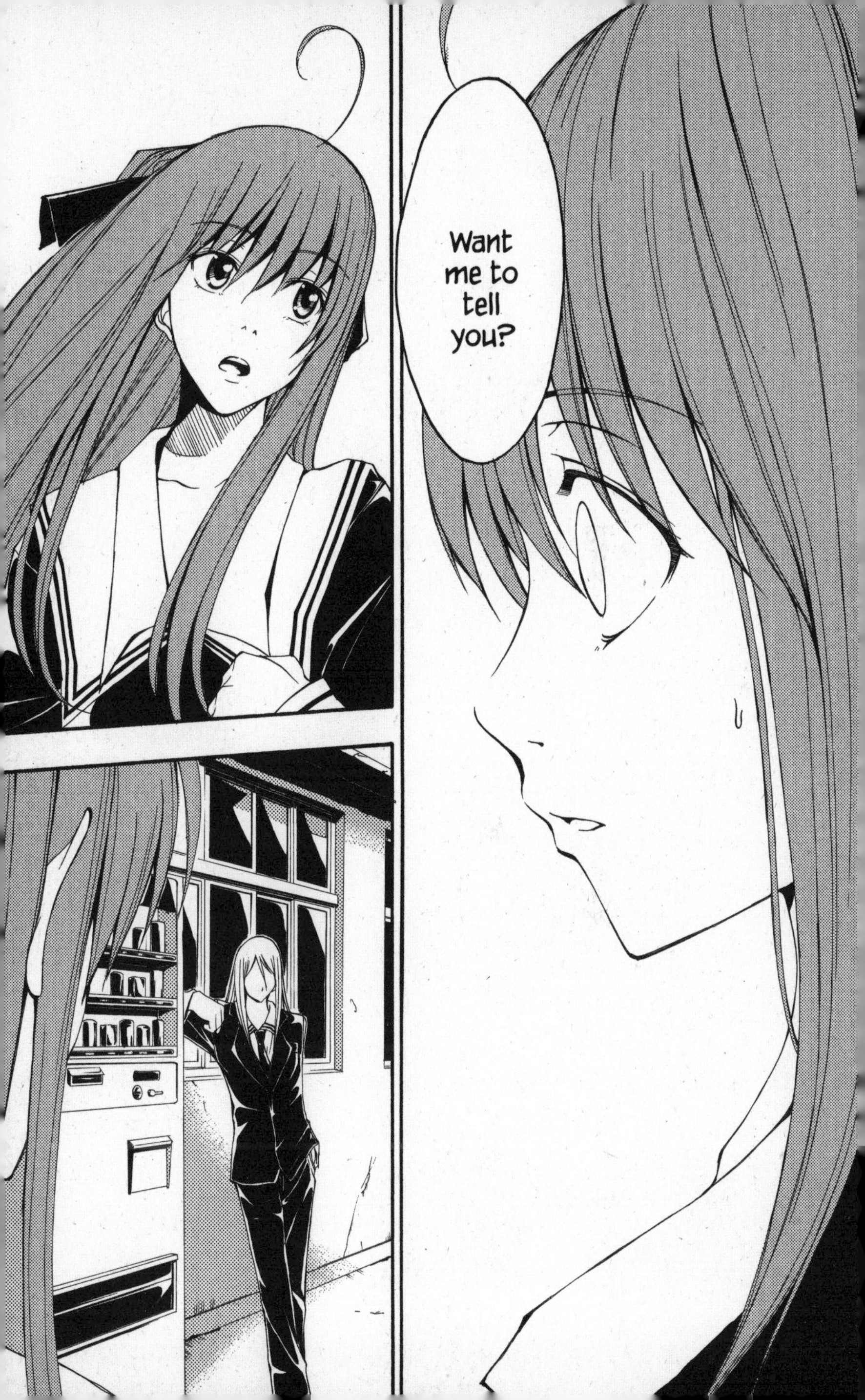
Want me to tell you?

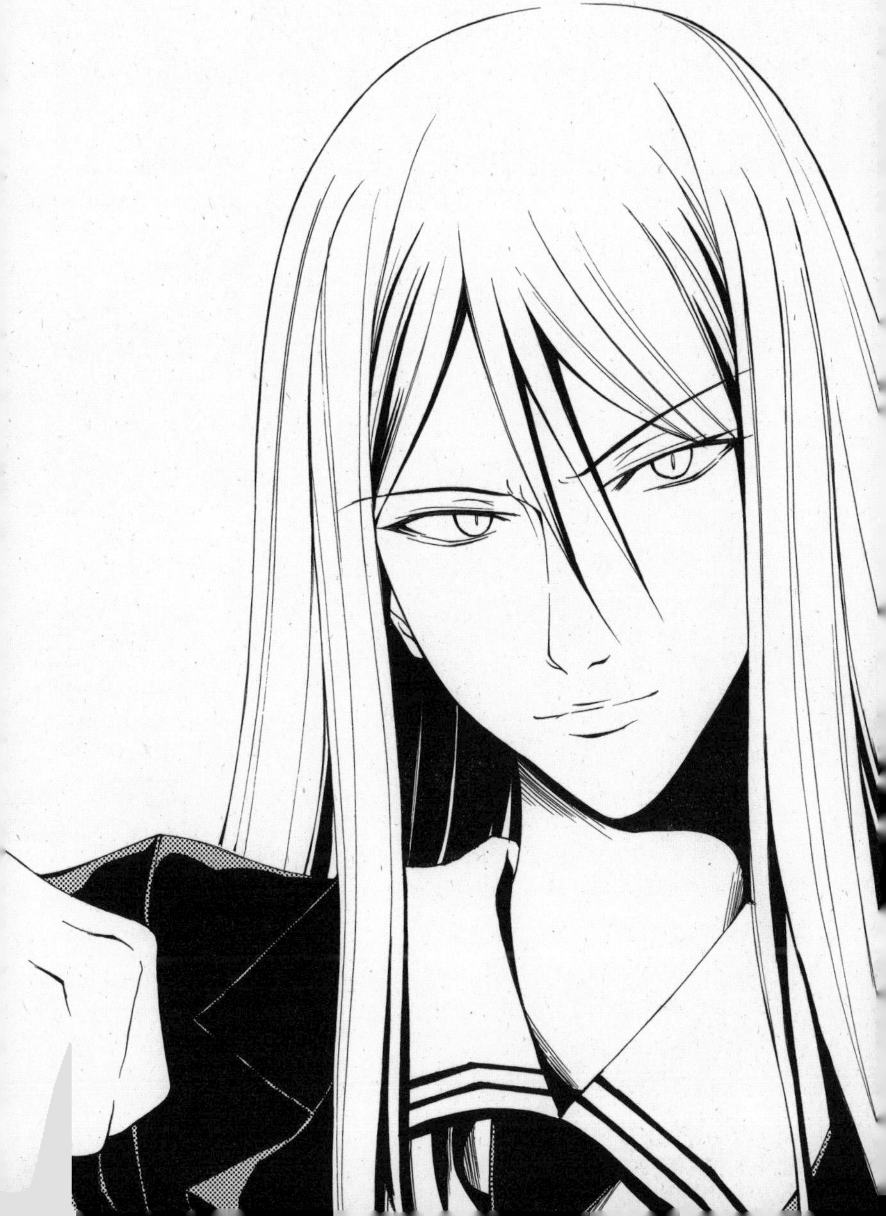

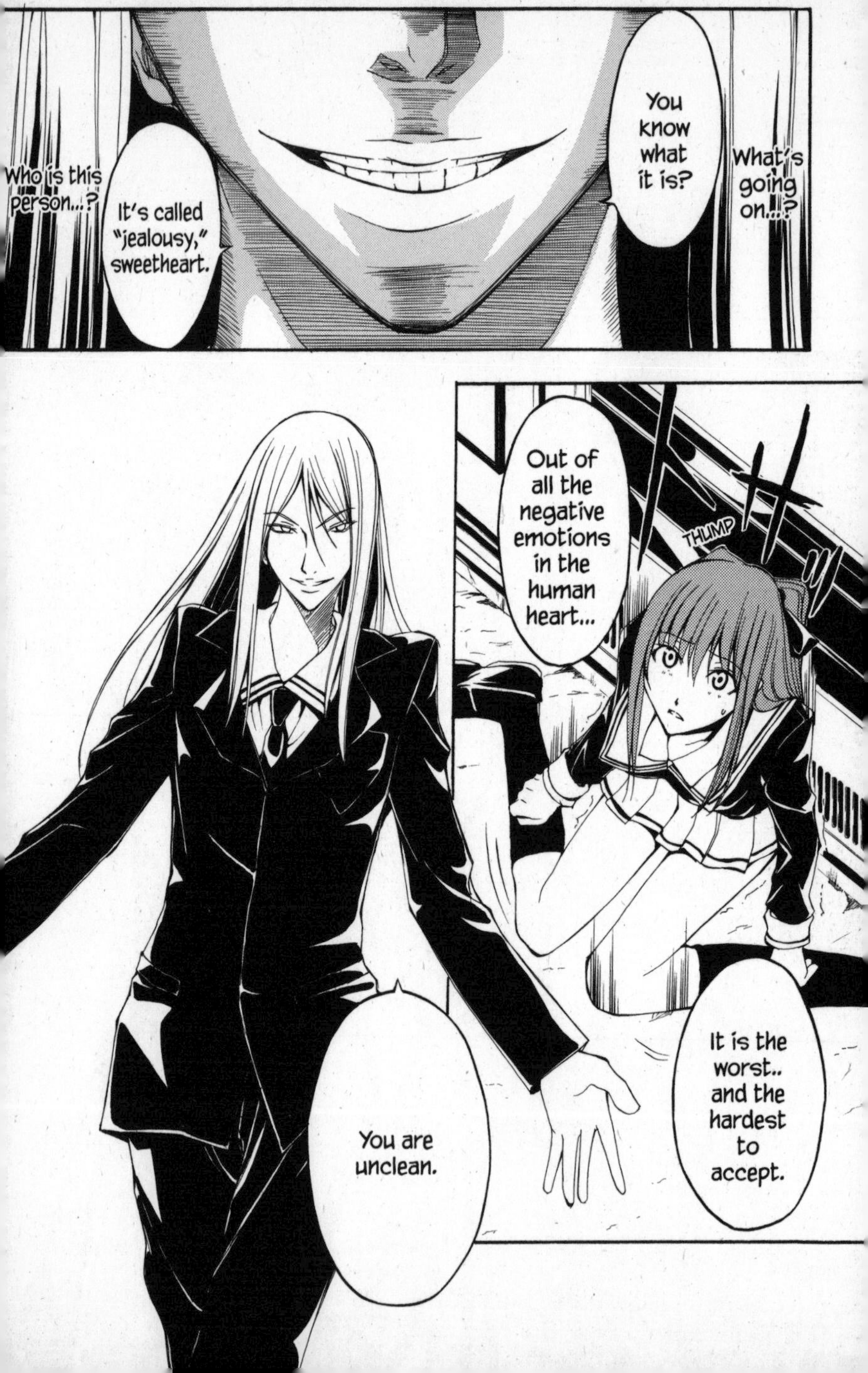
What's going on...?
You know what it is?
It's called "jealousy," sweetheart.
Who is this person...?
Out of all the negative emotions in the human heart...
THUMP
It is the worst.. and the hardest to accept.
You are unclean.

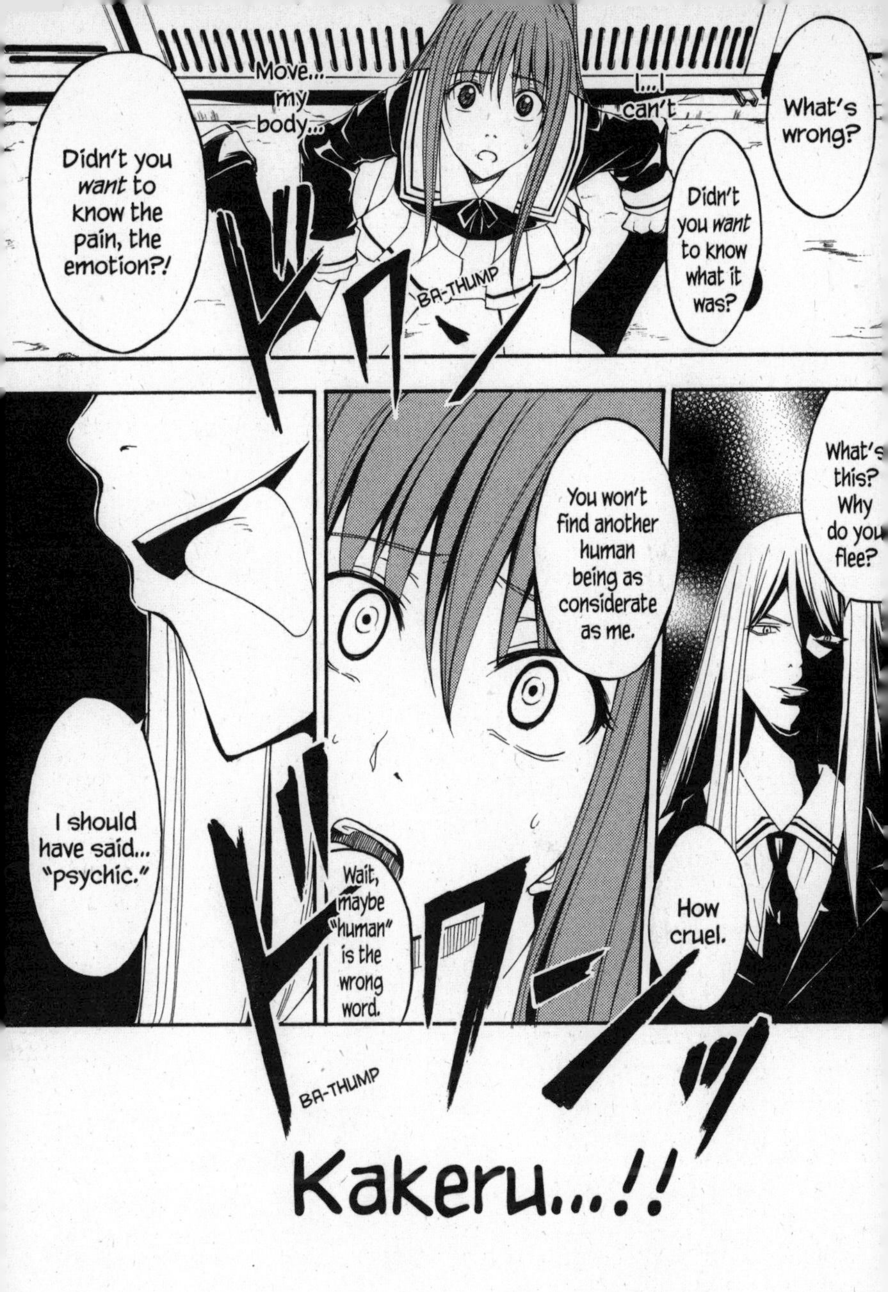
What's wrong?
Didn't you *want* to know what it was?
I...I can't
Move... my body...
BA-THUMP
Didn't you *want* to know the pain, the emotion?!
What's this? Why do you flee?
How cruel.
You won't find another human being as considerate as me.
Wait, maybe "human" is the wrong word.
I should have said... "psychic."
BA-THUMP
Kakeru...!!

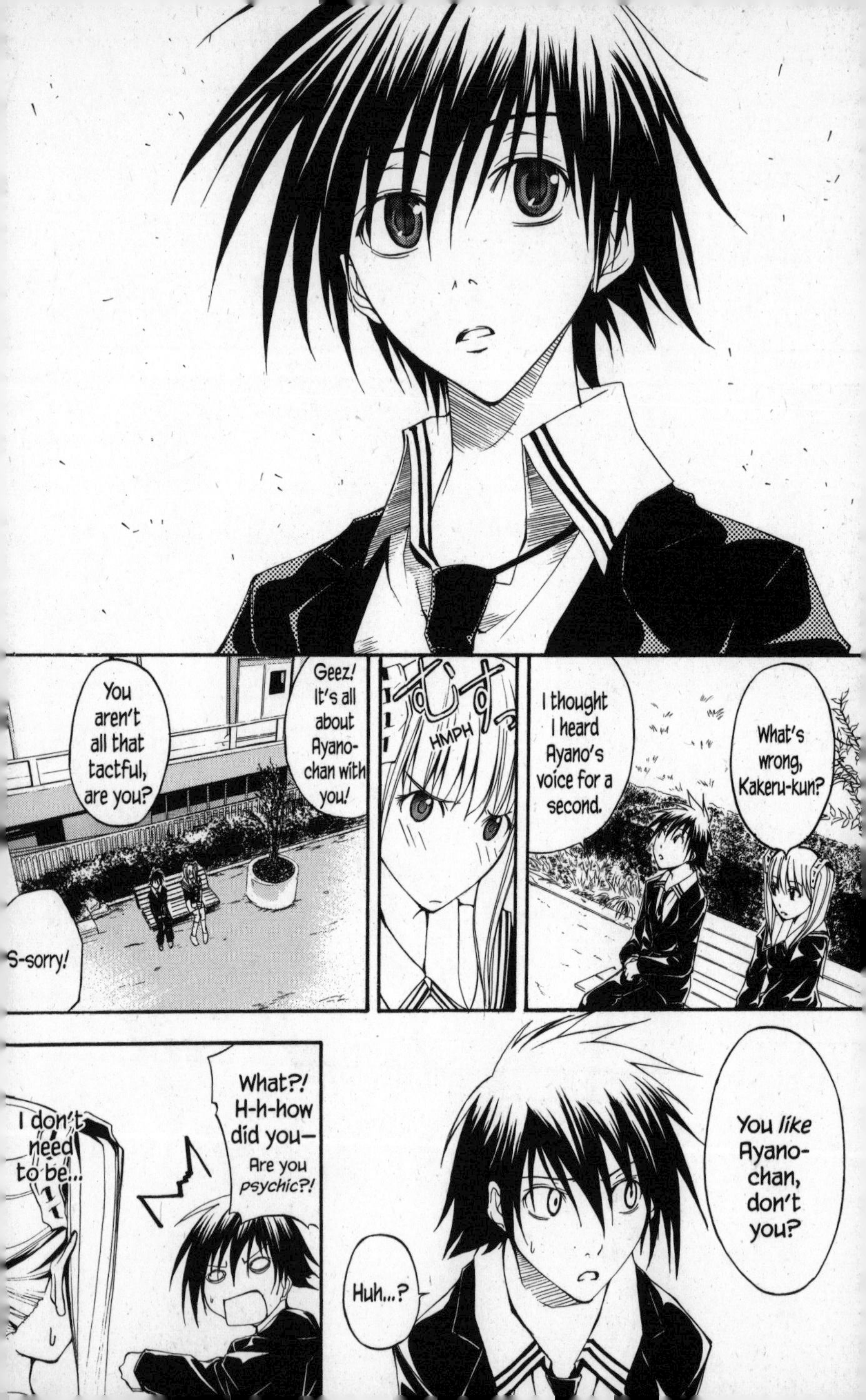
What's wrong, Kakeru-kun?
I thought I heard Ayano's voice for a second.
むすっ
HMPH
Geez! It's all about Ayano-chan with you!
You aren't all that tactful, are you?
S-sorry!
You like Ayano-chan, don't you?
Huh...?
What?! H-h-how did you— Are you psychic?!
I don't need to be...

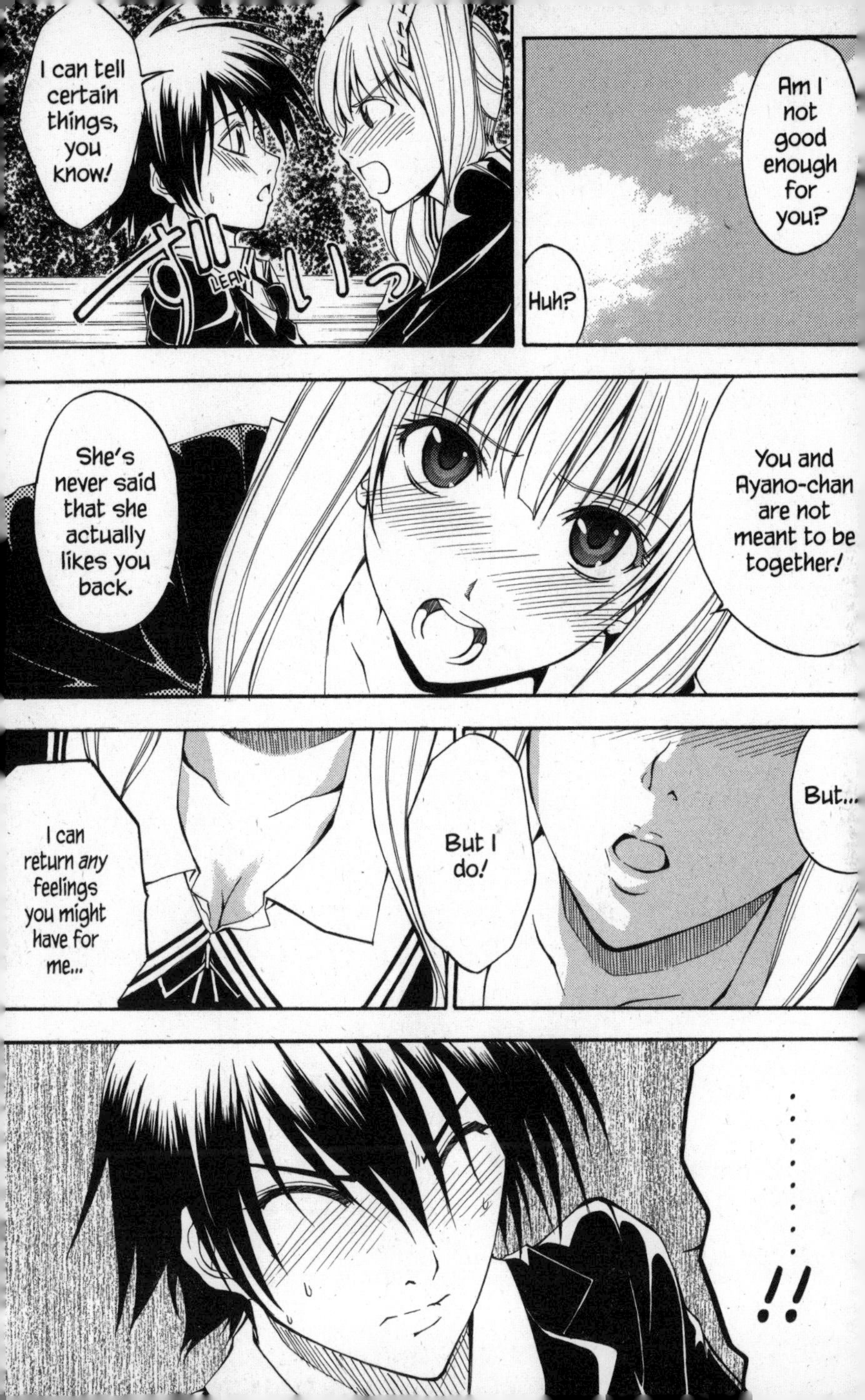
Am I not good enough for you?
Huh?
I can tell certain things, you know!
LEAN
You and Ayano-chan are not meant to be together!
She's never said that she actually likes you back.
But...
But I do!
I can return *any* feelings you might have for me...
......
!!

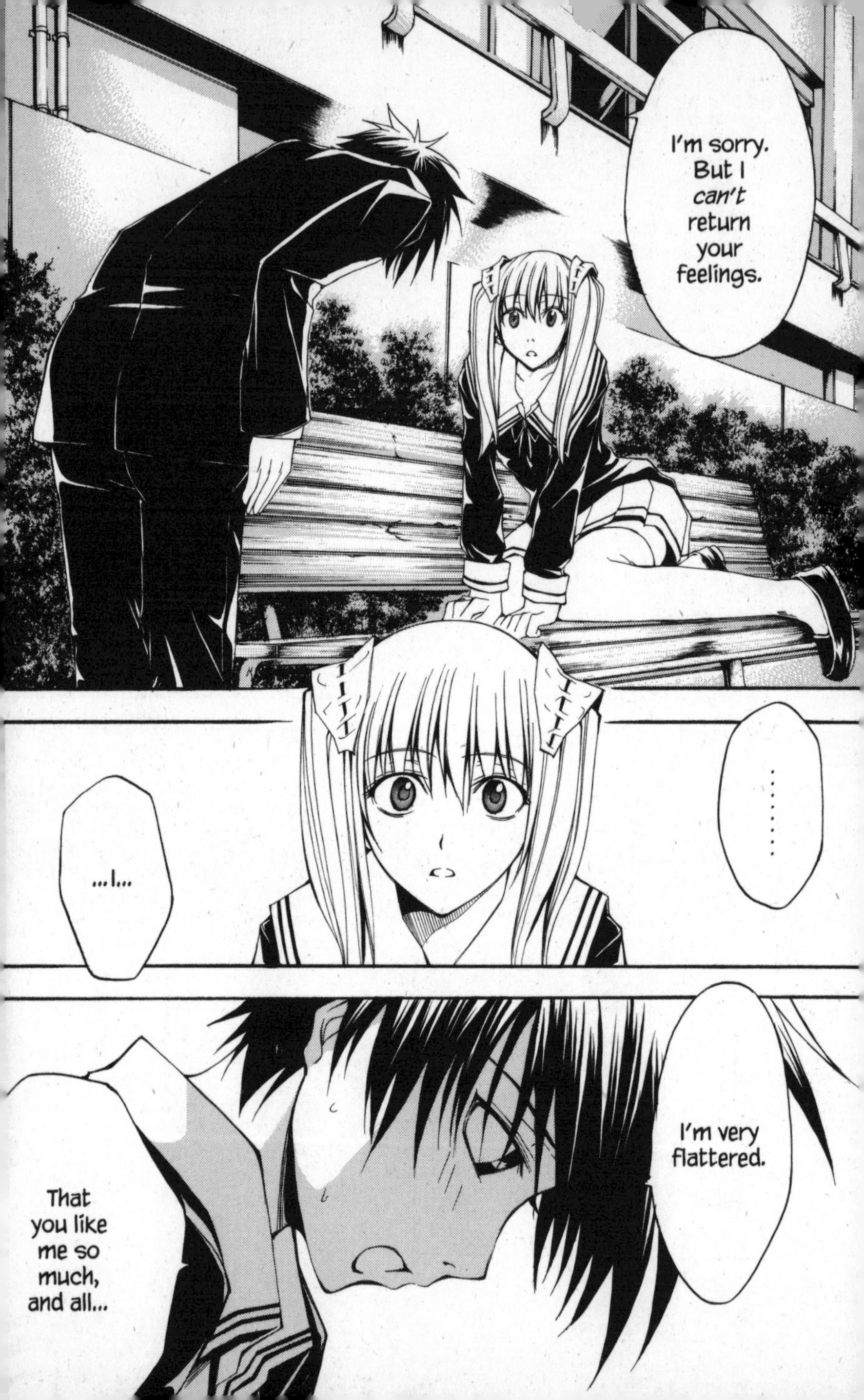
I'm sorry. But I *can't* return your feelings.
......
...I...
I'm very flattered.
That you like me so much, and all...

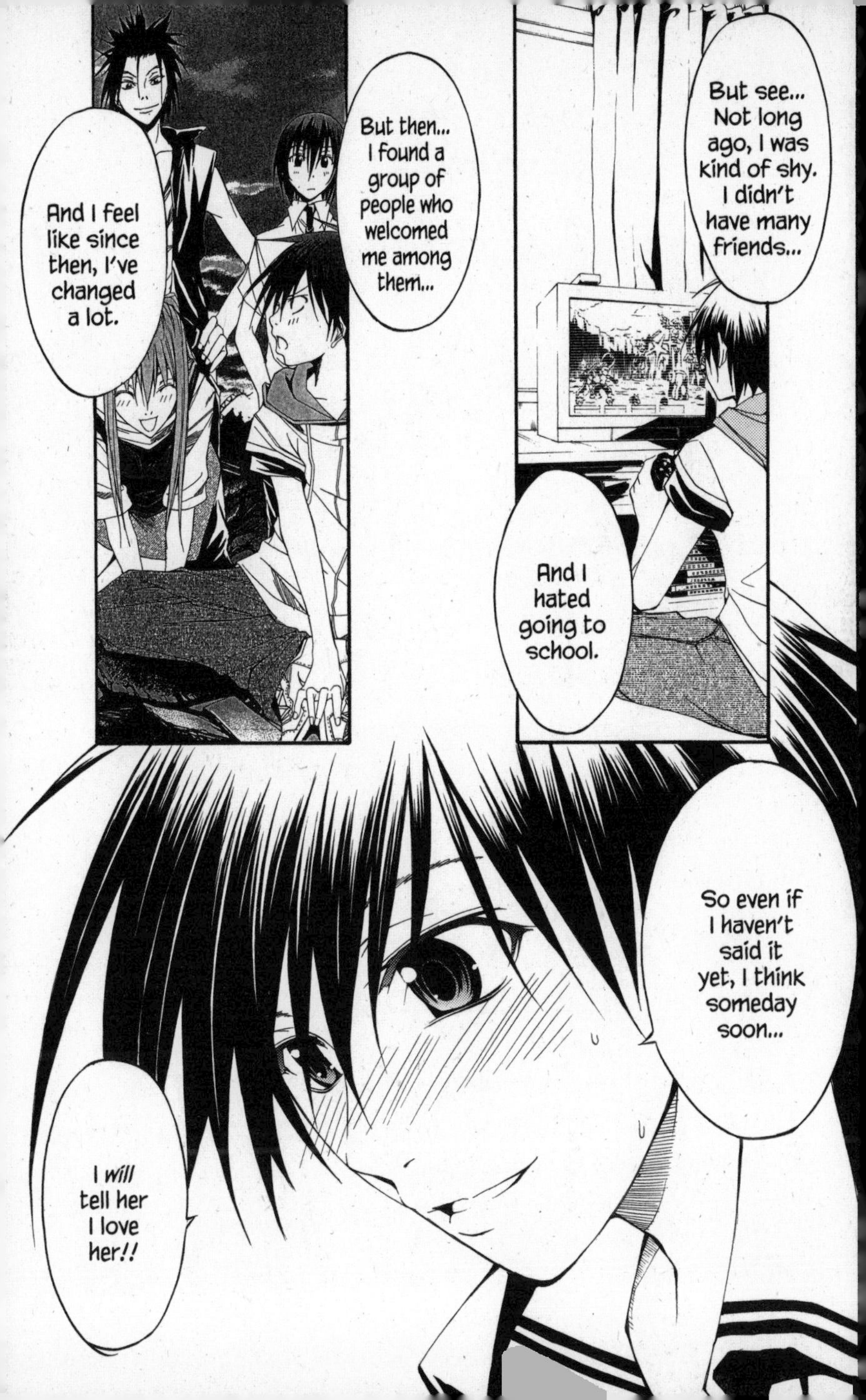
But see... Not long ago, I was kind of shy. I didn't have many friends...
And I hated going to school.
But then... I found a group of people who welcomed me among them...
And I feel like since then, I've changed a lot.
So even if I haven't said it yet, I think someday soon...
I *will* tell her I love her!!

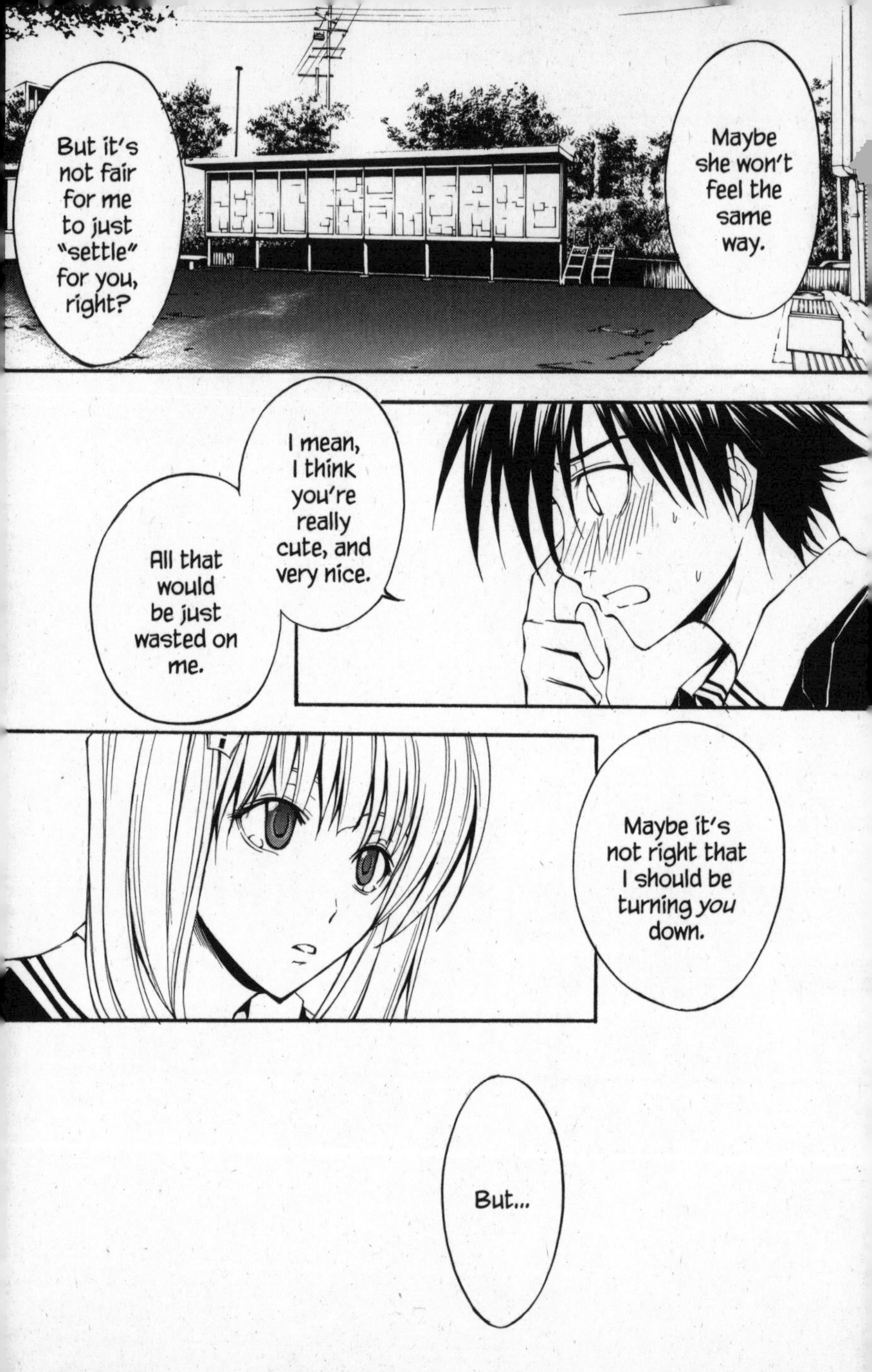
Maybe she won't feel the same way.
But it's not fair for me to just "settle" for you, right?
I mean, I think you're really cute, and very nice.
All that would be just wasted on me.
Maybe it's not right that I should be turning *you* down.
But...

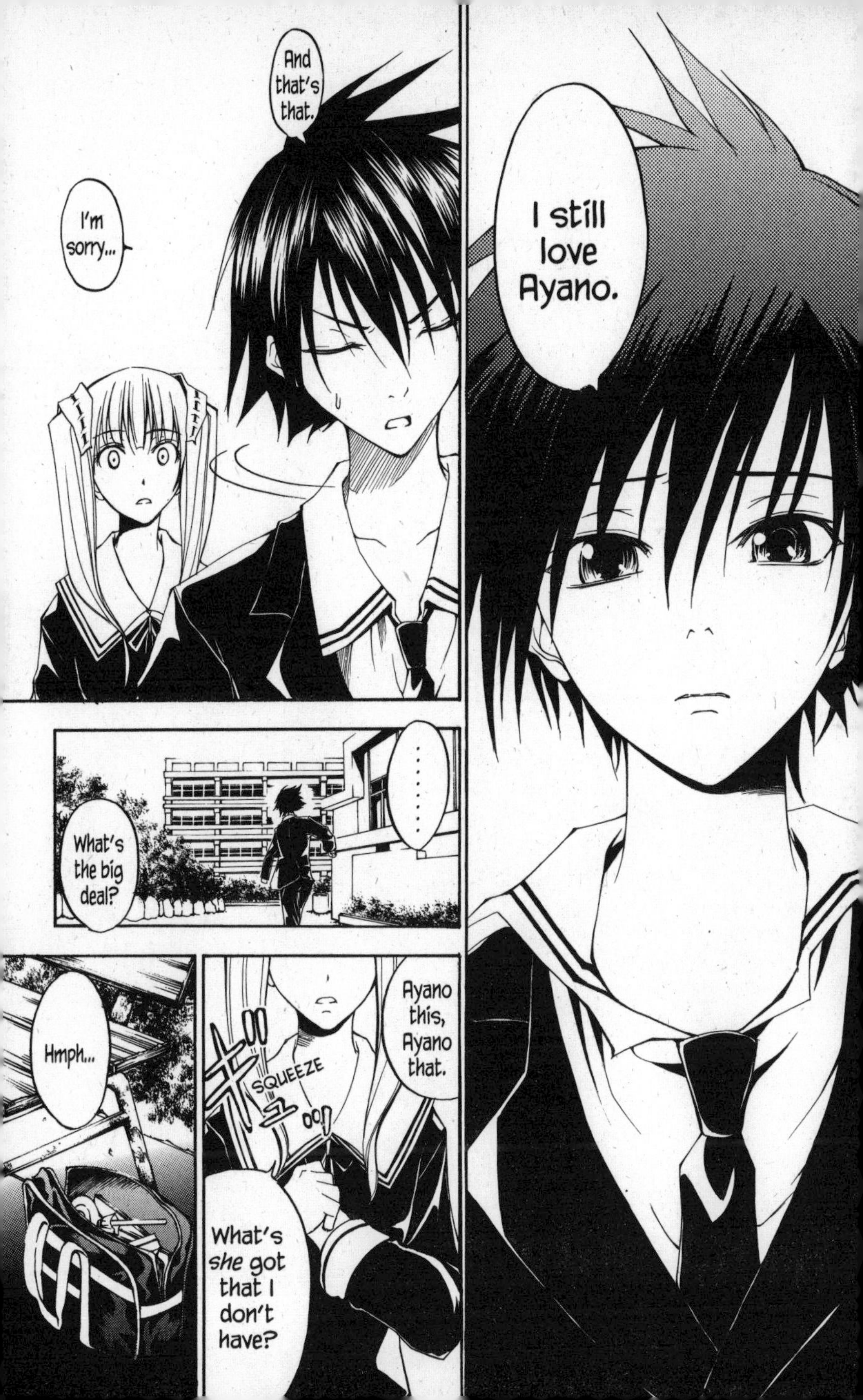
I still love Ayano.
And that's that.
I'm sorry...
......
What's the big deal?
Ayano this, Ayano that.
SQUEEZE
What's *she* got that I don't have?
Hmph...

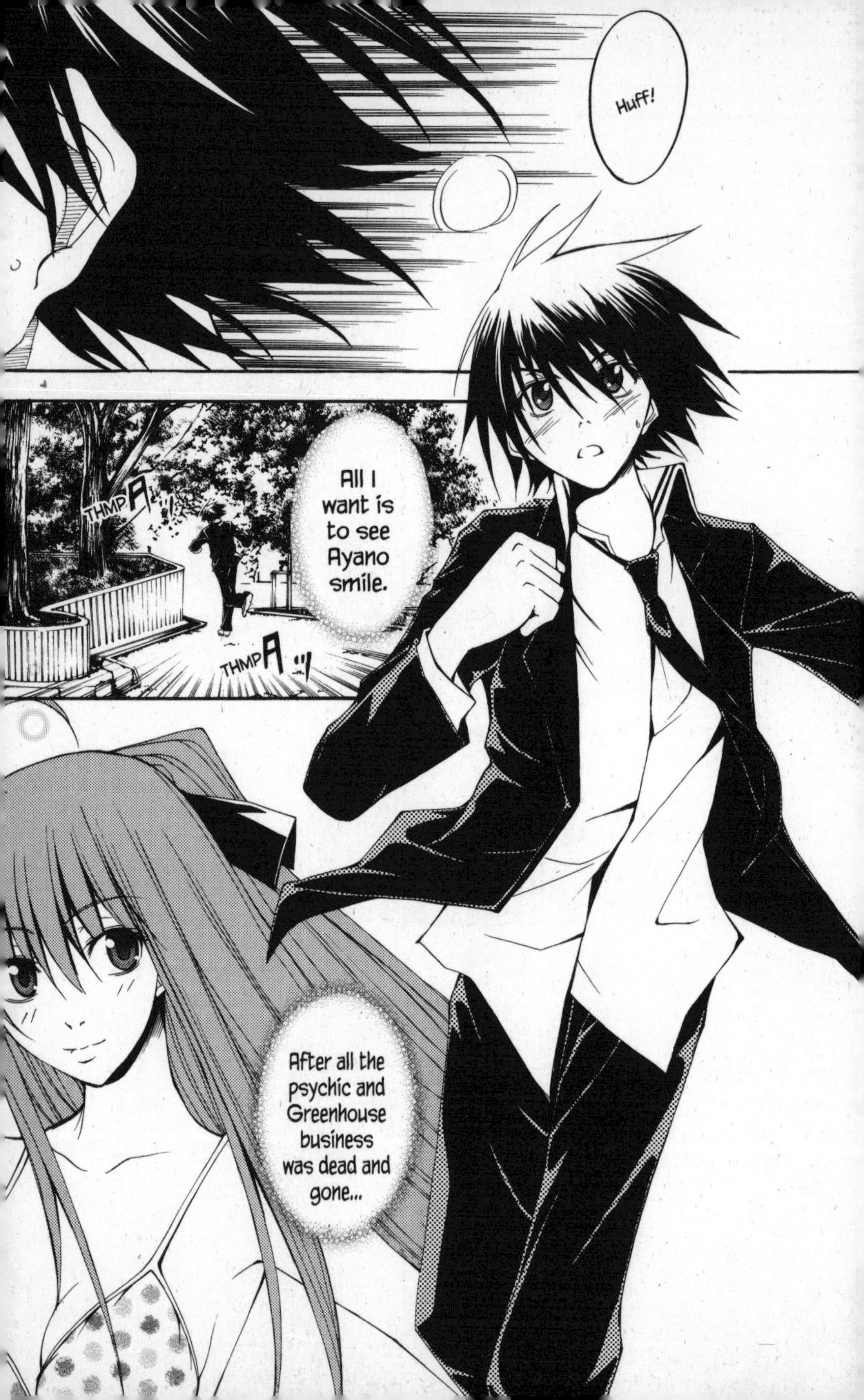
Huff!
All I want is to see Ayano smile.
THMP
THMP
After all the psychic and Greenhouse business was dead and gone...

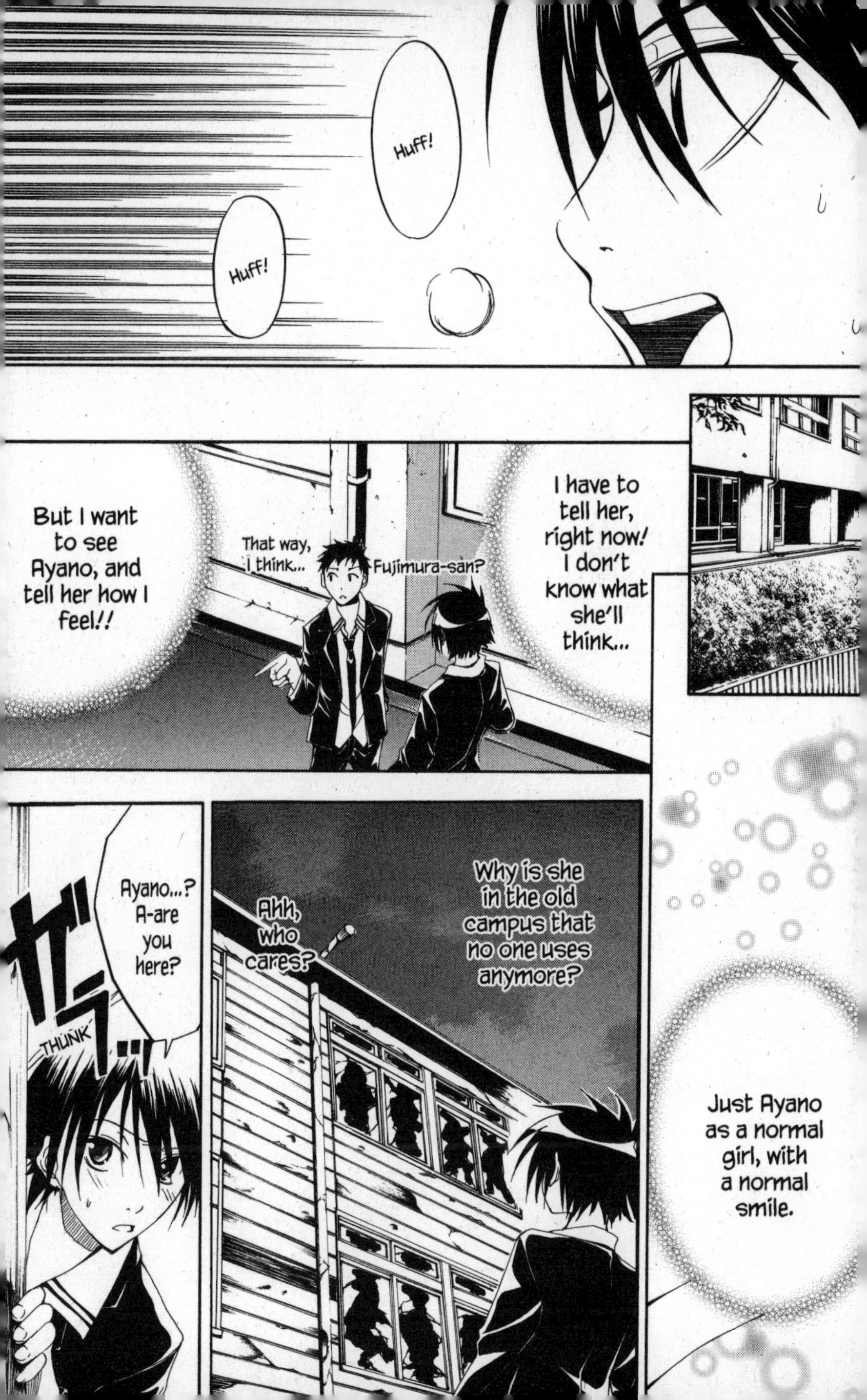
Huff!
Huff!
I have to tell her, right now! I don't know what she'll think...
Fujimura-san?
That way, I think...
But I want to see Ayano, and tell her how I feel!!
Just Ayano as a normal girl, with a normal smile.
Why is she in the old campus that no one uses anymore?
Ahh, who cares?
Ayano...? A-are you here?
THUNK

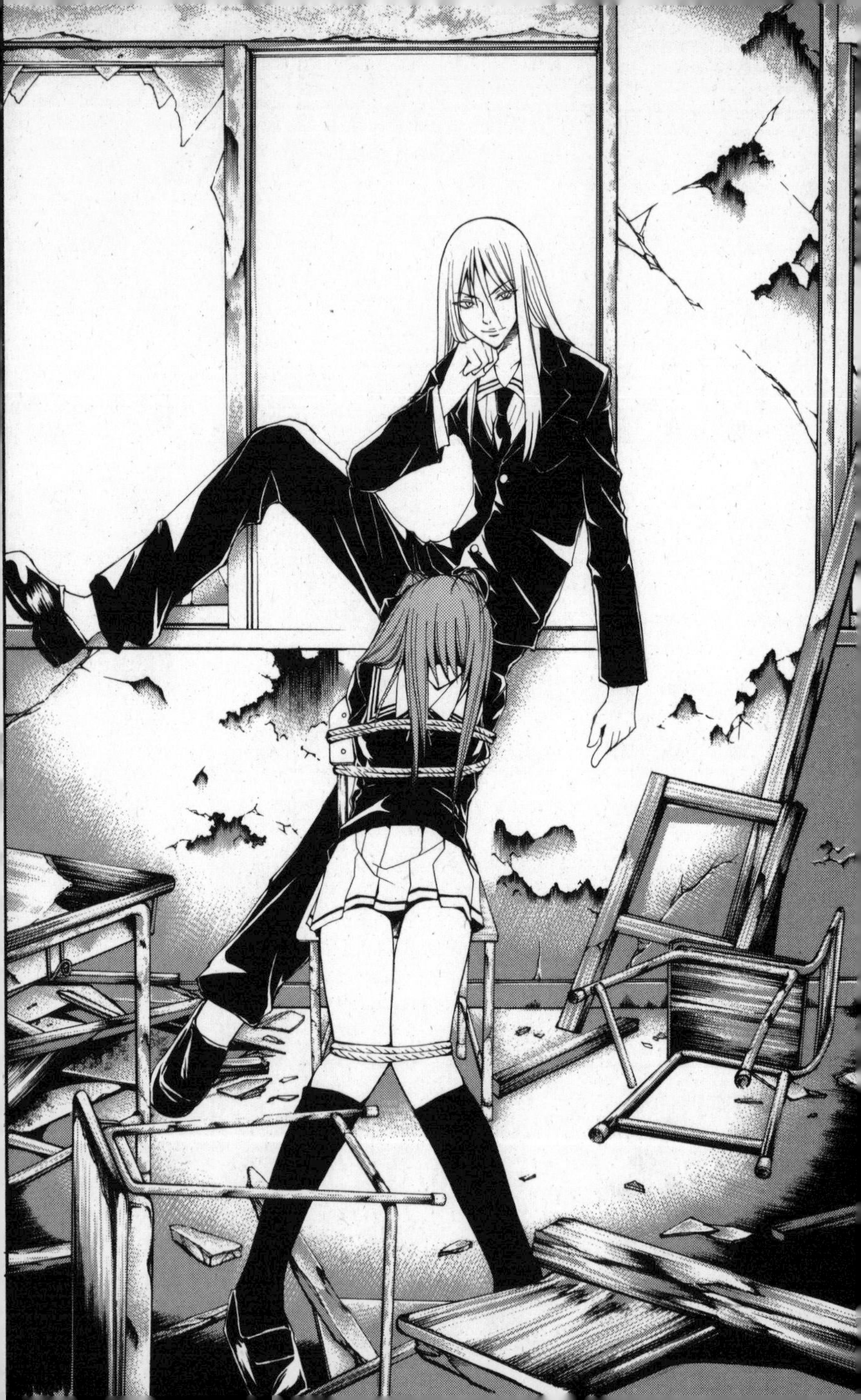

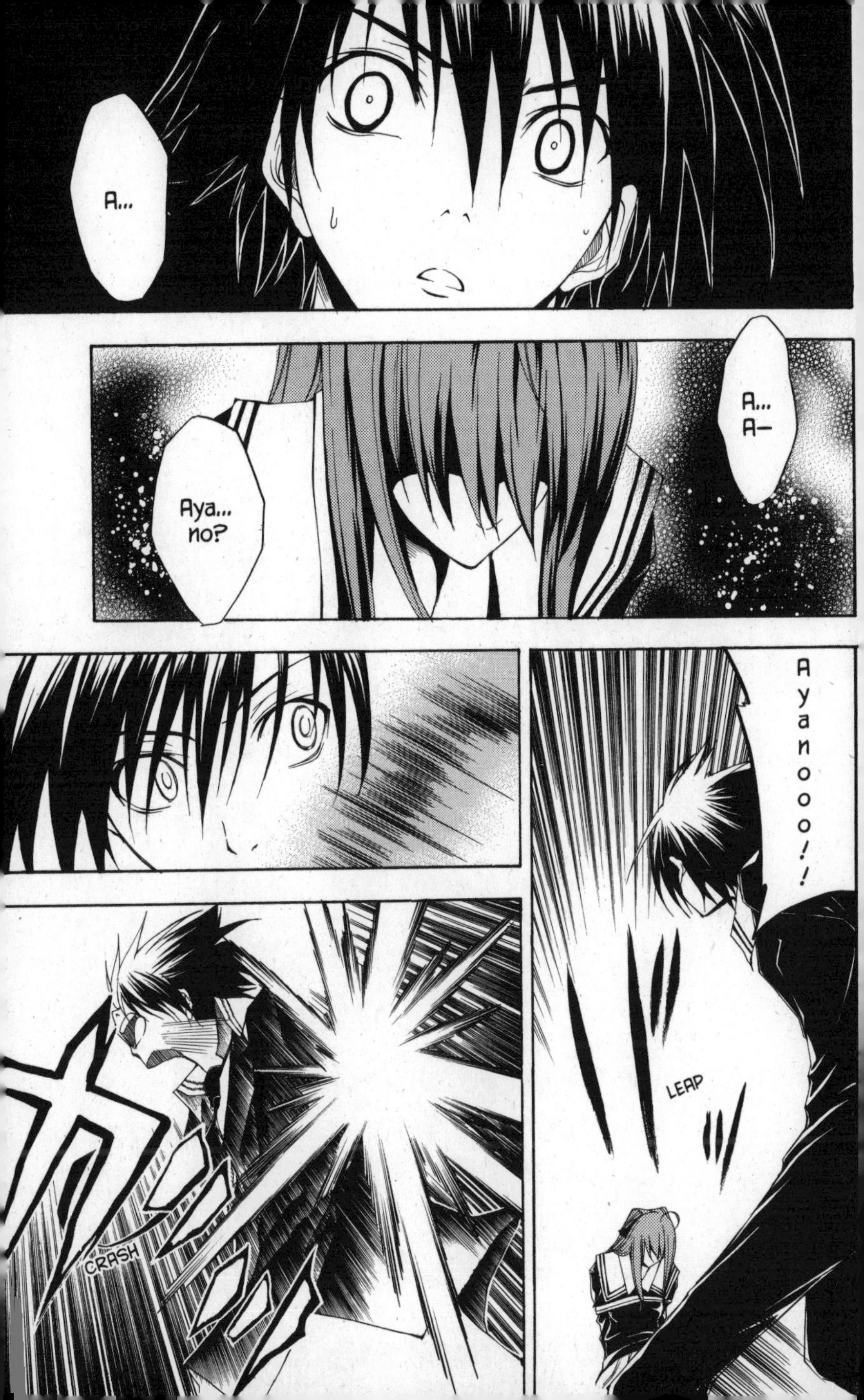
A...
A...
A—
Aya...
no?
Ayanooo!!
LEAP
CRASH

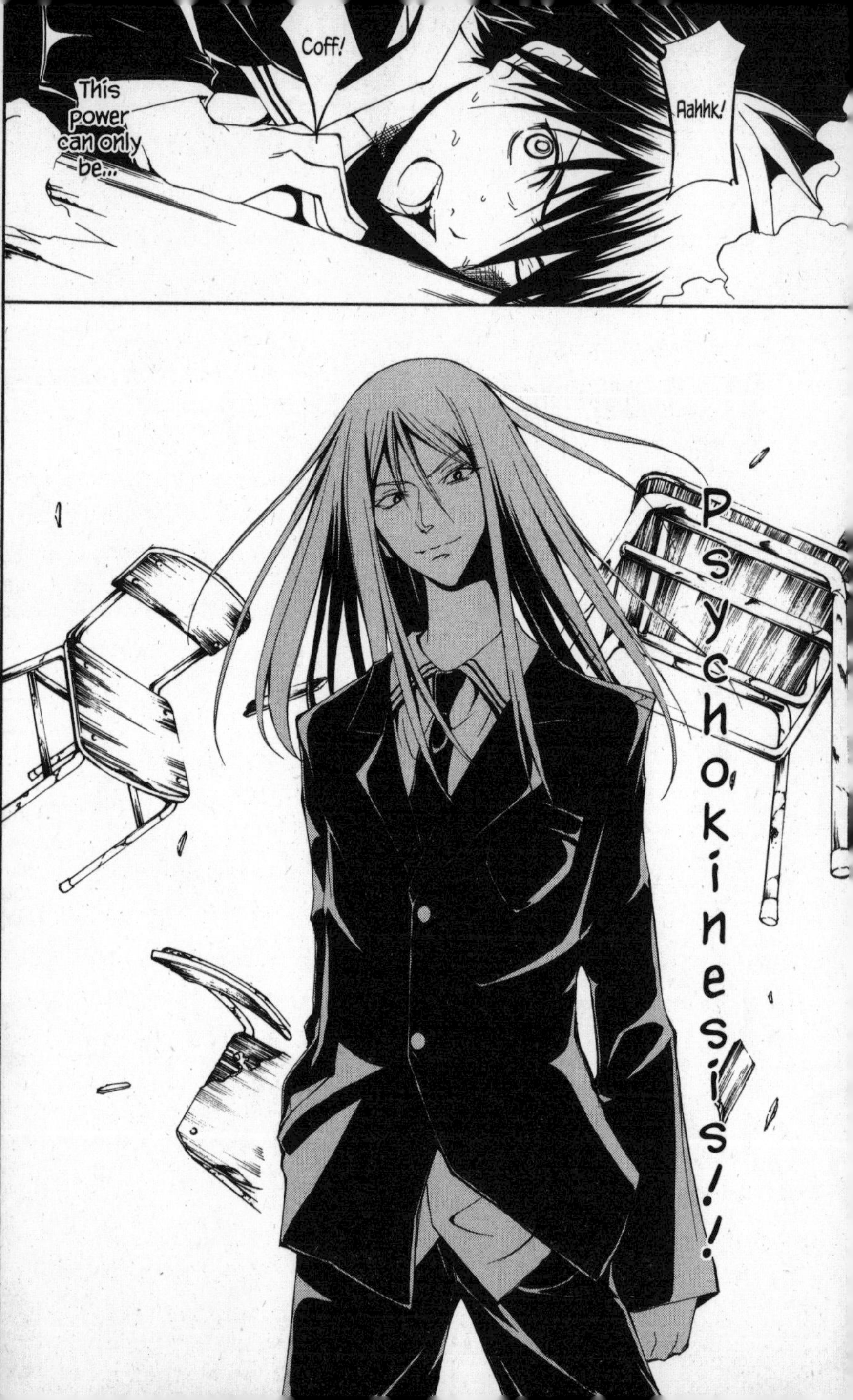
Aahhk!
Coff!
This power can only be...
Psychokinesis!!

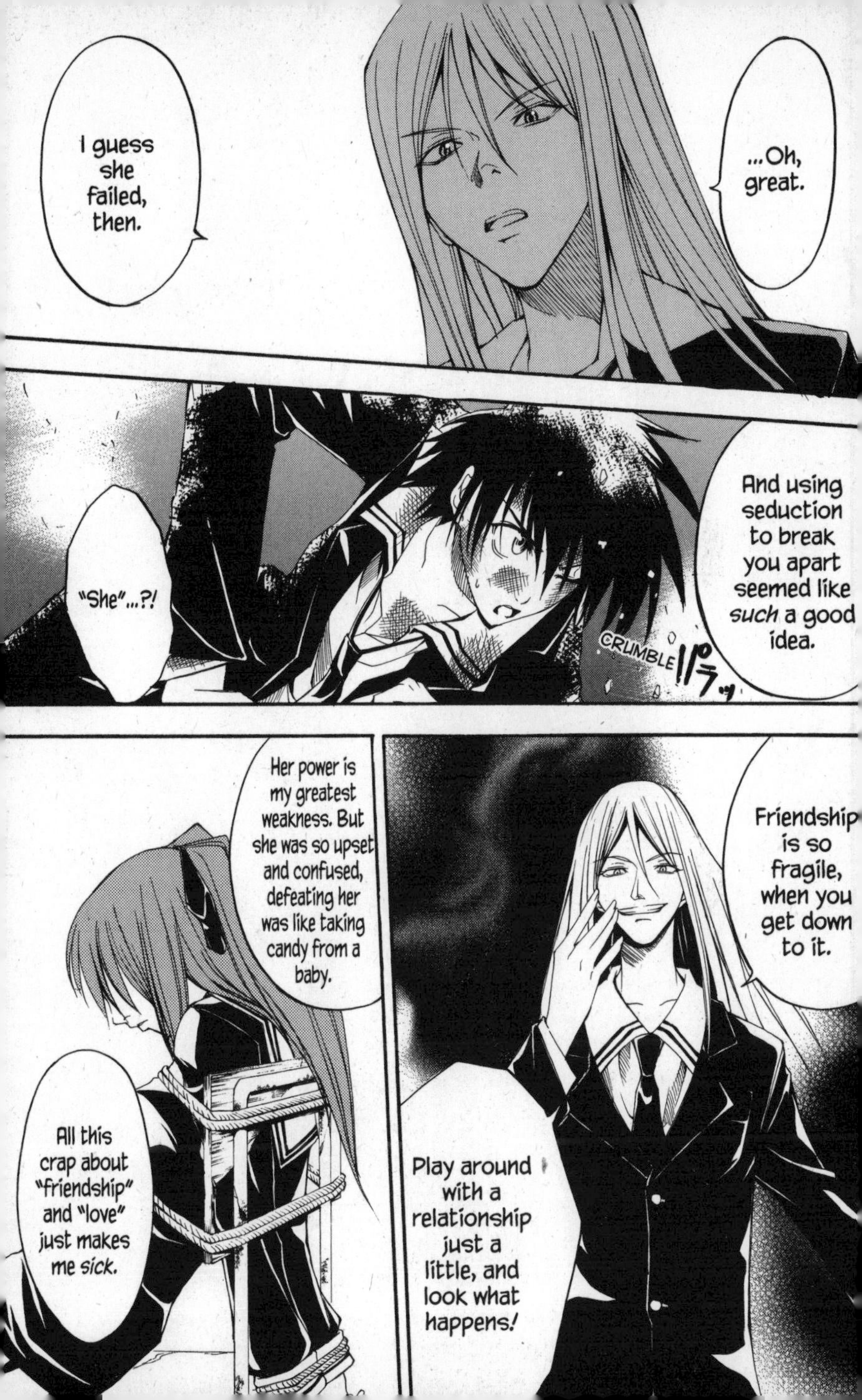
...Oh, great.
I guess she failed, then.
And using seduction to break you apart seemed like *such* a good idea.
CRUMBLE
"She"...?!
Friendship is so fragile, when you get down to it.
Play around with a relationship just a little, and look what happens!
Her power is my greatest weakness. But she was so upset and confused, defeating her was like taking candy from a baby.
All this crap about "friendship" and "love" just makes me *sick*.

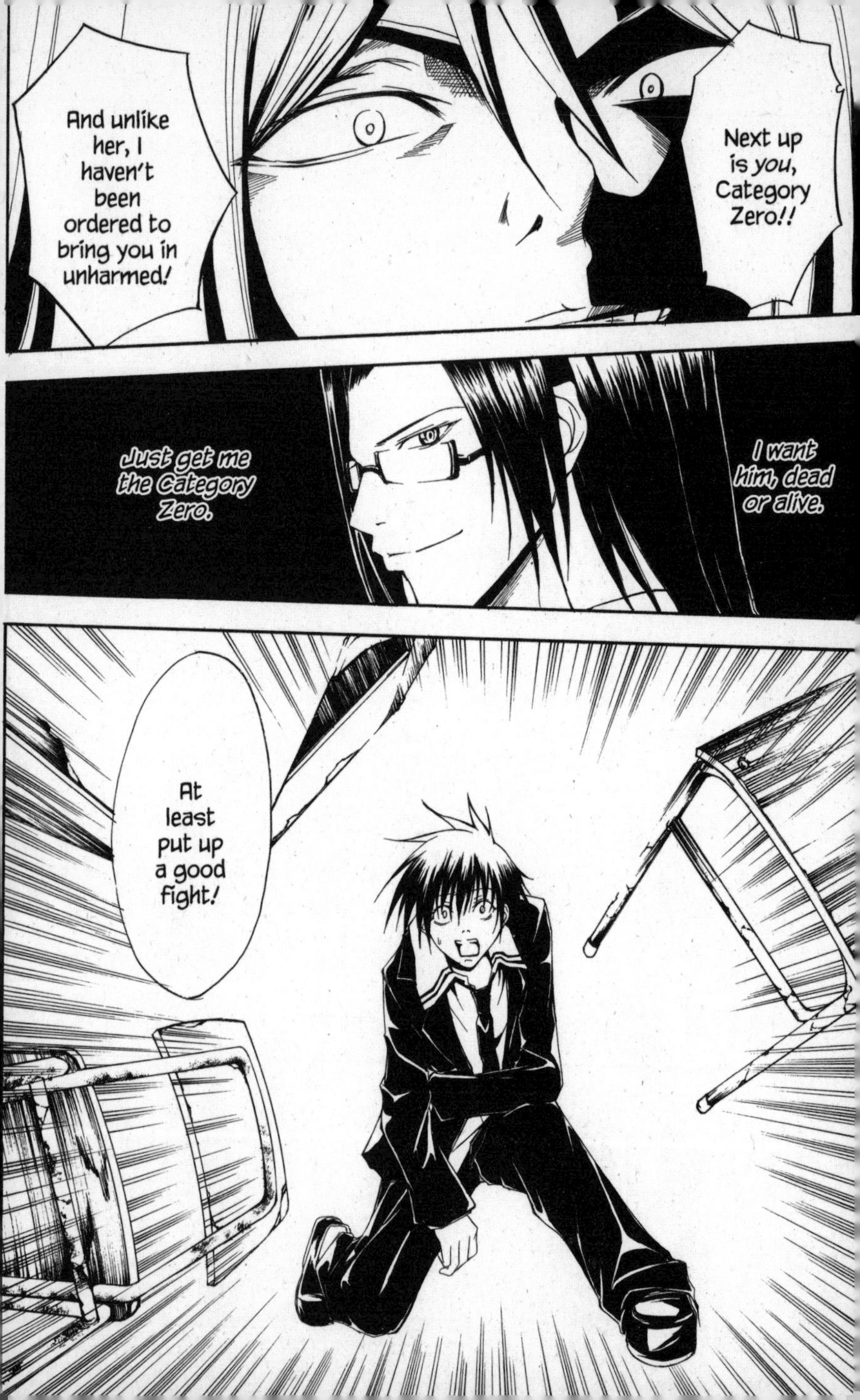
Next up is *you*, Category Zero!!
And unlike her, I haven't been ordered to bring you in unharmed!
I want him, dead or alive.
Just get me the Category Zero.
At least put up a good fight!

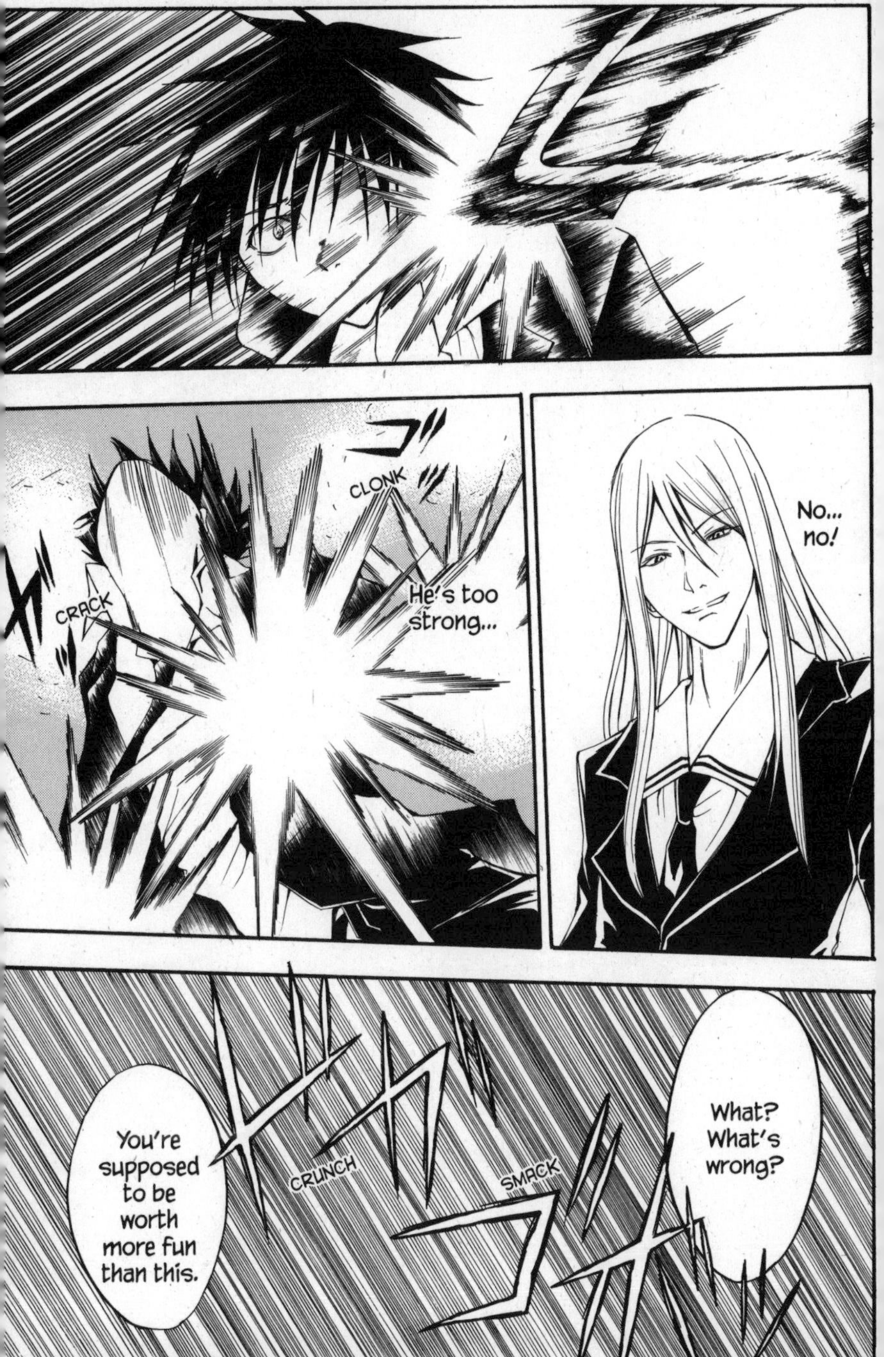
No... no!
CLONK
He's too strong...
CRACK
What? What's wrong?
SMACK
CRUNCH
You're supposed to be worth more fun than this.

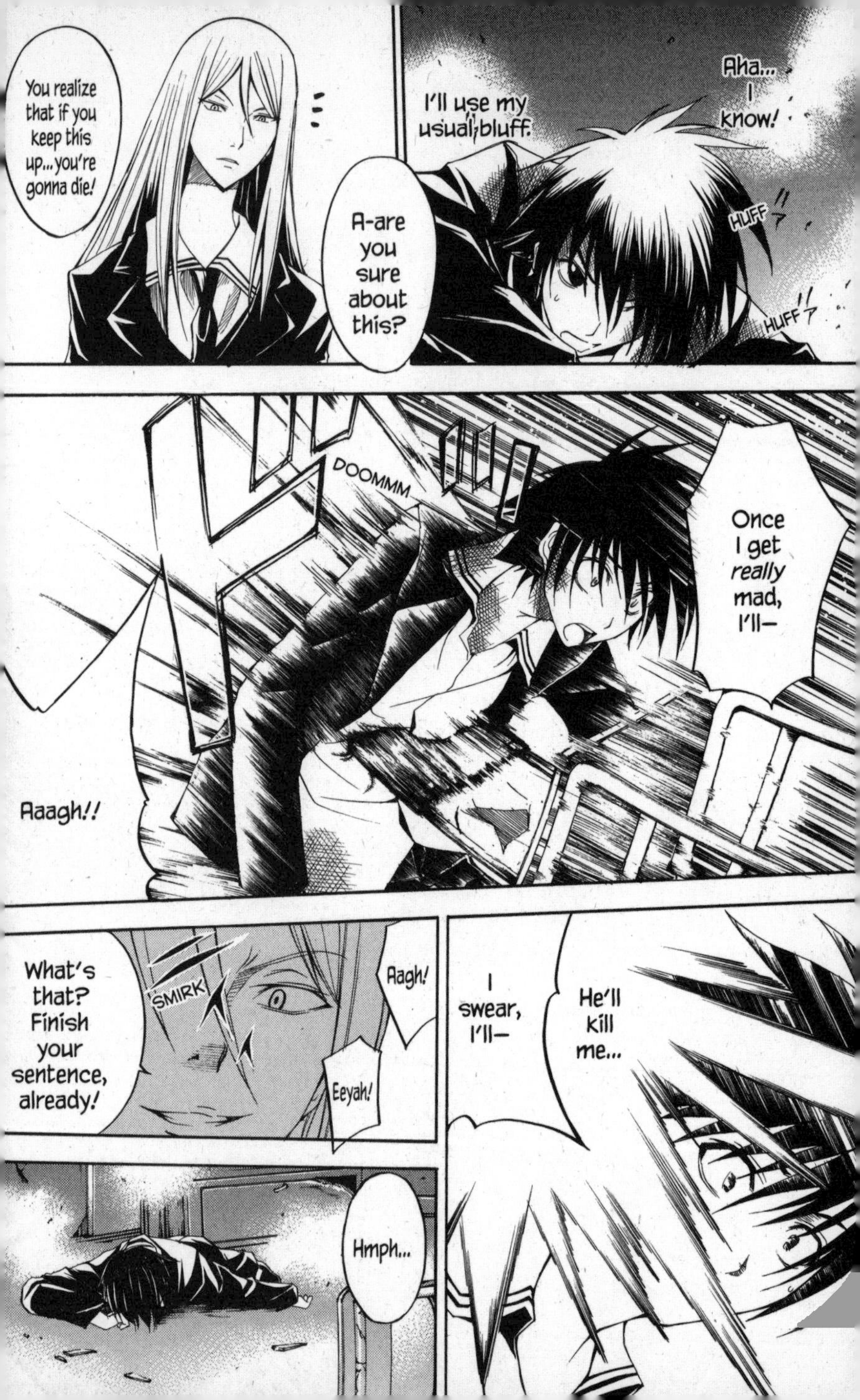
Aha... I know!
I'll use my usual bluff.
HUFF
HUFF
A-are you sure about this?
You realize that if you keep this up...you're gonna die!
Once I get *really* mad, I'll—
DOOMMM
Aaagh!!
He'll kill me...
I swear, I'll—
Aagh!
Eeyah!
SMIRK
What's that? Finish your sentence, already!
Hmph...

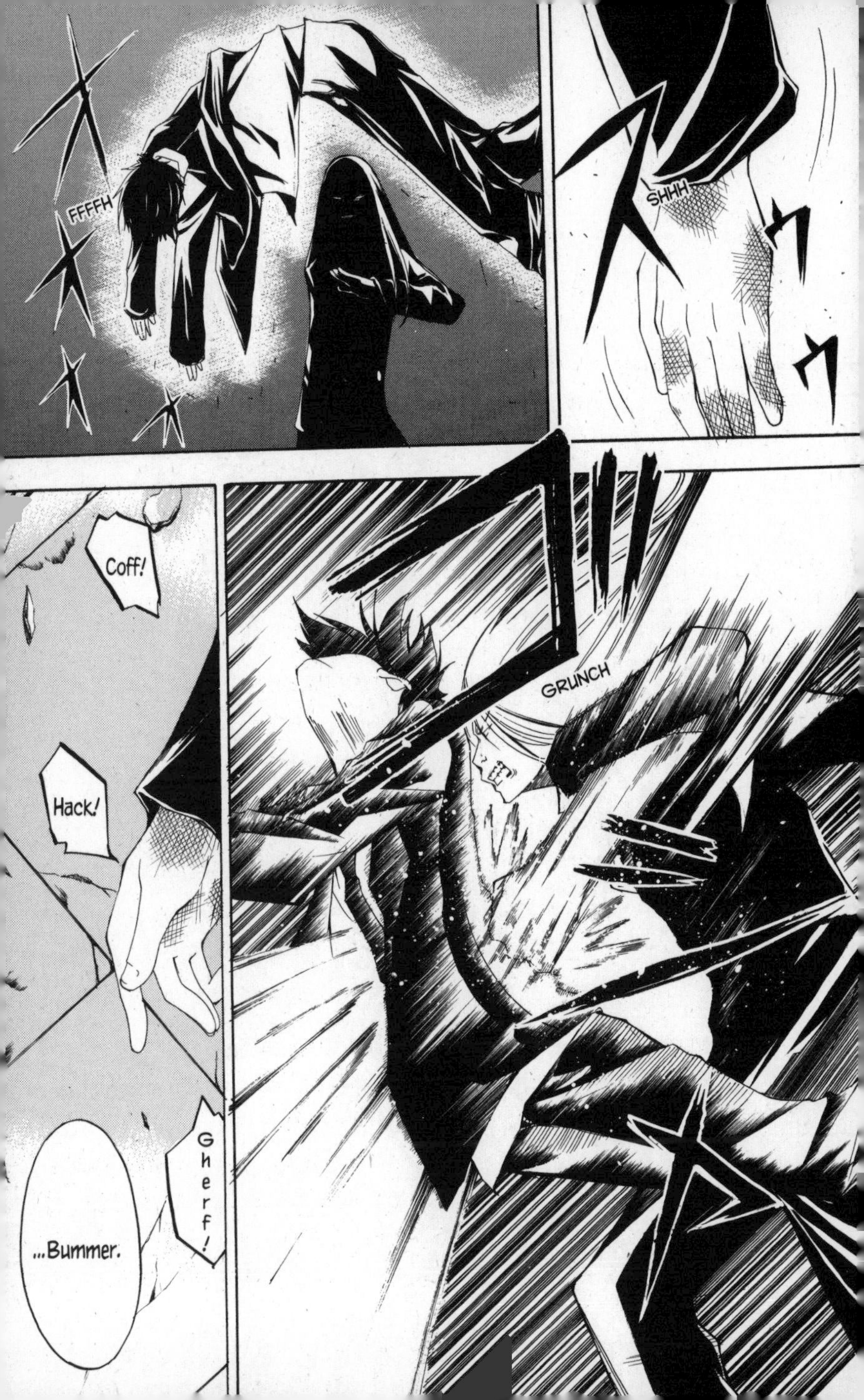
SHHH
FFFFH
GRUNCH
Coff!
Hack!
Gherf!
...Bummer.

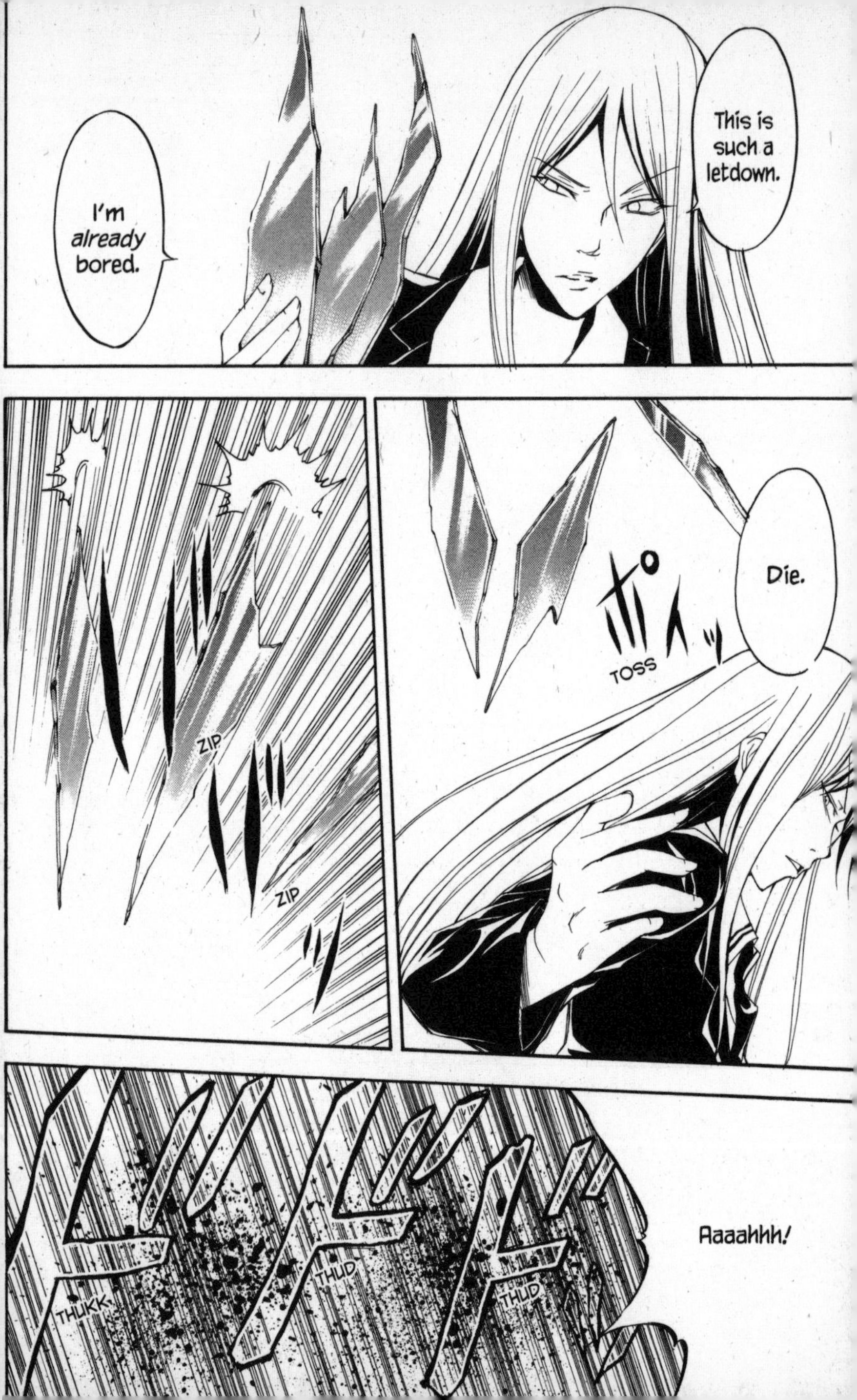
This is such a letdown.
I'm *already* bored.
Die.
TOSS
ZIP
ZIP
Aaaahhh!
THUD
THUD
THUKK

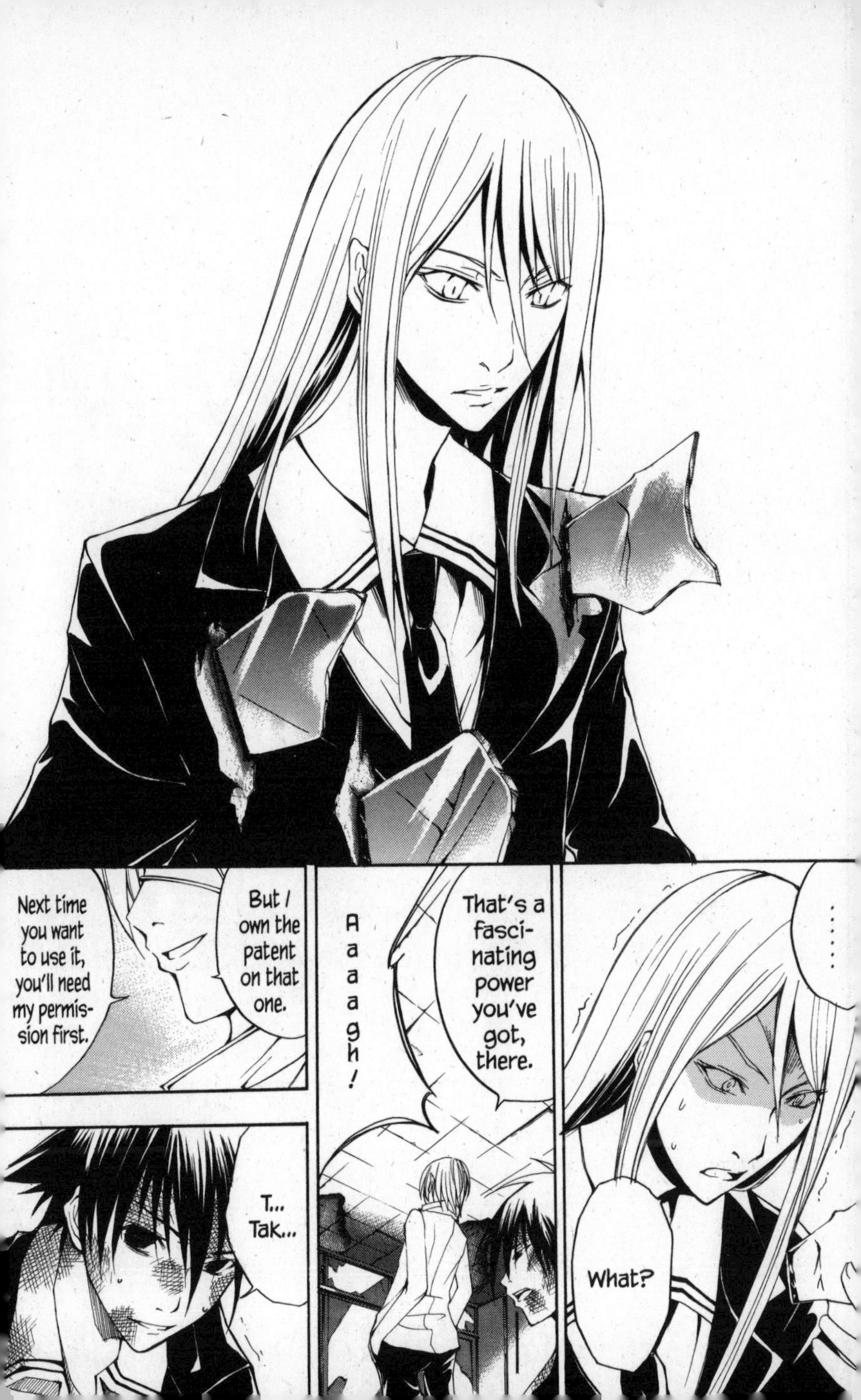
.....
What?
That's a fascinating power you've got, there.
Aaaagh!
But I own the patent on that one.
Next time you want to use it, you'll need my permission first.
T... Tak...

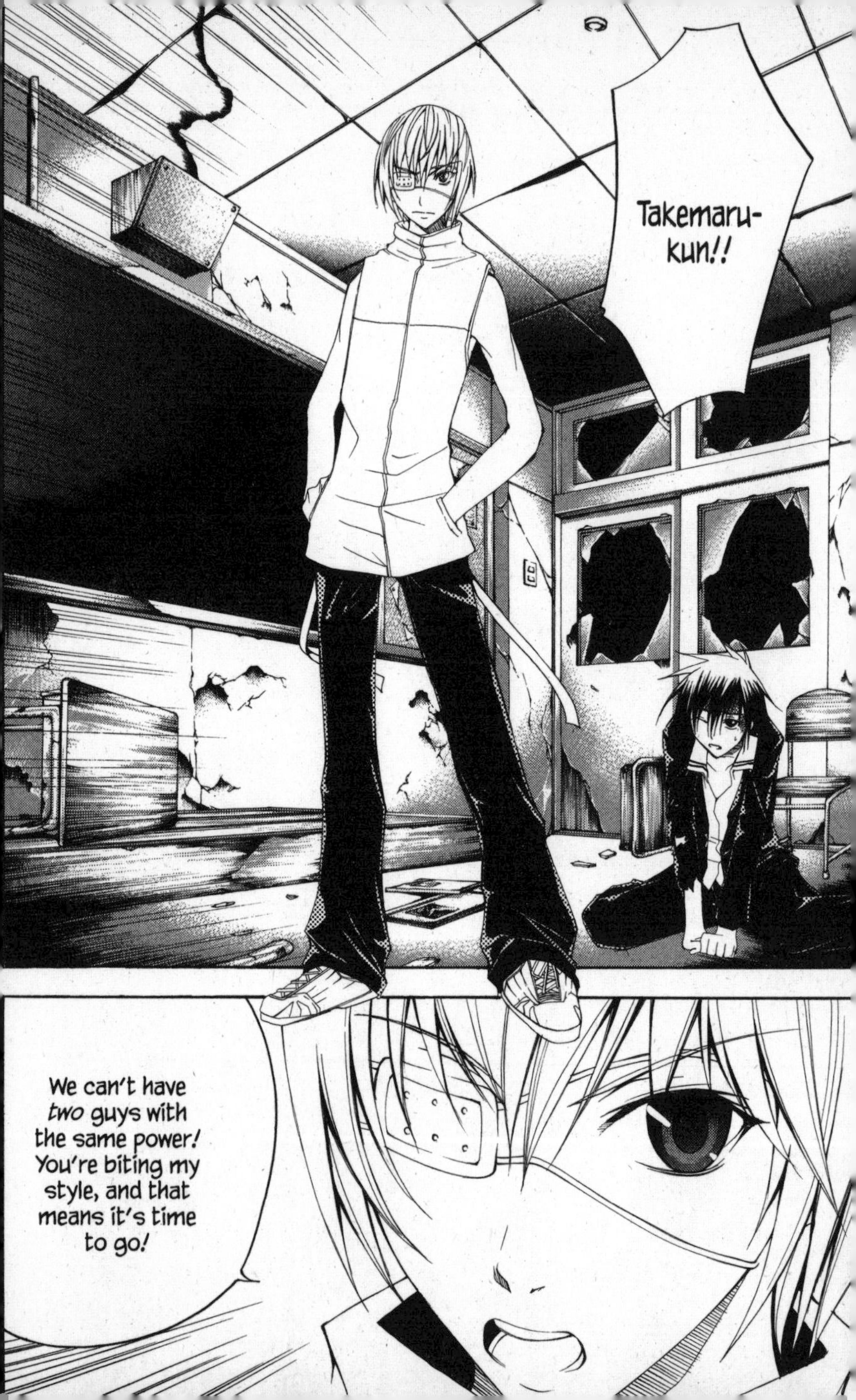
Takemaru-kun!!
We can't have *two* guys with the same power! You're biting my style, and that means it's time to go!

CASE 15 – Inhumanity

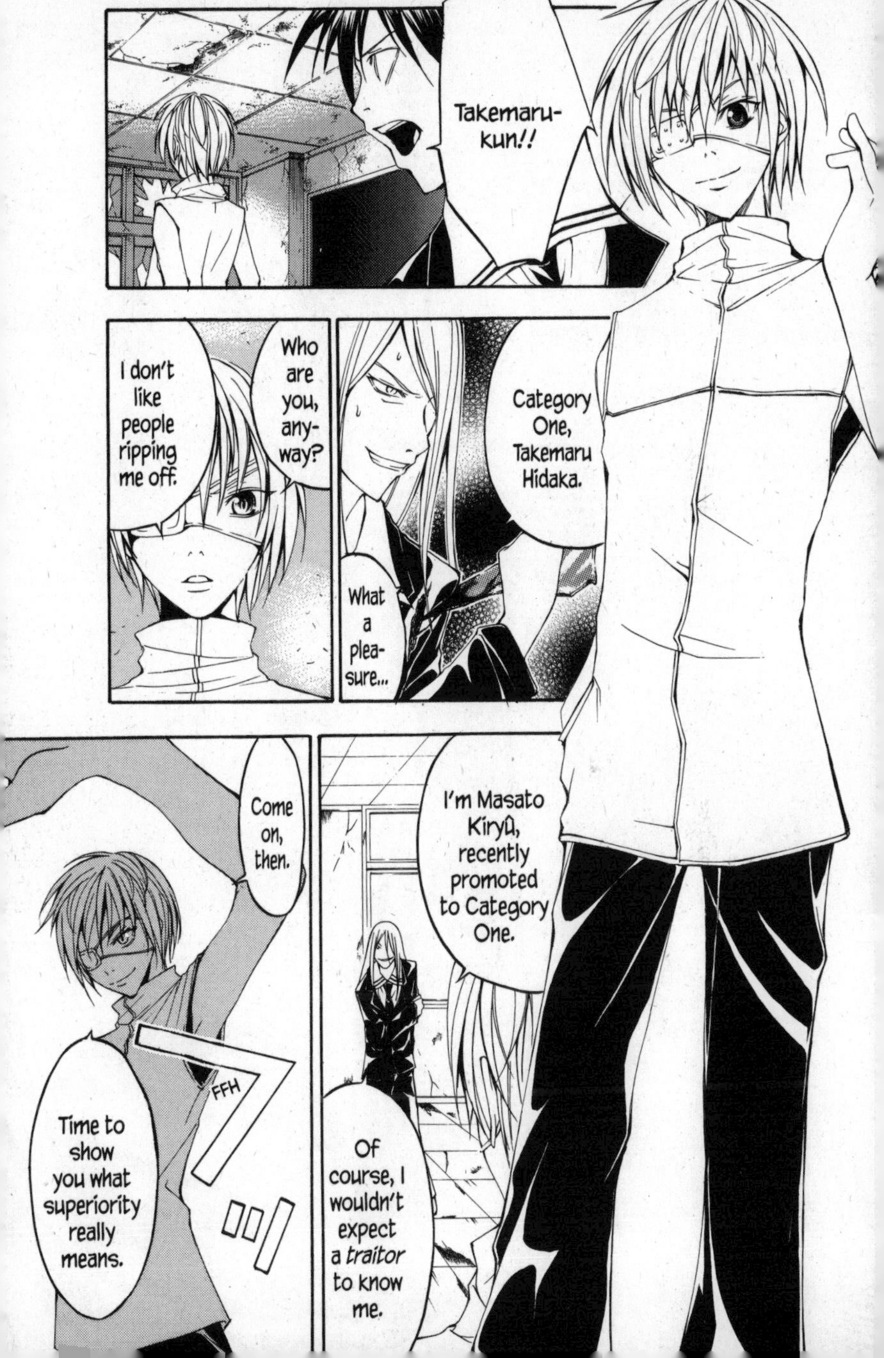

Takemaru-kun!!
Category One, Takemaru Hidaka.
What a pleasure...
Who are you, anyway?
I don't like people ripping me off.
I'm Masato Kiryû, recently promoted to Category One.
Of course, I wouldn't expect a *traitor* to know me.
Come on, then.
FFH
Time to show you what superiority really means.

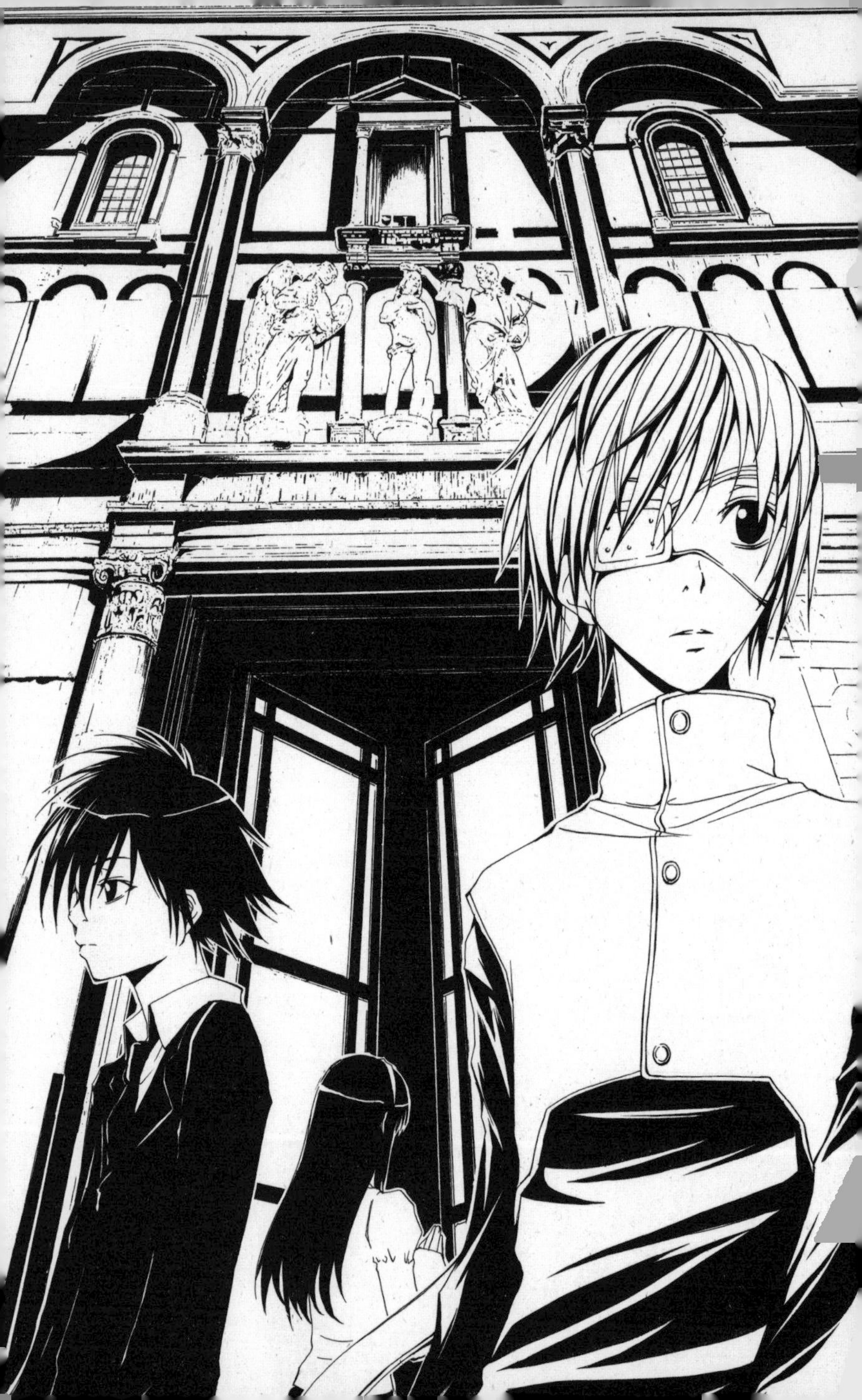

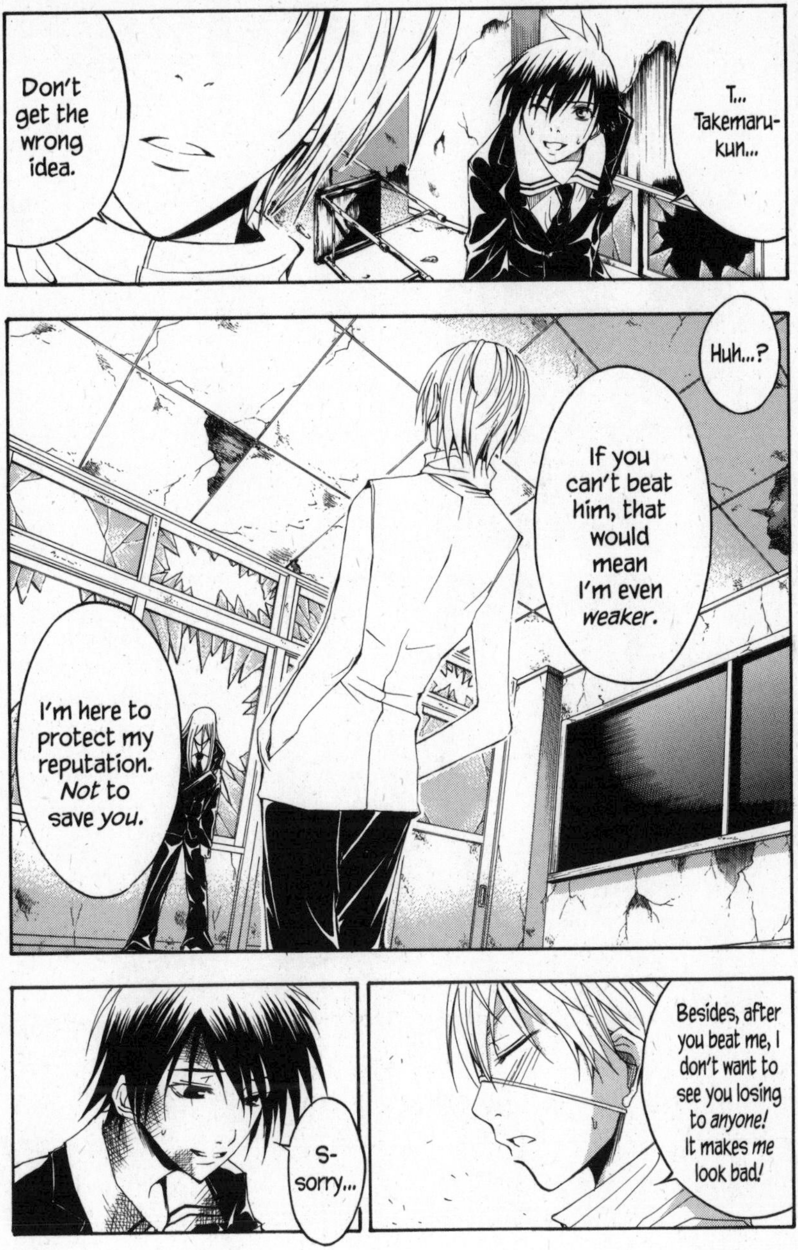
T... Takemaru-kun...
Don't get the wrong idea.
Huh...?
If you can't beat him, that would mean I'm even *weaker*.
I'm here to protect my reputation. *Not* to save *you*.
Besides, after you beat me, I don't want to see you losing to *anyone*! It makes *me* look bad!
S-sorry...

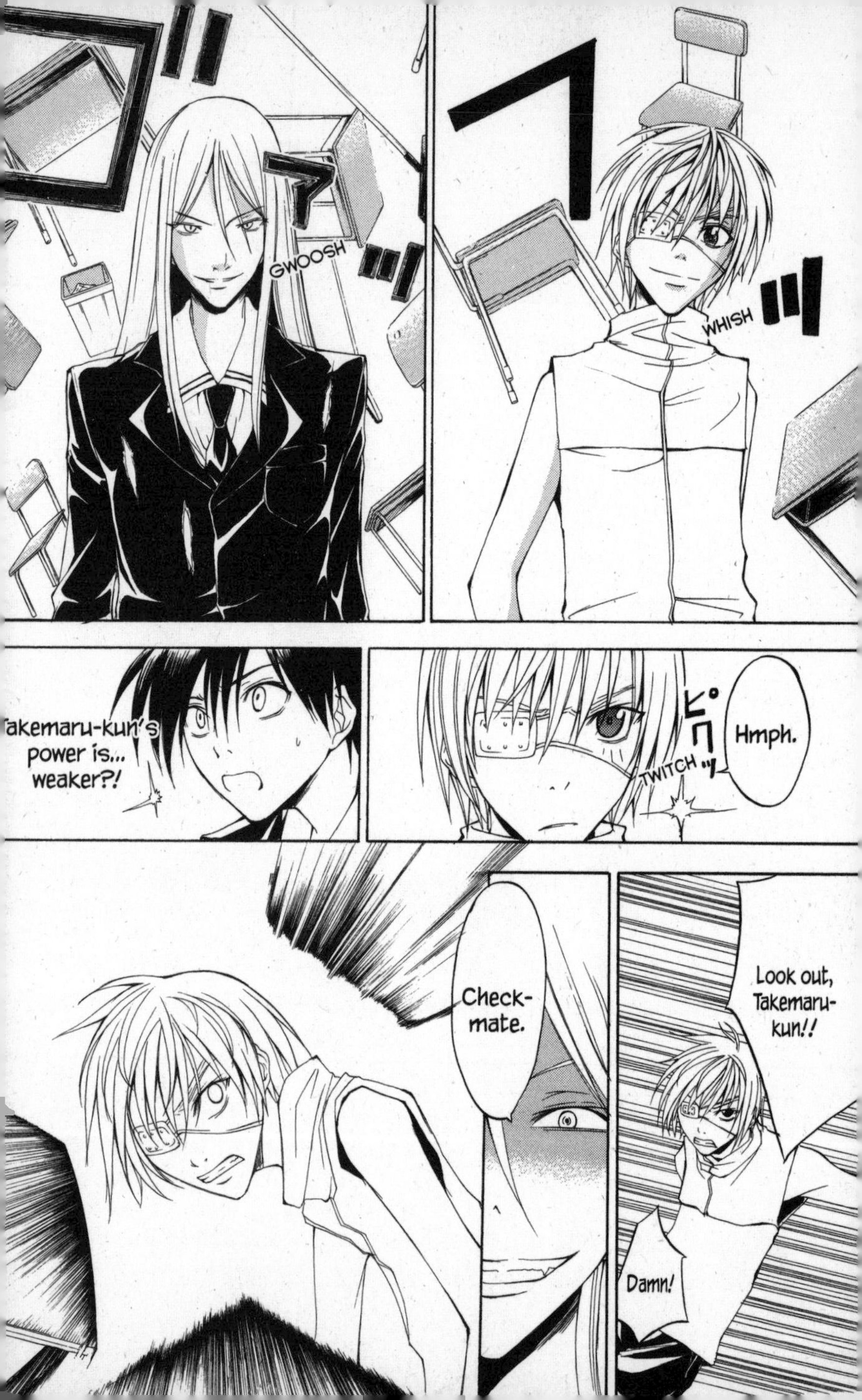
WHISH
GWOOSH
Hmph.
TWITCH
Takemaru-kun's power is... weaker?!
Look out, Takemaru-kun!!
Damn!
Check-mate.

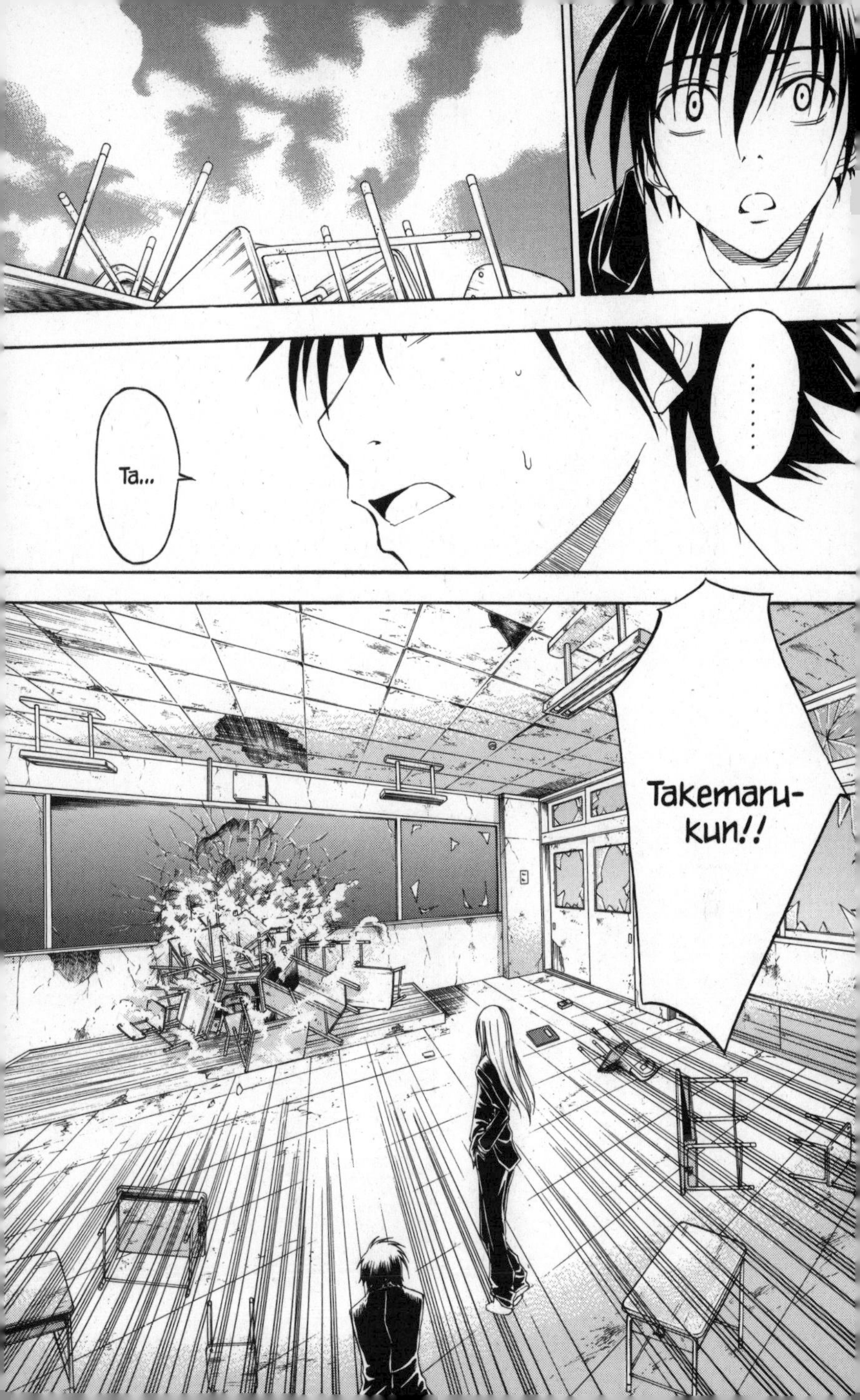
......
Ta...
Takemaru-kun!!

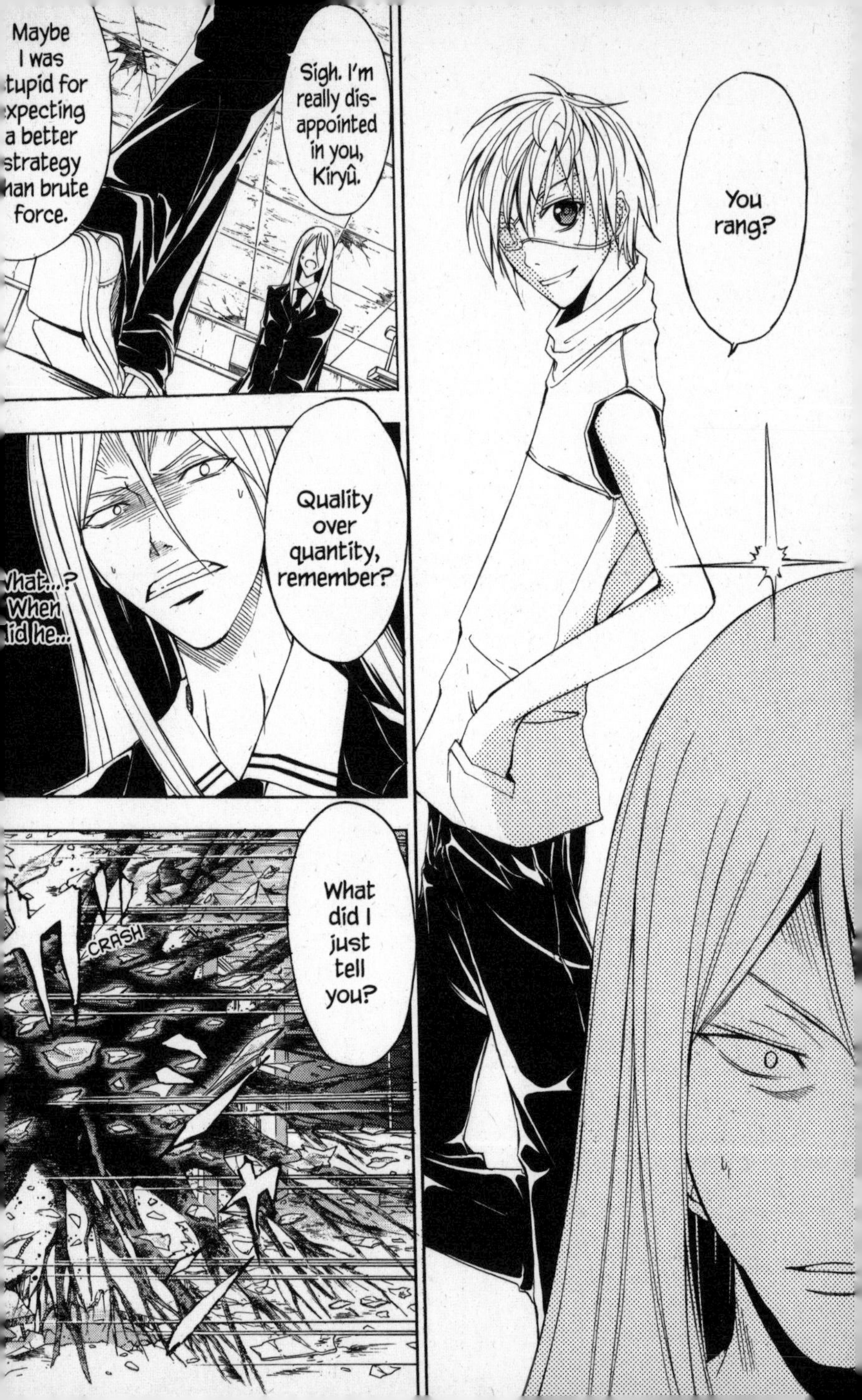

You rang?
Sigh. I'm really dis-appointed in you, Kiryû.
Maybe I was tupid for xpecting a better strategy han brute force.
Quality over quantity, remember?
hat...? When id he...
What did I just tell you?
CRASH

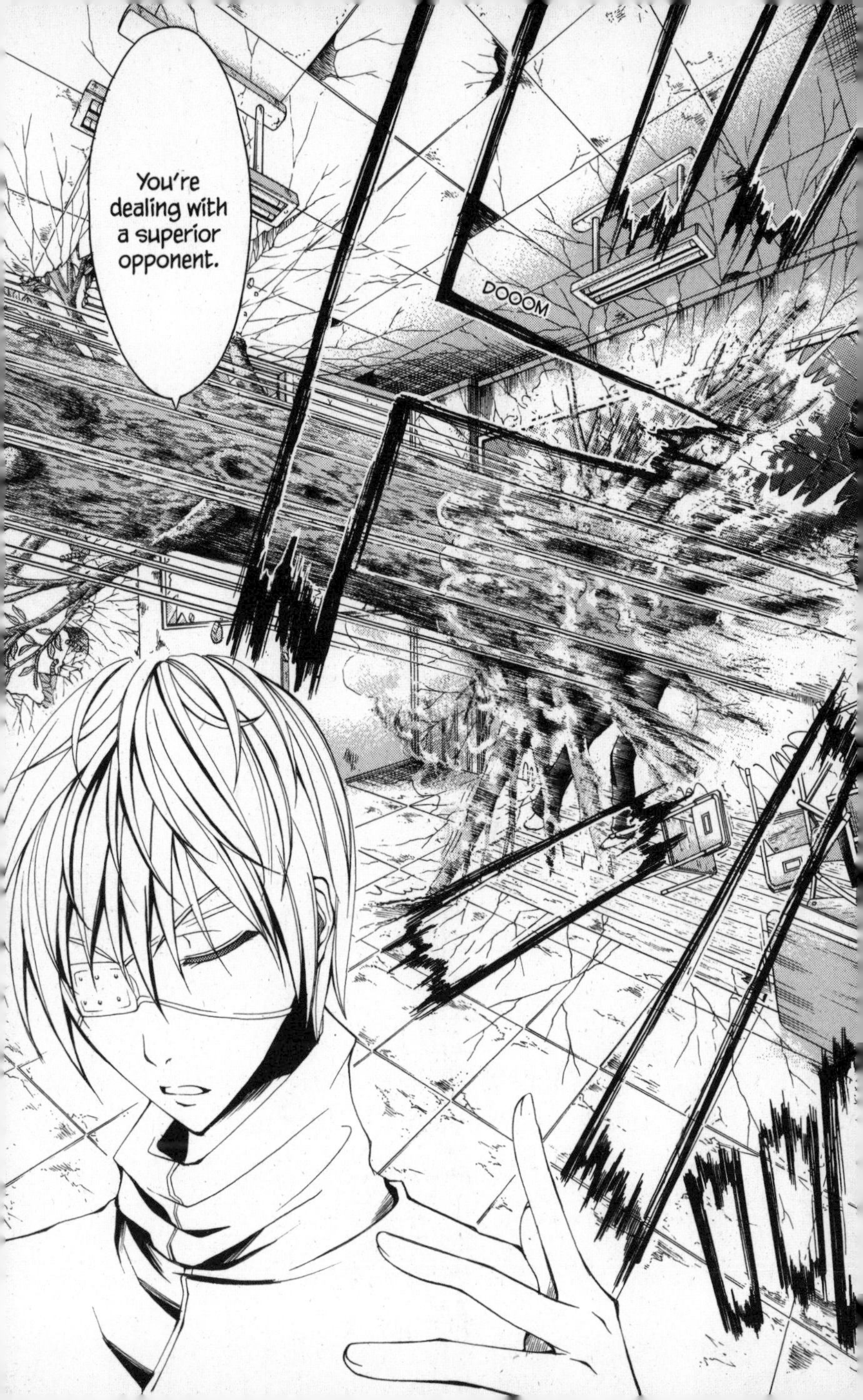
You're dealing with a superior opponent.
DOOOM

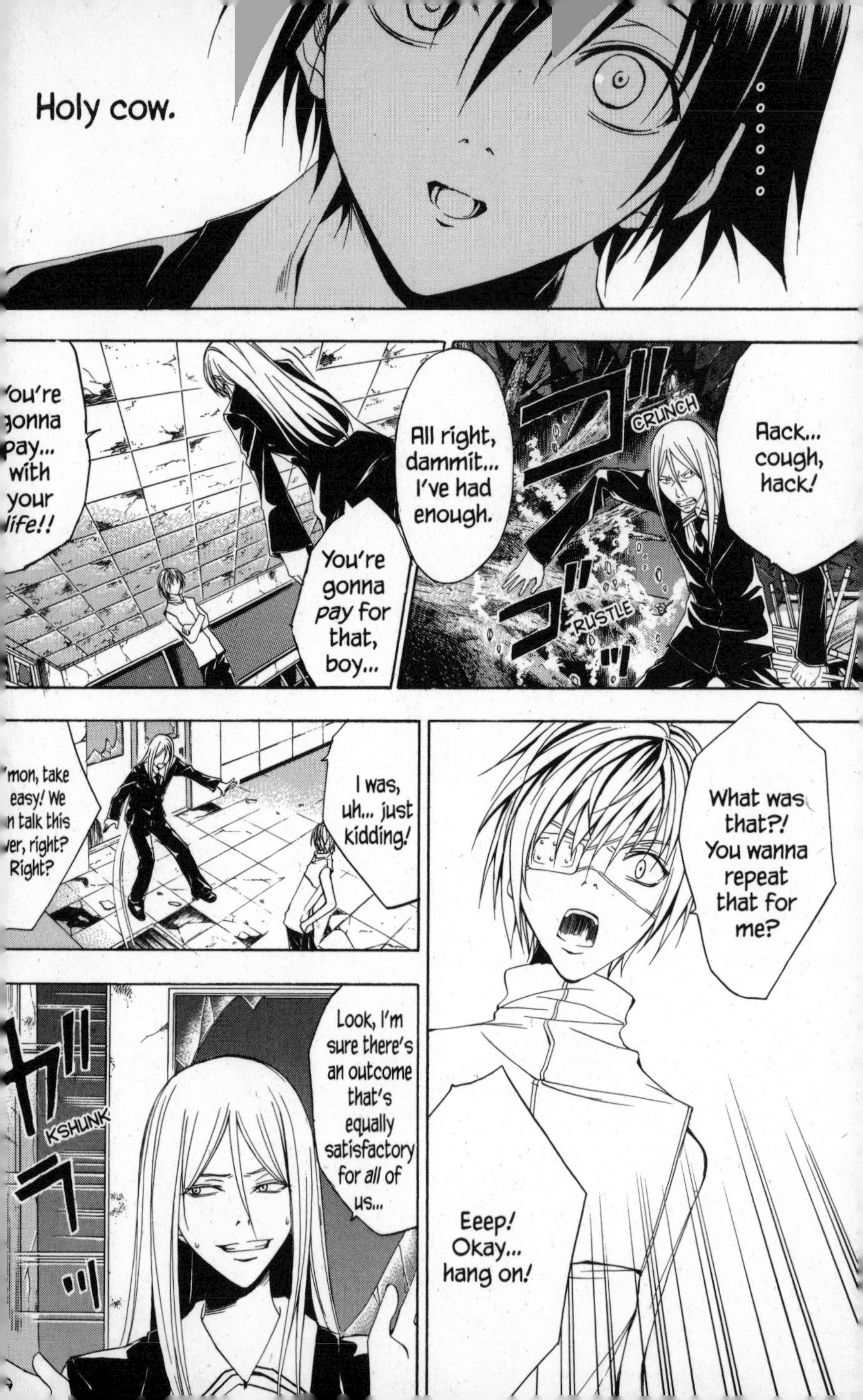

Holy cow.
Aack... cough, hack!
CRUNCH
RUSTLE
All right, dammit... I've had enough.
You're gonna pay for that, boy...
ou're gonna pay... with your ife!!
What was that?! You wanna repeat that for me?
Eeep! Okay... hang on!
I was, uh... just kidding!
'mon, take easy! We n talk this ver, right? Right?
KSHUNK
Look, I'm sure there's an outcome that's equally satisfactory for all of us...

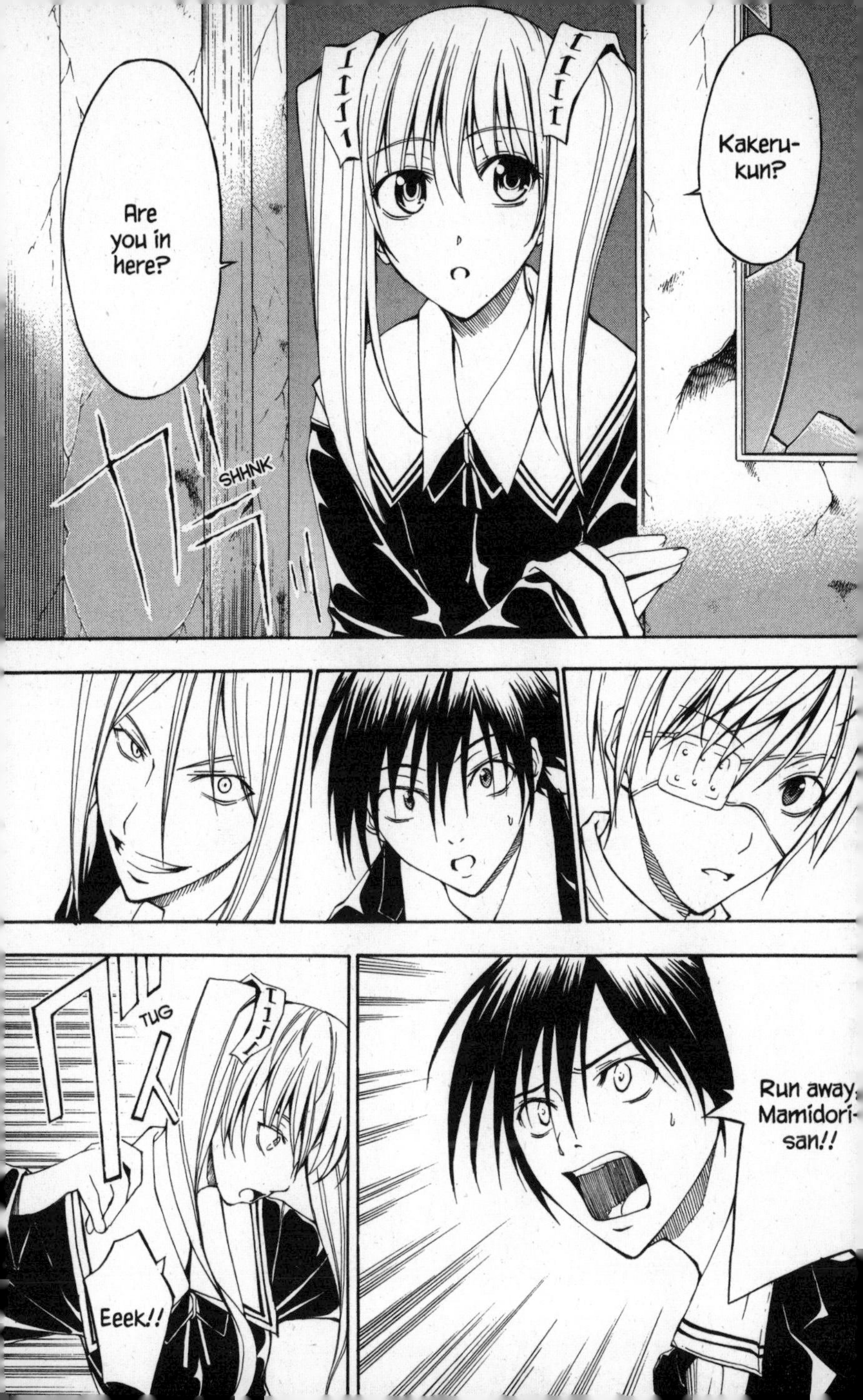
Kakeru-kun?
Are you in here?
SHHNK
Run away, Mamidori-san!!
TUG
Eeek!!

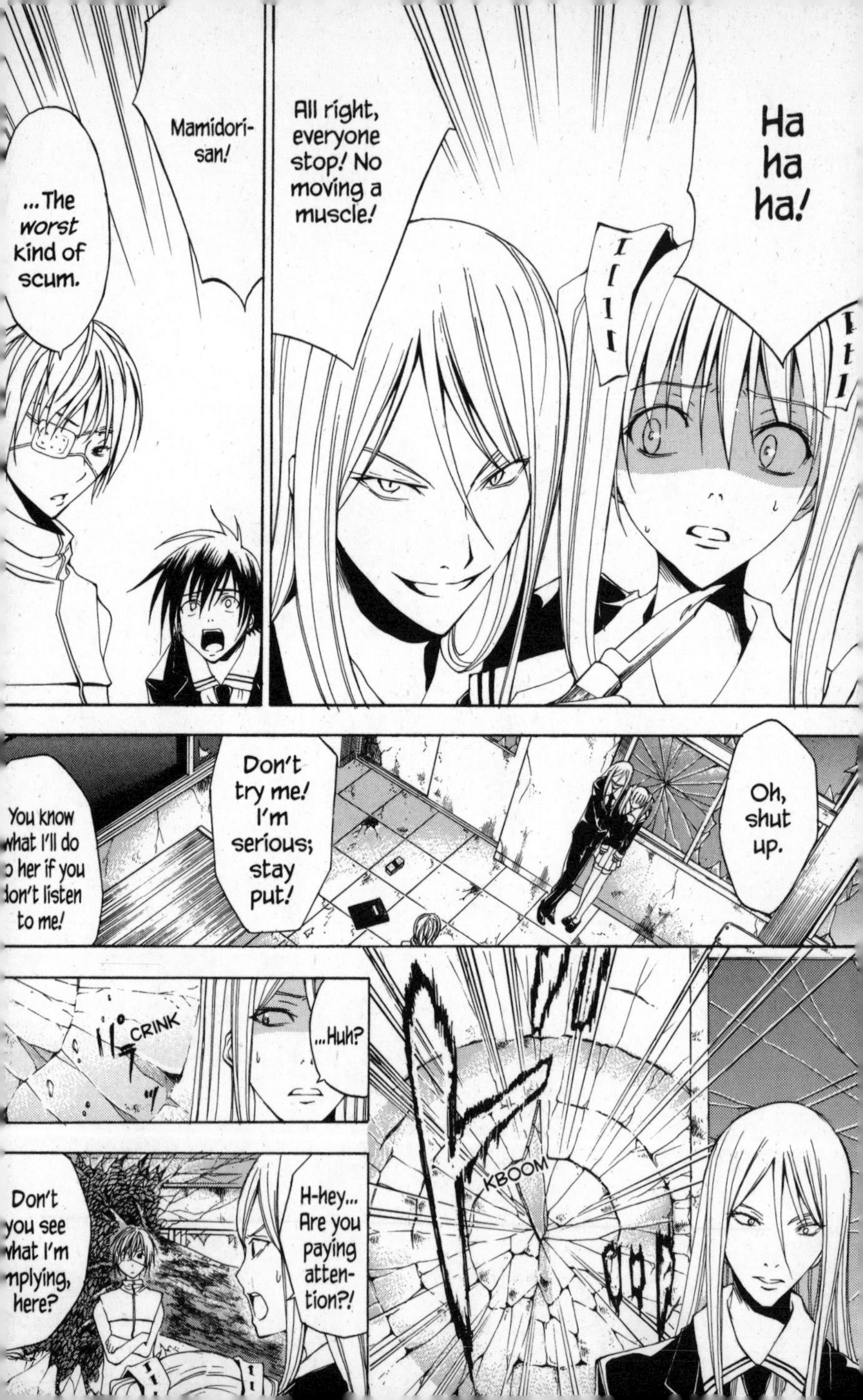
Ha ha ha!
All right, everyone stop! No moving a muscle!
Mamidori-san!
...The worst kind of scum.
Oh, shut up.
Don't try me! I'm serious; stay put!
You know hat I'll do o her if you on't listen to me!
KBOOM
CRINK
...Huh?
H-hey... Are you paying atten-tion?!
Don't you see hat I'm nplying, here?

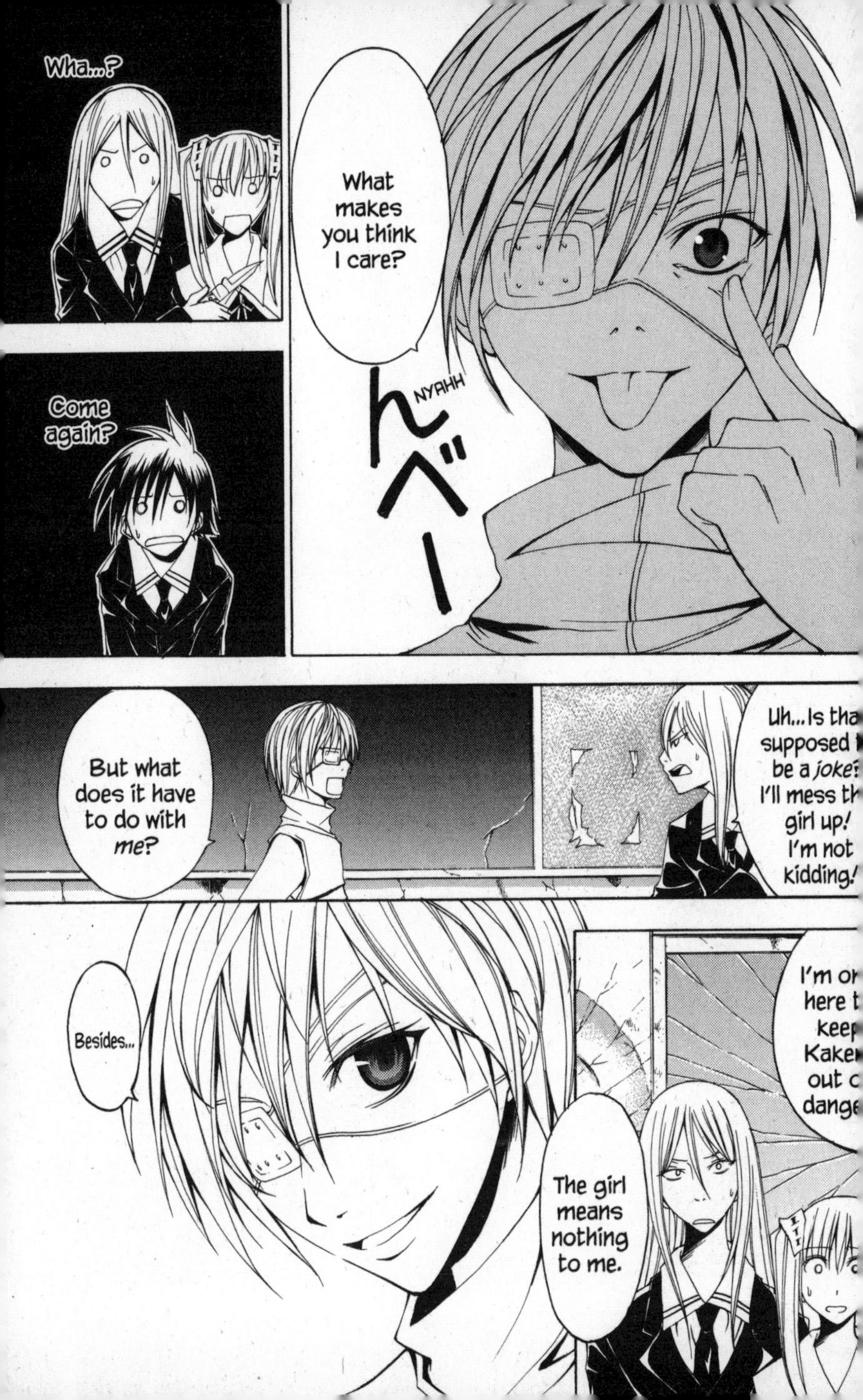
What makes you think I care?
んべー
NYAHH
Wha...?
Come again?
Uh...Is tha supposed be a joke? I'll mess th girl up! I'm not kidding!
But what does it have to do with *me*?
I'm or here t keep Kake out o dange
Besides...
The girl means nothing to me.

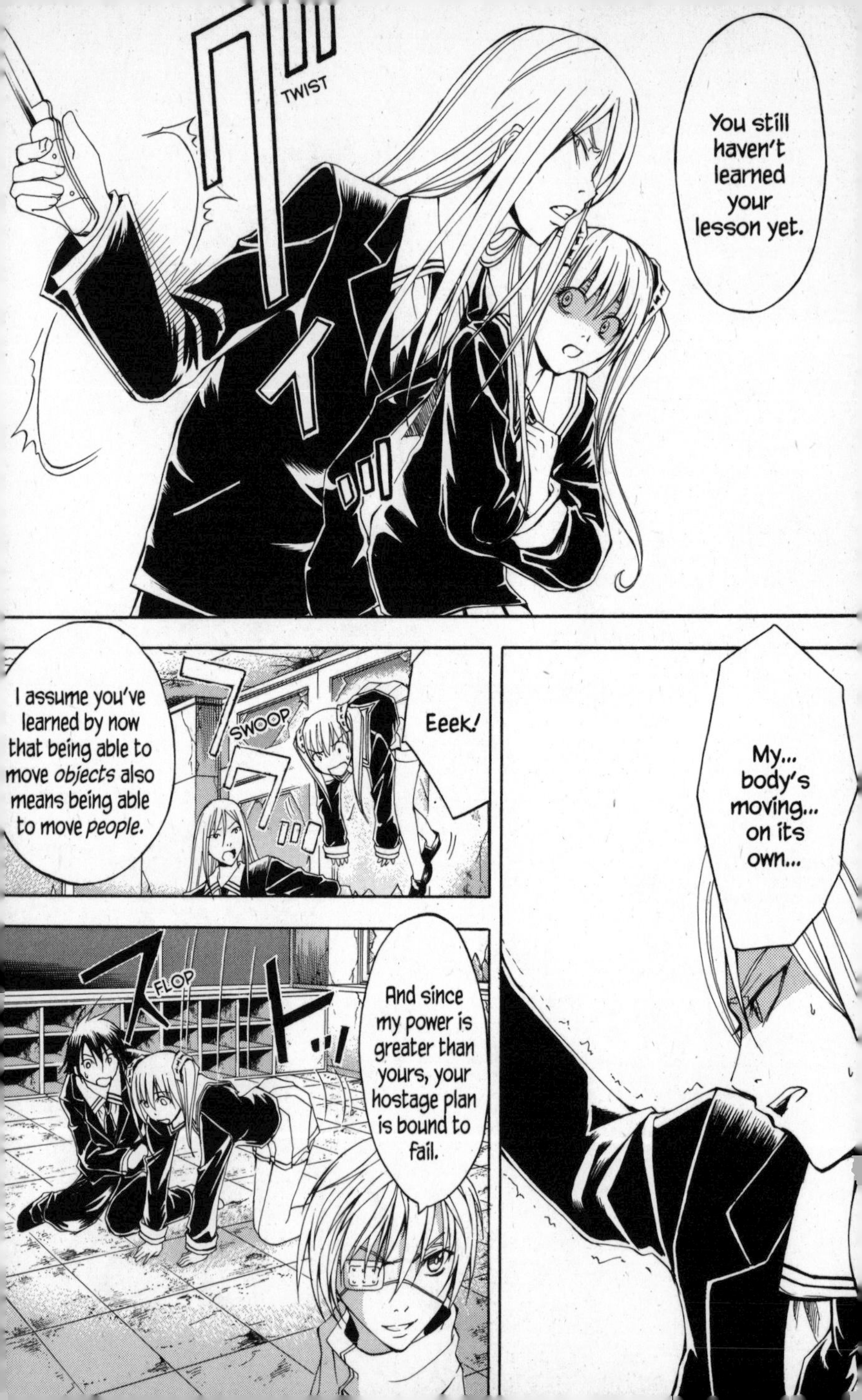
You still haven't learned your lesson yet.
TWIST
My... body's moving... on its own...
Eeek!
SWOOP
I assume you've learned by now that being able to move *objects* also means being able to move *people*.
And since my power is greater than yours, your hostage plan is bound to fail.
FLOP

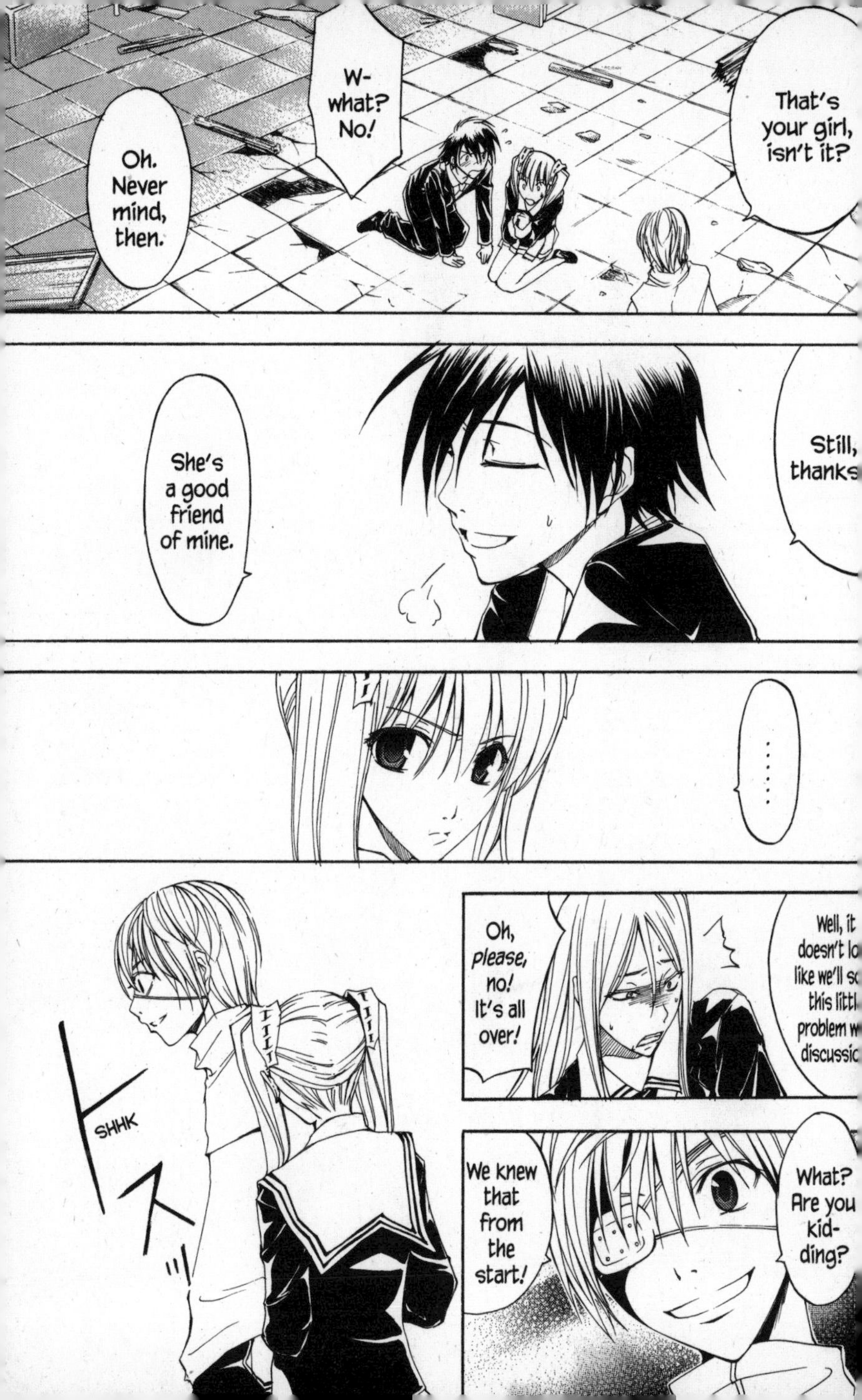
That's your girl, isn't it?
W- what? No!
Oh. Never mind, then.
Still, thanks
She's a good friend of mine.
......
Well, it doesn't lo like we'll sc this littl problem w discussic
Oh, *please*, no! It's all over!
What? Are you kid- ding?
We knew that from the start!
SHHK

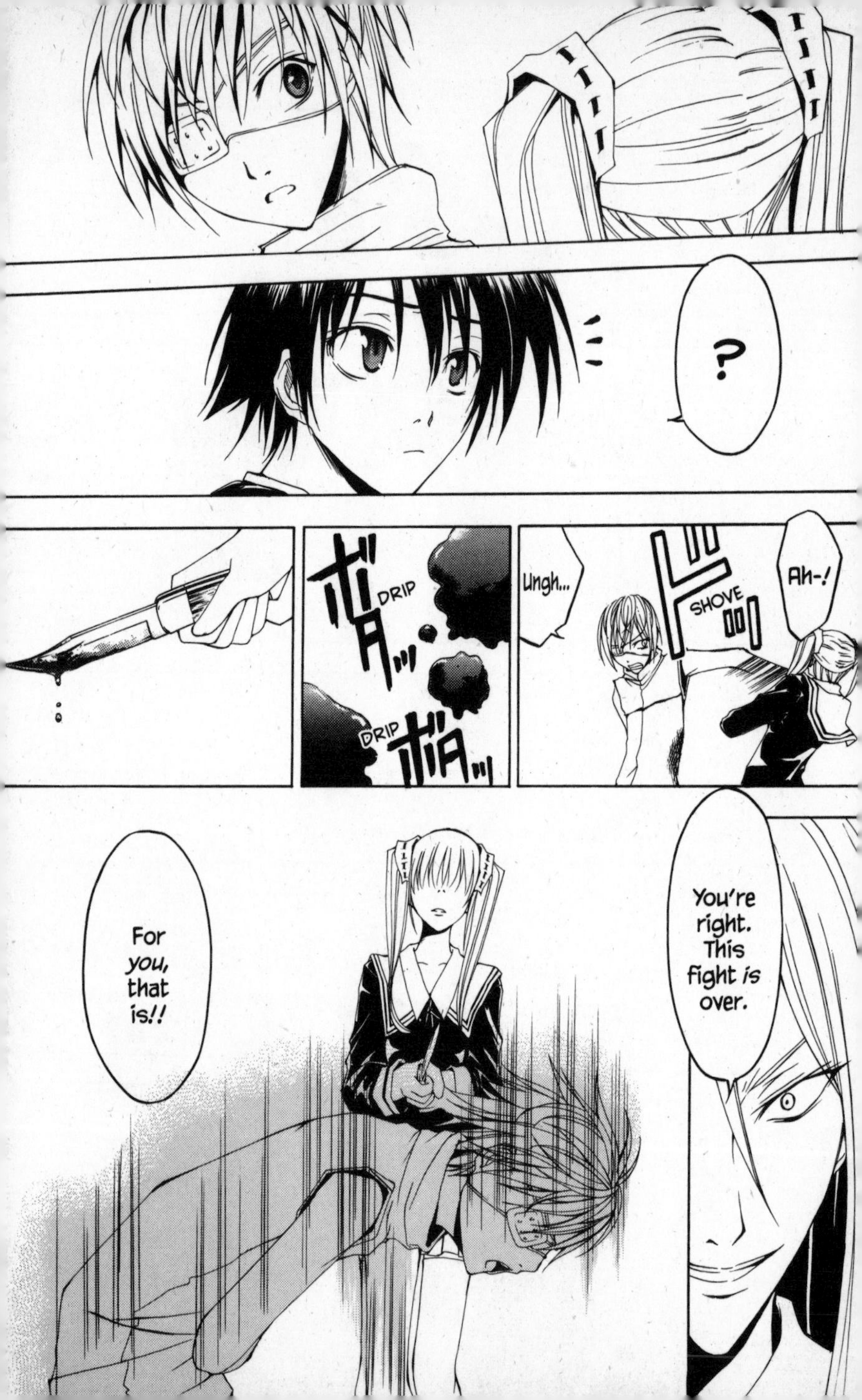
?
Ah-!
SHOVE
Ungh...
DRIP
DRIP
You're right. This fight *is* over.
For *you,* that is!!

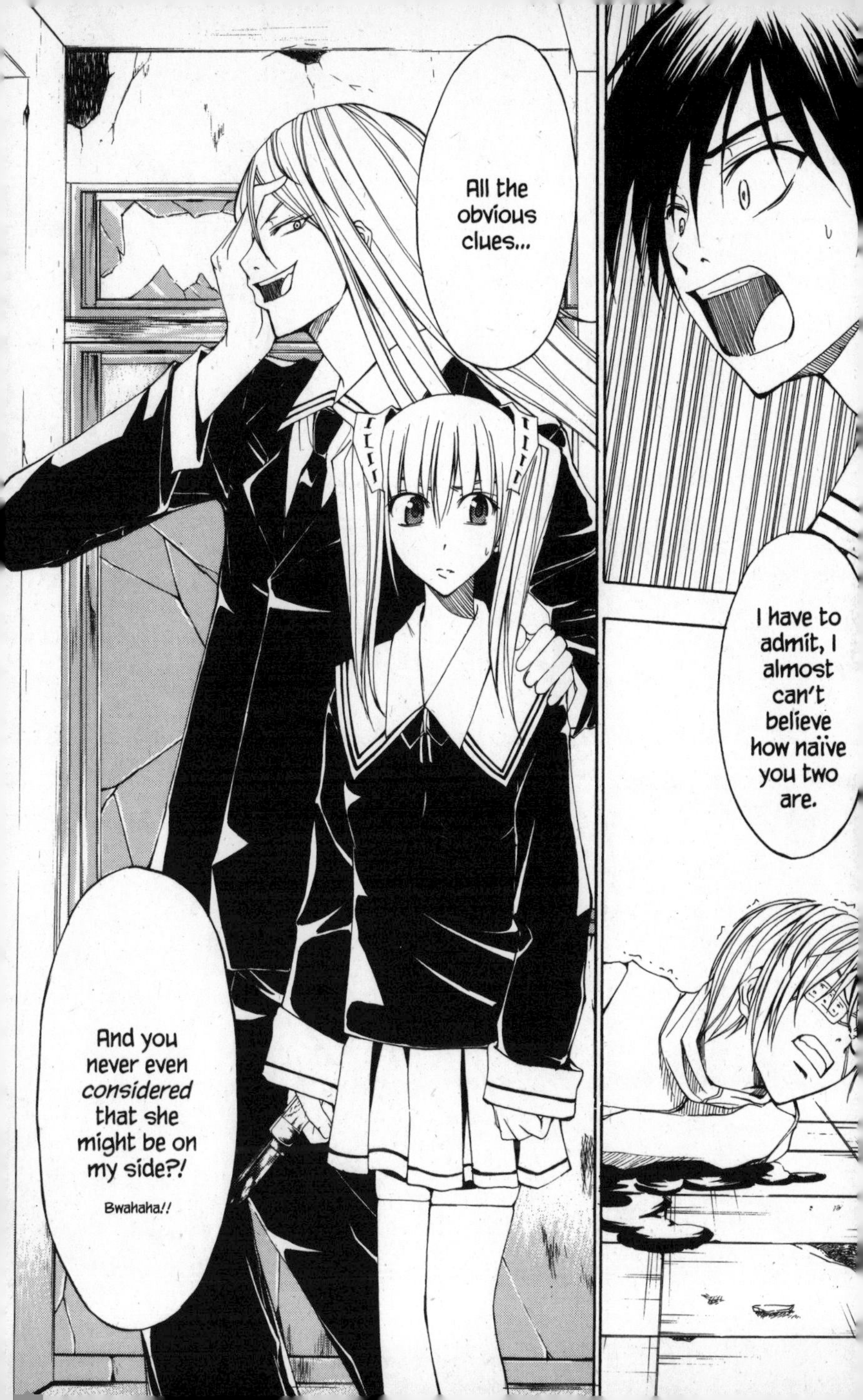
I have to admit, I almost can't believe how naïve you two are.
All the obvious clues...
And you never even *considered* that she might be on my side?!
Bwahaha!!

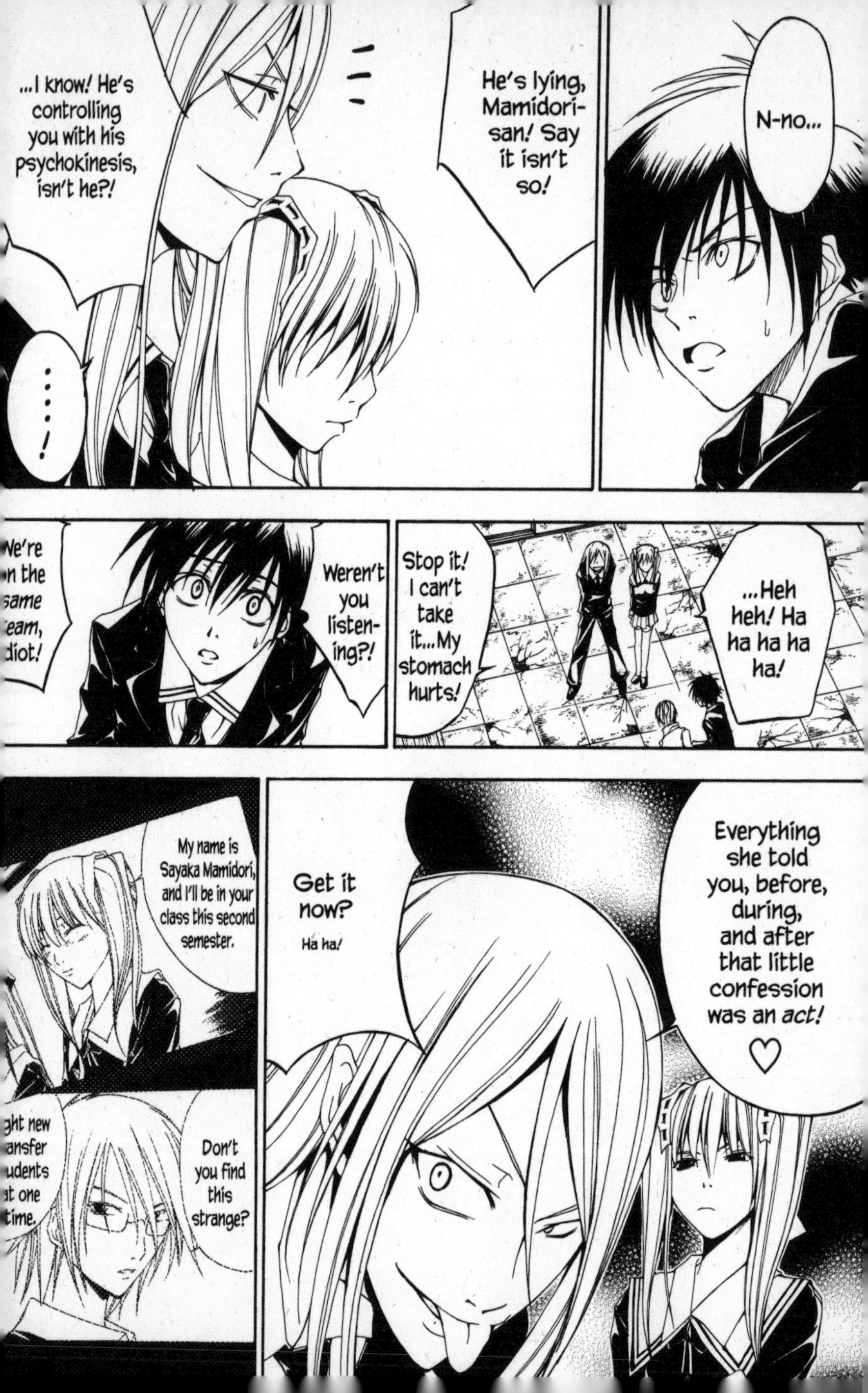
N-no...
He's lying, Mamidori-san! Say it isn't so!
...I know! He's controlling you with his psychokinesis, isn't he?!
......!
...Heh heh! Ha ha ha ha ha!
Stop it! I can't take it...My stomach hurts!
Weren't you listening?!
Ve're n the same eam, diot!
Everything she told you, before, during, and after that little confession was an act! ♡
Get it now?
Ha ha!
My name is Sayaka Mamidori, and I'll be in your class this second semester.
Don't you find this strange?
ght new ansfer udents at one time.

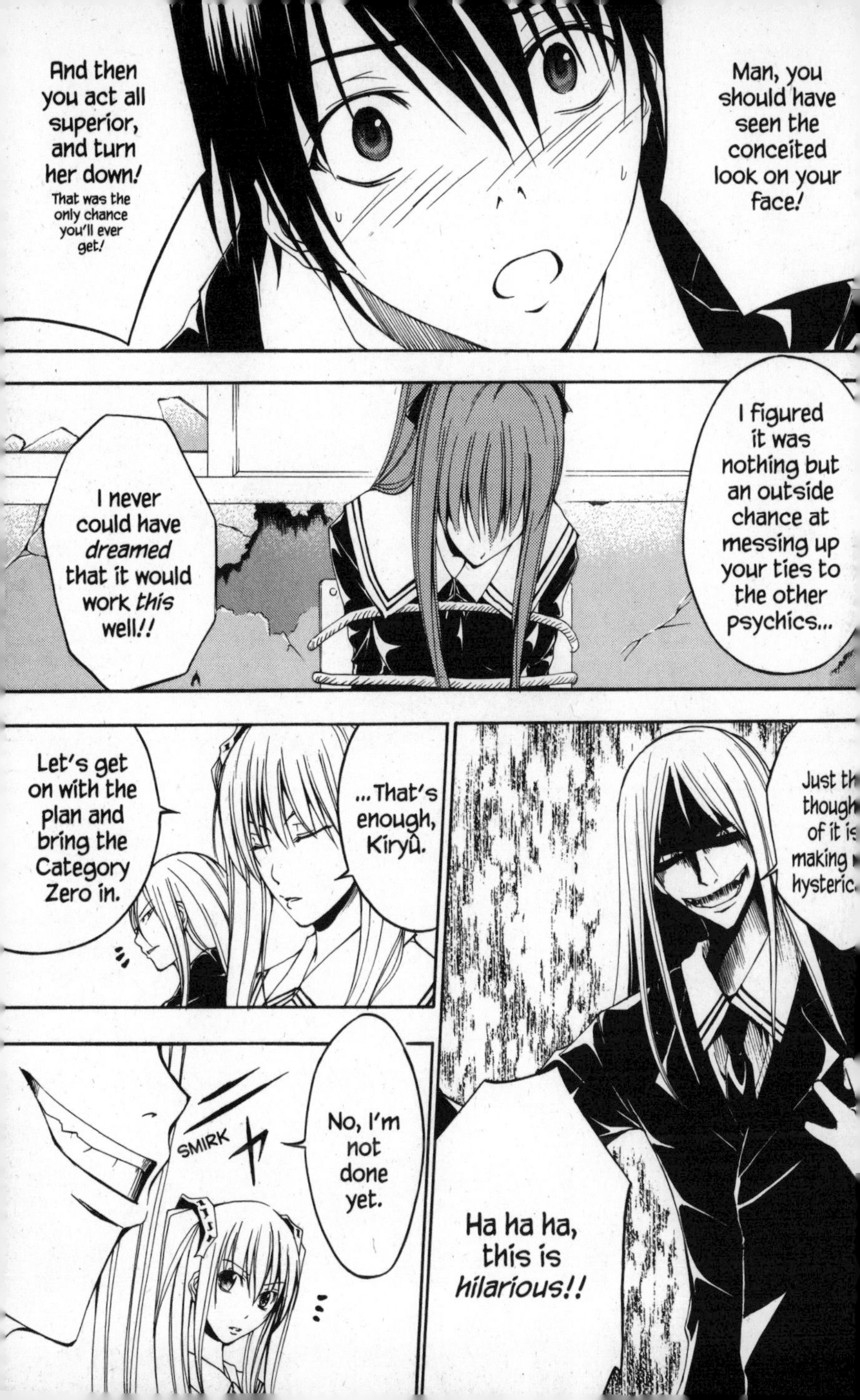

Man, you should have seen the conceited look on your face!
And then you act all superior, and turn her down!
That was the only chance you'll ever get!
I figured it was nothing but an outside chance at messing up your ties to the other psychics...
I never could have dreamed that it would work this well!!
Just th though of it is making hysteric
Ha ha ha, this is hilarious!!
...That's enough, Kiryû.
Let's get on with the plan and bring the Category Zero in.
No, I'm not done yet.
SMIRK

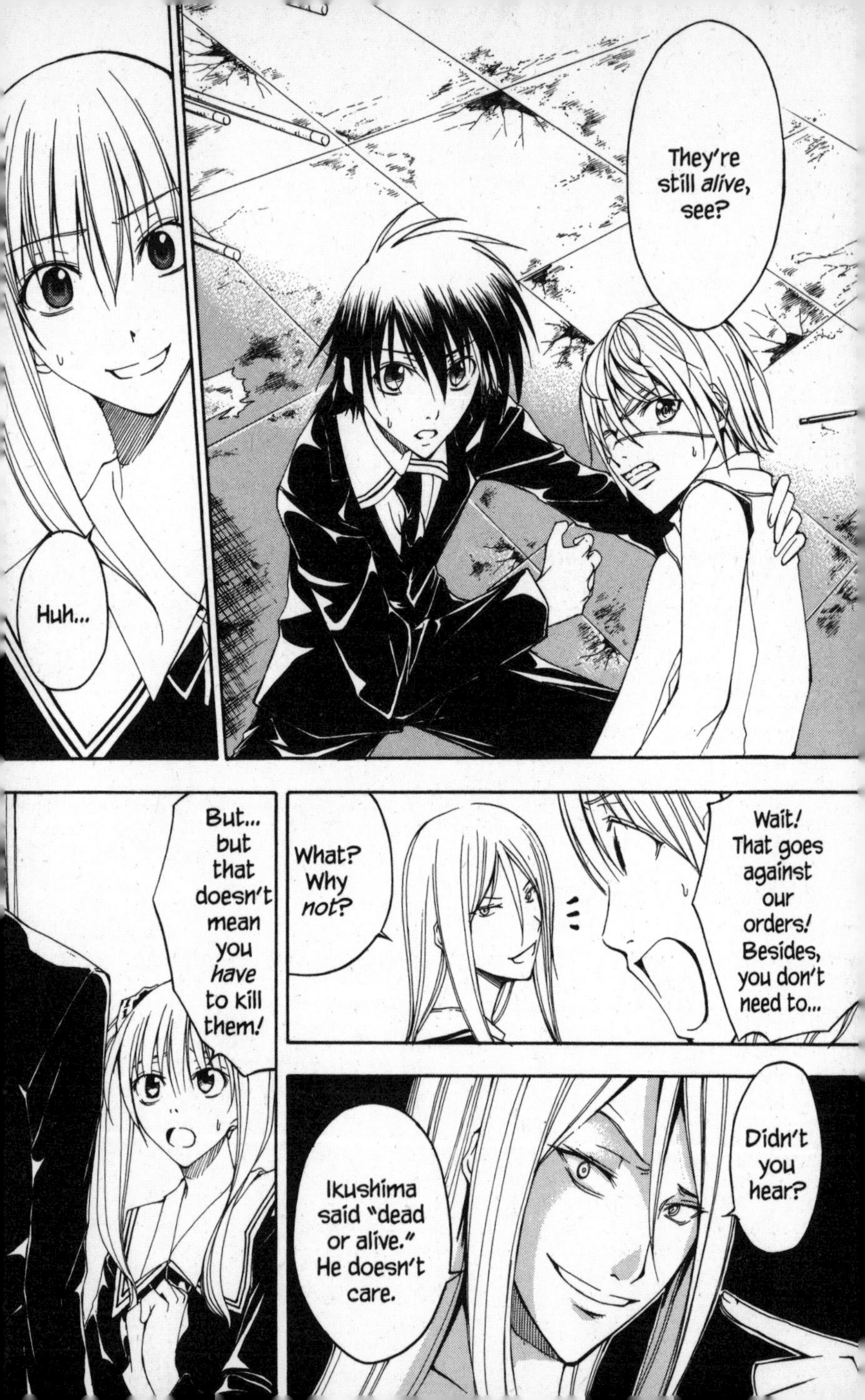
They're still *alive*, see?
Huh...
Wait! That goes against our orders! Besides, you don't need to...
What? Why *not*?
Didn't you hear?
Ikushima said "dead or alive." He doesn't care.
But... but that doesn't mean you *have* to kill them!

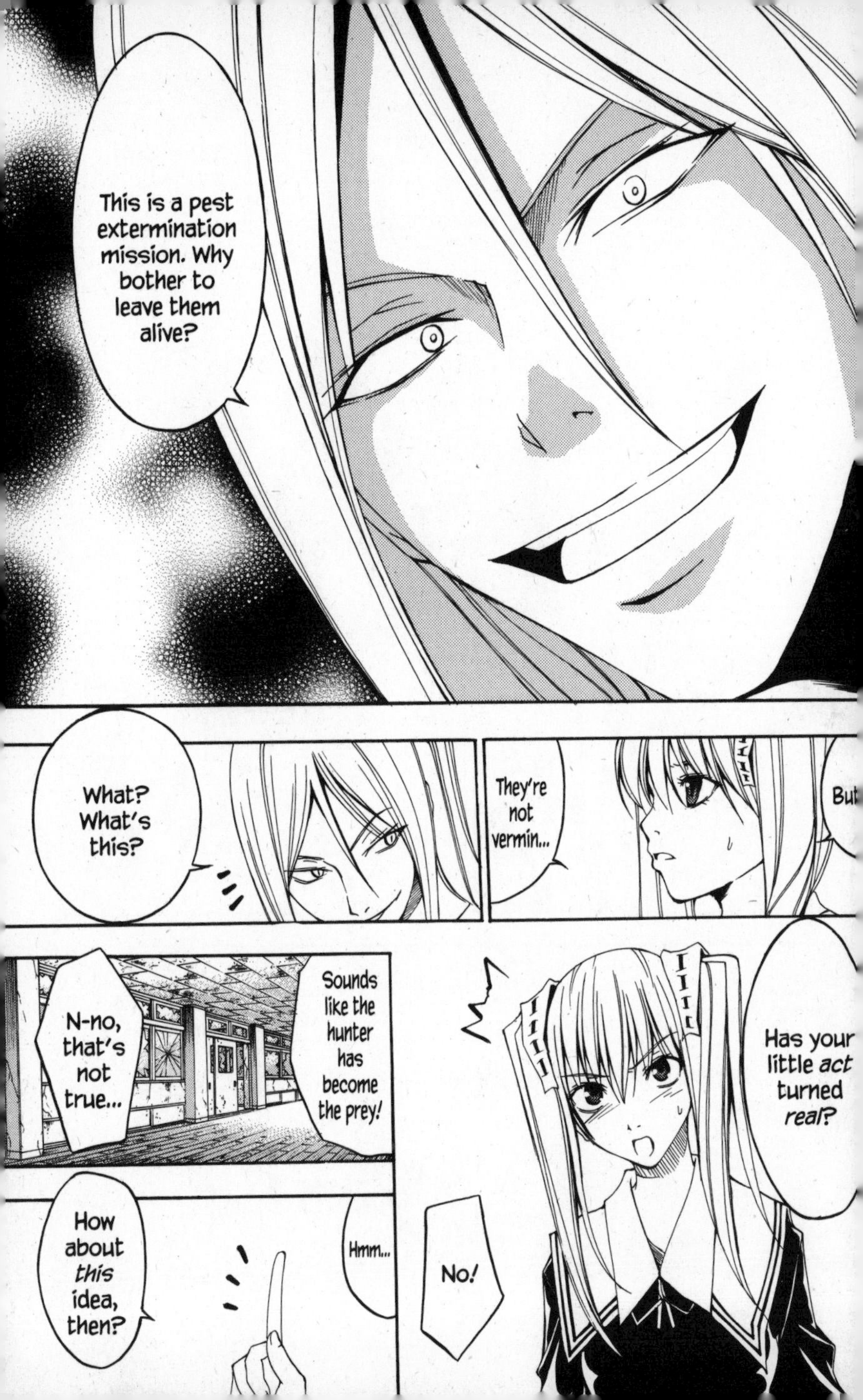
This is a pest extermination mission. Why bother to leave them alive?
Bu
They're not vermin...
What? What's this?
Has your little *act* turned *real*?
No!
Sounds like the hunter has become the prey!
N-no, that's not true...
Hmm...
How about *this* idea, then?

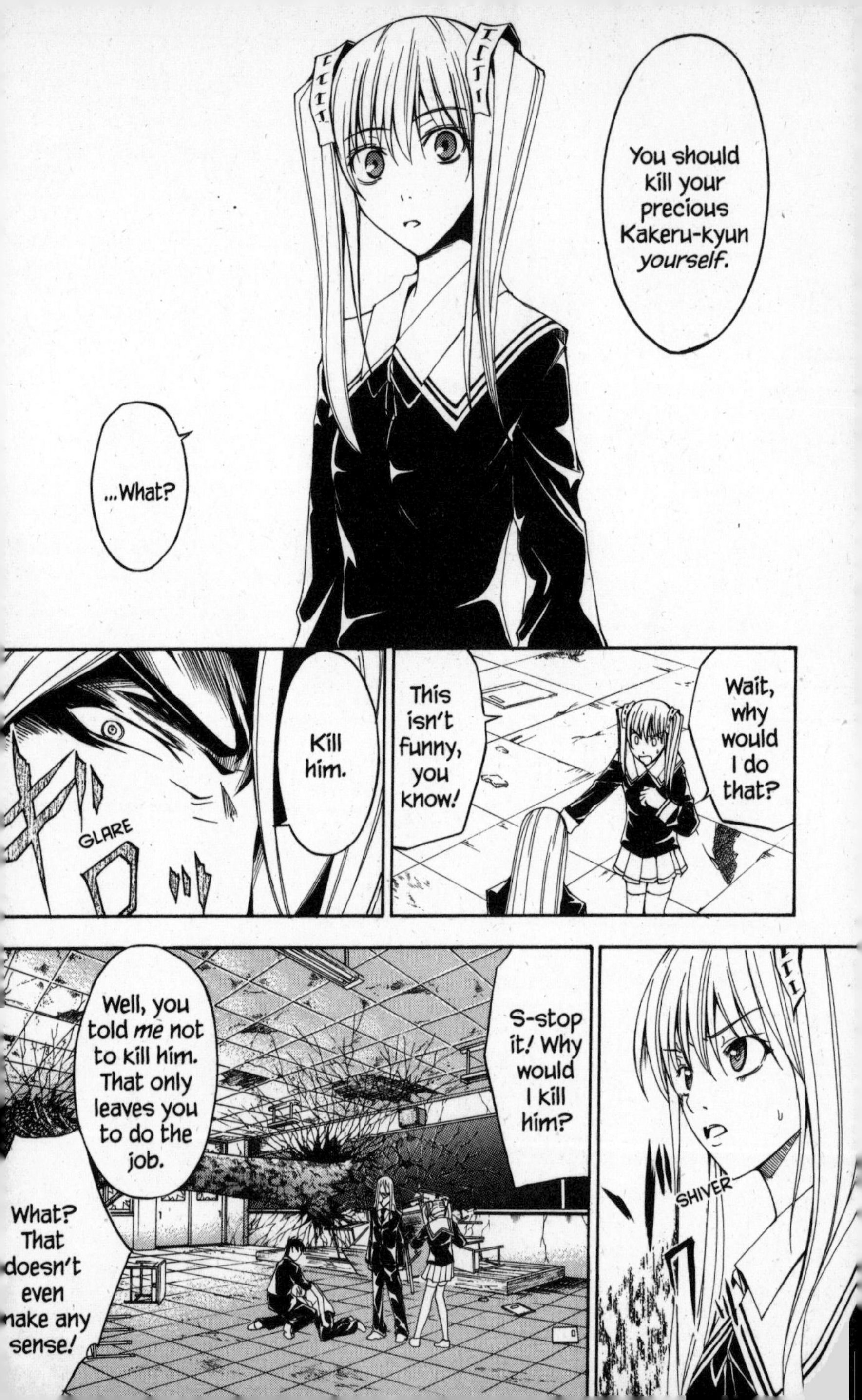
You should kill your precious Kakeru-kyun *yourself*.
...What?
Wait, why would I do that?
This isn't funny, you know!
Kill him.
GLARE
S-stop it! Why would I kill him?
SHIVER
Well, you told *me* not to kill him. That only leaves you to do the job.
What? That doesn't even make any sense!

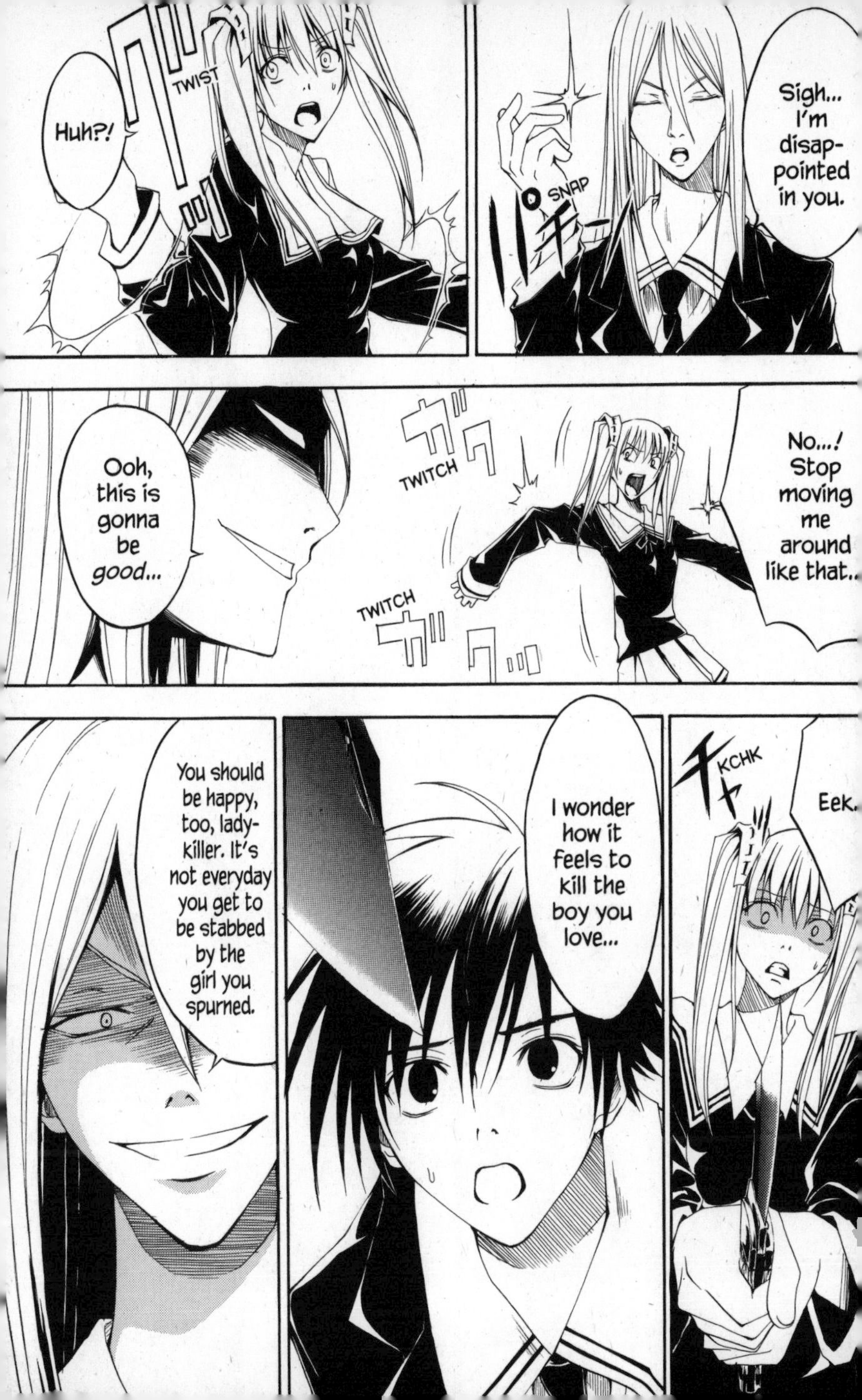
Sigh... I'm disap-pointed in you.
SNAP
TWIST
Huh?!
No...! Stop moving me around like that..
TWITCH
TWITCH
Ooh, this is gonna be *good*...
KCHK
Eek.
I wonder how it feels to kill the boy you love...
You should be happy, too, lady-killer. It's not everyday you get to be stabbed by the girl you spurned.

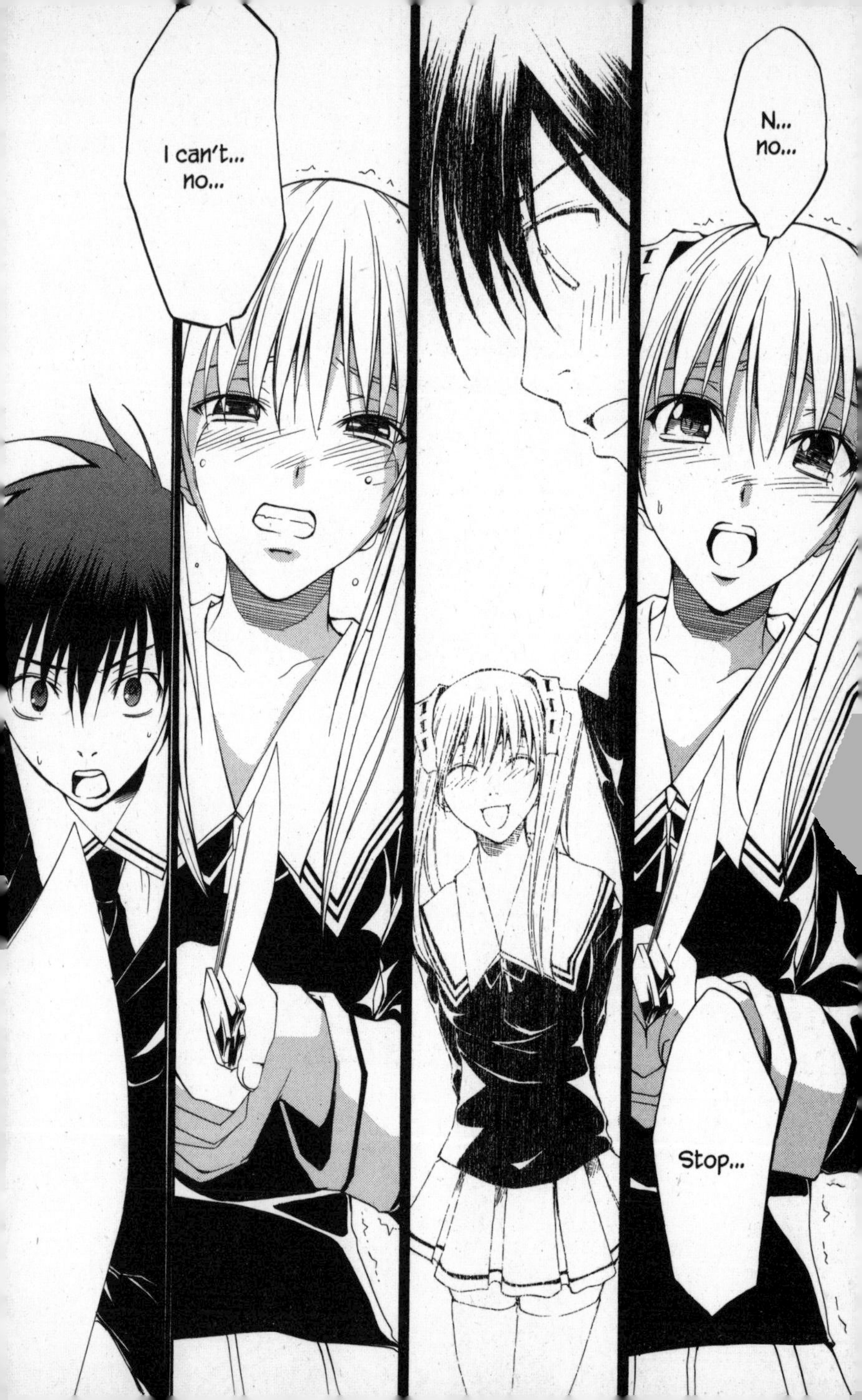
N... no...
Stop...
I can't... no...

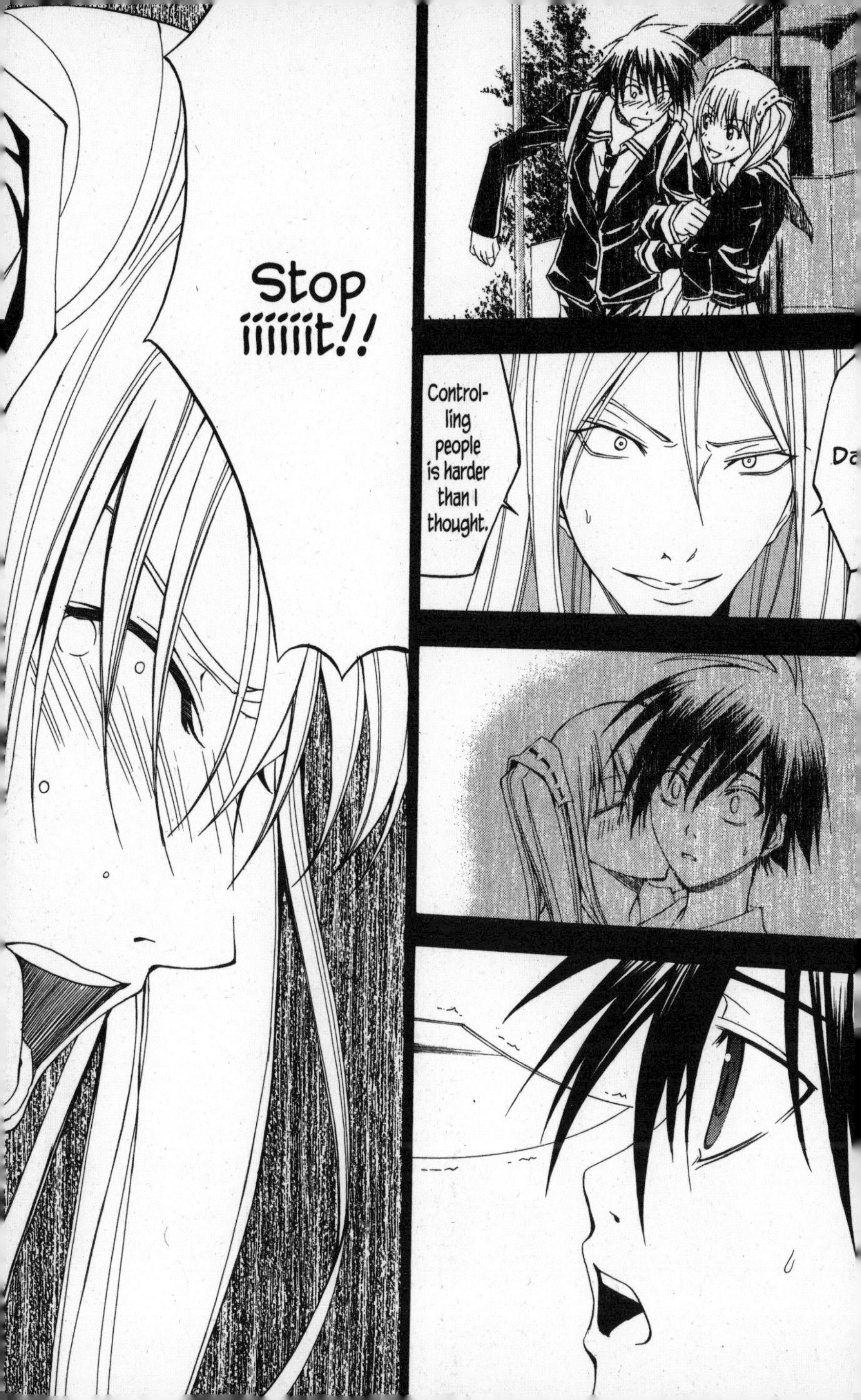
Da
Controlling people is harder than I thought.
Stop iiiiiit!!

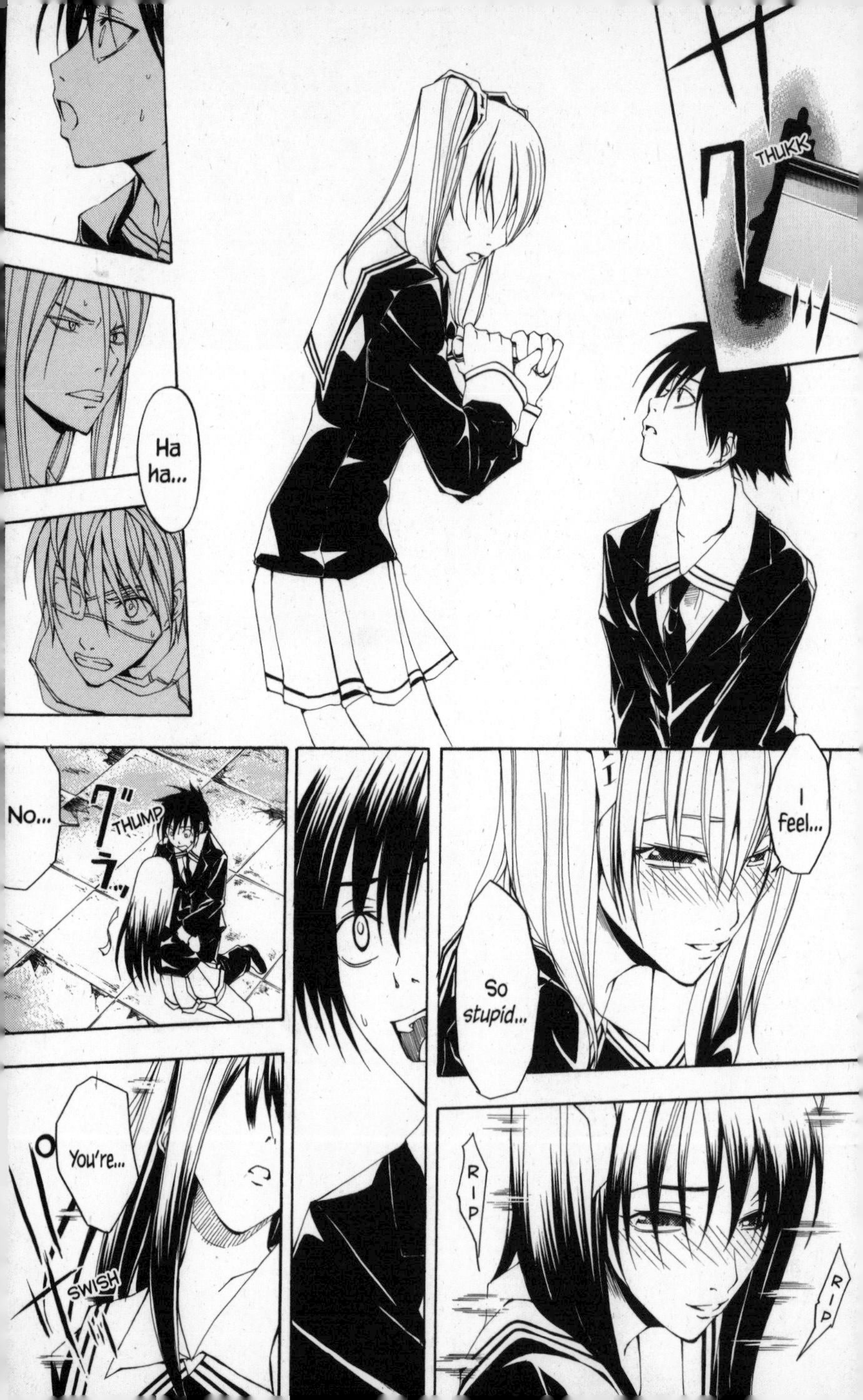
THUKK
Ha ha...
I feel...
So stupid...
No...
THUMP
RIP
RIP
You're...
SWISH

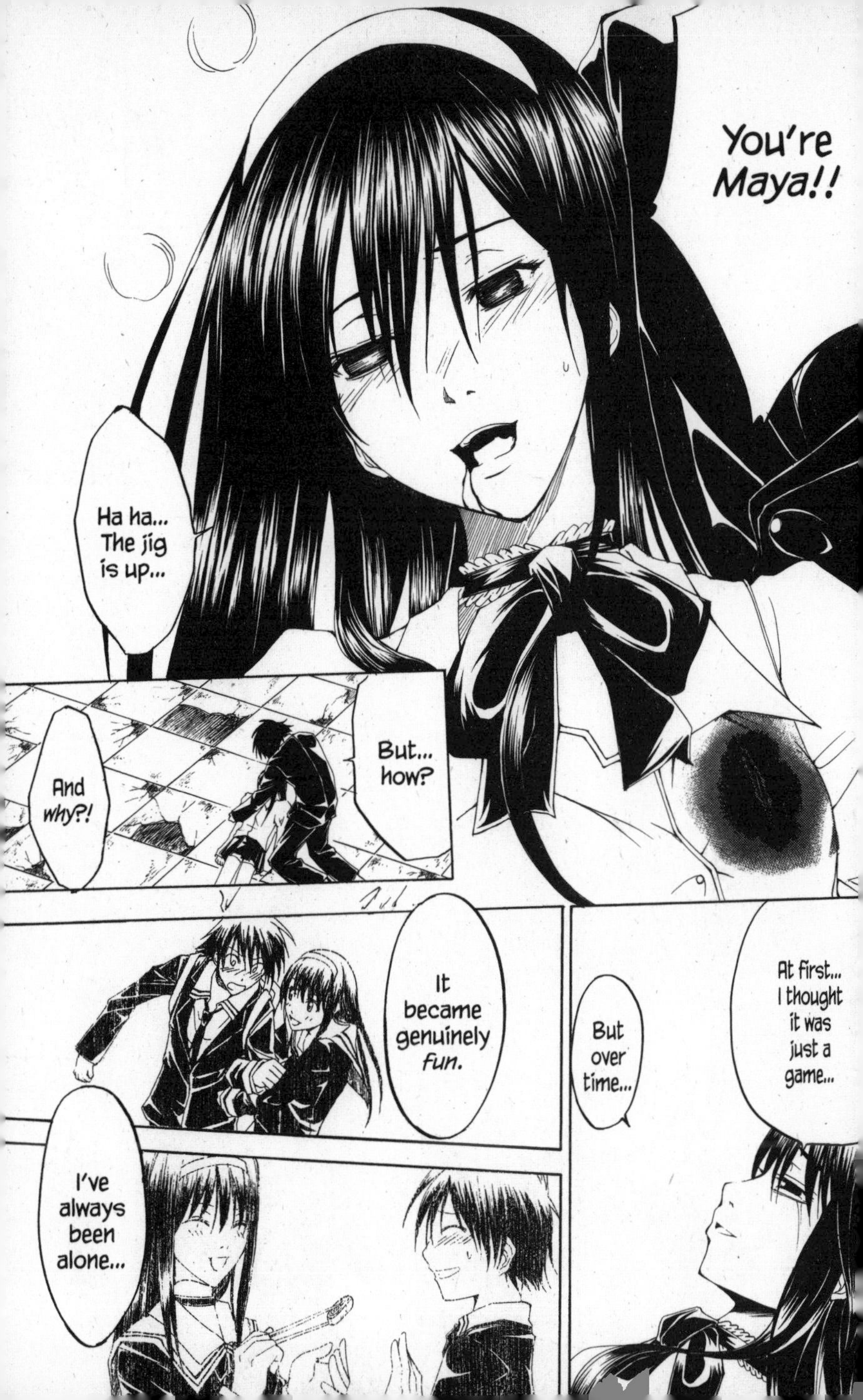
You're *Maya!!*
Ha ha... The jig is up...
But... how?
And *why?!*
At first... I thought it was just a game...
But over time...
It became genuinely *fun.*
I've always been alone...

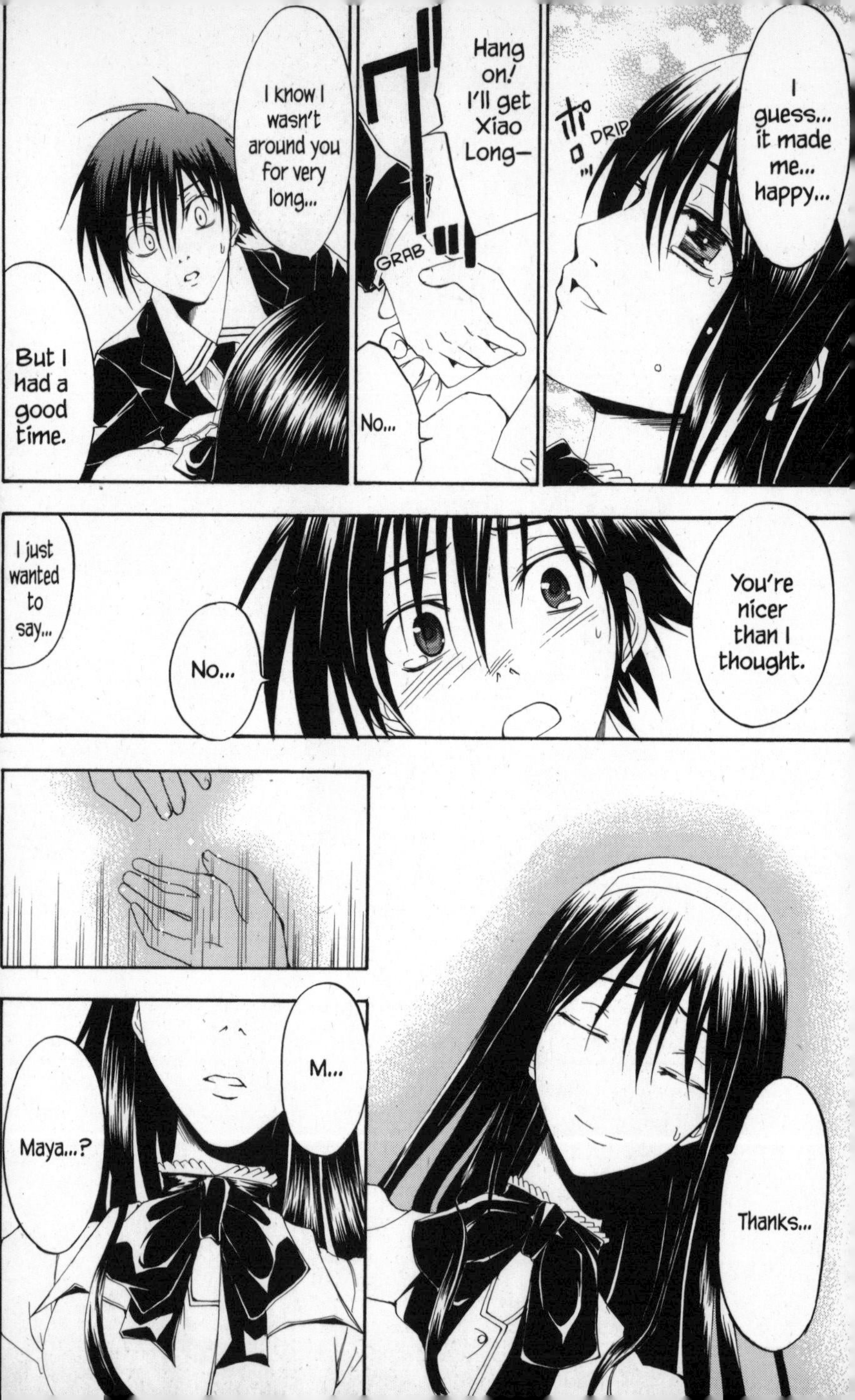
I guess... it made me... happy...
DRIP
Hang on! I'll get Xiao Long—
GRAB
No...
I know I wasn't around you for very long...
But I had a good time.
You're nicer than I thought.
No...
I just wanted to say...
Thanks...
M...
Maya...?

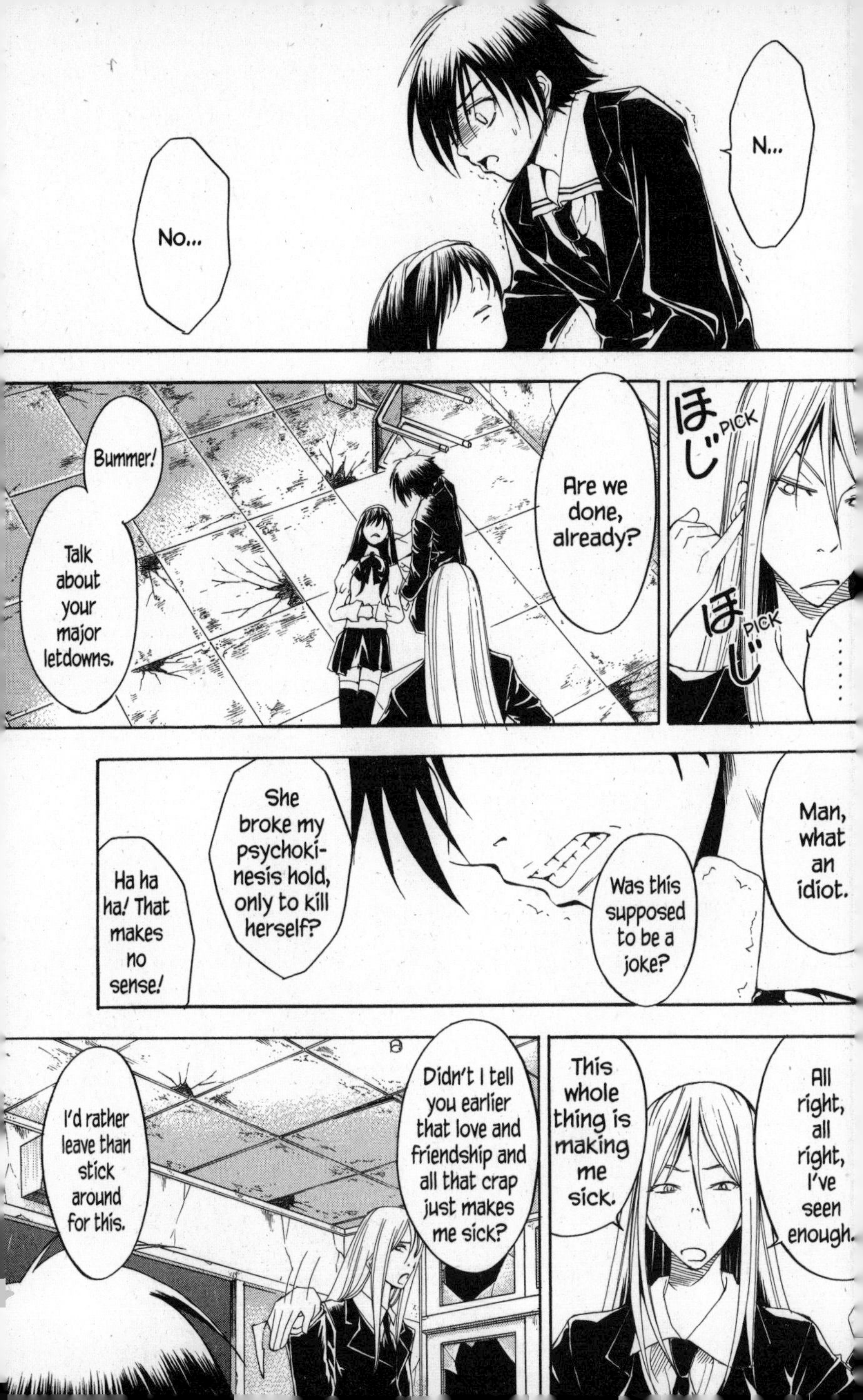
N...
No...
ほじ PICK
ほじ PICK
.....
Are we done, already?
Bummer!
Talk about your major letdowns.
Man, what an idiot.
Was this supposed to be a joke?
She broke my psychokinesis hold, only to kill herself?
Ha ha ha! That makes no sense!
All right, all right, I've seen enough.
This whole thing is making me sick.
Didn't I tell you earlier that love and friendship and all that crap just makes me sick?
I'd rather leave than stick around for this.

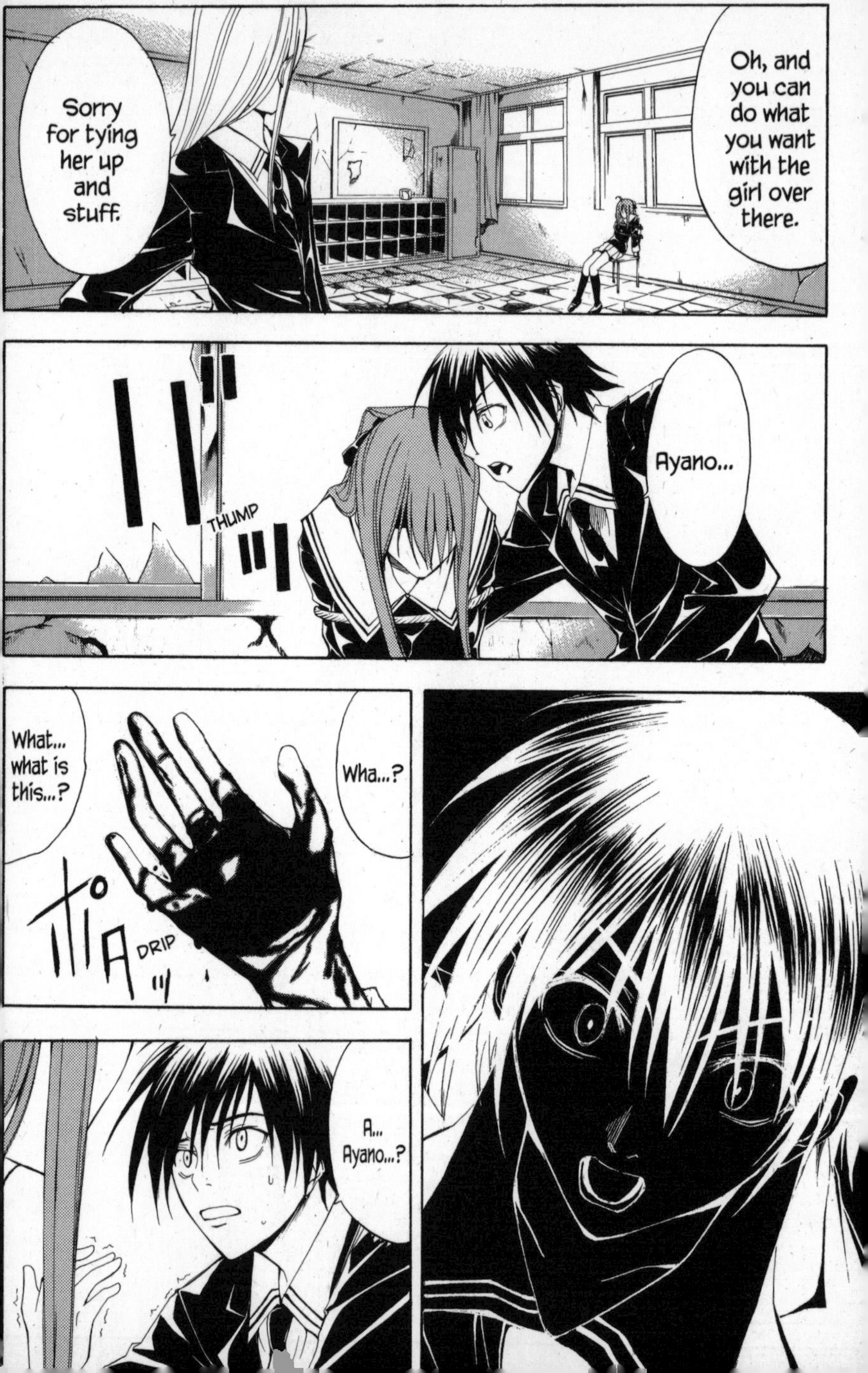
Oh, and you can do what you want with the girl over there.
Sorry for tying her up and stuff.
Ayano...
THUMP
Wha...?
What... what is this...?
DRIP
A... Ayano...?

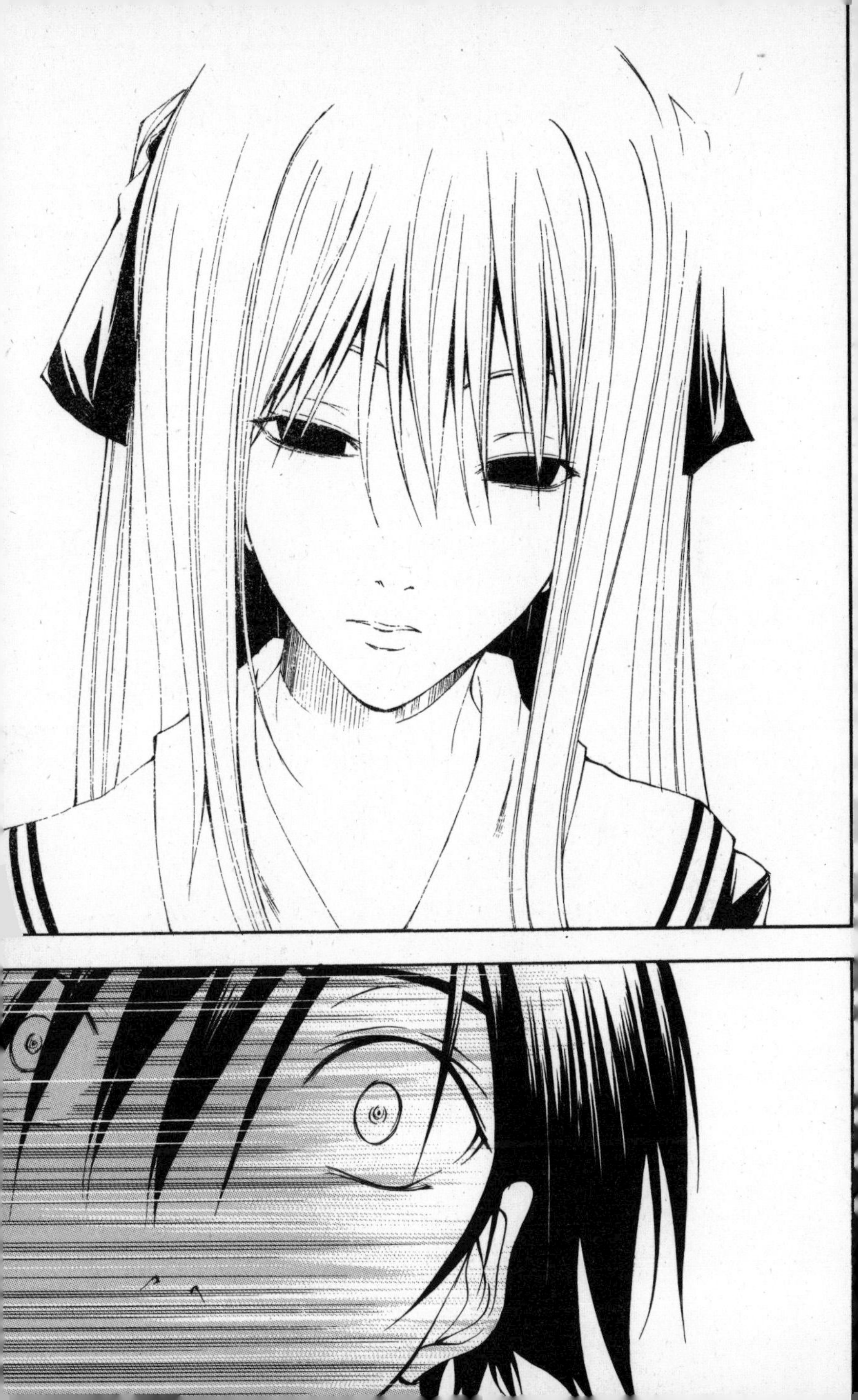

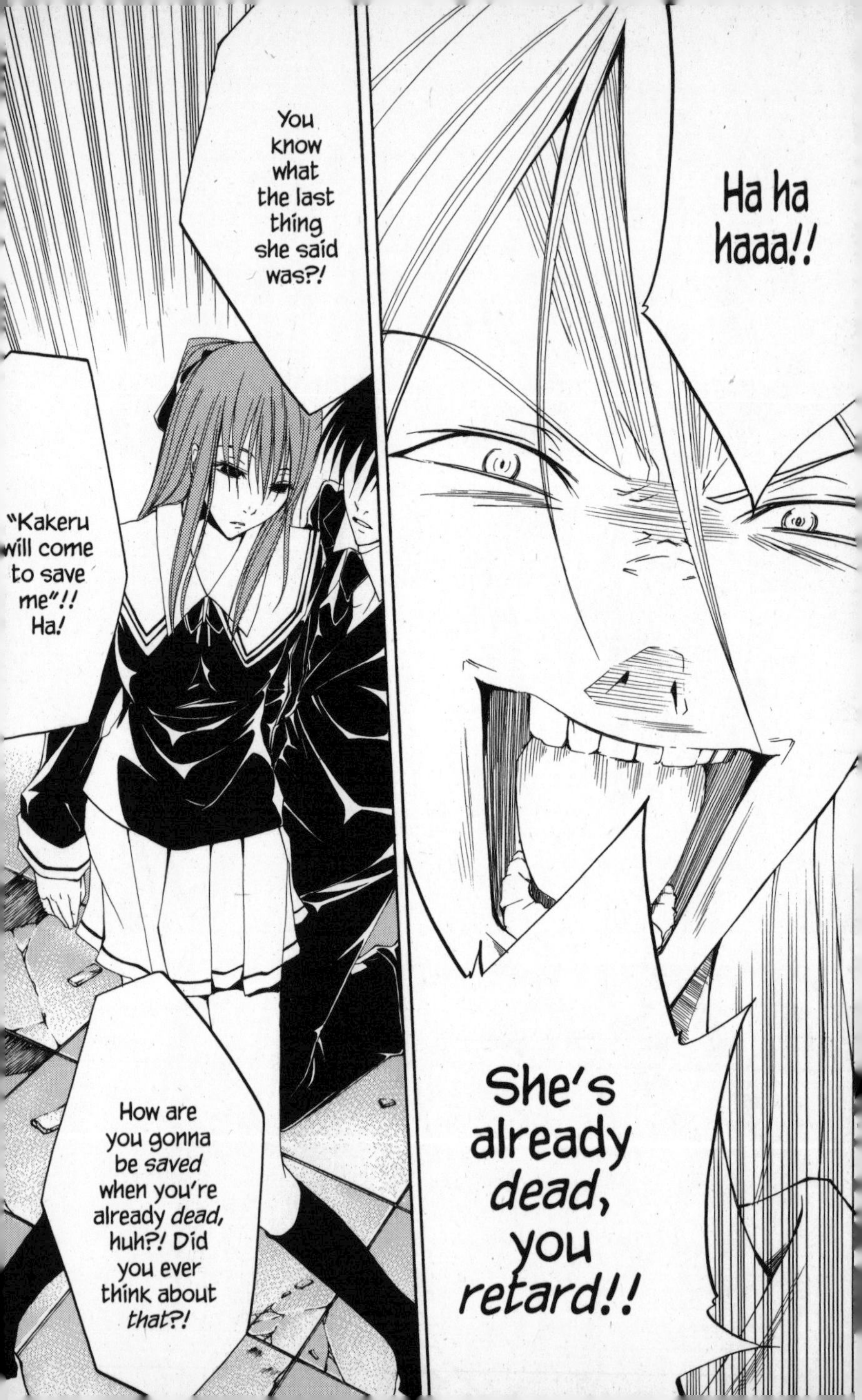
Ha ha haaa!!
She's already *dead*, you *retard!!*
You know what the last thing she said was?!
"Kakeru will come to save me"!! Ha!
How are you gonna be *saved* when you're already *dead*, huh?! Did you ever think about *that*?!

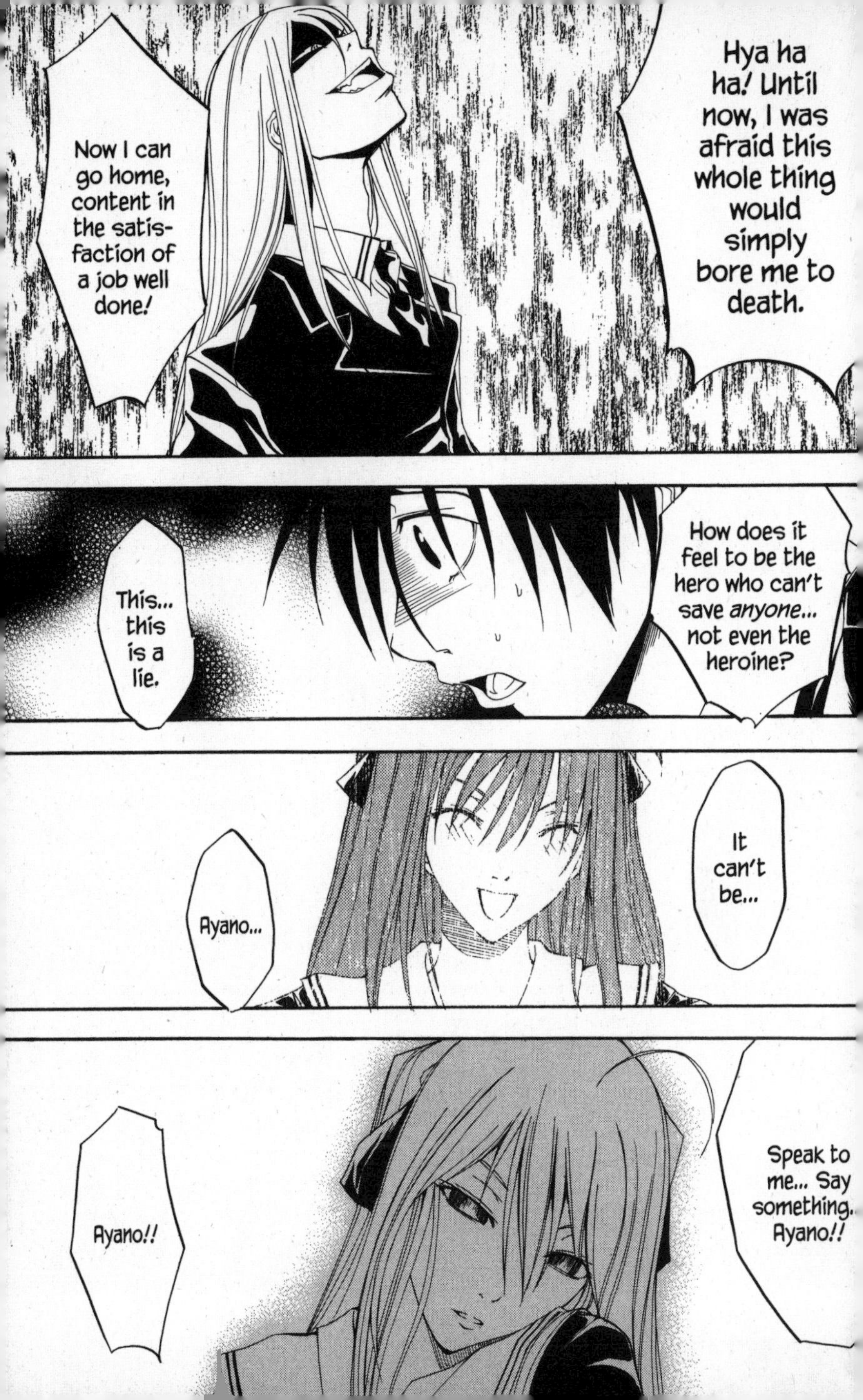
Hya ha ha! Until now, I was afraid this whole thing would simply bore me to death.
Now I can go home, content in the satis-faction of a job well done!
How does it feel to be the hero who can't save *anyone*... not even the heroine?
This... this is a lie.
It can't be...
Ayano...
Speak to me... Say something. Ayano!!
Ayano!!

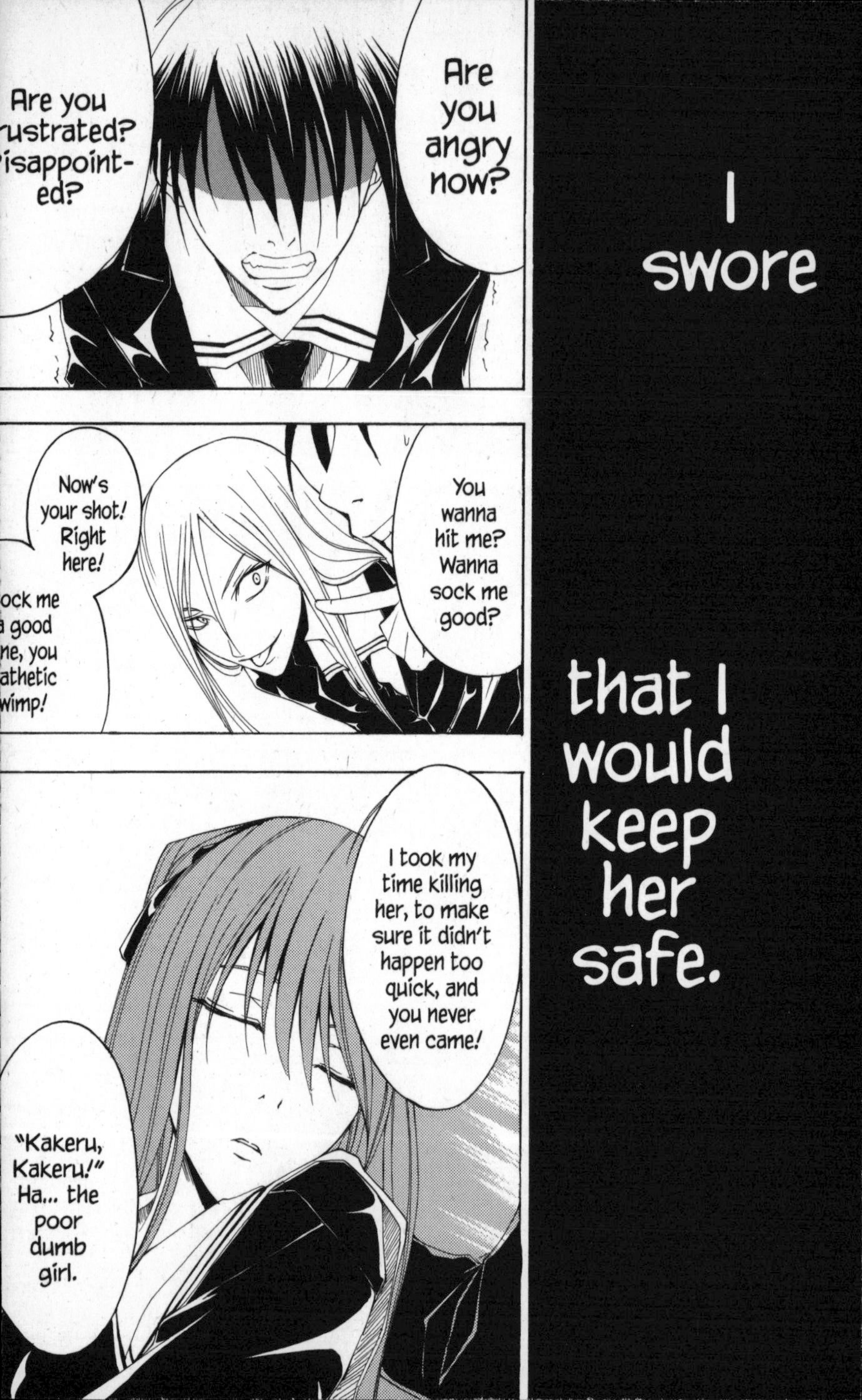
I swore
that I would keep her safe.
Are you angry now?
Are you rustrated? isappoint-ed?
You wanna hit me? Wanna sock me good?
Now's your shot! Right here!
ock me a good ne, you athetic wimp!
I took my time killing her, to make sure it didn't happen too quick, and you never even came!
"Kakeru, Kakeru!" Ha... the poor dumb girl.

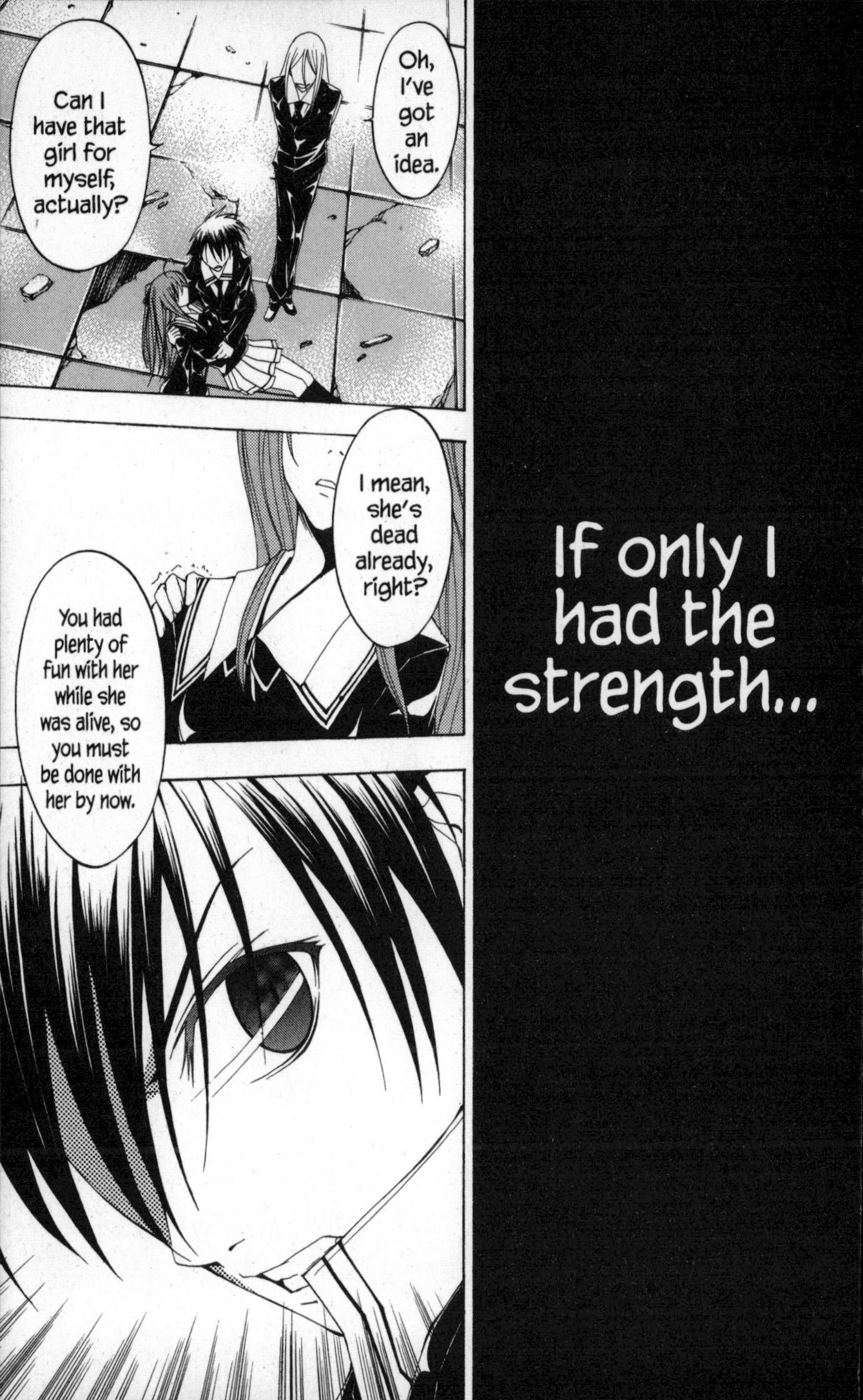
If only I had the strength...
Oh, I've got an idea.
Can I have that girl for myself, actually?
I mean, she's dead already, right?
You had plenty of fun with her while she was alive, so you must be done with her by now.

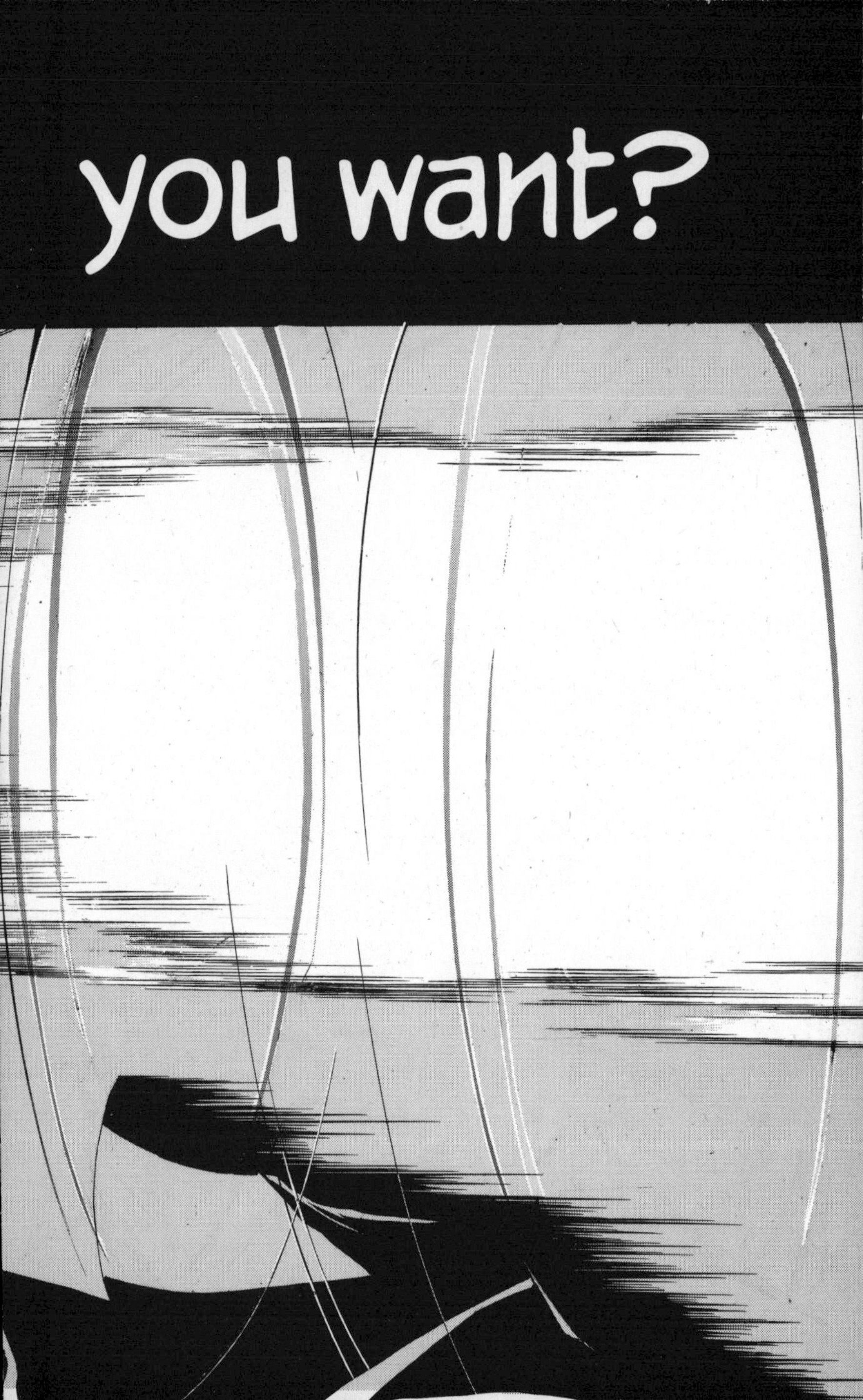
you want?

Is it strength

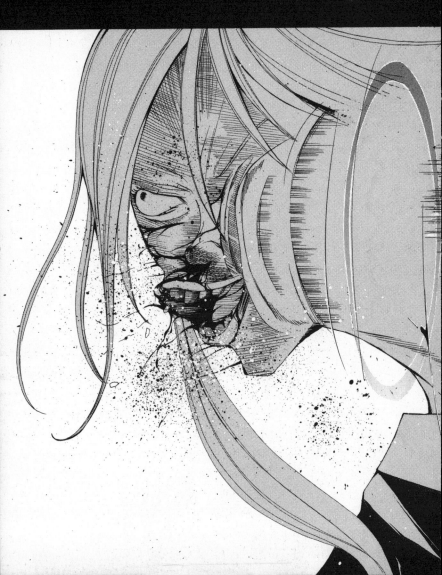

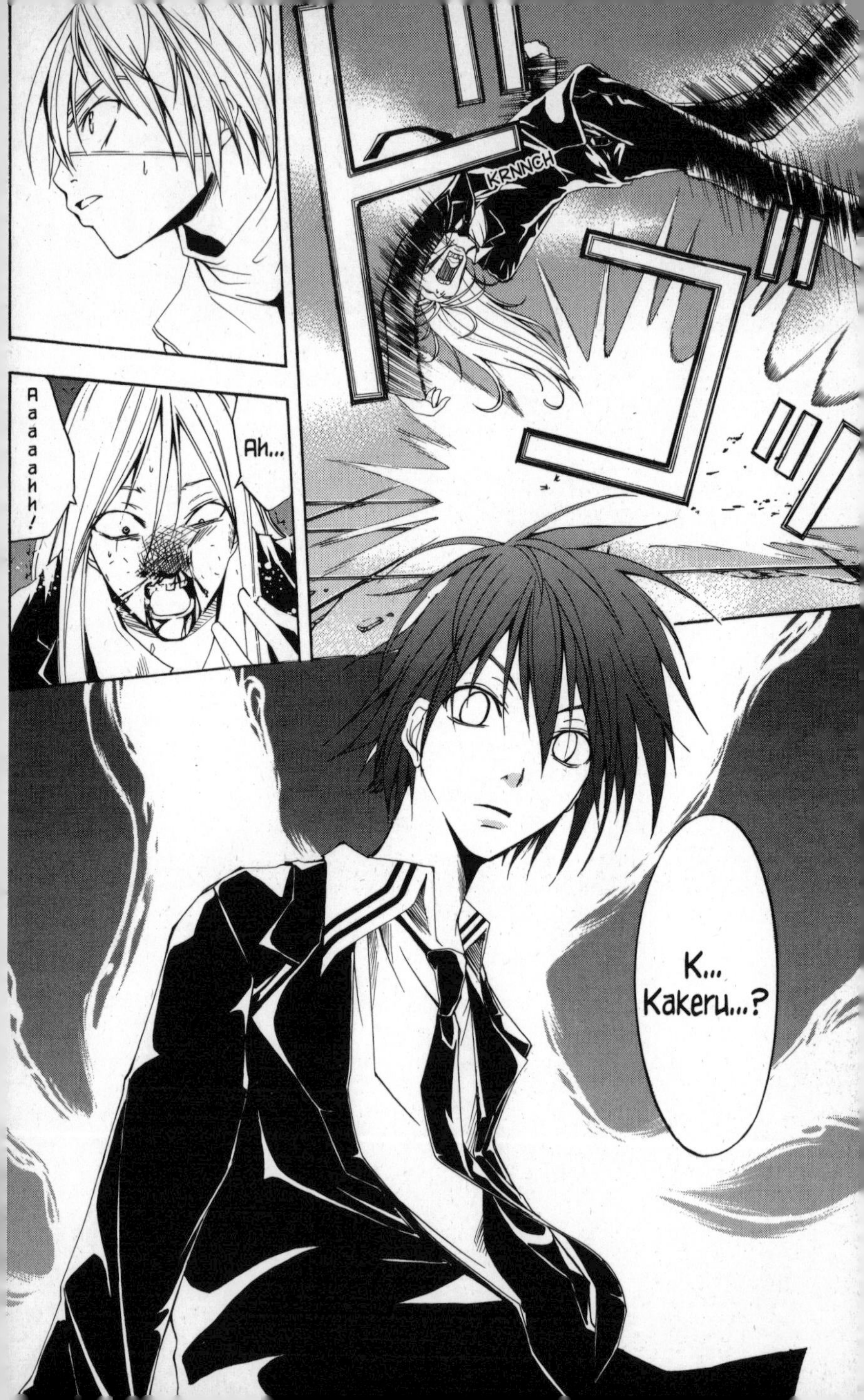
KRNNCH
Ah...
Aaaaahh!
K... Kakeru...?

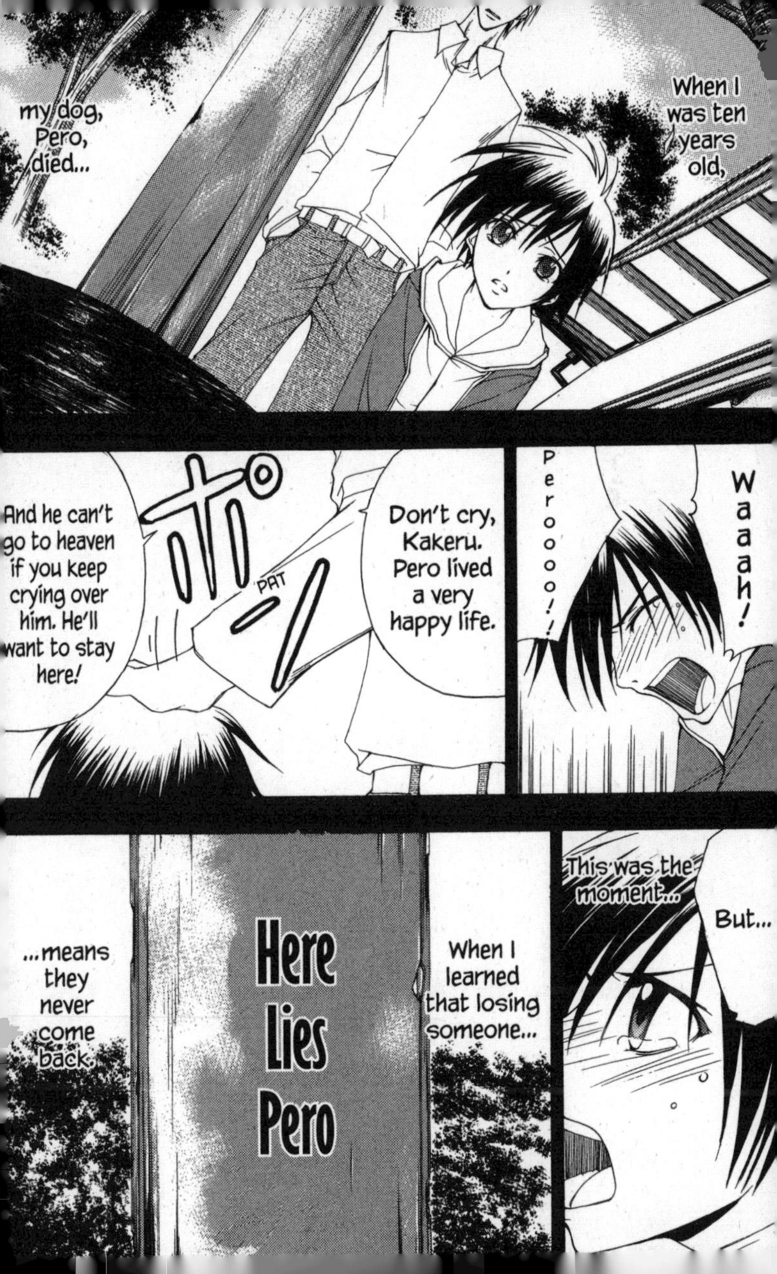
When I was ten years old,
my dog, Pero, died...
Waaah!
Perooooo!!
Don't cry, Kakeru. Pero lived a very happy life.
PAT
And he can't go to heaven if you keep crying over him. He'll want to stay here!
But...
This was the moment...
When I learned that losing someone...
Here Lies Pero
...means they never come back.

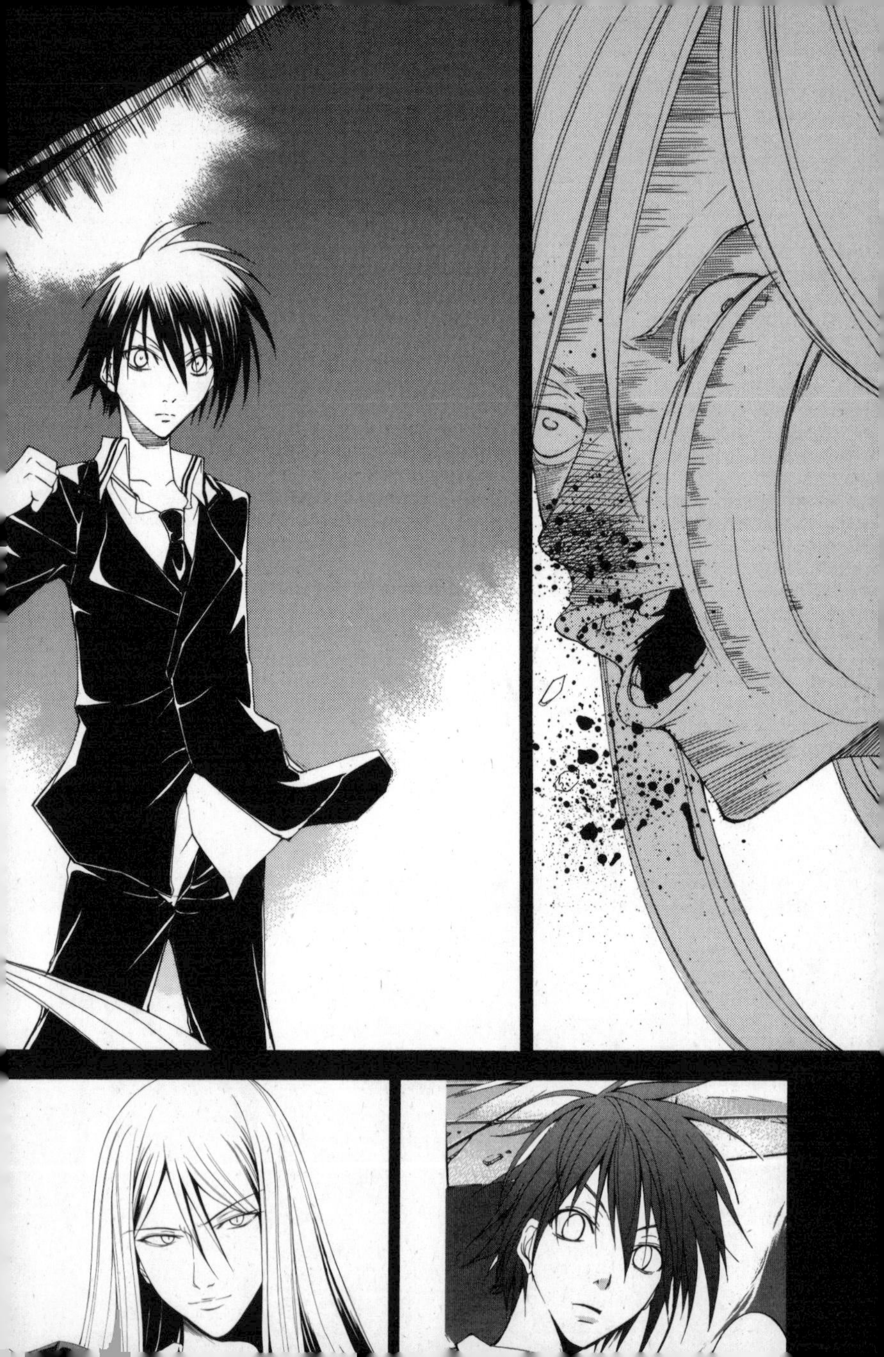

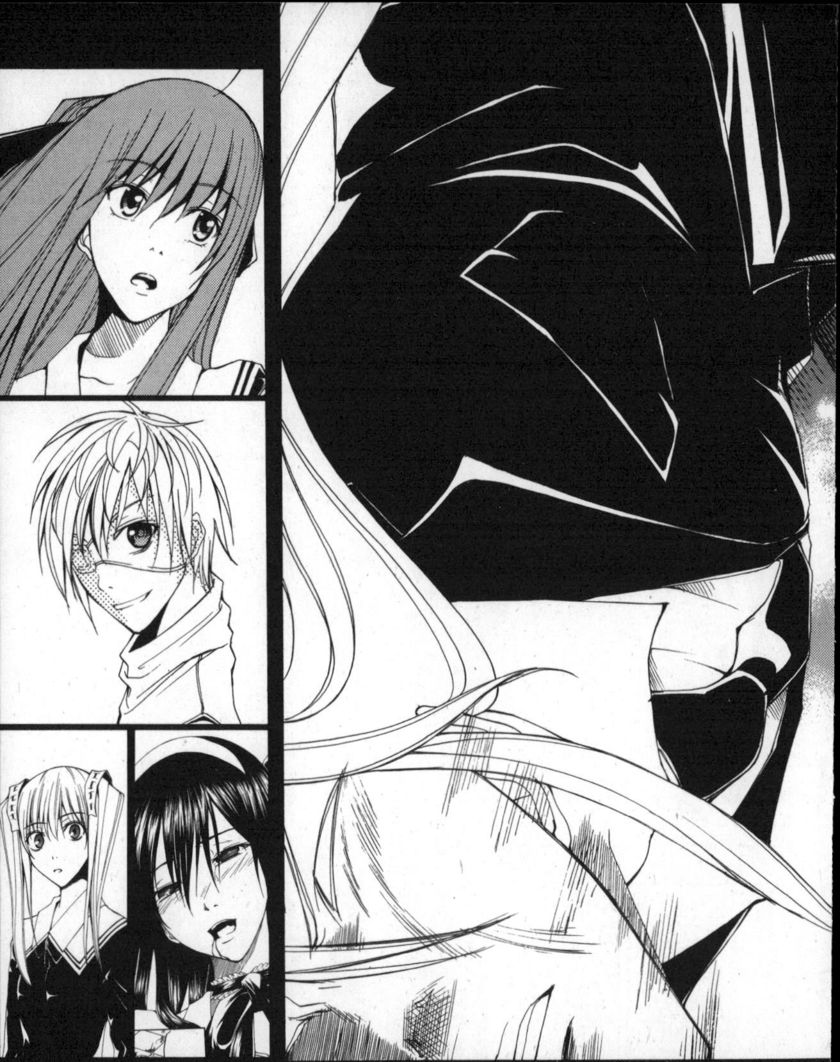

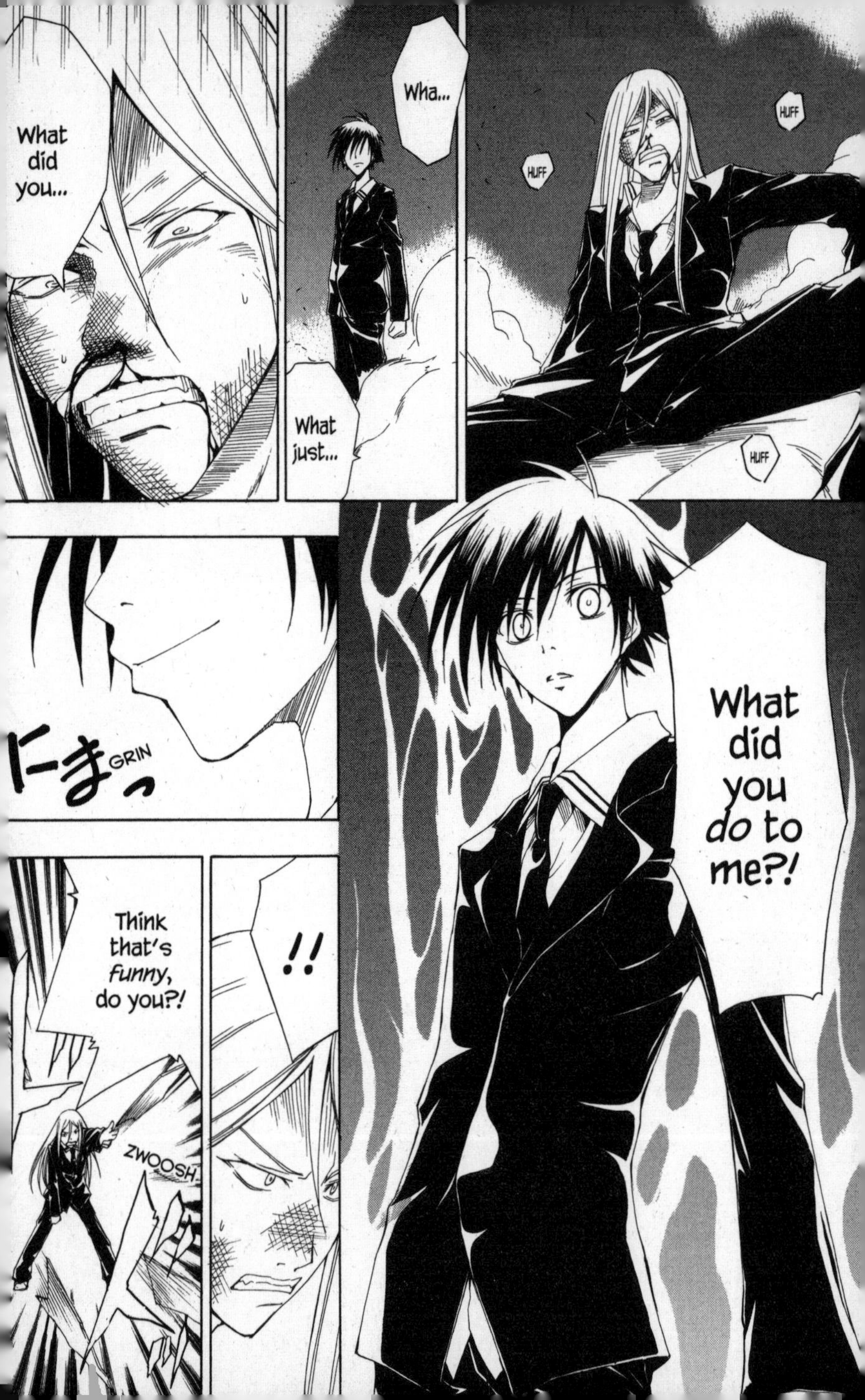
HUFF
HUFF
HUFF
Wha...
What just...
What did you...
What did you *do* to me?!
にまっ GRIN
!!
Think that's *funny*, do you?!
ZWOOSH

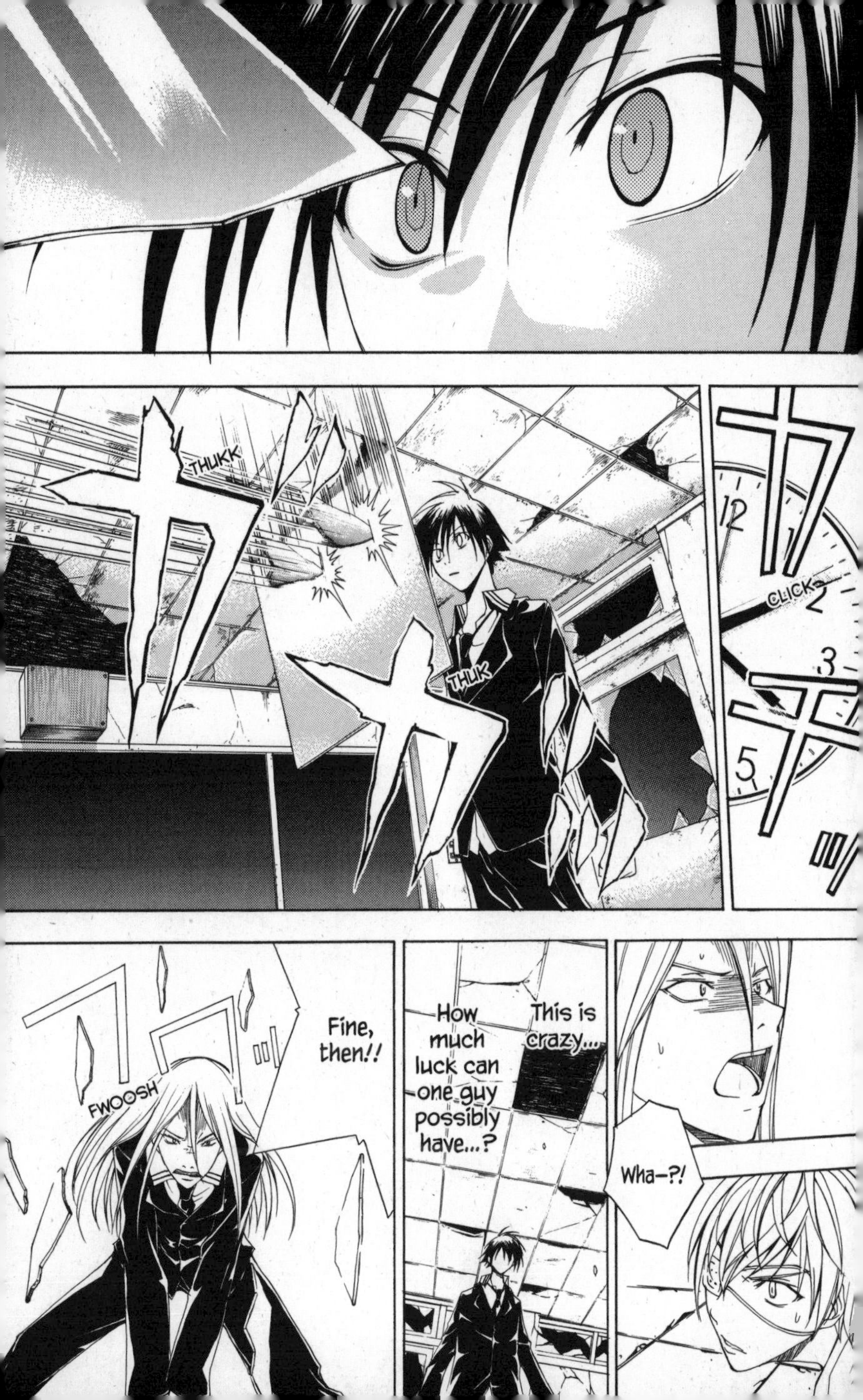
CLICK
THUKK
THUK
Wha-?!
This is crazy...
How much luck can one guy possibly have...?
Fine, then!!
FWOOSH

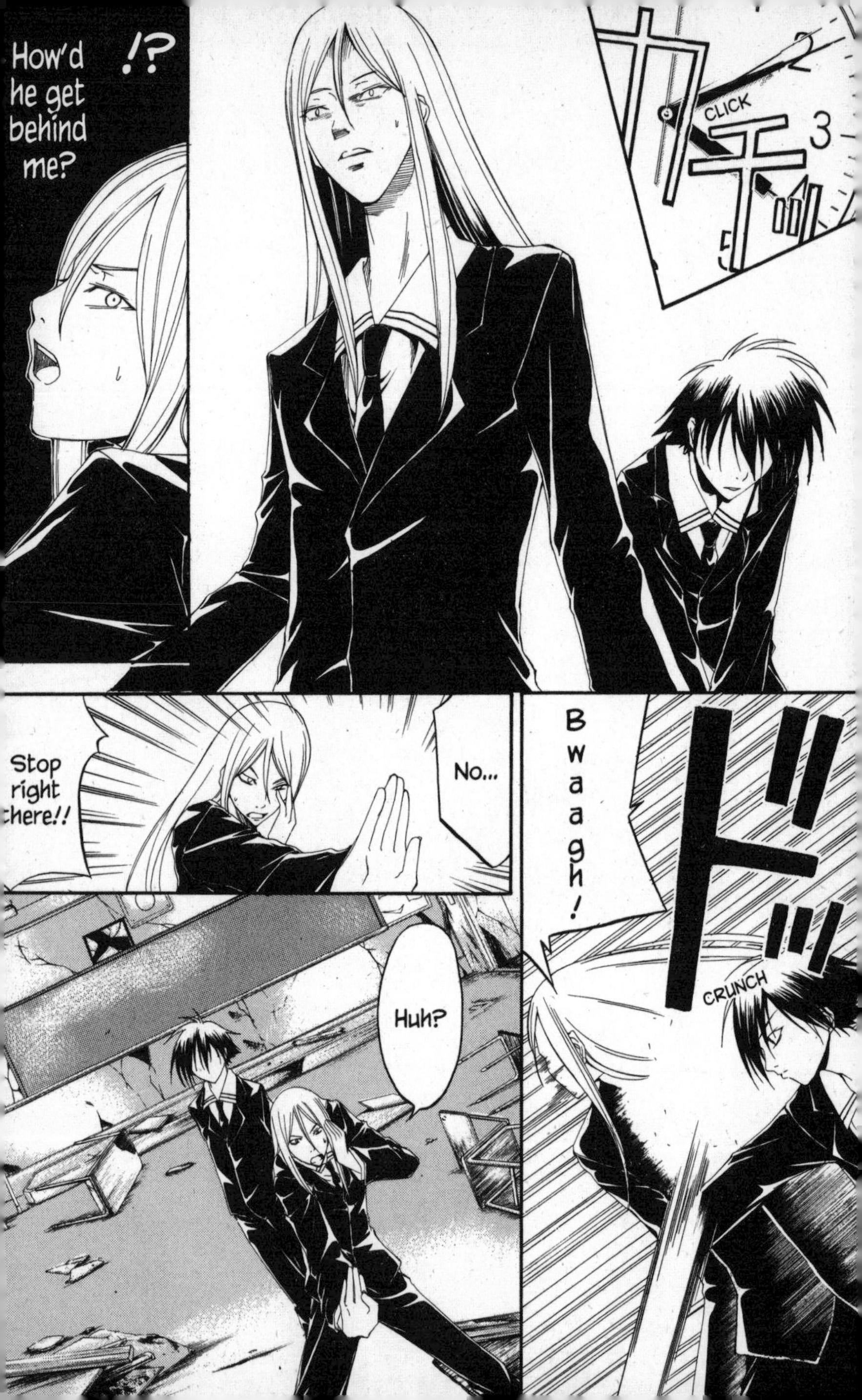
CLICK
!?
How'd he get behind me?
Bwaagh!
CRUNCH
No...
Stop right there!!
Huh?

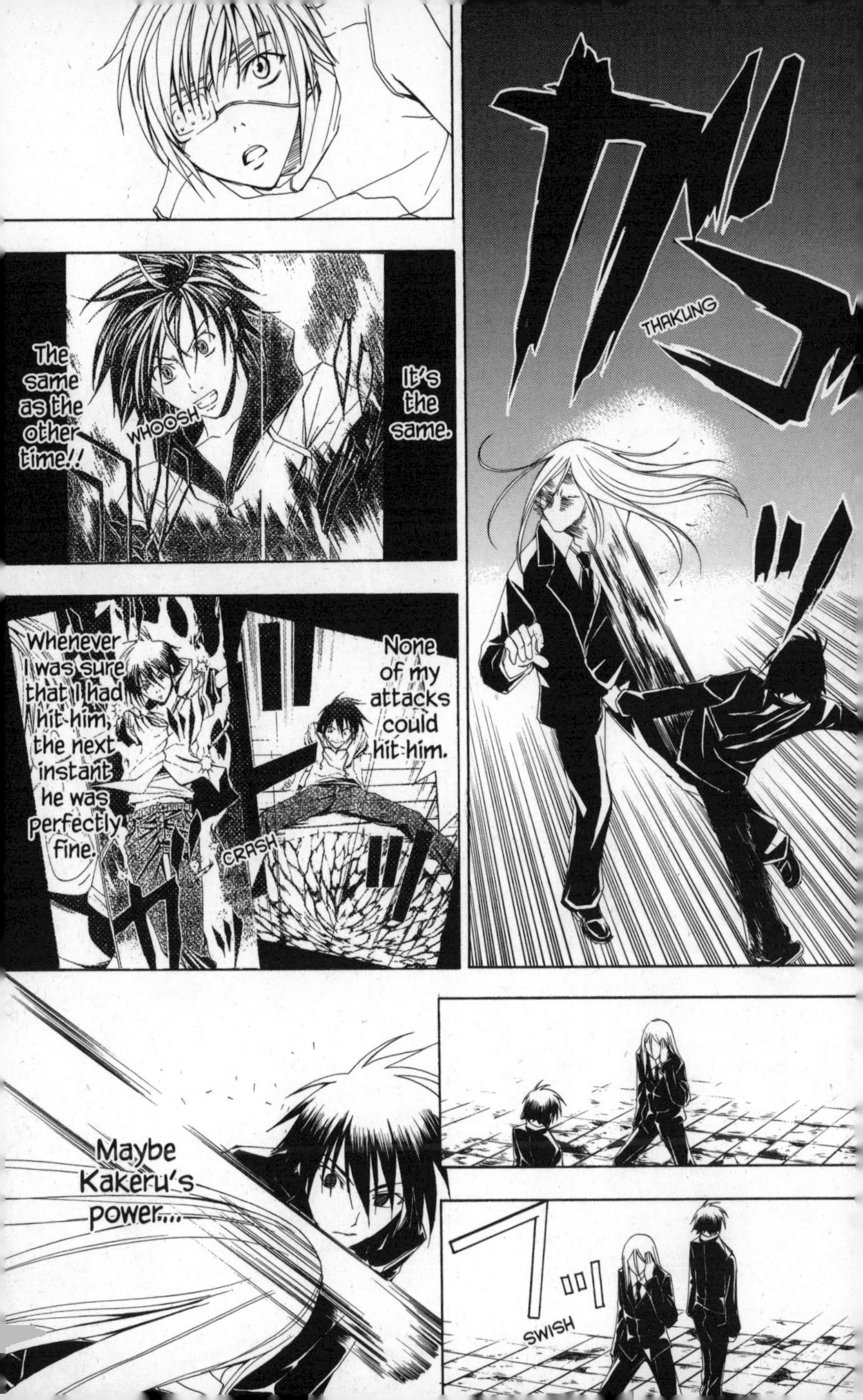
THAKUNG
It's the same.
WHOOSH
The same as the other time!!
None of my attacks could hit him.
Whenever I was sure that I had hit him, the next instant he was perfectly fine.
CRASH
SWISH
Maybe Kakeru's power....

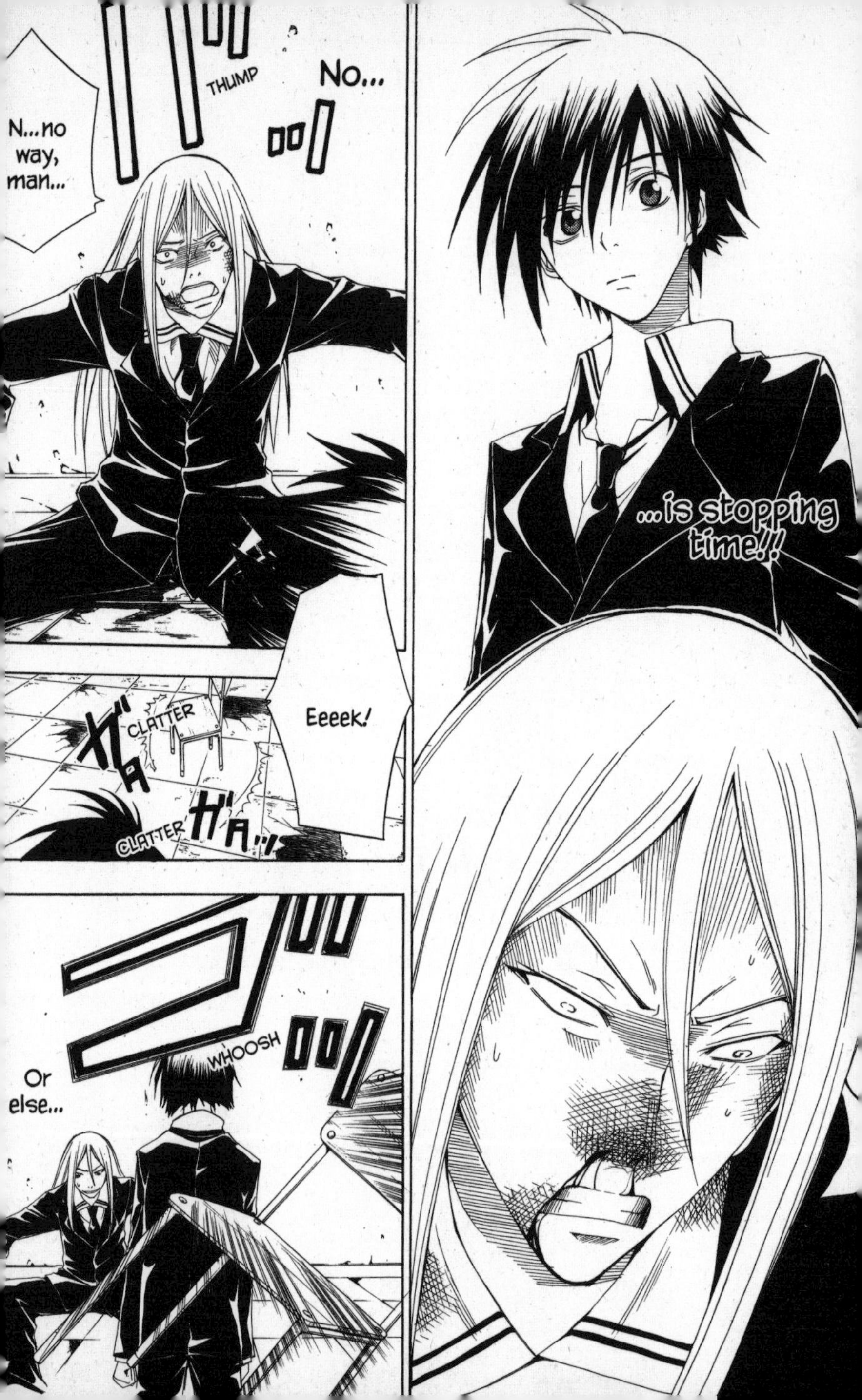
...is stopping time!!
No...
THUMP
N...no way, man...
Eeeek!
CLATTER
CLATTER
WHOOSH
Or else...

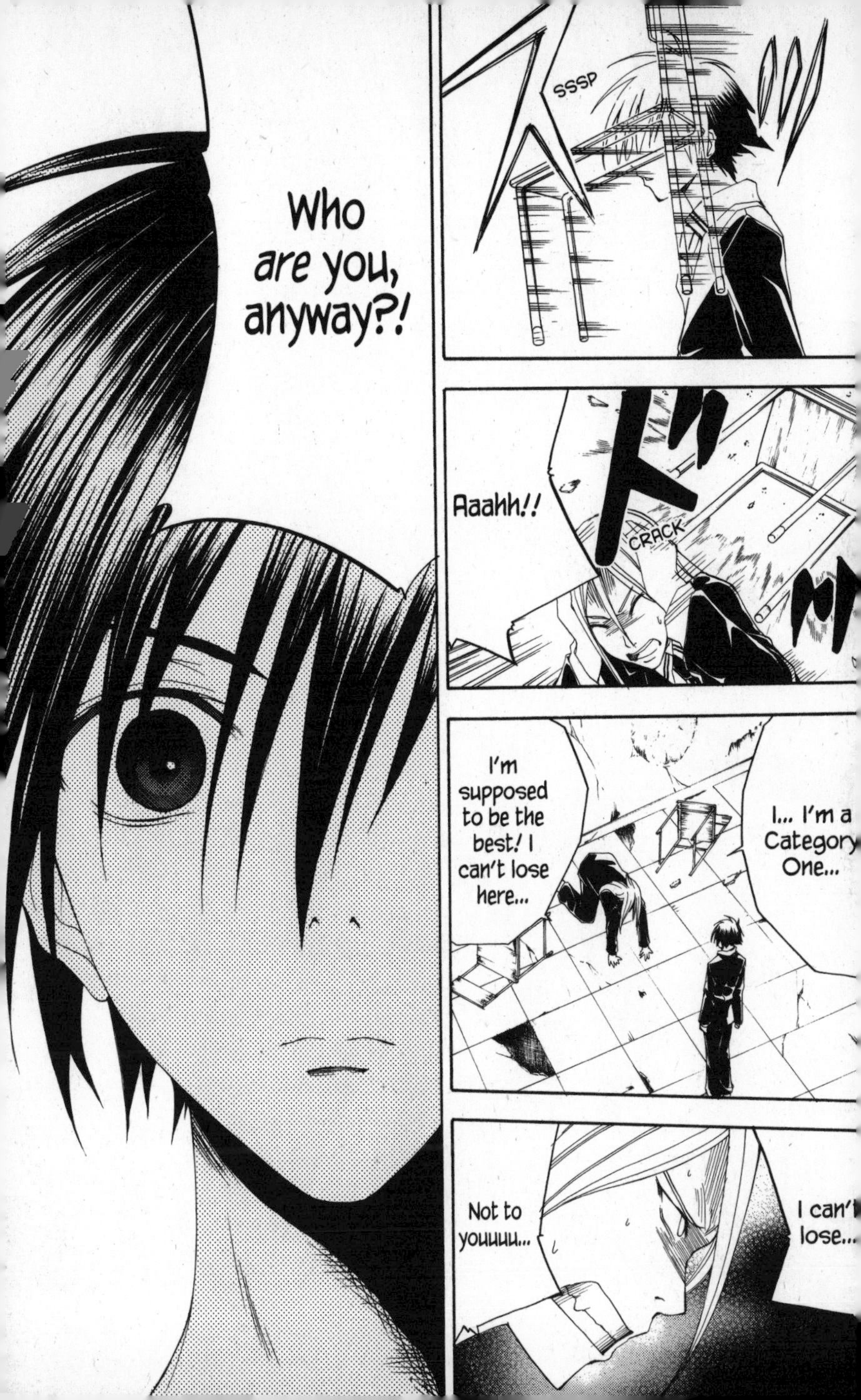
SSSP
Aaahh!!
CRACK
I... I'm a Category One...
I'm supposed to be the best! I can't lose here...
I can't lose...
Not to youuuu...
Who are you, anyway?!

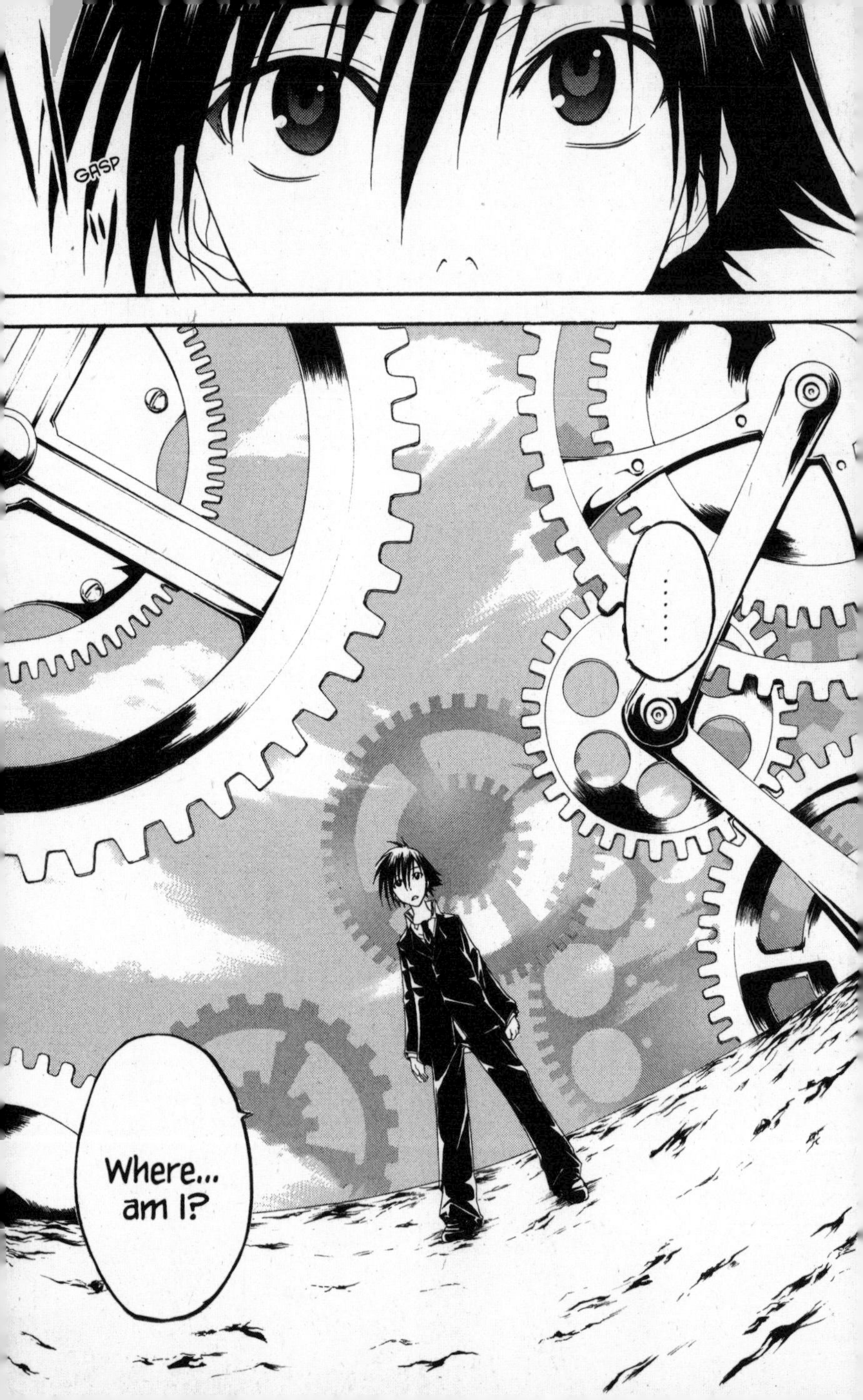
GASP
......
Where... am I?

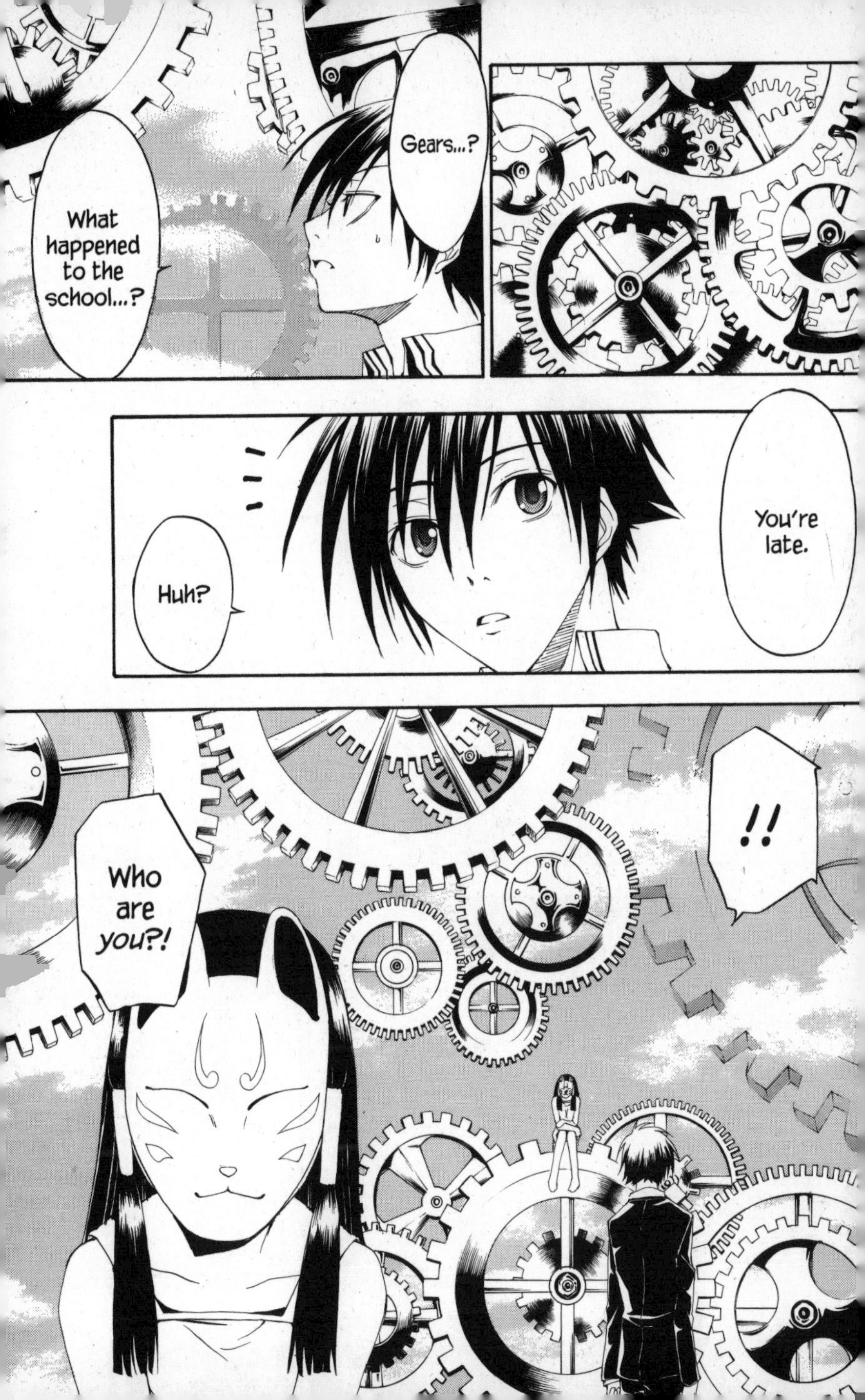
Gears...?
What happened to the school...?
You're late.
Huh?
!!
Who are *you*?!

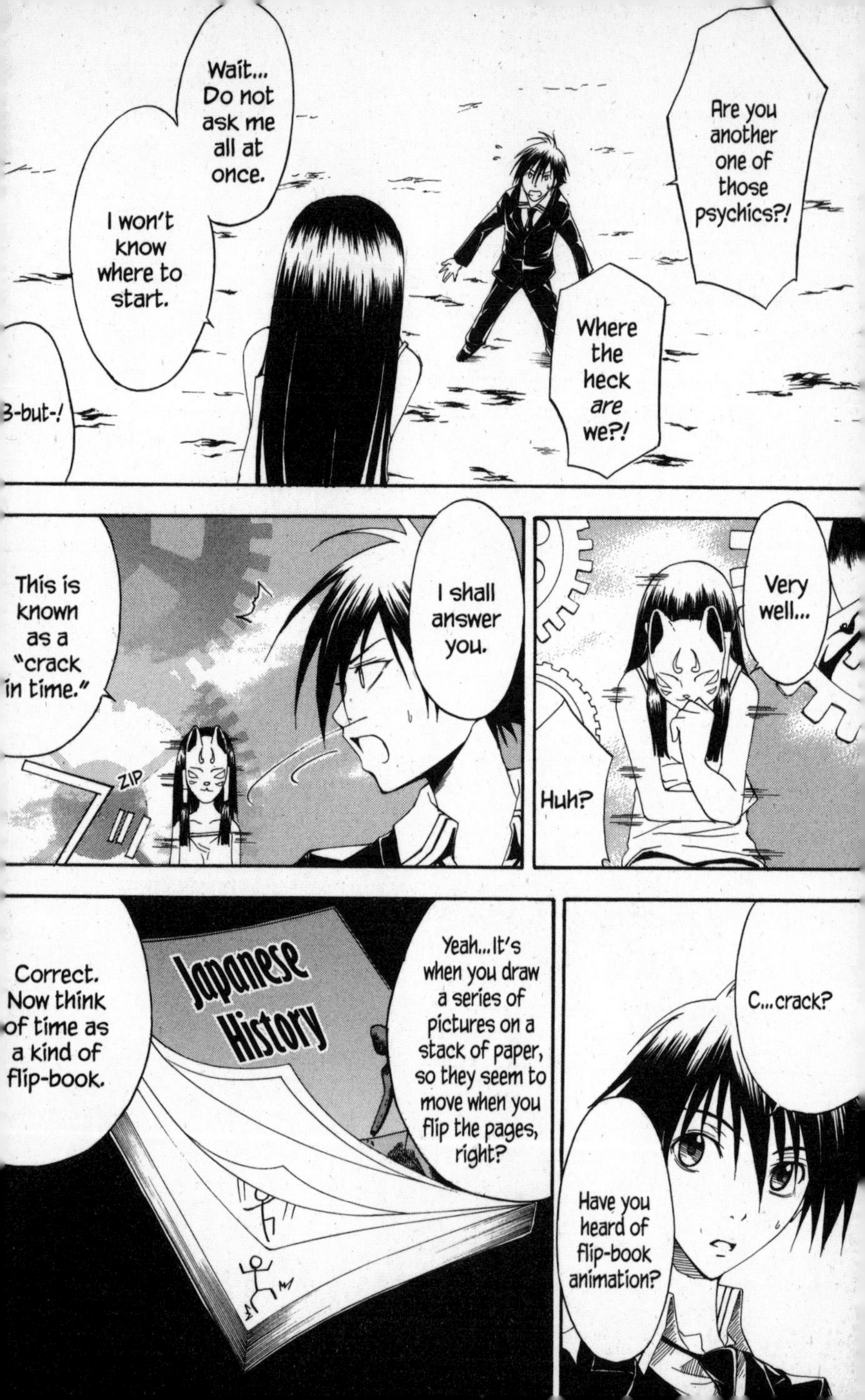

Are you another one of those psychics?!
Where the heck *are* we?!
Wait... Do not ask me all at once.
I won't know where to start.
-but-!
Very well...
Huh?
I shall answer you.
This is known as a "crack in time."
ZIP
C...crack?
Have you heard of flip-book animation?
Yeah... It's when you draw a series of pictures on a stack of paper, so they seem to move when you flip the pages, right?
Japanese History
Correct. Now think of time as a kind of flip-book.

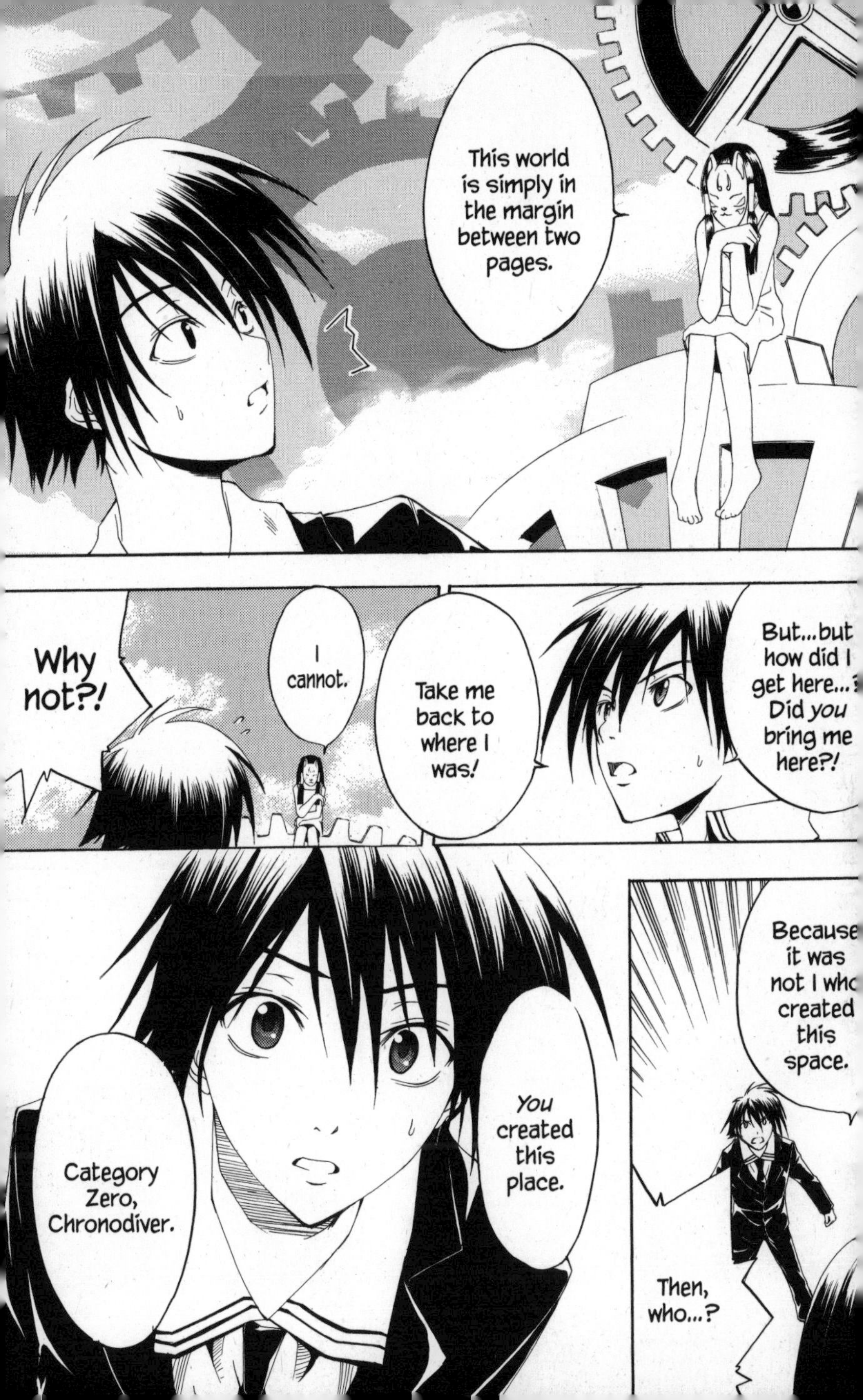
This world is simply in the margin between two pages.
But...but how did I get here...? Did *you* bring me here?!
Take me back to where I was!
I cannot.
Why not?!
Because it was not I who created this space.
Then, who...?
You created this place.
Category Zero, Chronodiver.

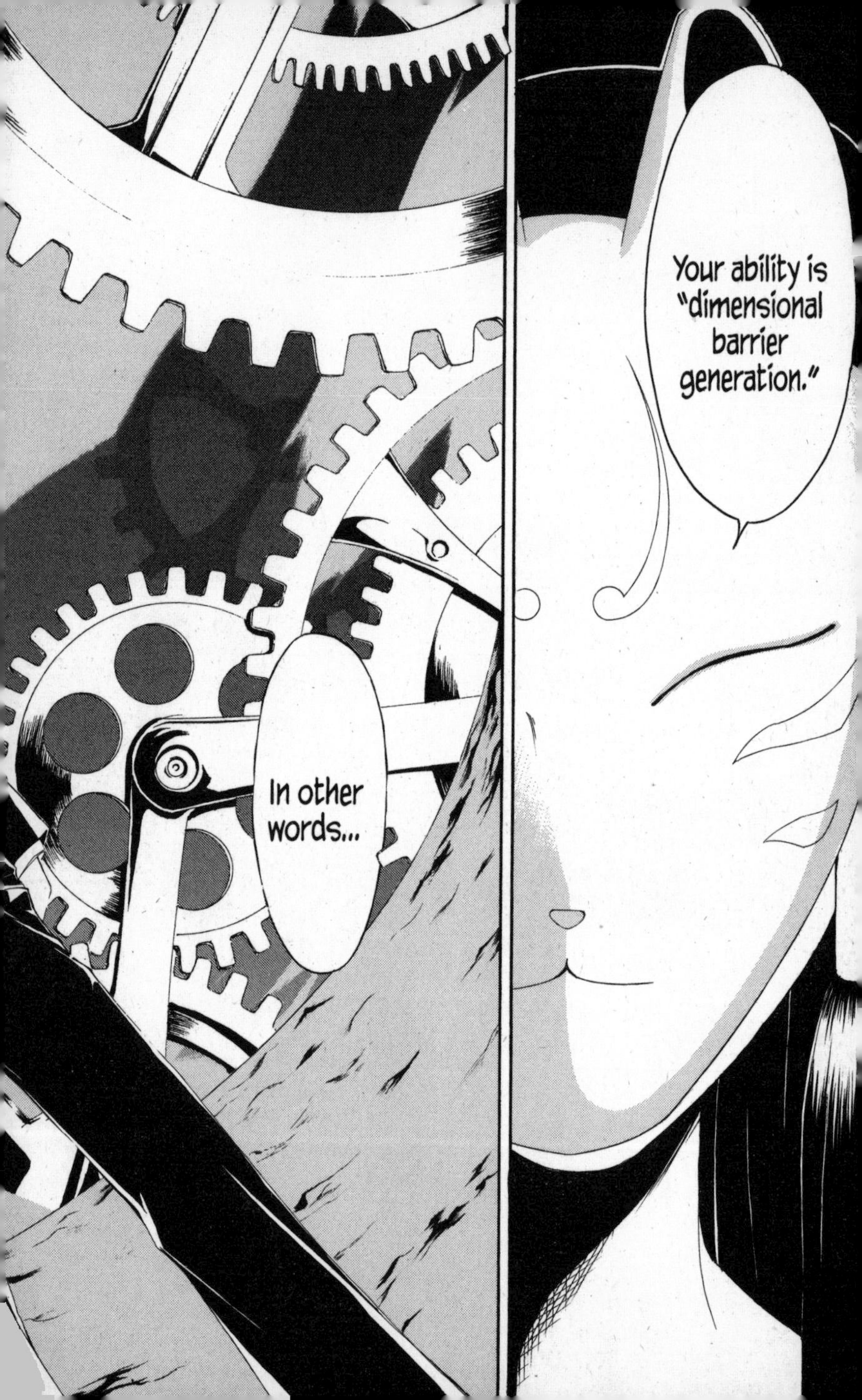
Your ability is "dimensional barrier generation."
In other words...

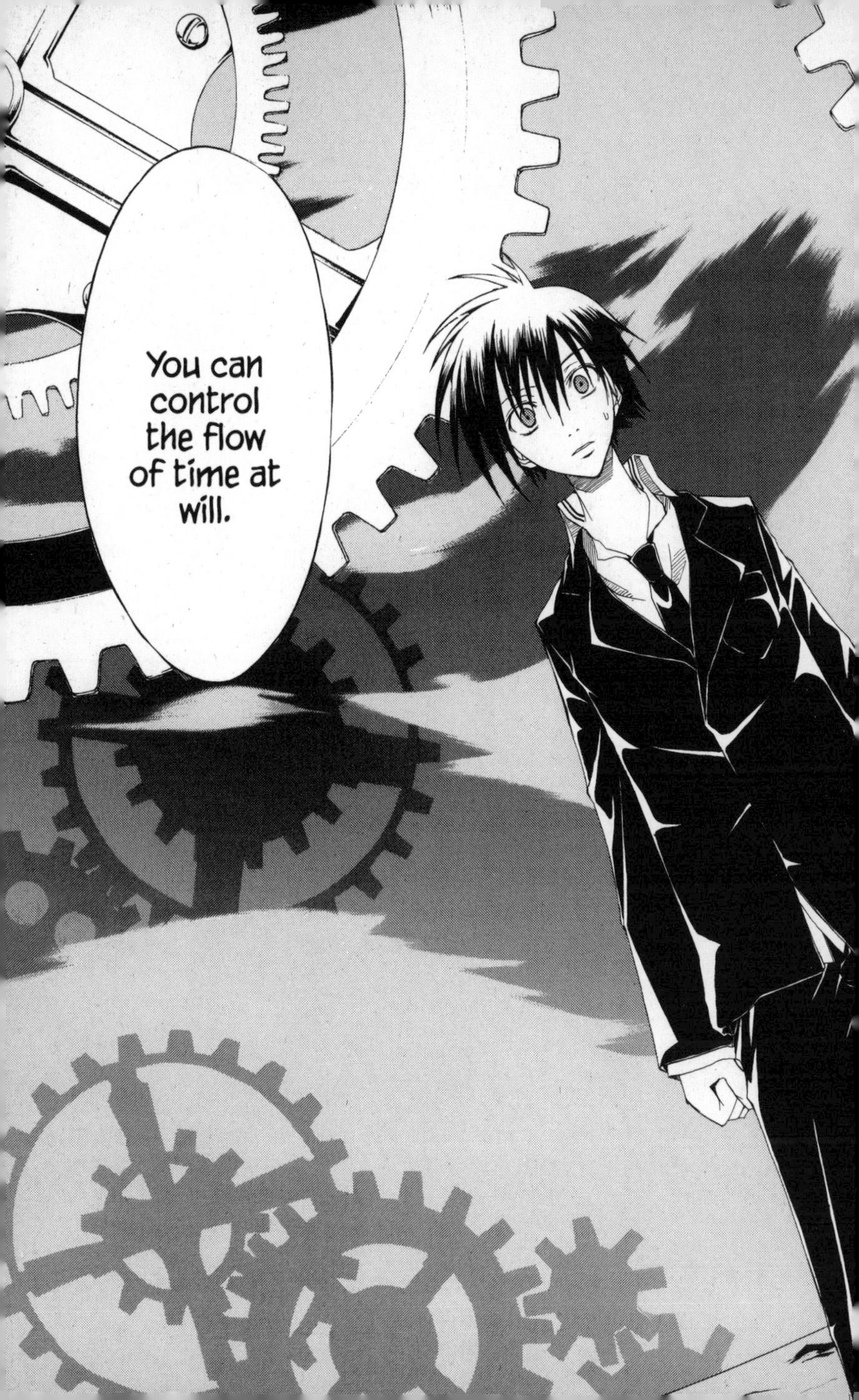
You can control the flow of time at will.

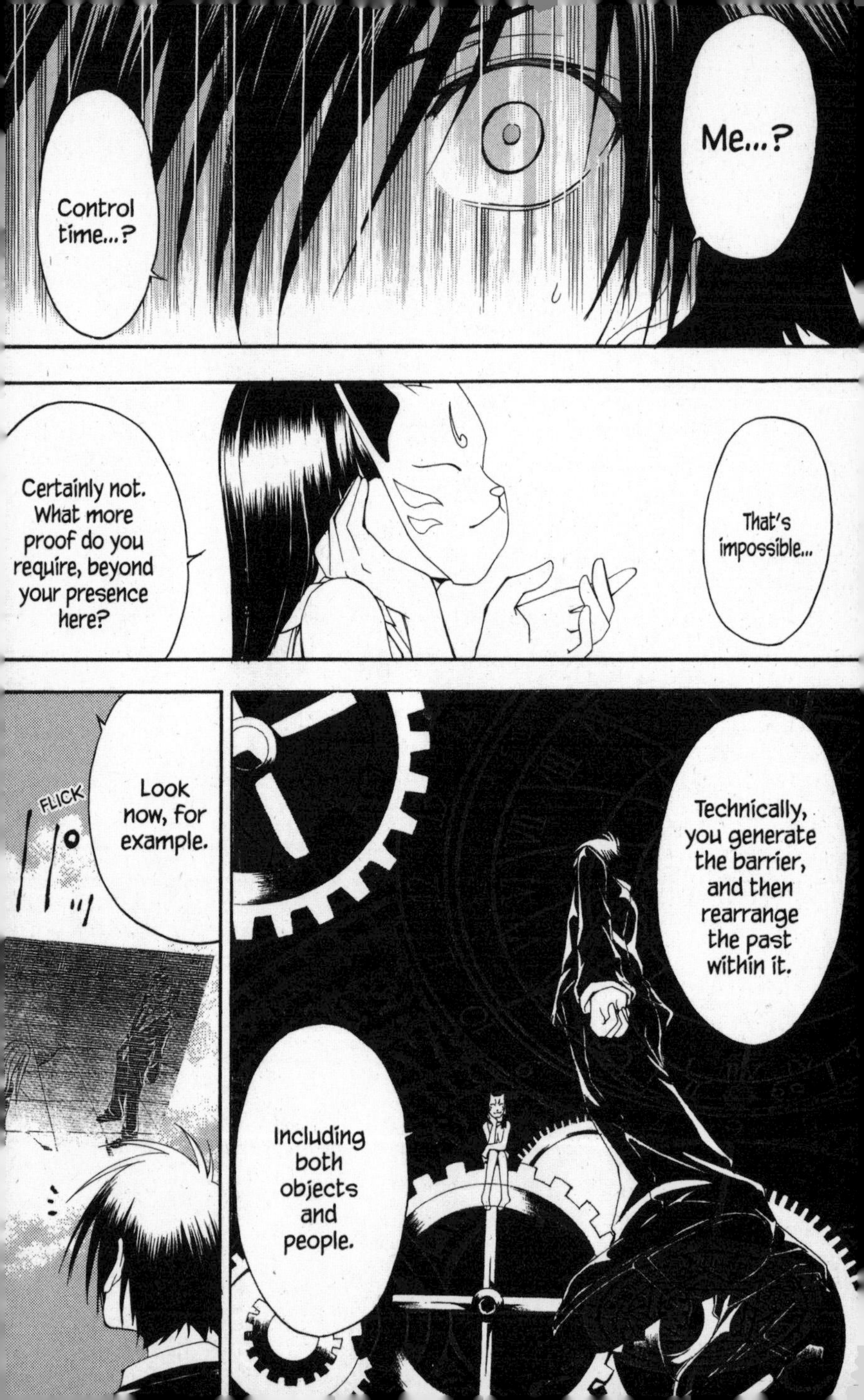
Me...?
Control time...?
That's impossible...
Certainly not. What more proof do you require, beyond your presence here?
Technically, you generate the barrier, and then rearrange the past within it.
Including both objects and people.
Look now, for example.
FLICK

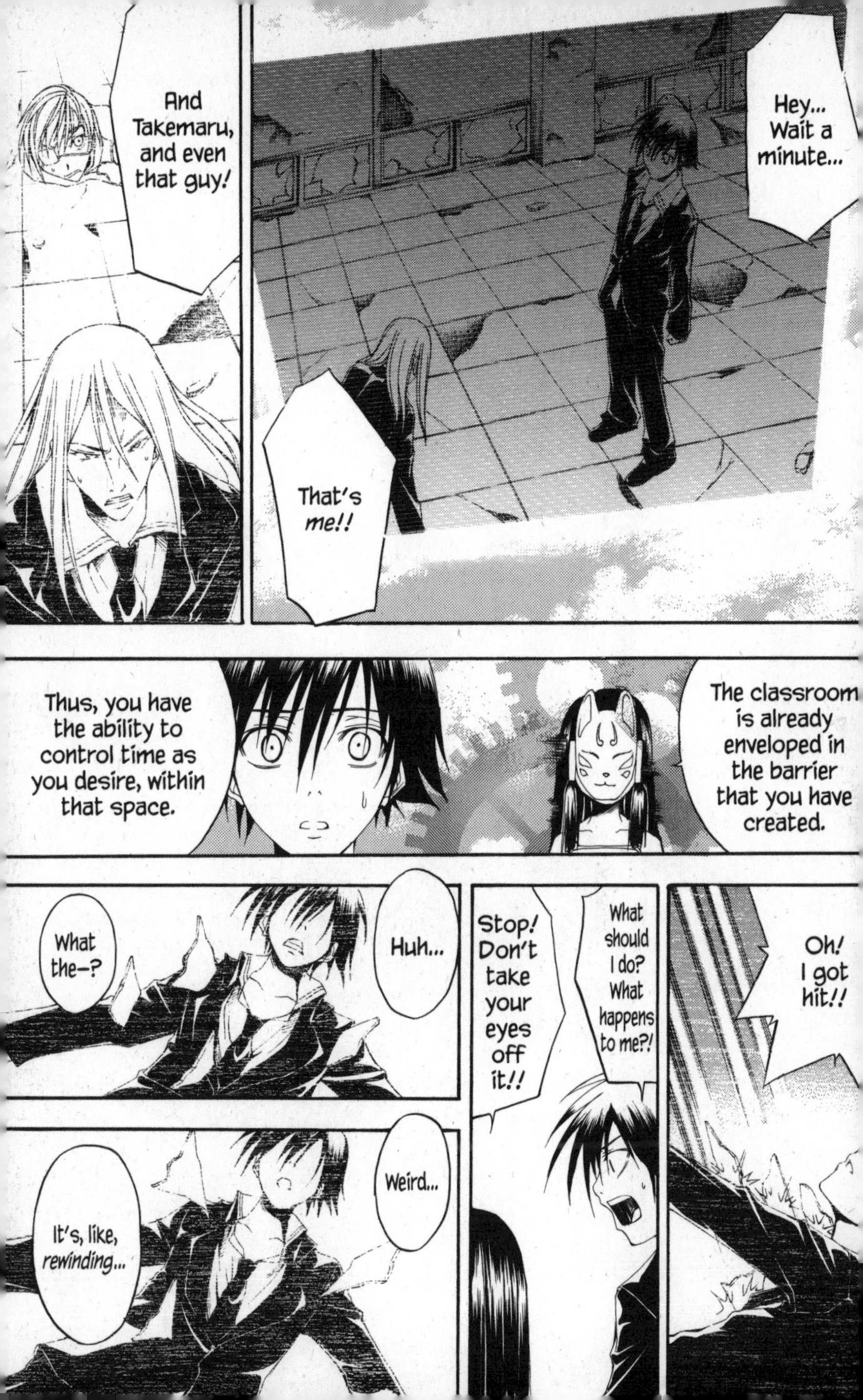
Hey... Wait a minute...
That's *me!!*
And Takemaru, and even that guy!
The classroom is already enveloped in the barrier that you have created.
Thus, you have the ability to control time as you desire, within that space.
Oh! I got hit!!
What should I do? What happens to me?!
Stop! Don't take your eyes off it!!
Huh...
What the–?
Weird...
It's, like, *rewinding...*

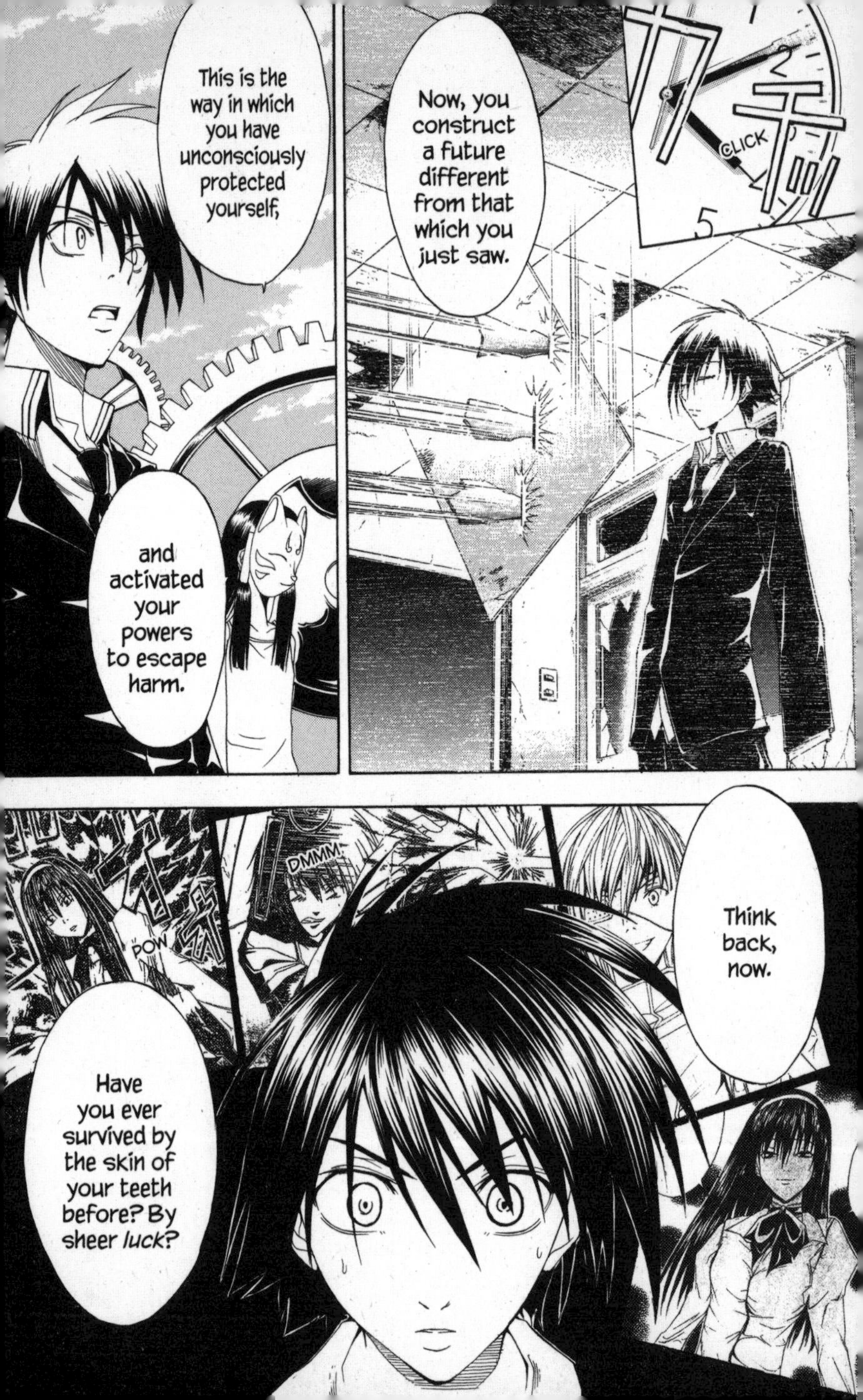
CLICK
Now, you construct a future different from that which you just saw.
This is the way in which you have unconsciously protected yourself,
and activated your powers to escape harm.
Think back, now.
DMMM
POW
Have you ever survived by the skin of your teeth before? By sheer *luck*?

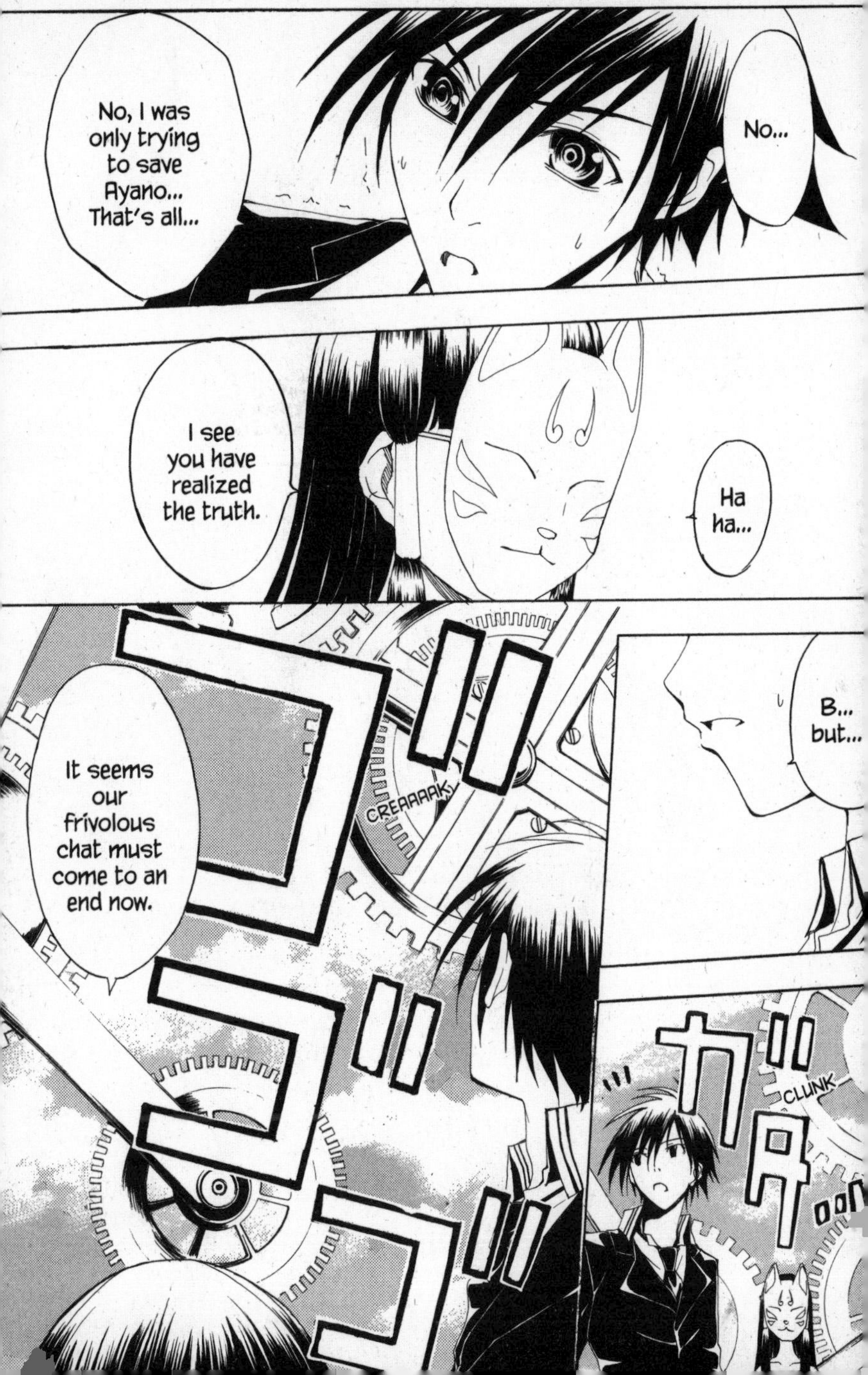
No...
No, I was only trying to save Ayano... That's all...
Ha ha...
I see you have realized the truth.
B... but...
CLUNK
It seems our frivolous chat must come to an end now.
CREAAAAK

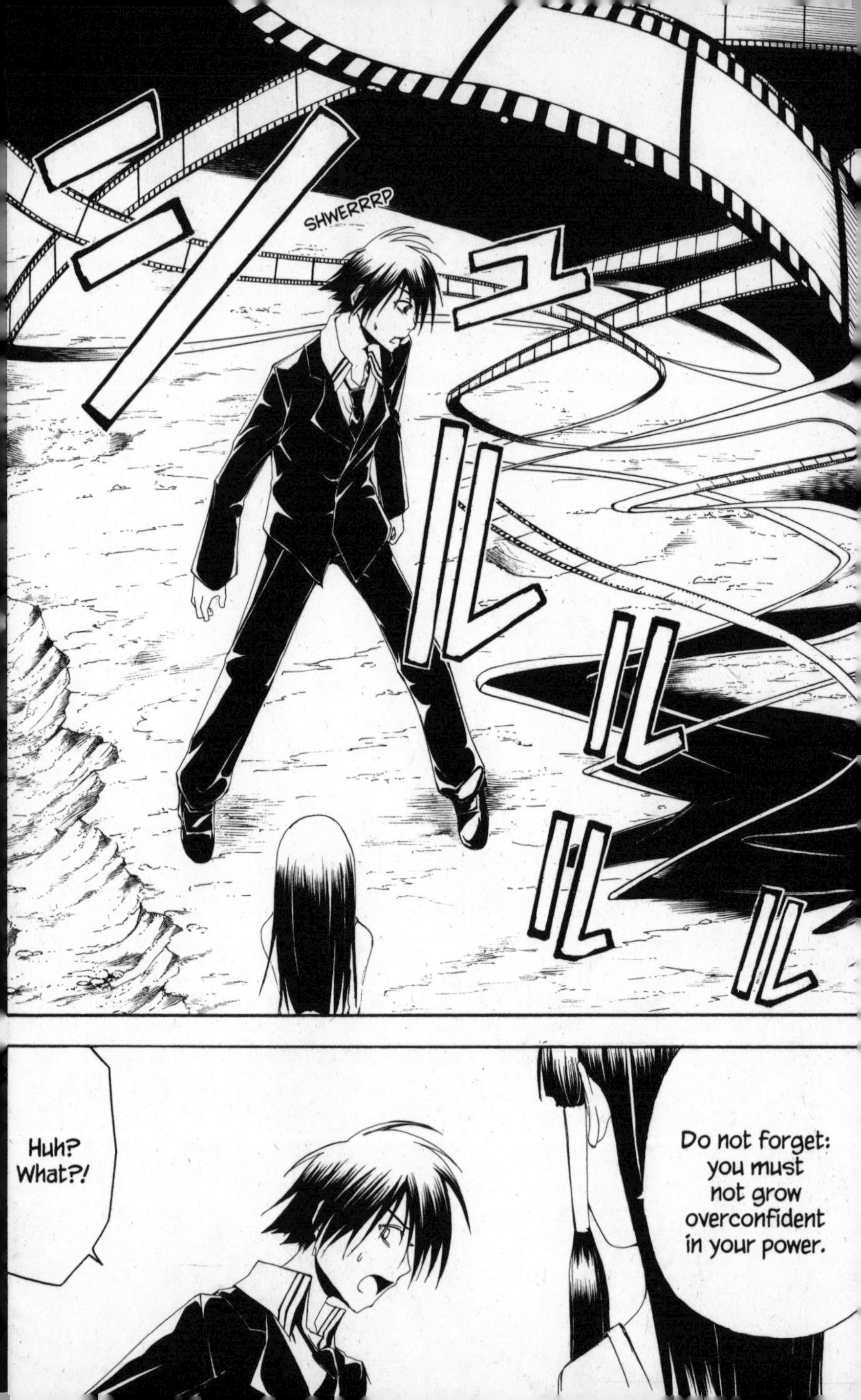
SHWERRRP
Do not forget: you must not grow overconfident in your power.
Huh? What?!

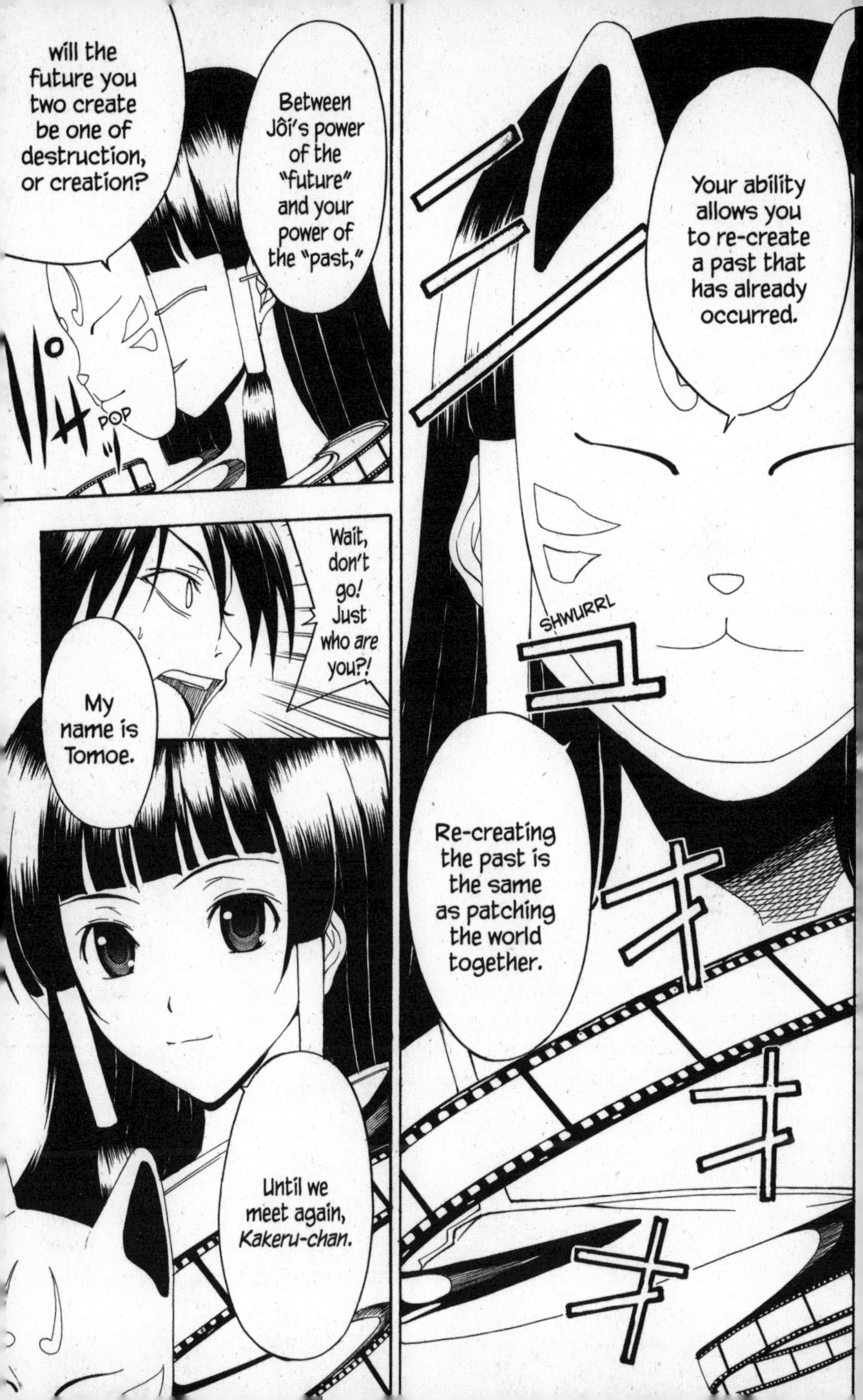

Your ability allows you to re-create a past that has already occurred.
SHWURRL
Re-creating the past is the same as patching the world together.
Between Jôi's power of the "future" and your power of the "past,"
will the future you two create be one of destruction, or creation?
POP
Wait, don't go! Just who are you?!
My name is Tomoe.
Until we meet again, Kakeru-chan.

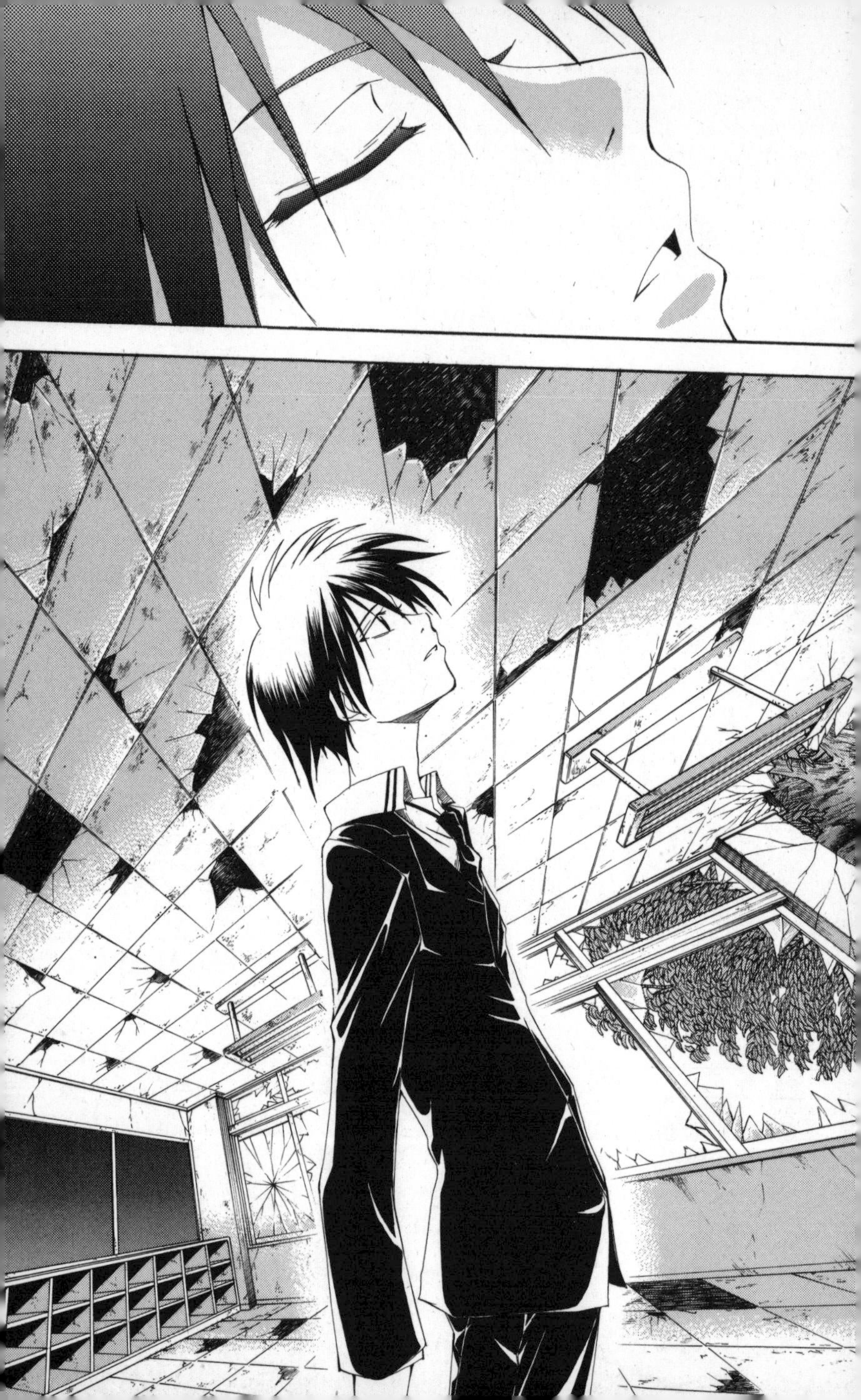

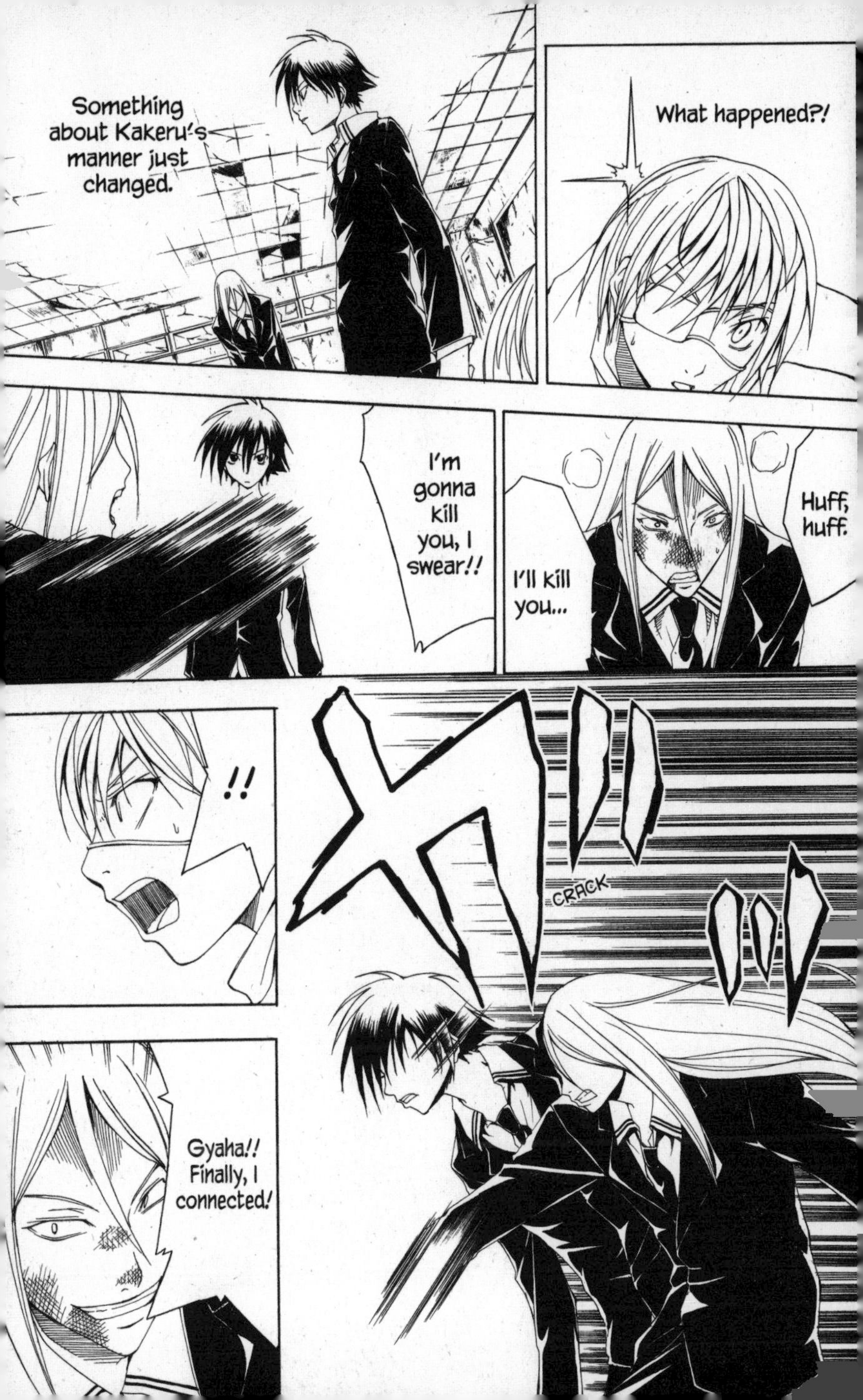
What happened?!
Something about Kakeru's manner just changed.
Huff, huff.
I'll kill you...
I'm gonna kill you, I swear!!
CRACK
!!
Gyaha!! Finally, I connected!

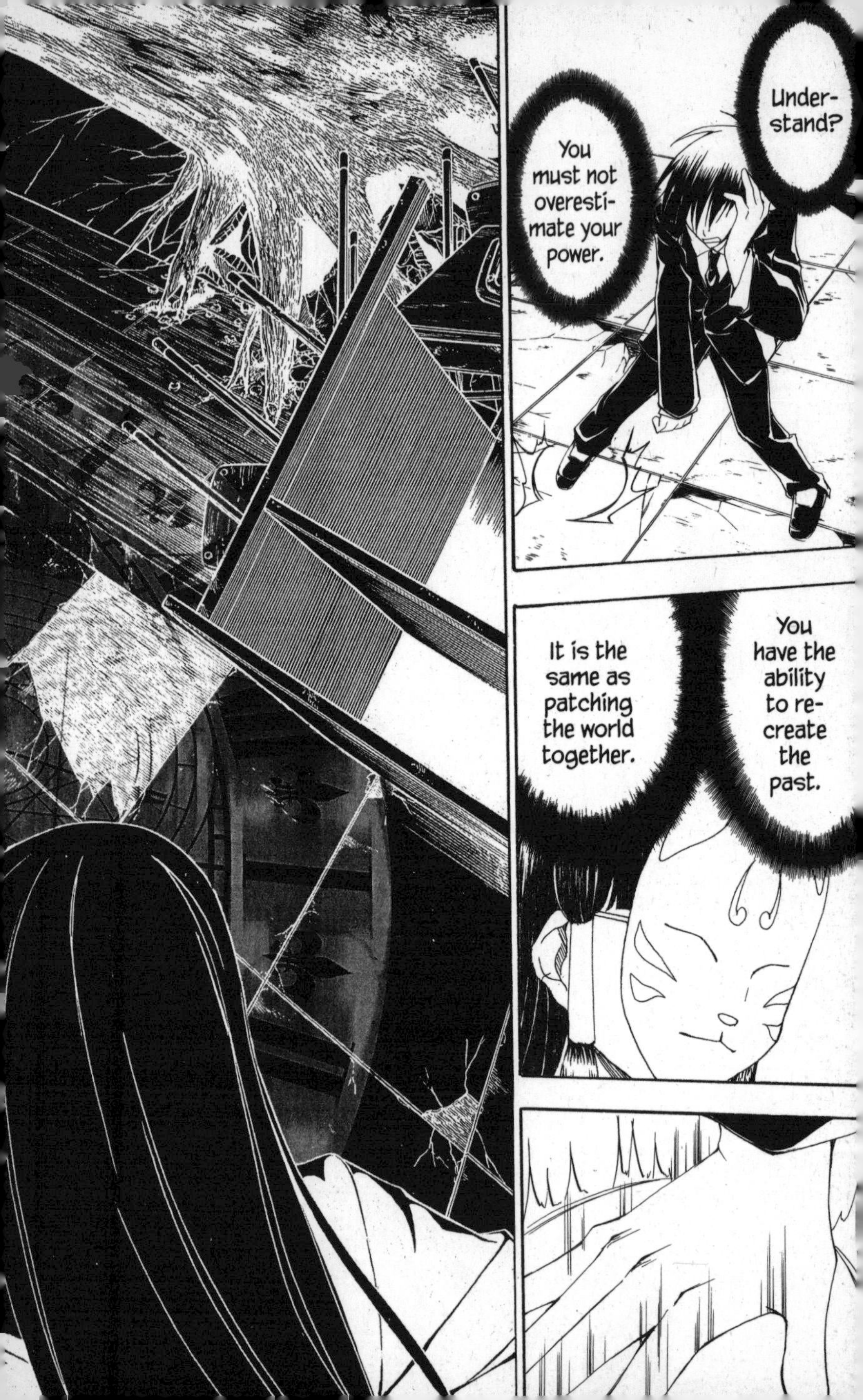
Under-stand?
You must not overesti-mate your power.
You have the ability to re-create the past.
It is the same as patching the world together.

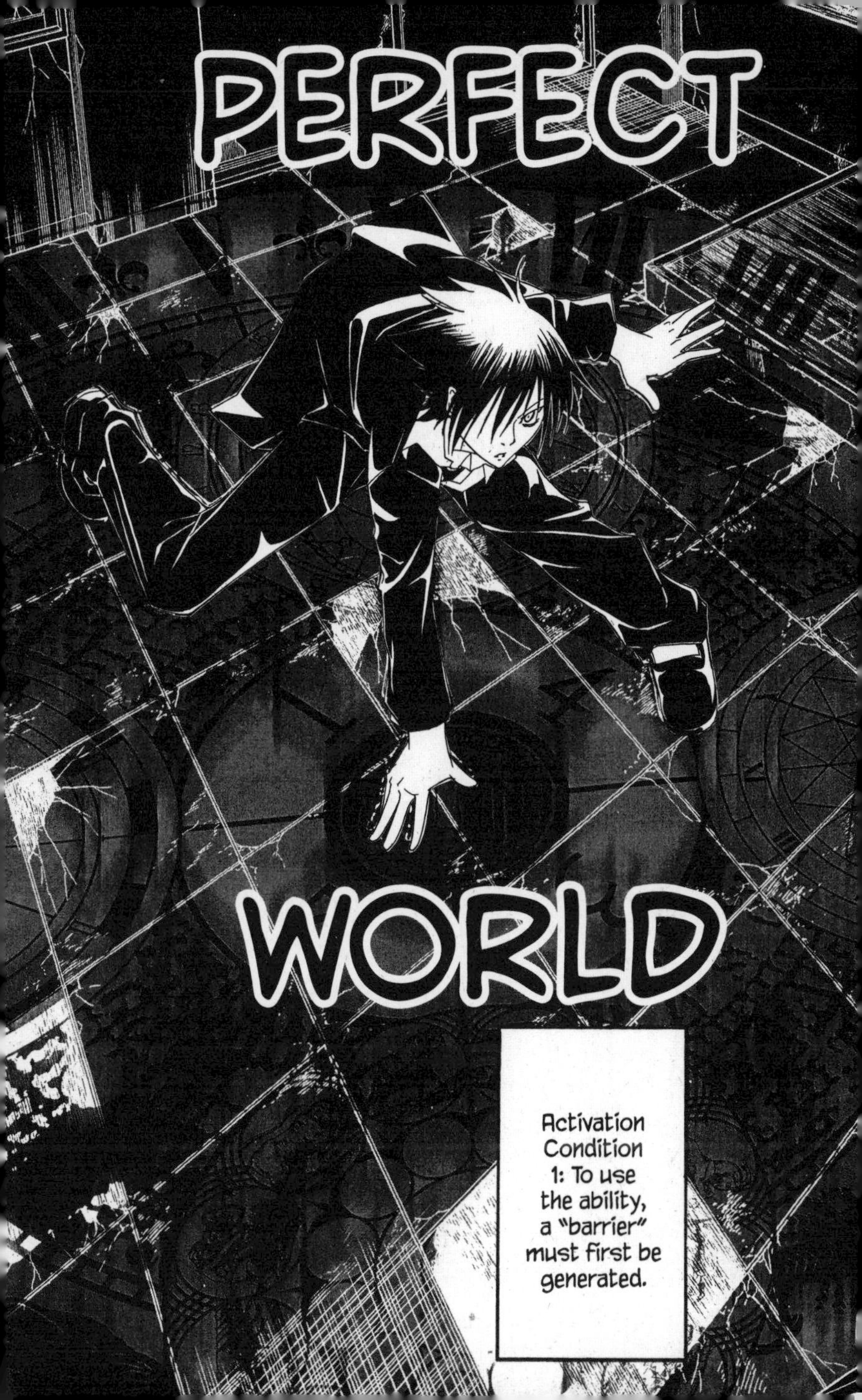
PERFECT
WORLD
Activation Condition 1: To use the ability, a "barrier" must first be generated.

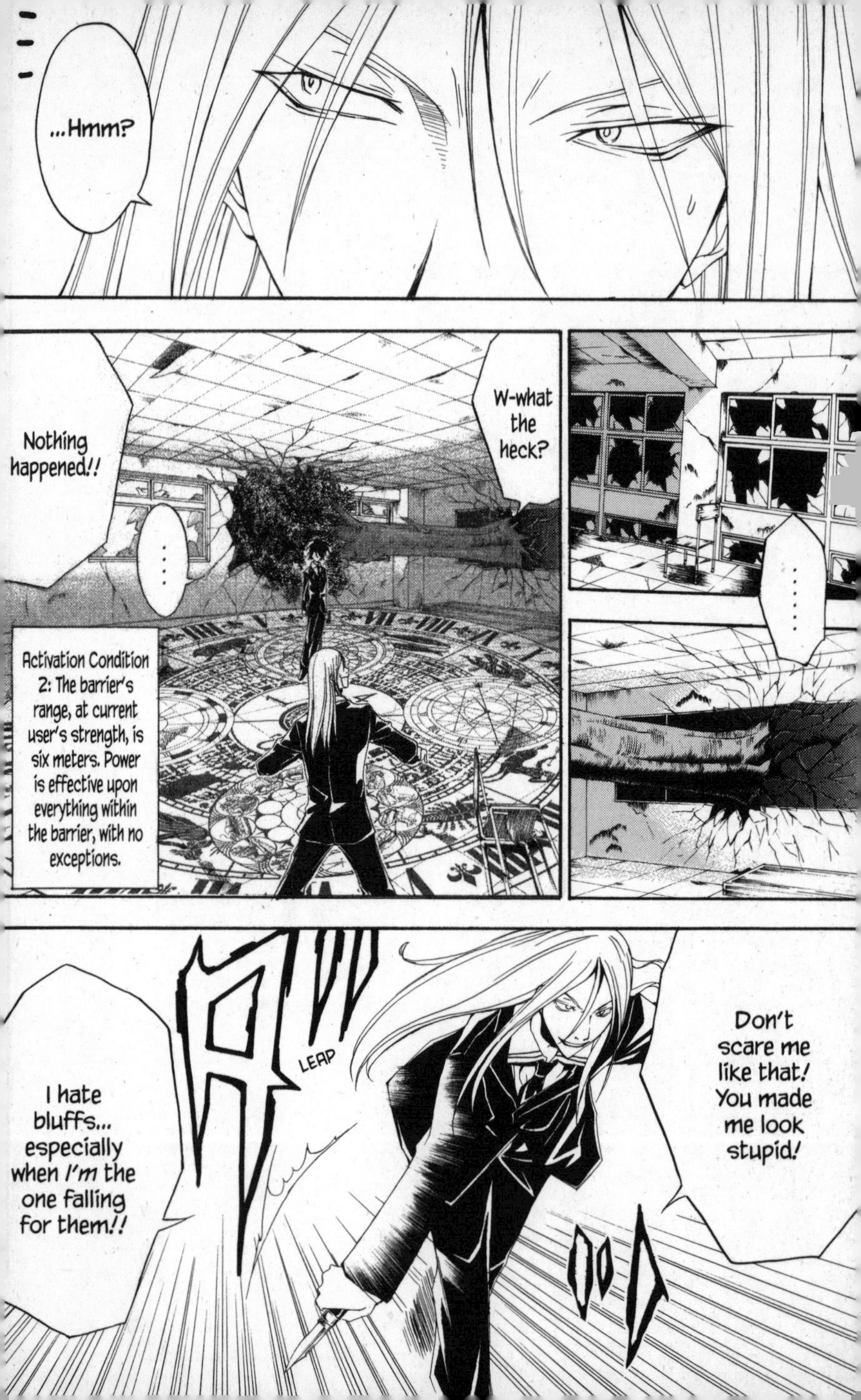

...Hmm?
...
W-what the heck?
Nothing happened!!
...
Activation Condition 2: The barrier's range, at current user's strength, is six meters. Power is effective upon everything within the barrier, with no exceptions.
Don't scare me like that! You made me look stupid!
LEAP
I hate bluffs... especially when I'm the one falling for them!!

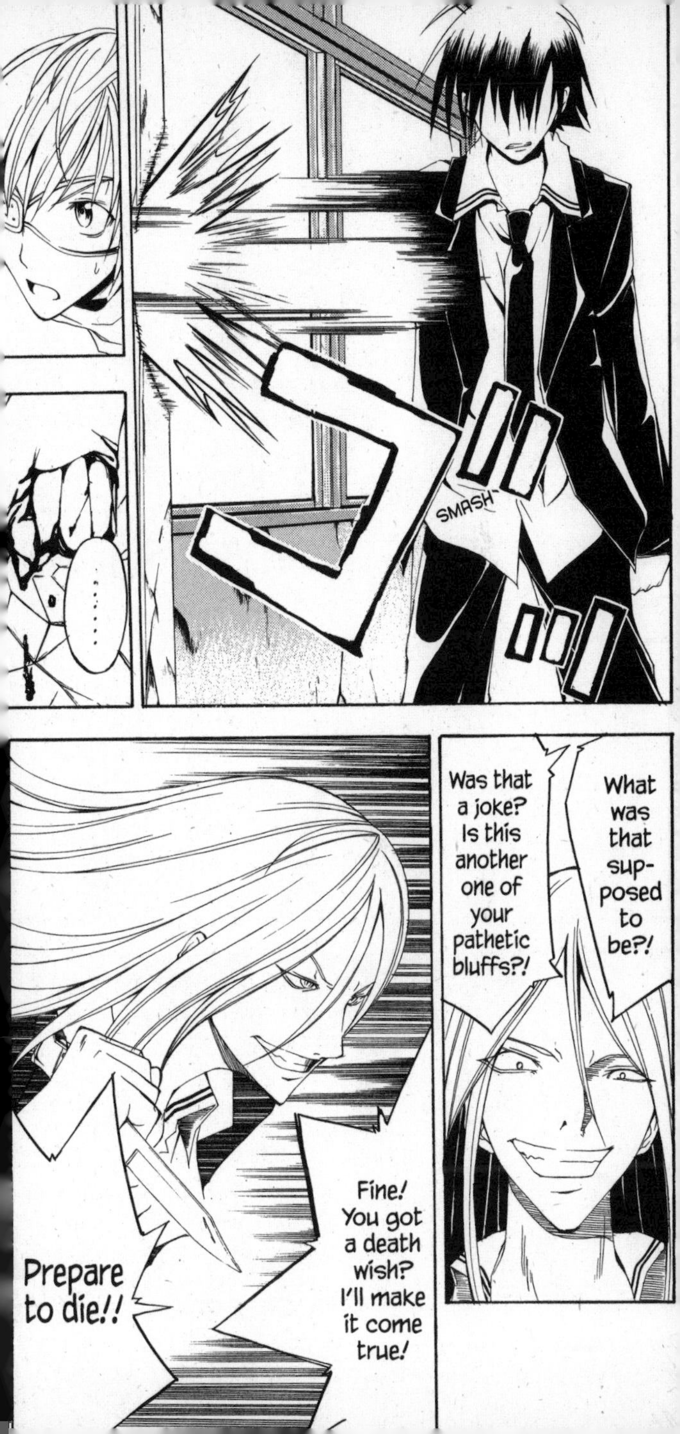
SMASH
......
What was that sup-posed to be?!
Was that a joke? Is this another one of your pathetic bluffs?!
Fine! You got a death wish? I'll make it come true!
Prepare to die!!

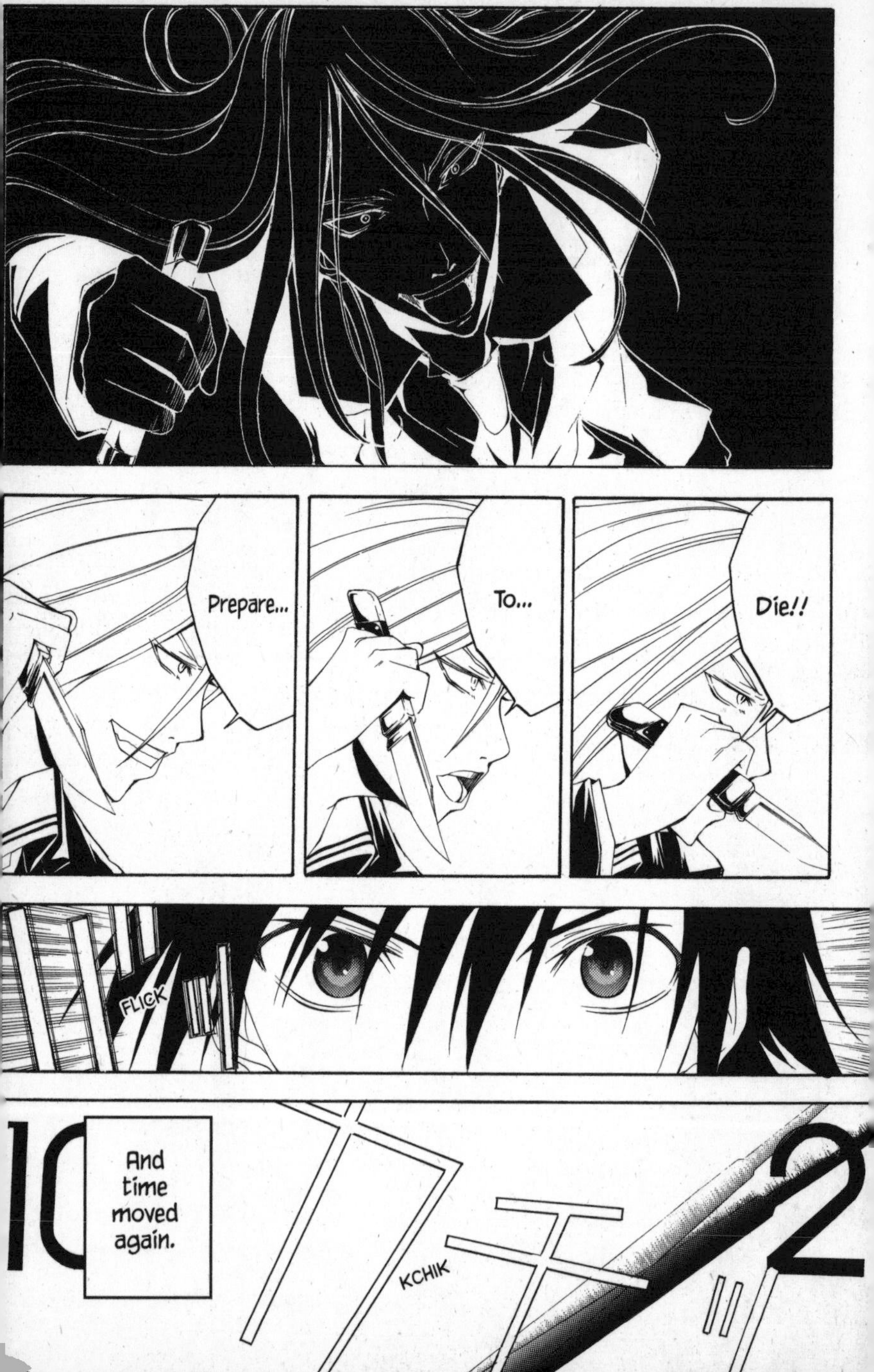

Die!!
To...
Prepare...
FLICK
KCHIK
And time moved again.

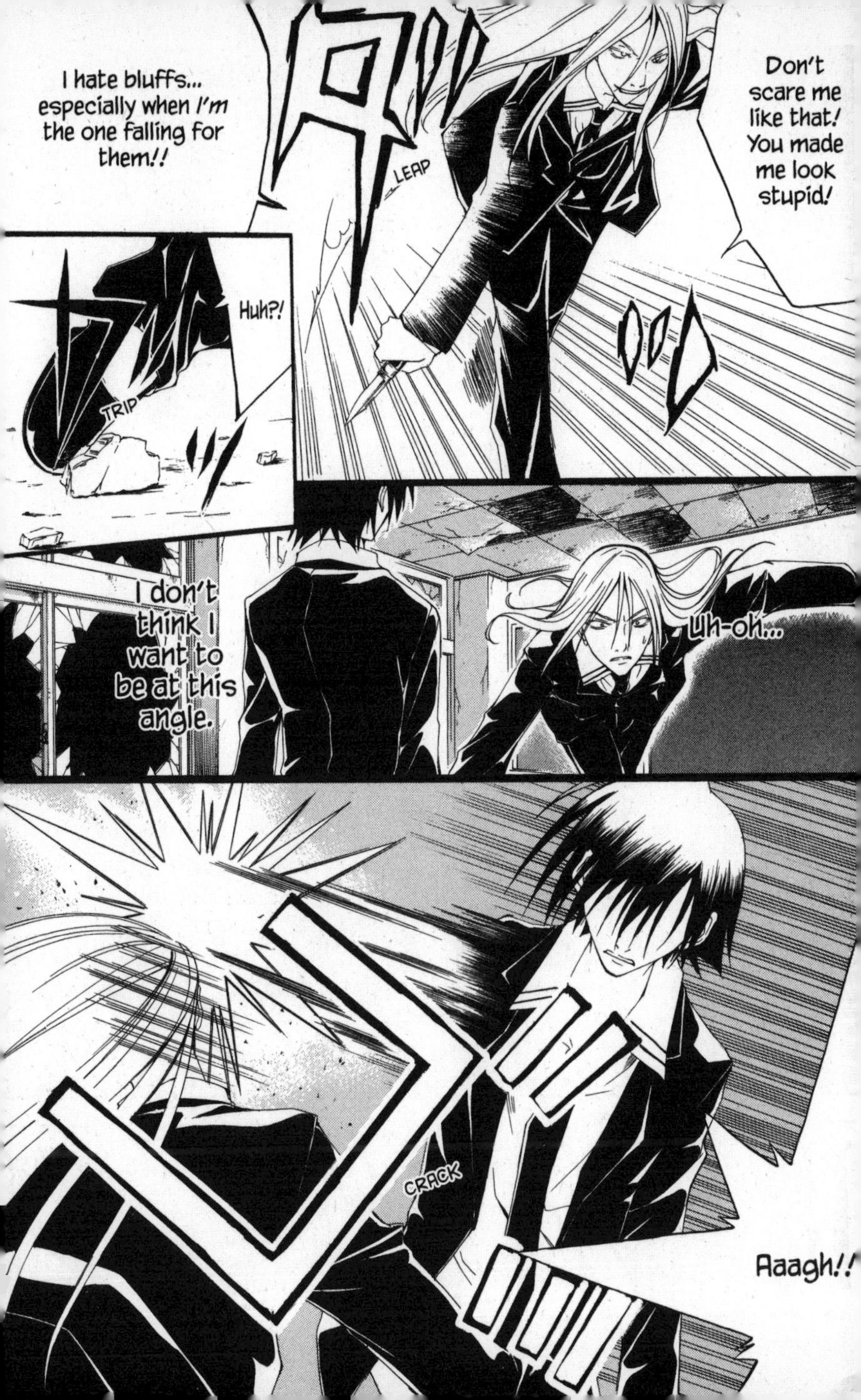
Don't scare me like that! You made me look stupid!
I hate bluffs... especially when I'm the one falling for them!!
LEAP
Huh?!
TRIP
Uh-oh...
I don't think I want to be at this angle.
Aaagh!!
CRACK

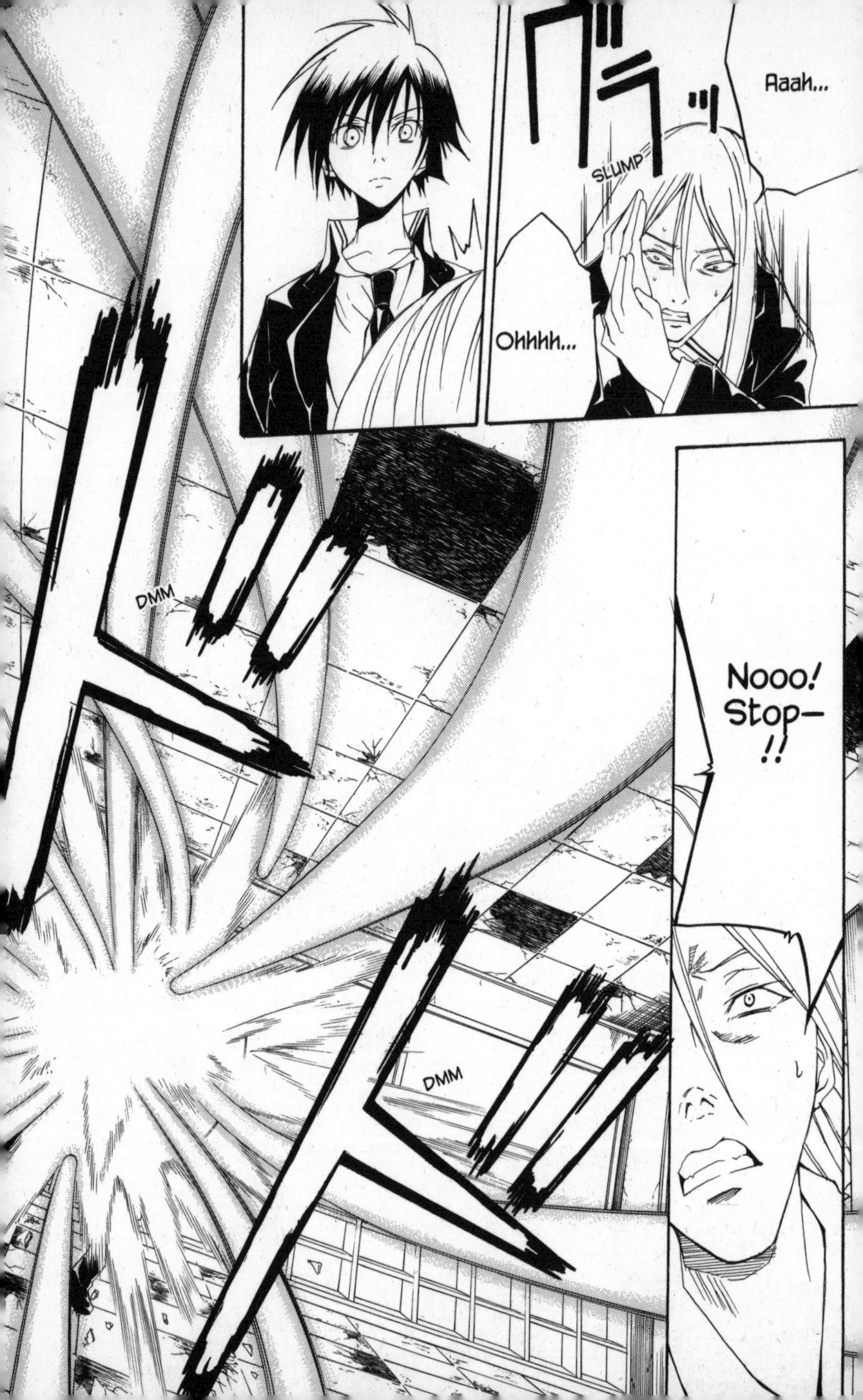
Aaah...
SLUMP
Ohhhh...
Nooo! Stop—!!
DMM
DMM

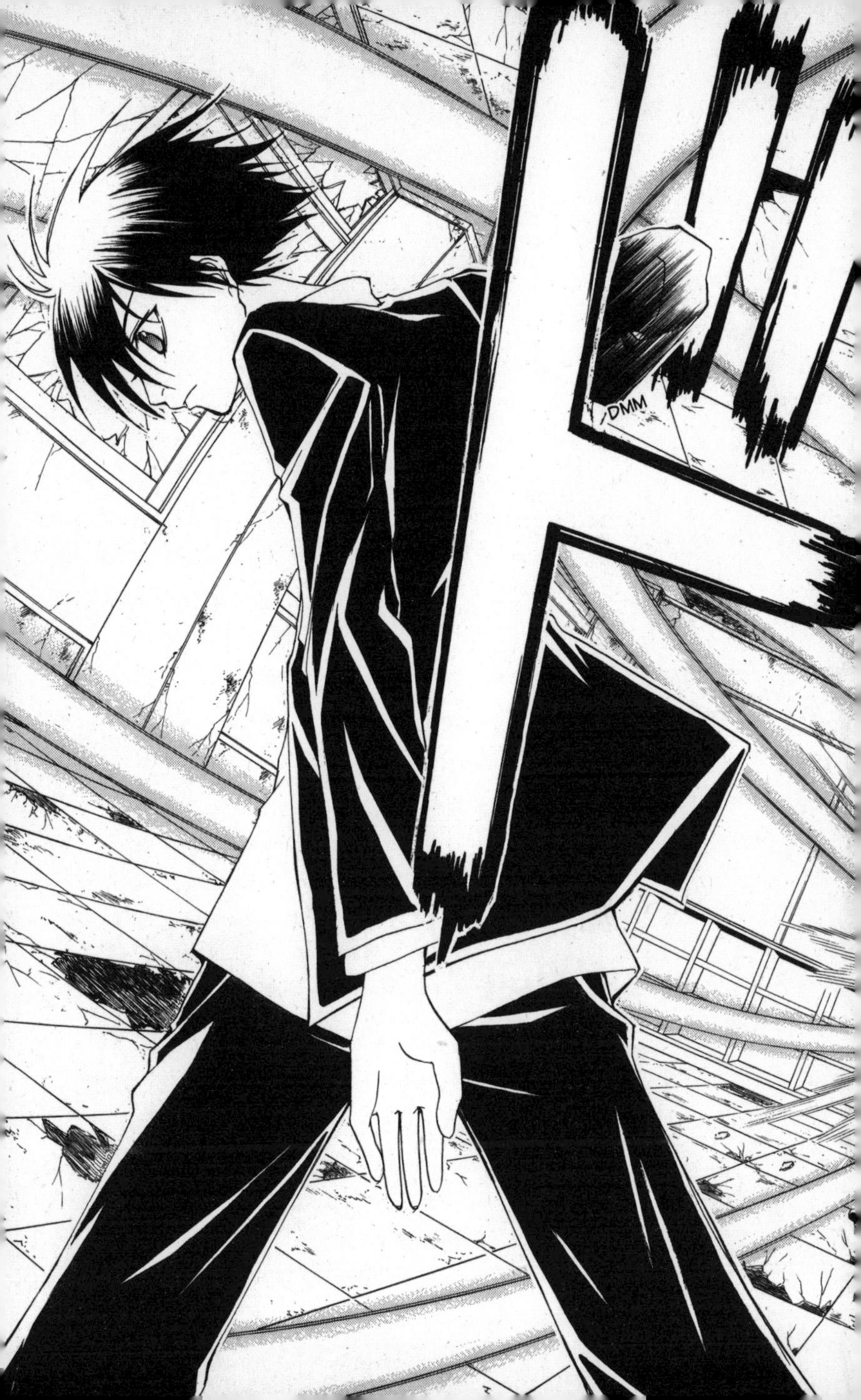
DMM

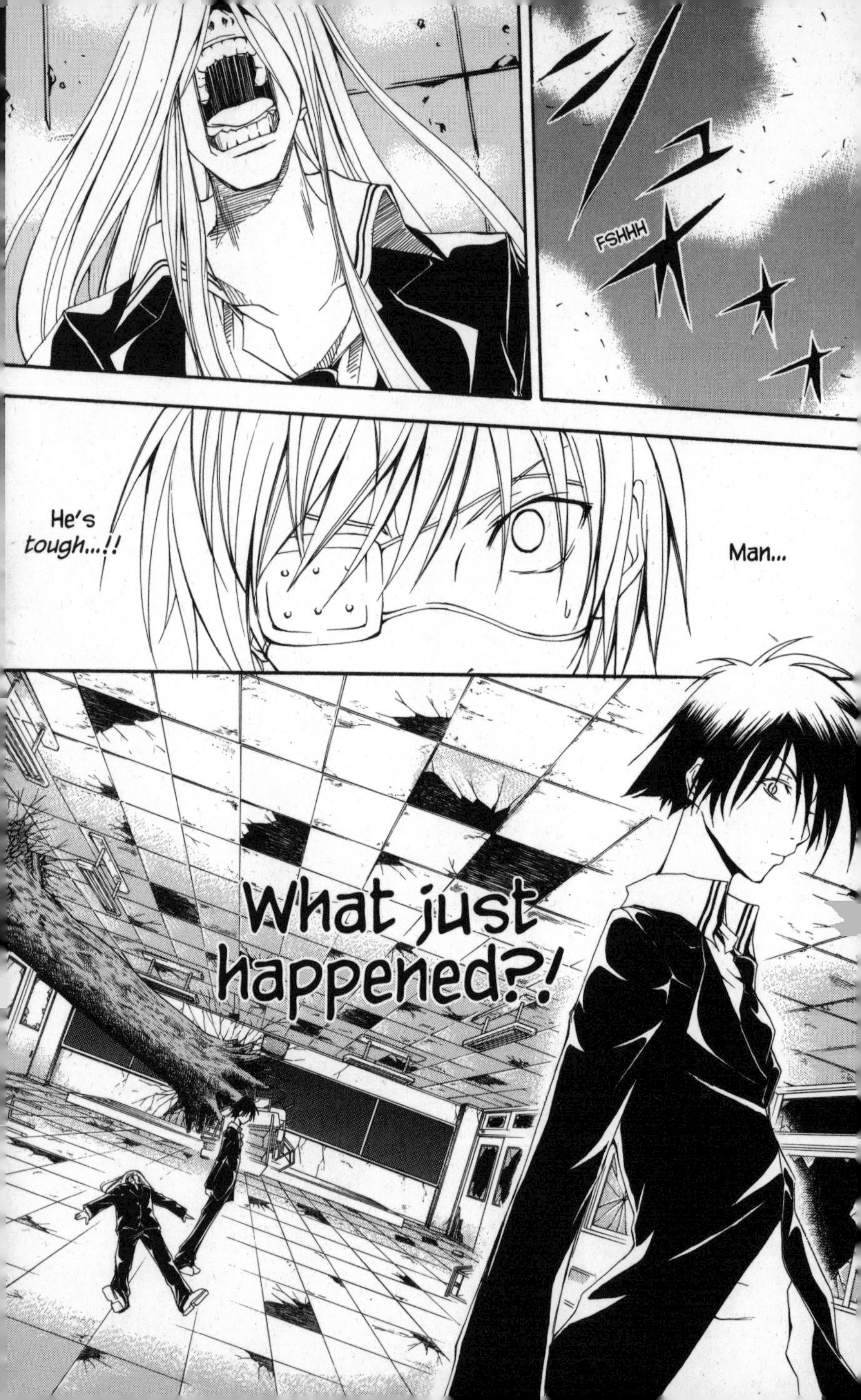
FSHHH
Man...
He's tough...!!
What just happened?!

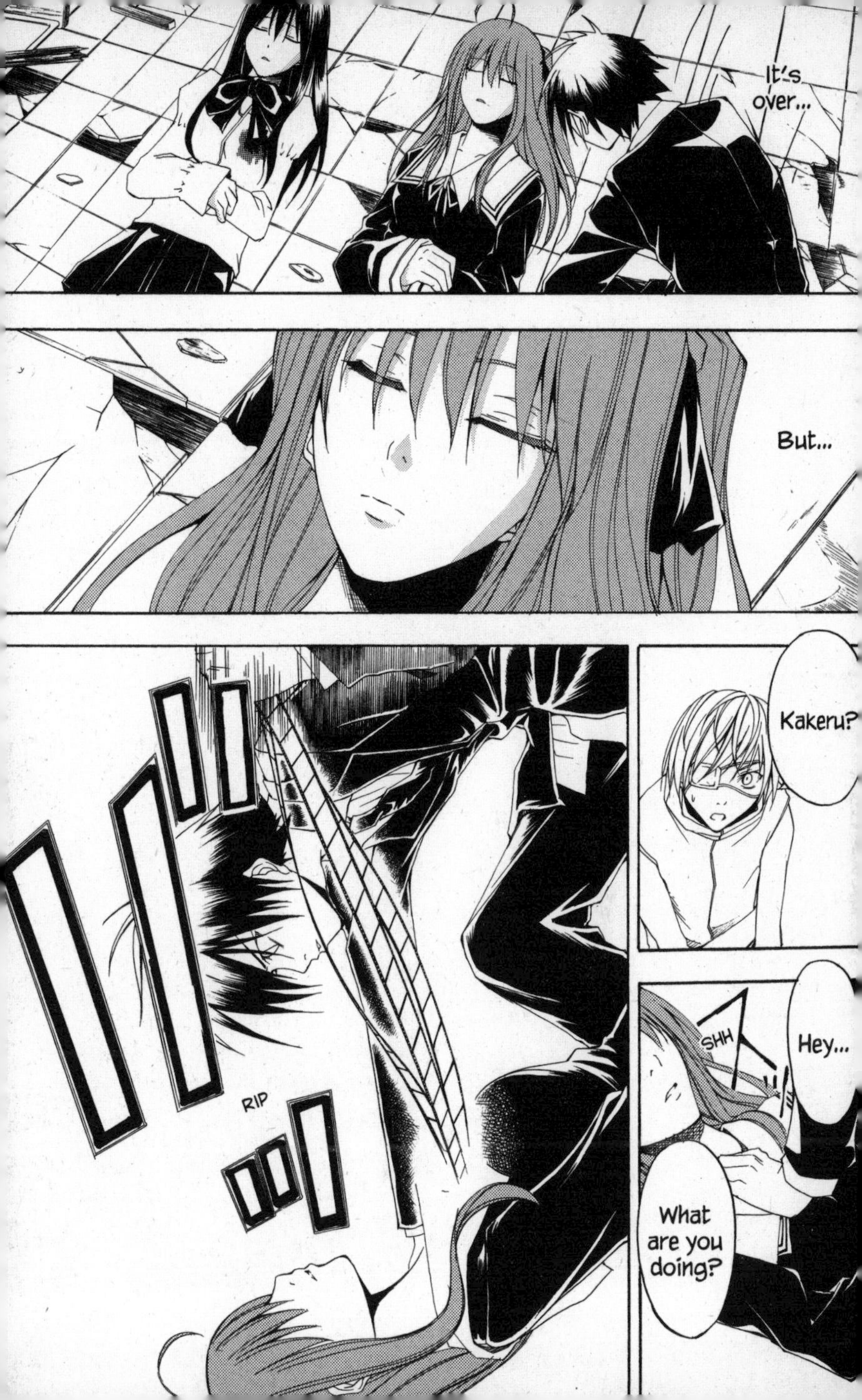
It's over...
But...
Kakeru?
Hey...
SHH
What are you doing?
RIP

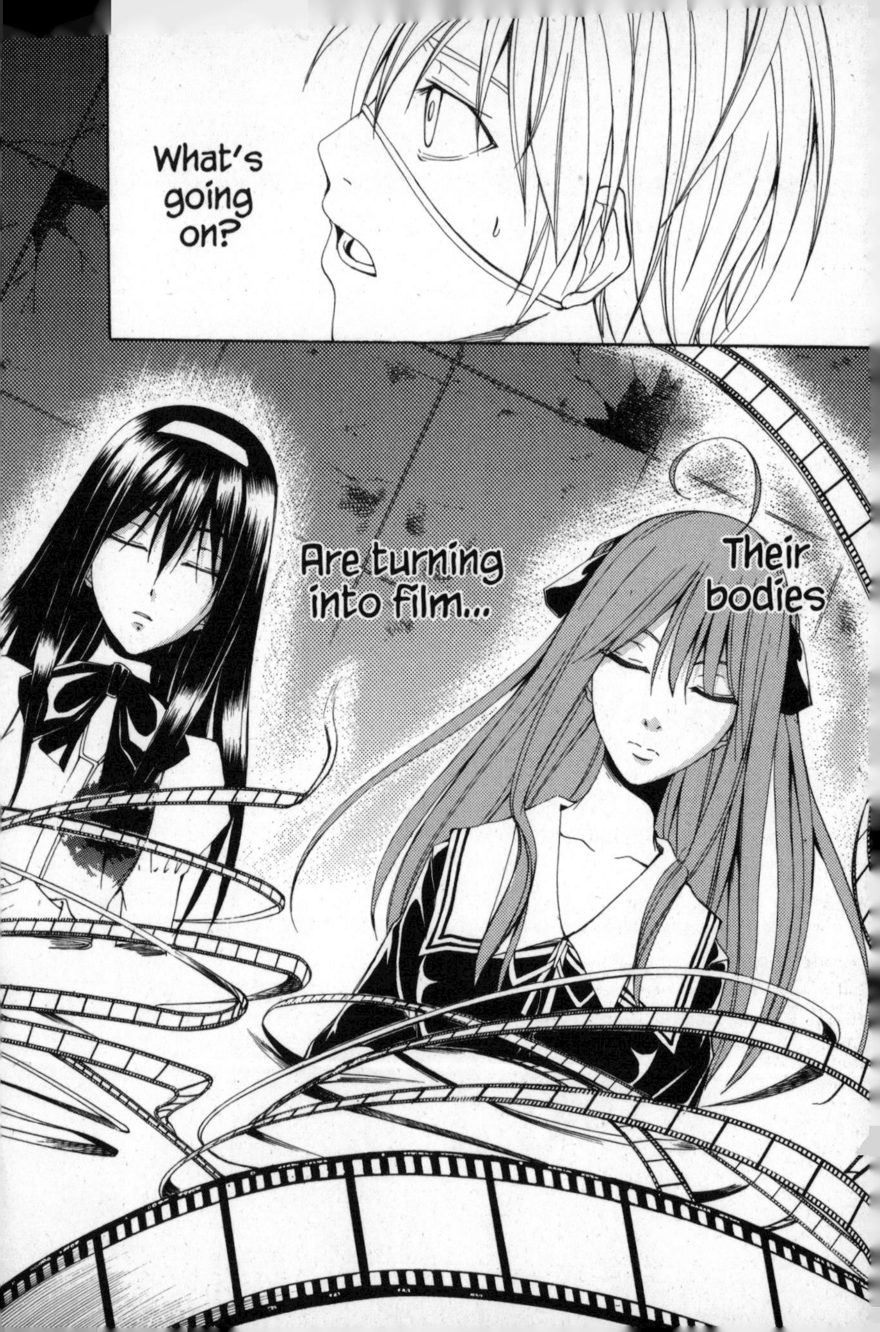
What's going on?
Their bodies
Are turning into film...

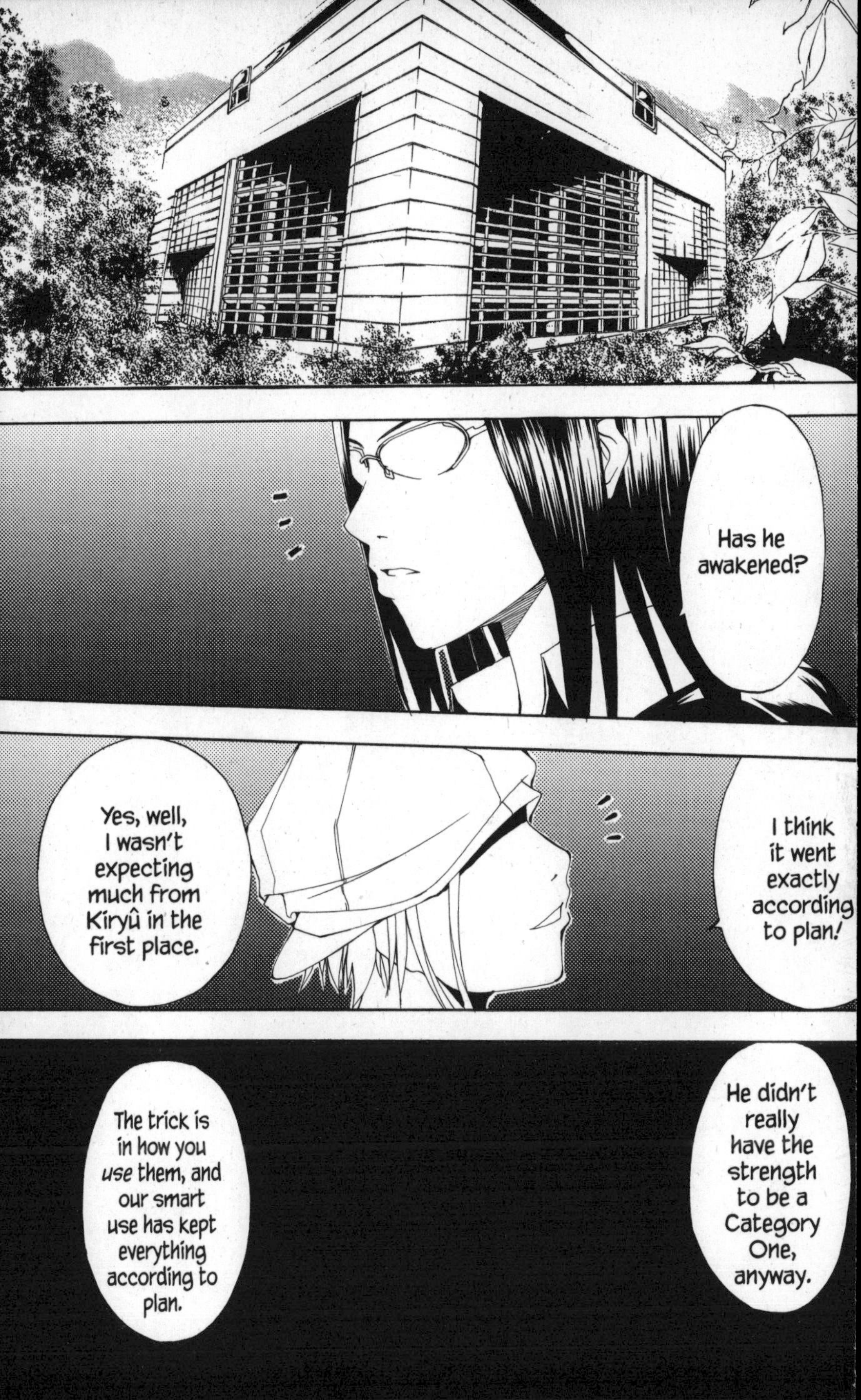
Has he awakened?
I think it went exactly according to plan!
Yes, well, I wasn't expecting much from Kiryû in the first place.
He didn't really have the strength to be a Category One, anyway.
The trick is in how you *use* them, and our smart use has kept everything according to plan.

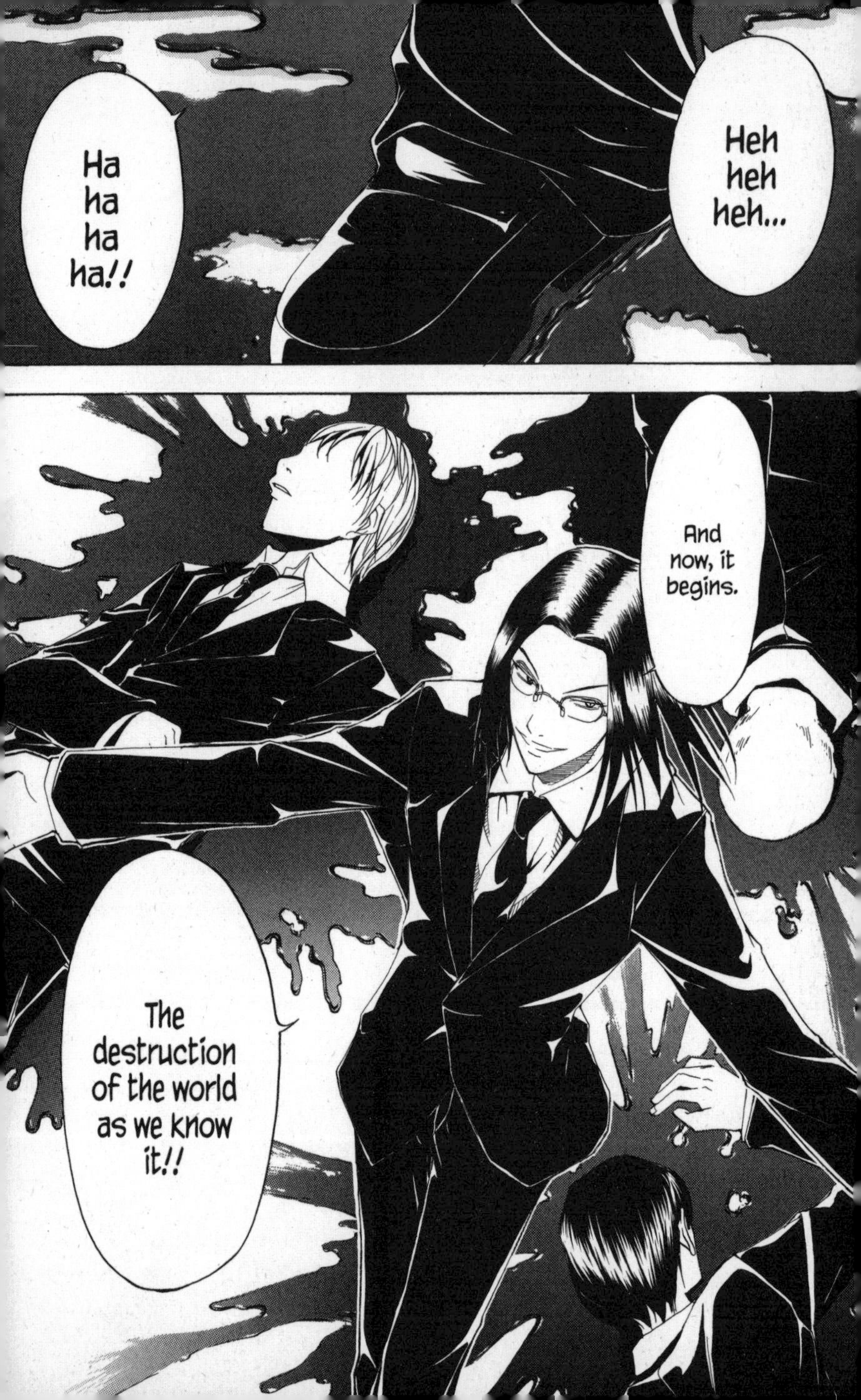
Heh heh heh...
Ha ha ha ha!!
And now, it begins.
The destruction of the world as we know it!!

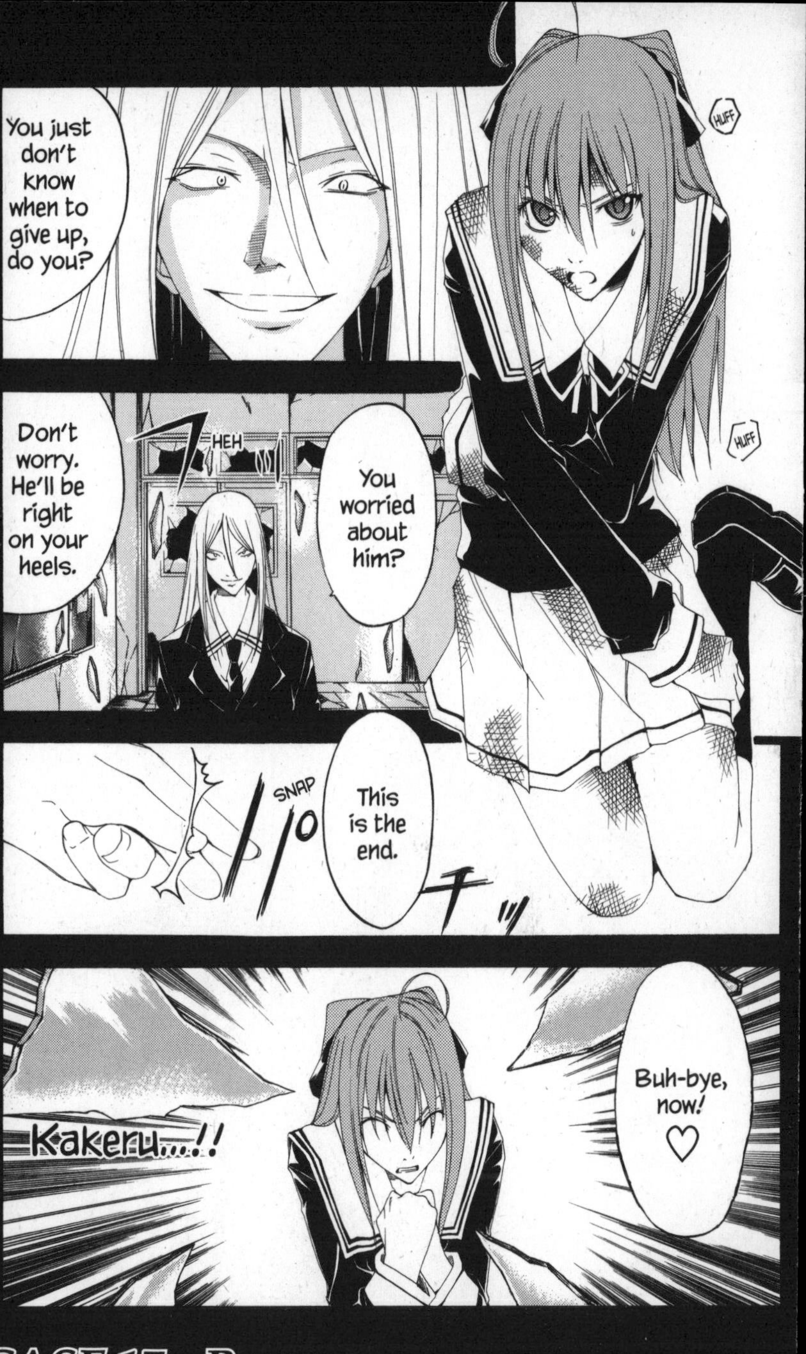
HUFF
HUFF
You just don't know when to give up, do you?
You worried about him?
HEH
Don't worry. He'll be right on your heels.
This is the end.
SNAP
チッ
Buh-bye, now! ♡
Kakeru...!!

CASE 17 – Progress

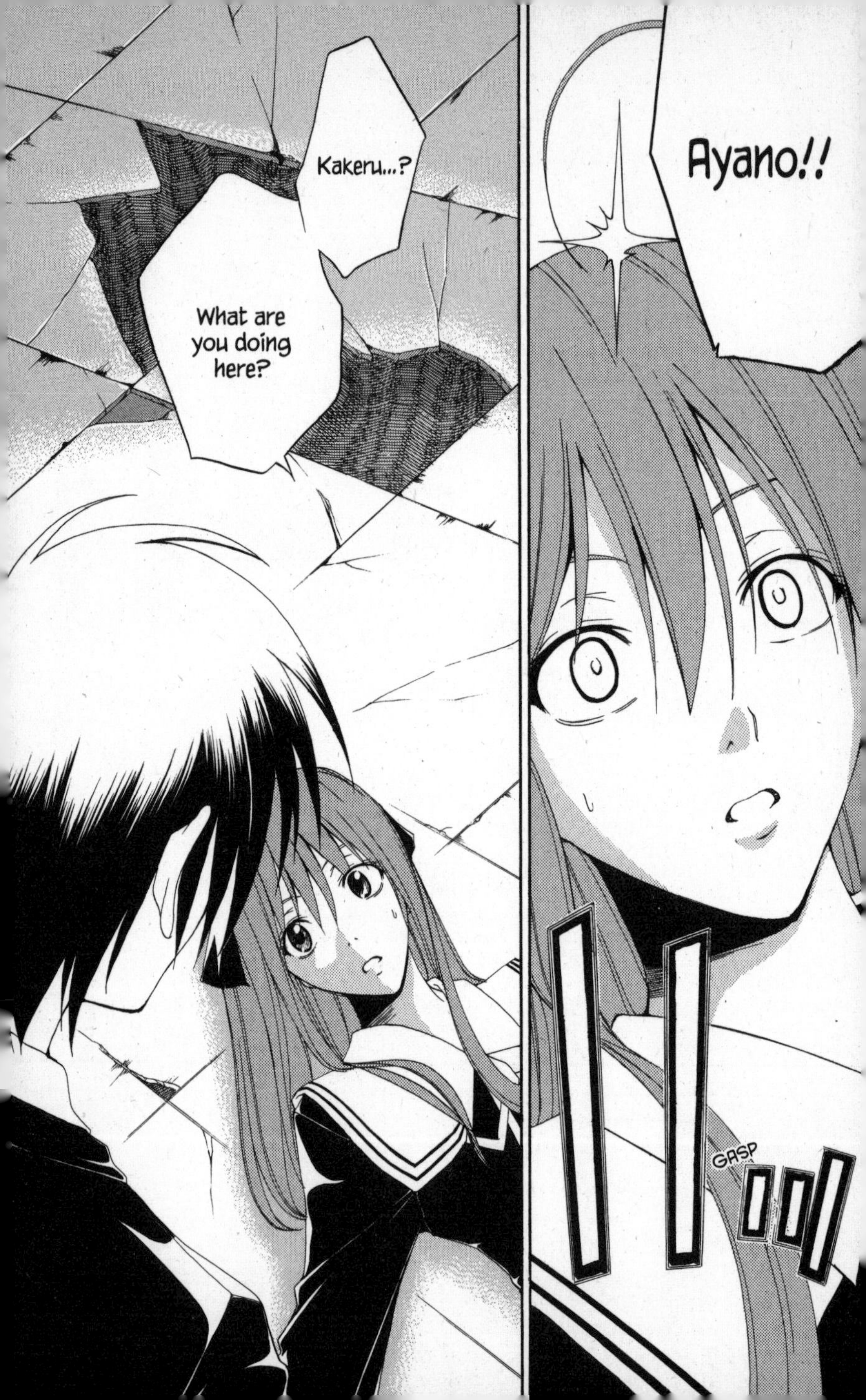
Ayano!!
GASP
Kakeru...?
What are you doing here?

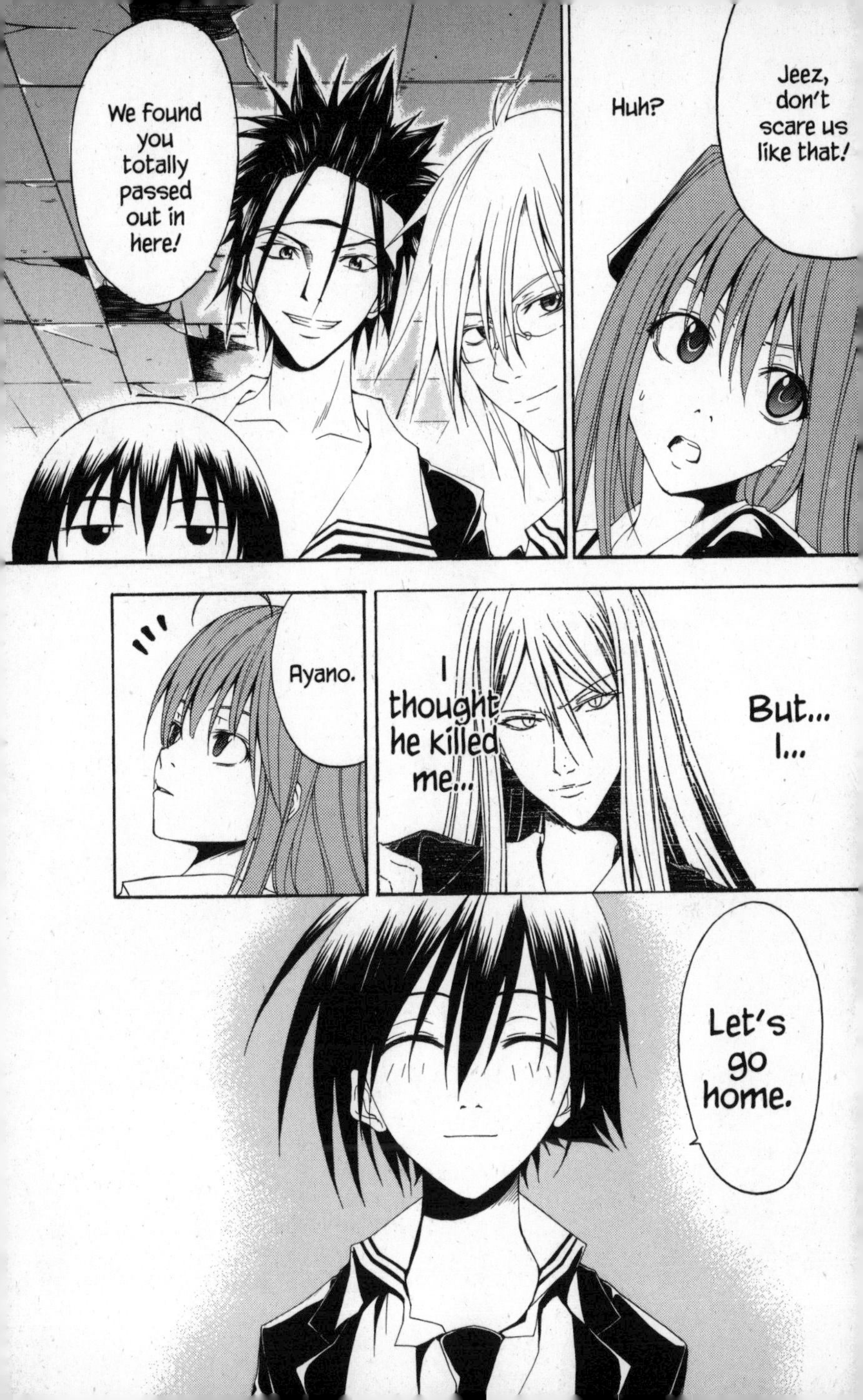
Jeez, don't scare us like that!
Huh?
We found you totally passed out in here!
But... I...
I thought he killed me...
Ayano.
Let's go home.

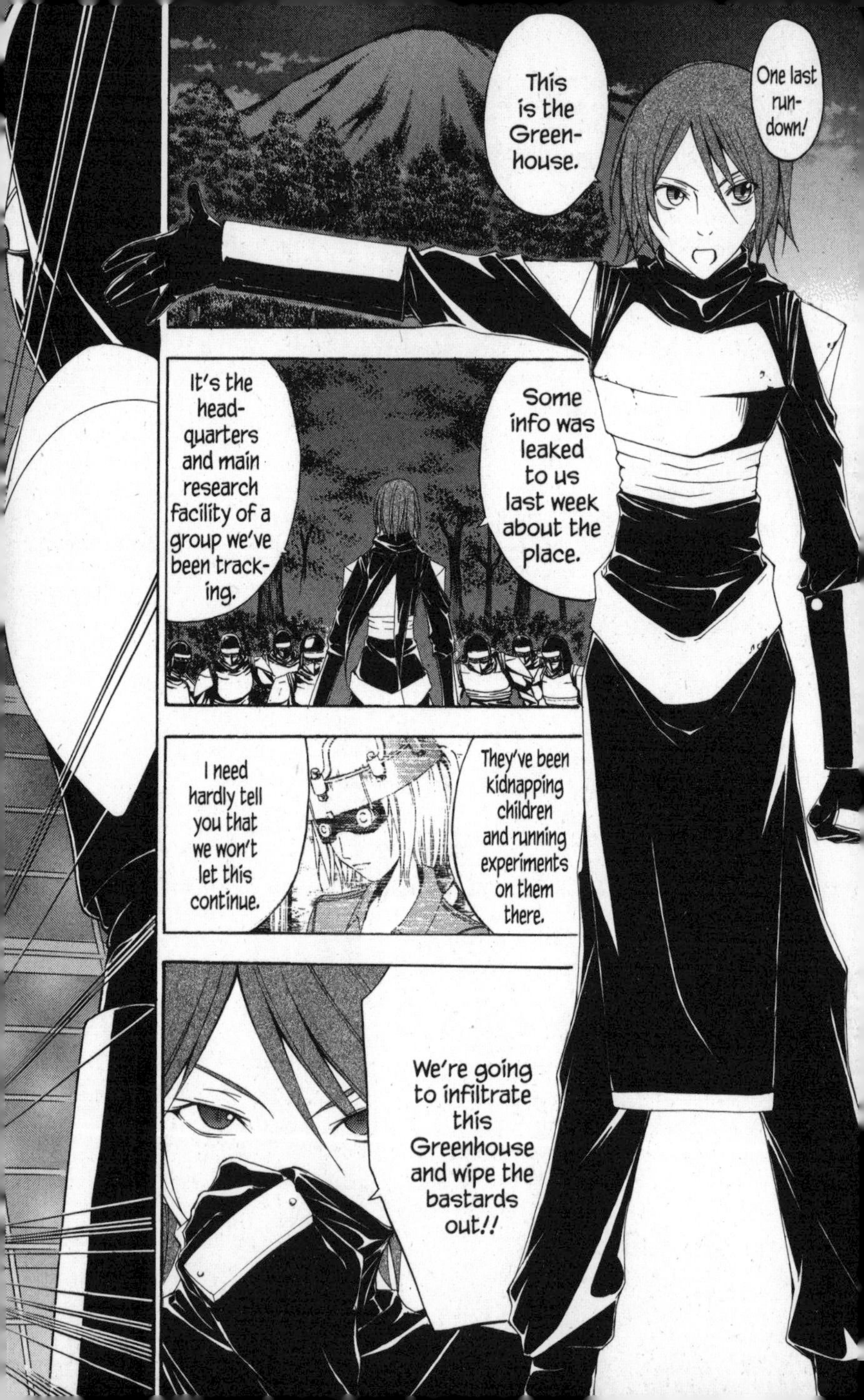
One last run-down!
This is the Green-house.
Some info was leaked to us last week about the place.
It's the head-quarters and main research facility of a group we've been track-ing.
They've been kidnapping children and running experiments on them there.
I need hardly tell you that we won't let this continue.
We're going to infiltrate this Greenhouse and wipe the bastards out!!

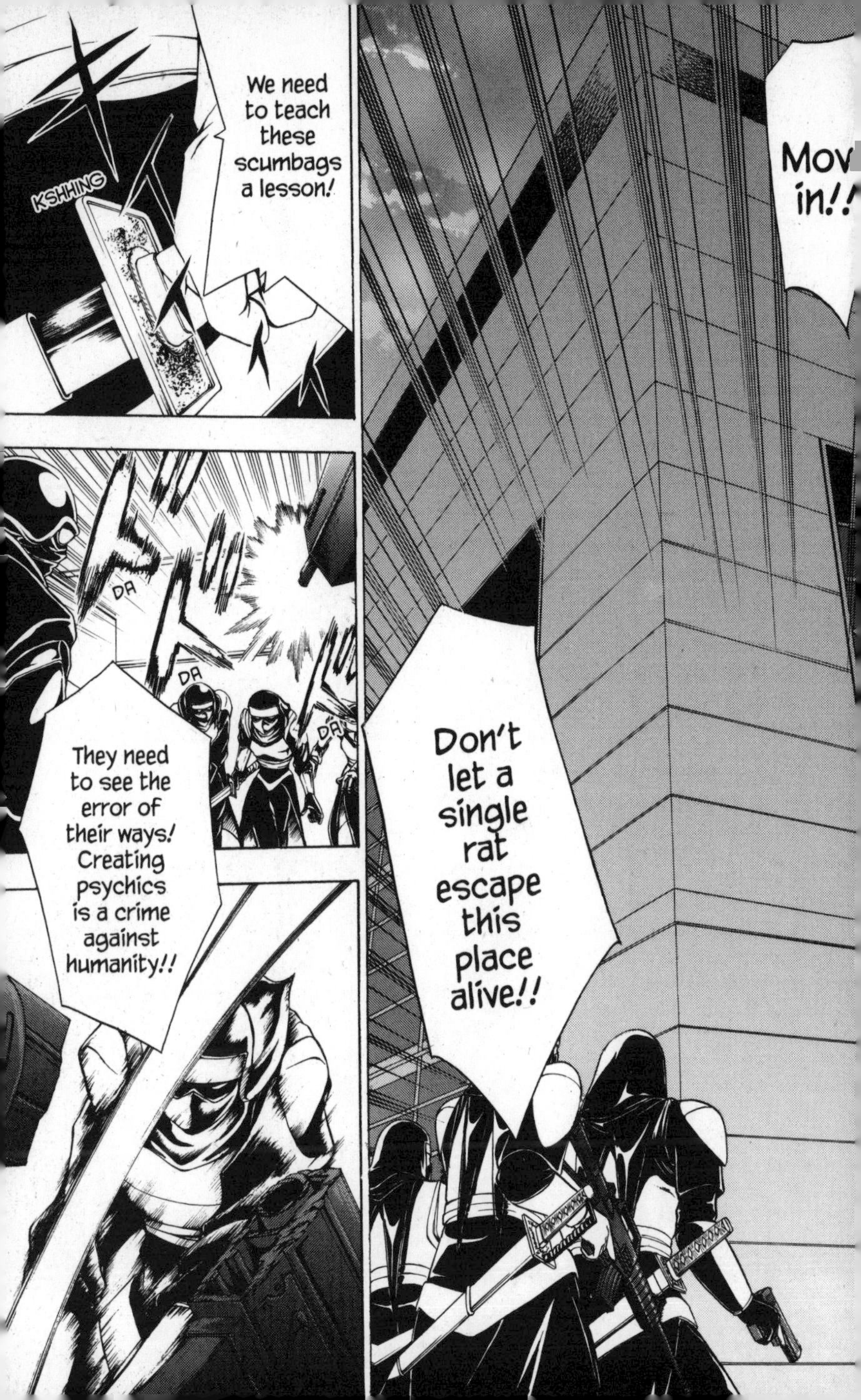
Mov in!!
Don't let a single rat escape this place alive!!
We need to teach these scumbags a lesson!
KSHHING
DA
DA
DA
They need to see the error of their ways! Creating psychics is a crime against humanity!!

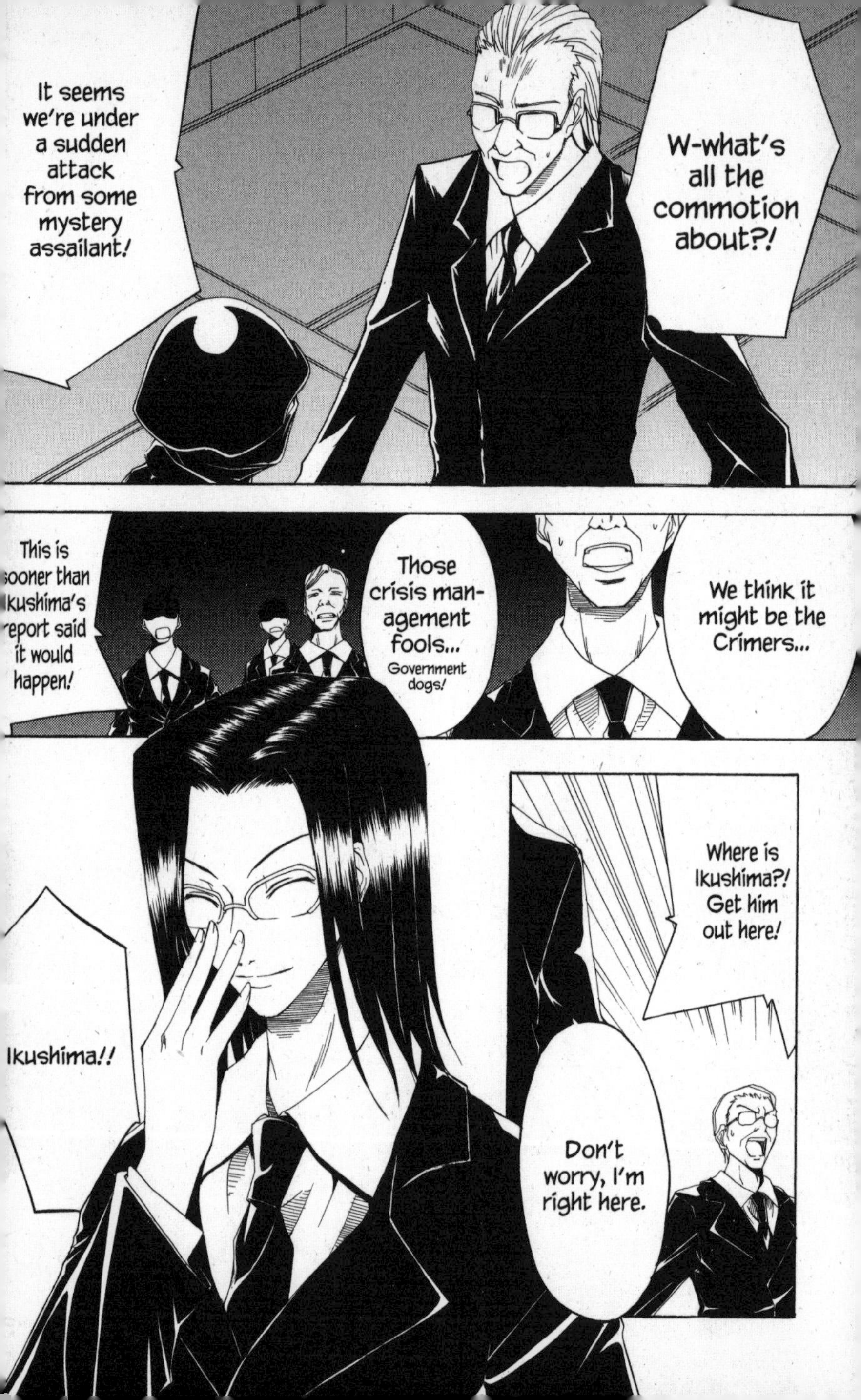
W-what's all the commotion about?!
It seems we're under a sudden attack from some mystery assailant!
We think it might be the Crimers...
Those crisis management fools... Government dogs!
This is sooner than Ikushima's report said it would happen!
Where is Ikushima?! Get him out here!
Don't worry, I'm right here.
Ikushima!!

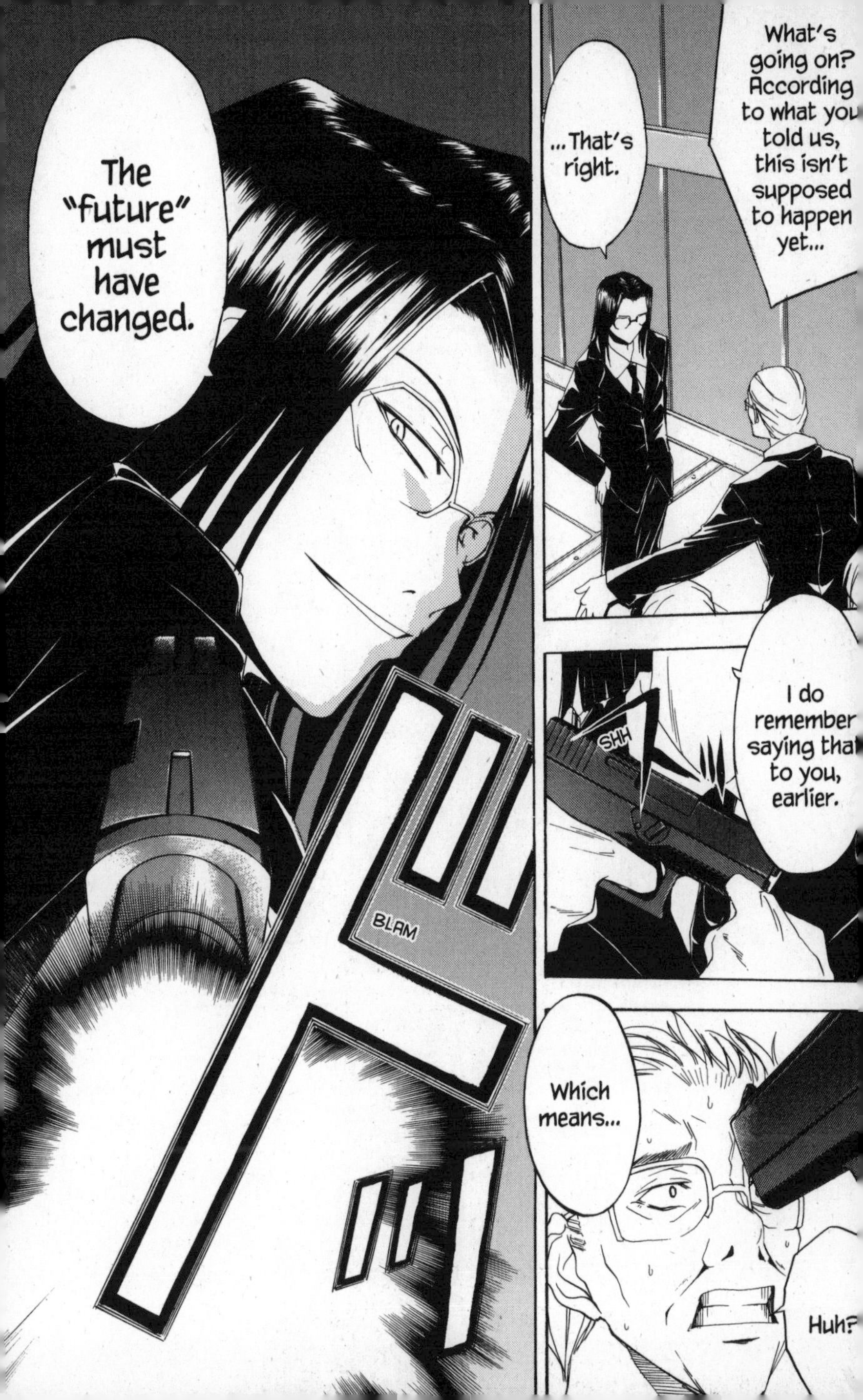
What's going on? According to what you told us, this isn't supposed to happen yet...
...That's right.
I do remember saying that to you, earlier.
SHH
Which means...
Huh?
The "future" must have changed.
BLAM

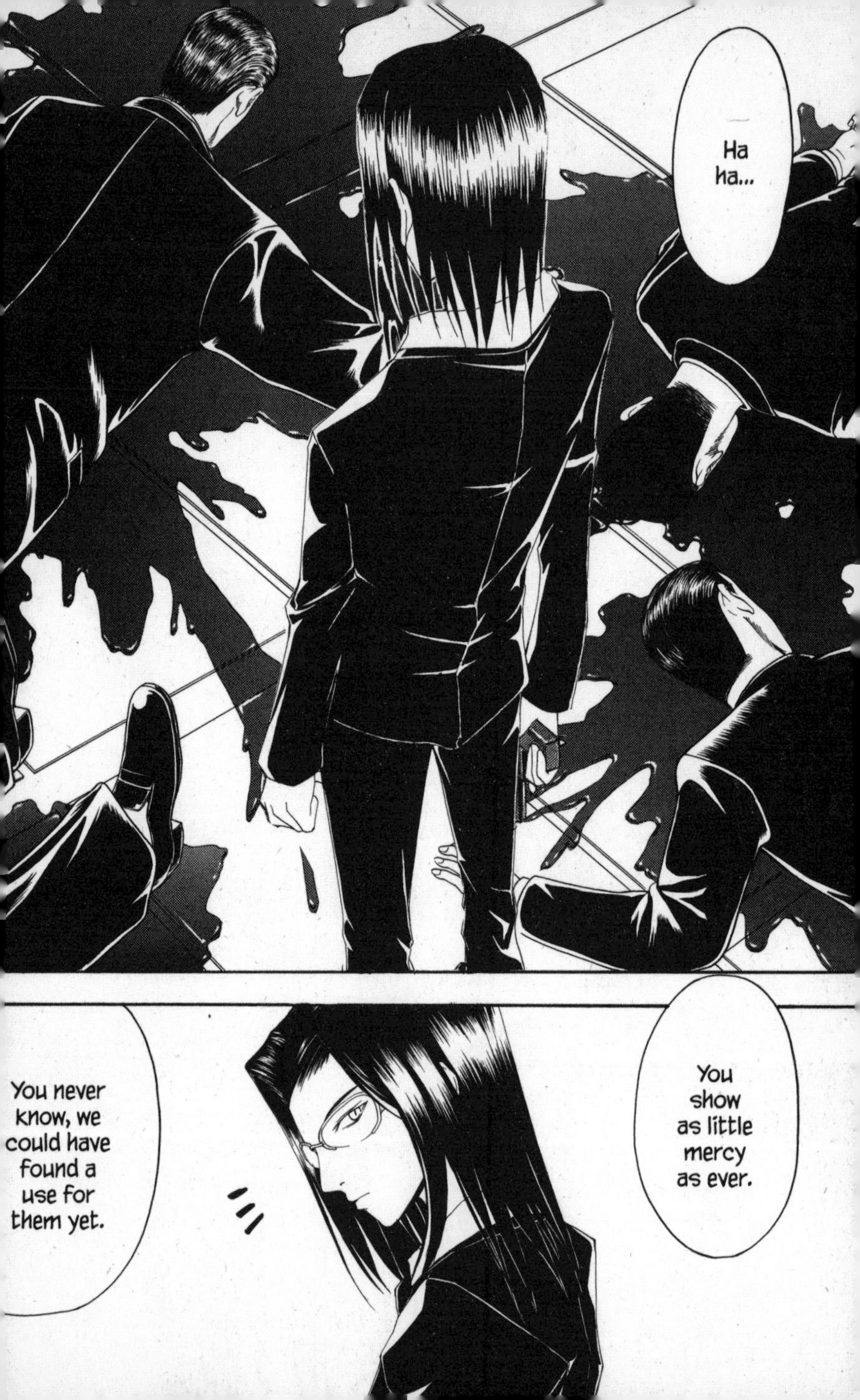
Ha ha...
You show as little mercy as ever.
You never know, we could have found a use for them yet.

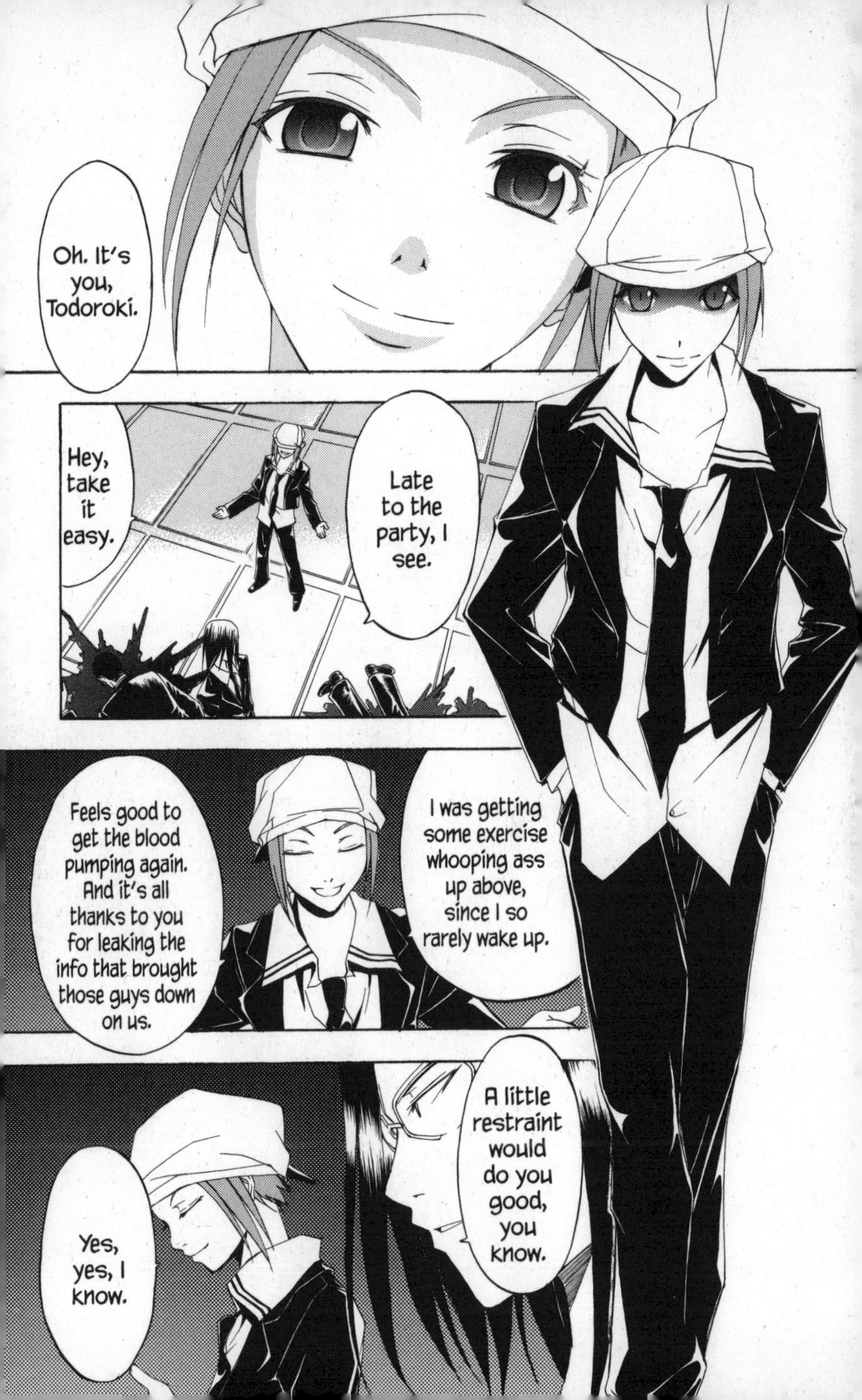
Oh. It's you, Todoroki.
Late to the party, I see.
Hey, take it easy.
I was getting some exercise whooping ass up above, since I so rarely wake up.
Feels good to get the blood pumping again. And it's all thanks to you for leaking the info that brought those guys down on us.
A little restraint would do you good, you know.
Yes, yes, I know.

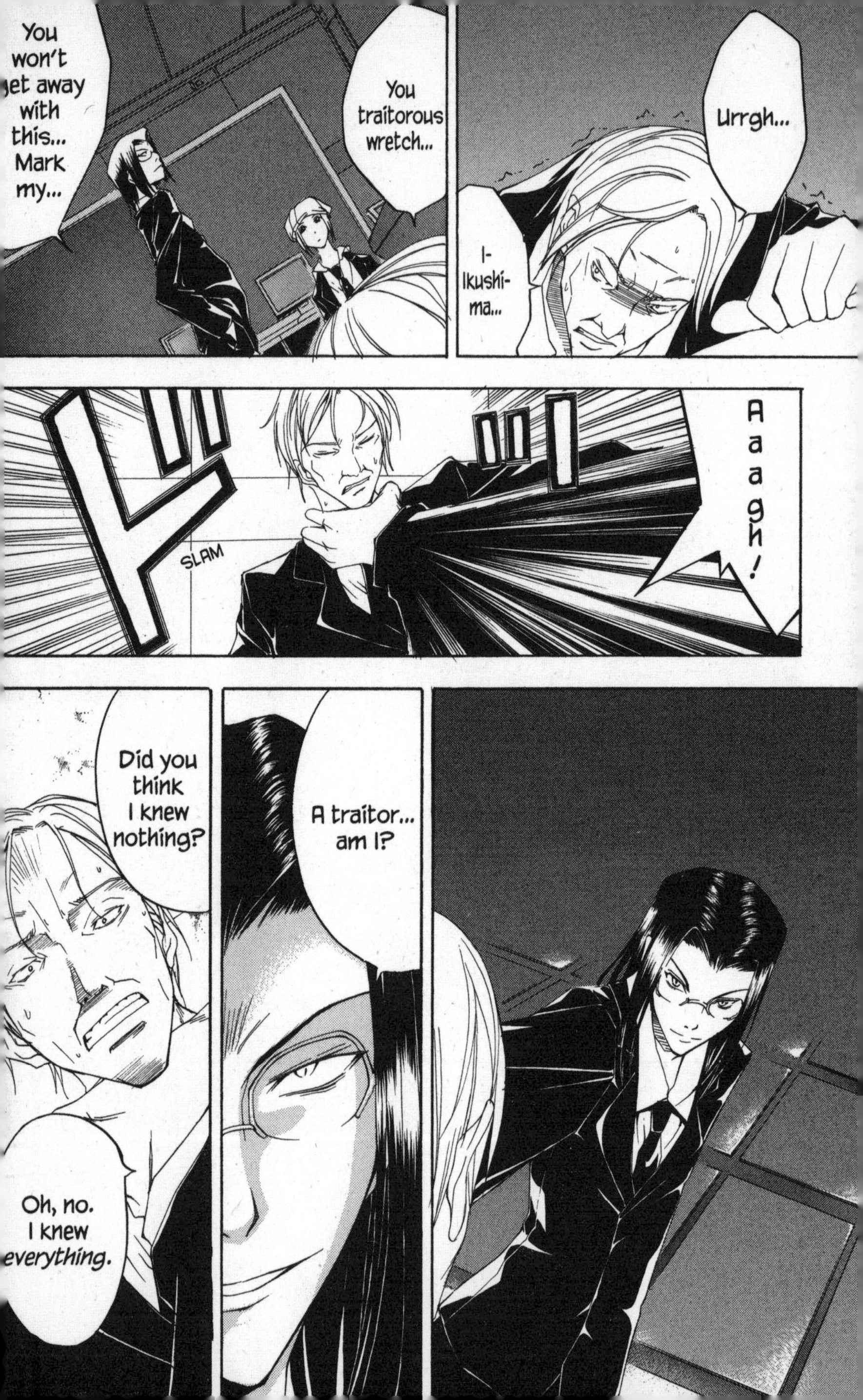

Urrgh...
I- Ikushi-ma...
You traitorous wretch...
You won't get away with this... Mark my...
Aaagh!
SLAM
A traitor... am I?
Did you think I knew nothing?
Oh, no. I knew everything.

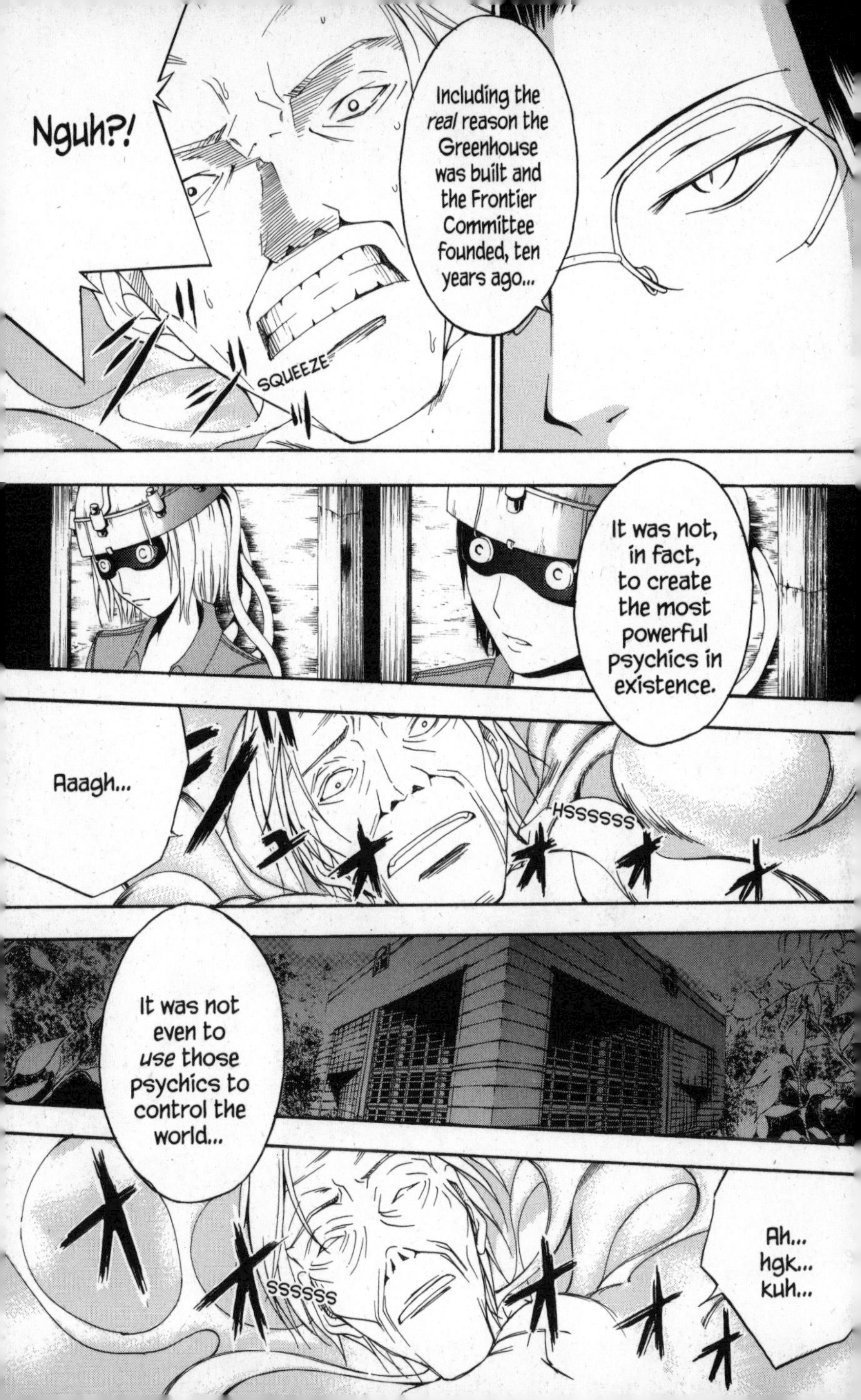
Including the *real* reason the Greenhouse was built and the Frontier Committee founded, ten years ago...
Nguh?!
SQUEEZE
It was not, in fact, to create the most powerful psychics in existence.
Aaagh...
HSSSSSS
It was not even to *use* those psychics to control the world...
Ah... hgk... kuh...
SSSSSS

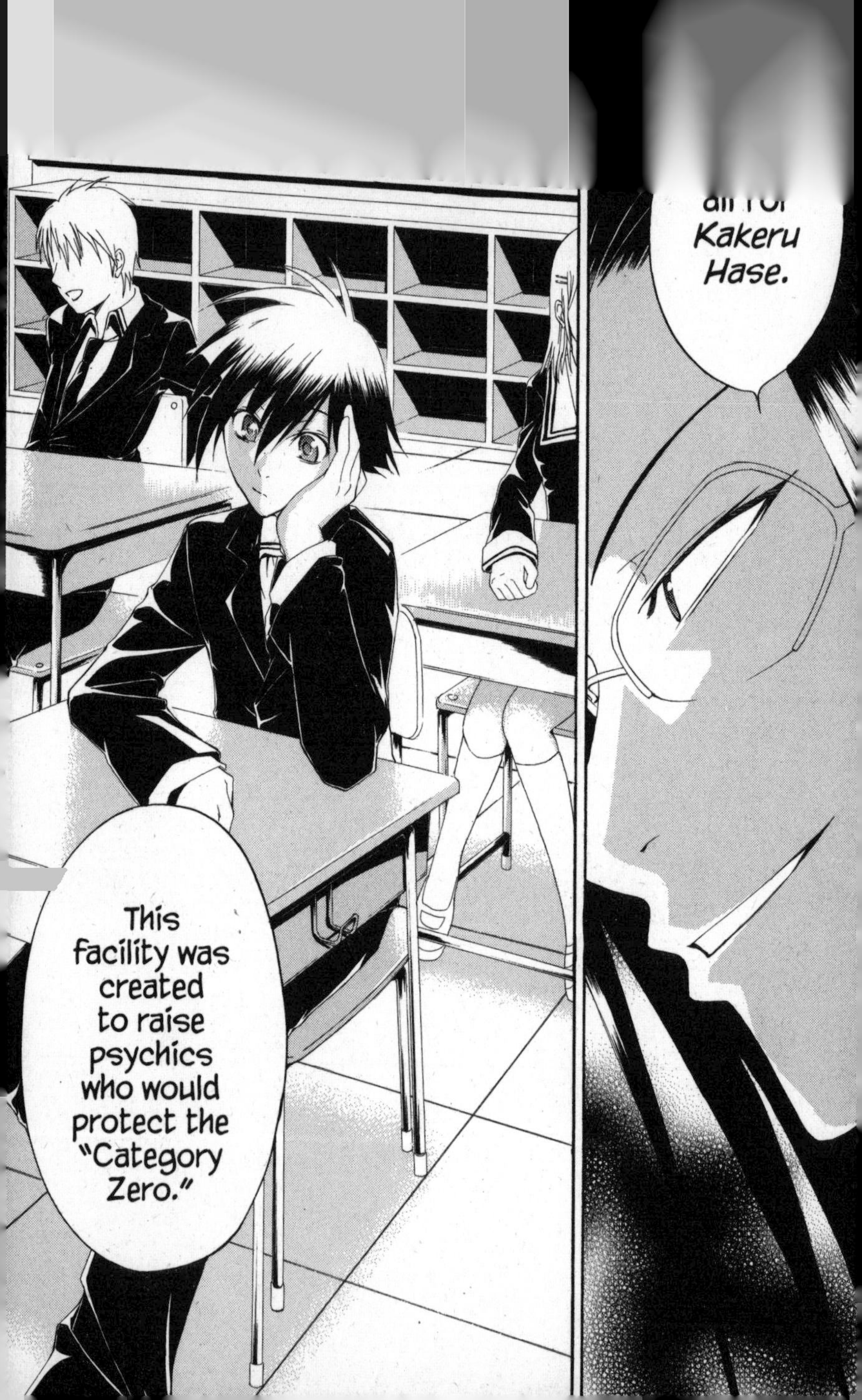
Kakeru Hase.
This facility was created to raise psychics who would protect the "Category Zero."

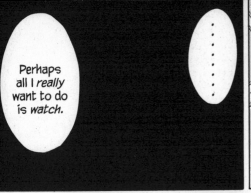

Perhaps
all I *really*
want to do
is *watch*.

THUMP

Watch the
end of
this false
reality,

and the
"true
future"
which
ought to
be woven.

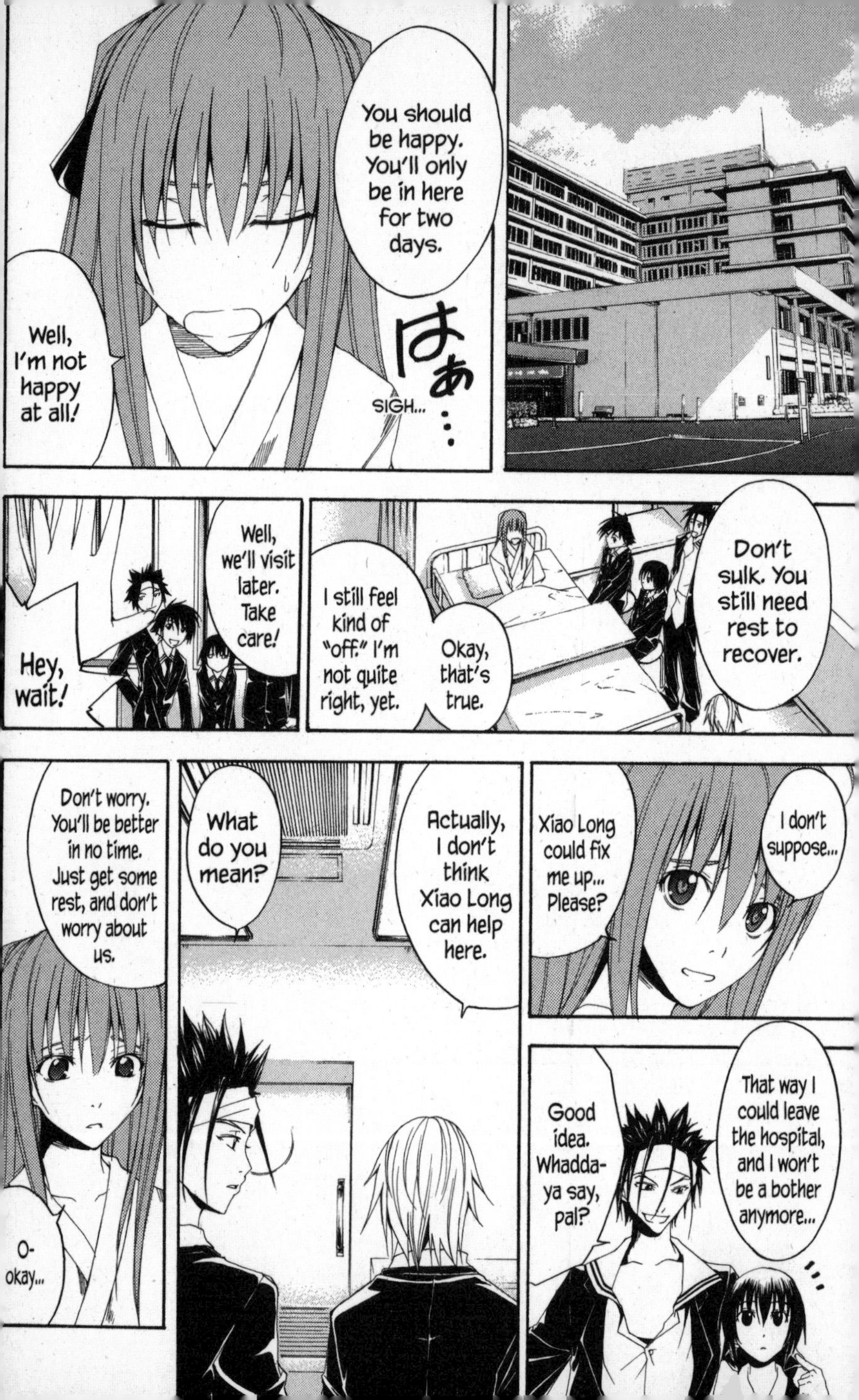
You should be happy. You'll only be in here for two days.
はぁ…
SIGH...
Well, I'm not happy at all!
Don't sulk. You still need rest to recover.
Okay, that's true.
I still feel kind of "off." I'm not quite right, yet.
Well, we'll visit later. Take care!
Hey, wait!
I don't suppose...
Xiao Long could fix me up... Please?
That way I could leave the hospital, and I won't be a bother anymore...
Good idea. Whadda-ya say, pal?
Actually, I don't think Xiao Long can help here.
What do you mean?
Don't worry. You'll be better in no time. Just get some rest, and don't worry about us.
O-okay...

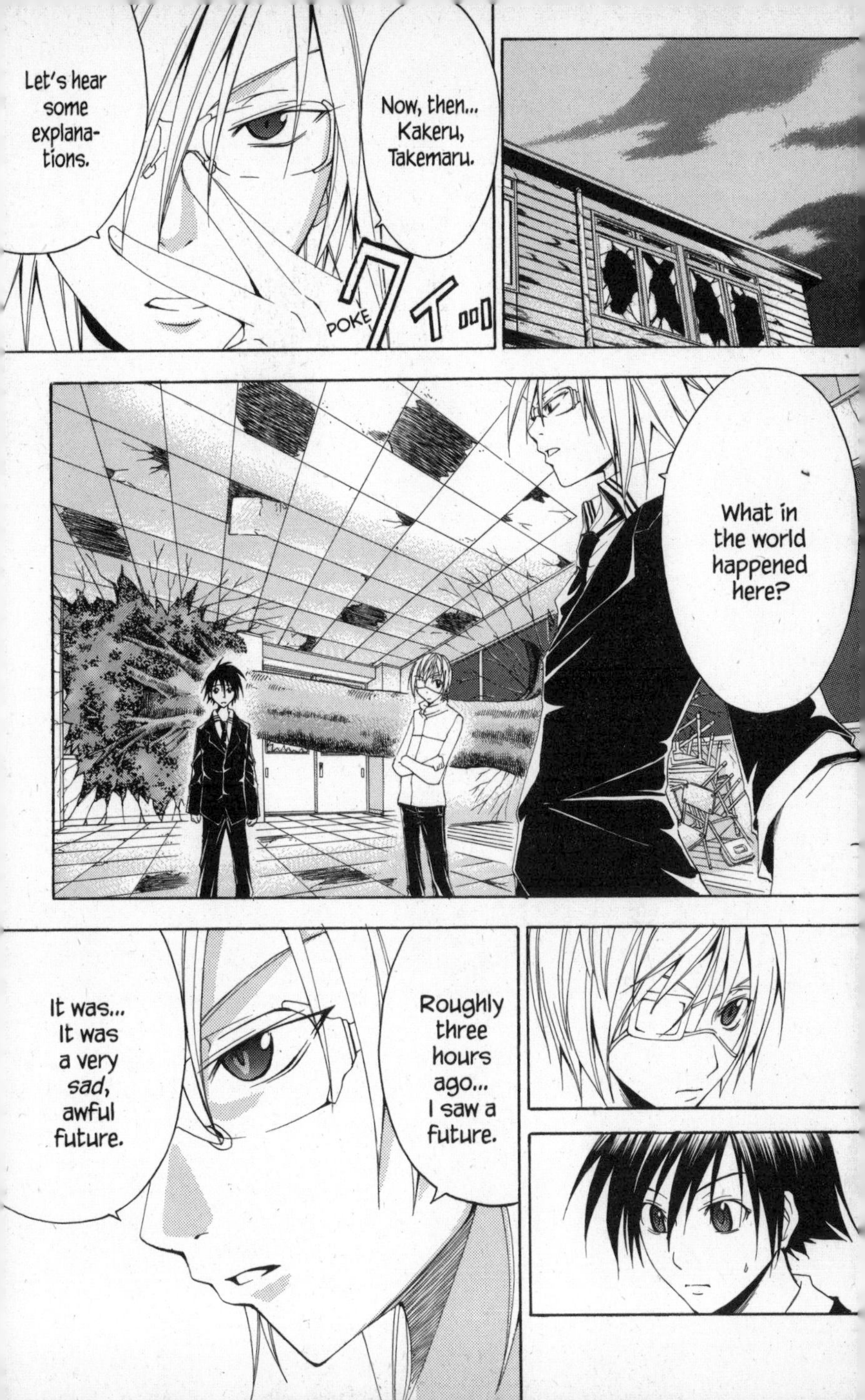
Now, then... Kakeru, Takemaru.
Let's hear some explana-tions.
POKE
What in the world happened here?
Roughly three hours ago... I saw a future.
It was... It was a very *sad*, awful future.

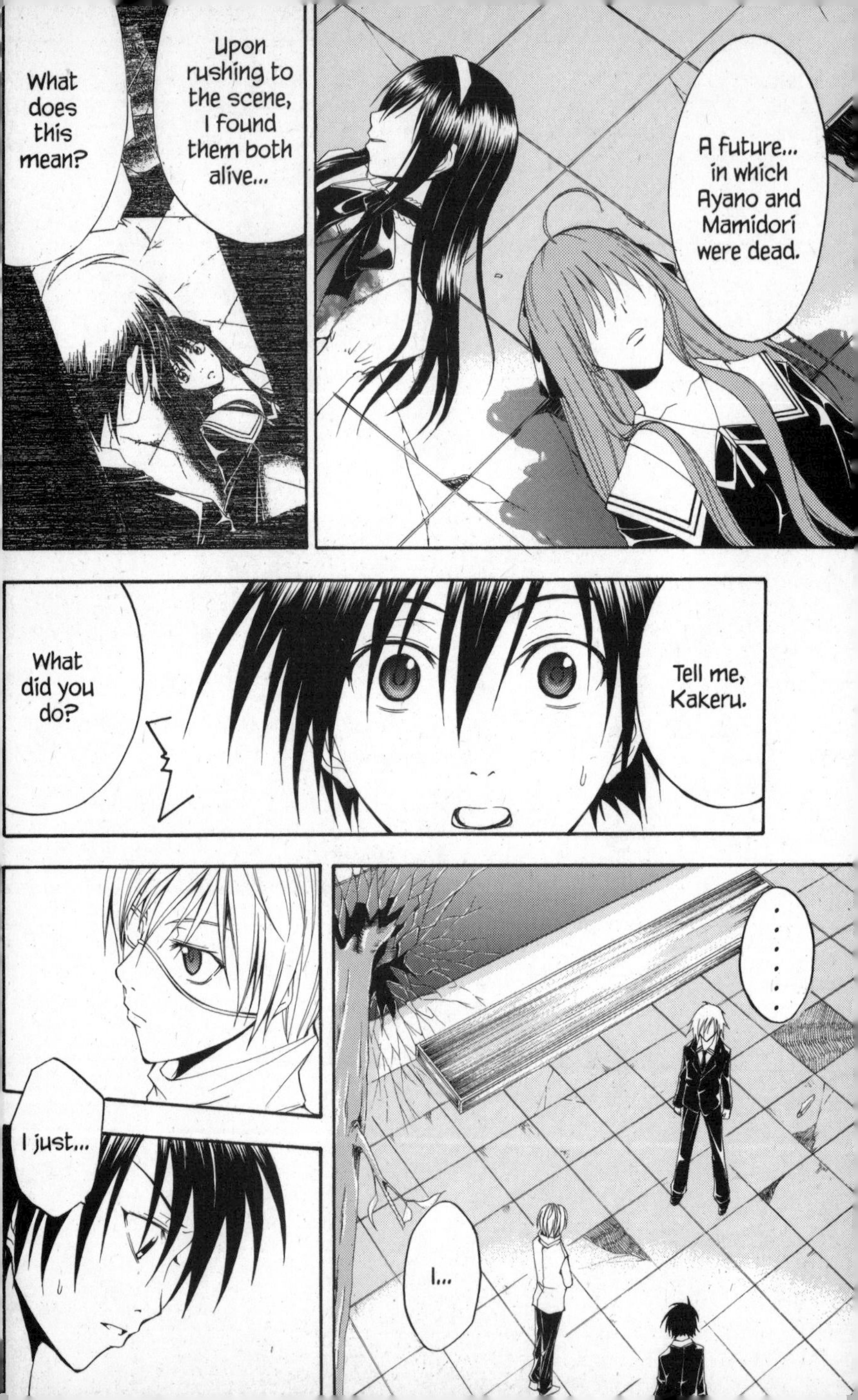
A future... in which Ayano and Mamidori were dead.
Upon rushing to the scene, I found them both alive...
What does this mean?
Tell me, Kakeru.
What did you do?
......
I...
I just...

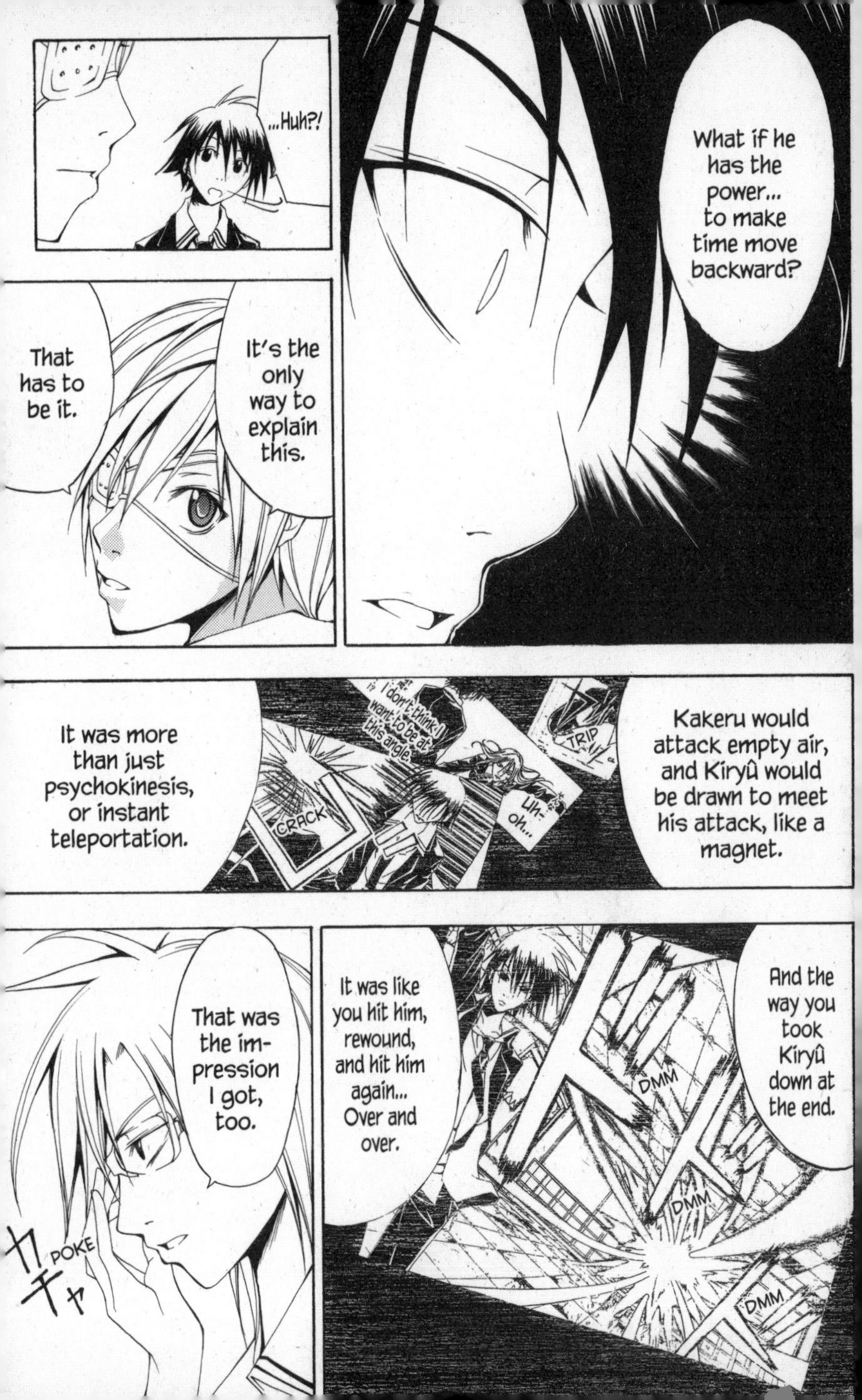
What if he has the power... to make time move backward?
...Huh?!
It's the only way to explain this.
That has to be it.
Kakeru would attack empty air, and Kiryû would be drawn to meet his attack, like a magnet.
TRIP
I don't think I want to be at this angle.
Uh-oh...
CRACK
It was more than just psychokinesis, or instant teleportation.
And the way you took Kiryû down at the end.
DMM
DMM
DMM
It was like you hit him, rewound, and hit him again... Over and over.
That was the impression I got, too.
POKE
カチャ

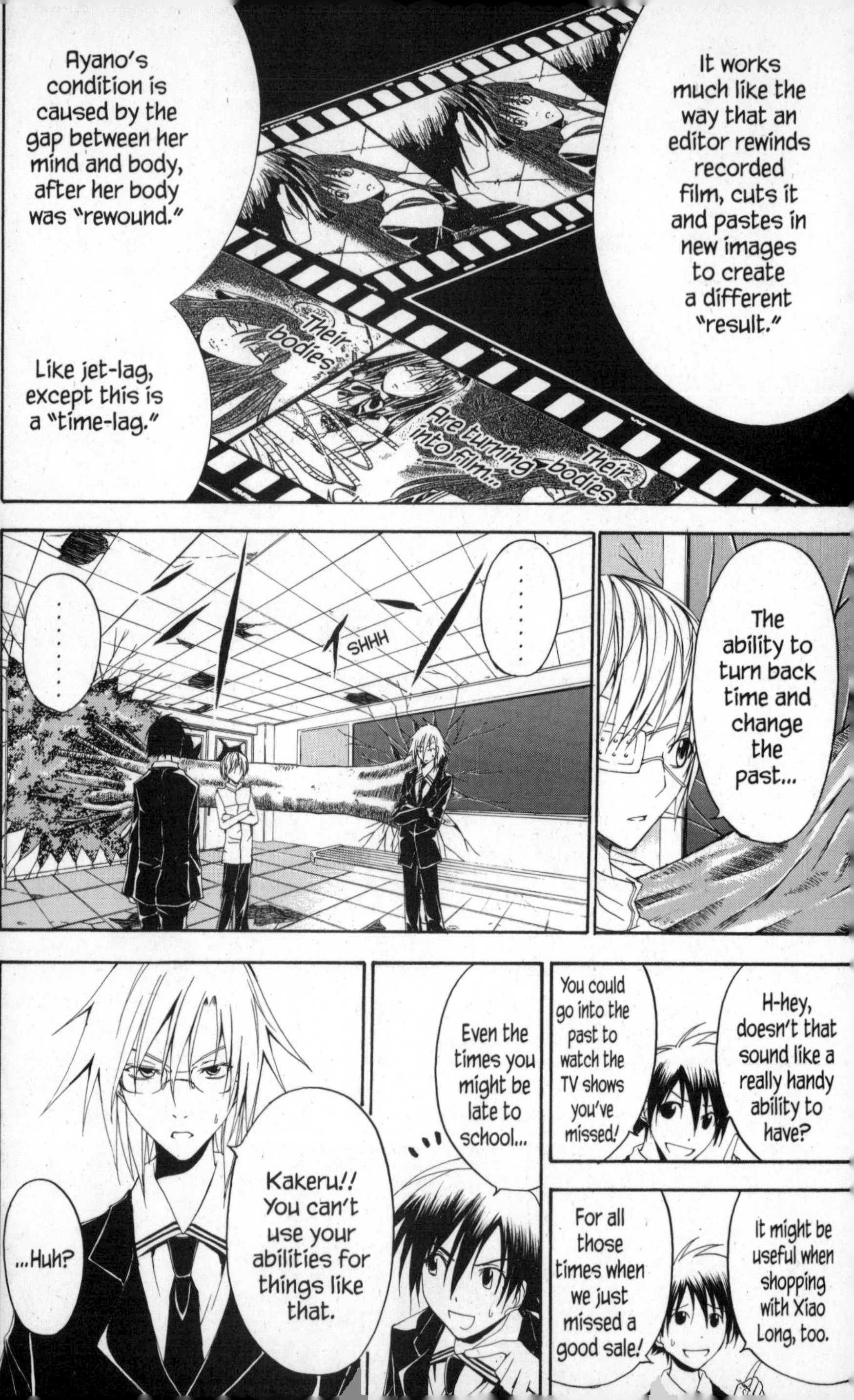
It works much like the way that an editor rewinds recorded film, cuts it and pastes in new images to create a different "result."
Their bodies
Their bodies
Are turning into film...
Ayano's condition is caused by the gap between her mind and body, after her body was "rewound."
Like jet-lag, except this is a "time-lag."
The ability to turn back time and change the past...
......
SHHH
......
H-hey, doesn't that sound like a really handy ability to have?
You could go into the past to watch the TV shows you've missed!
It might be useful when shopping with Xiao Long, too.
For all those times when we just missed a good sale!
Even the times you might be late to school...
...
Kakeru!! You can't use your abilities for things like that.
...Huh?

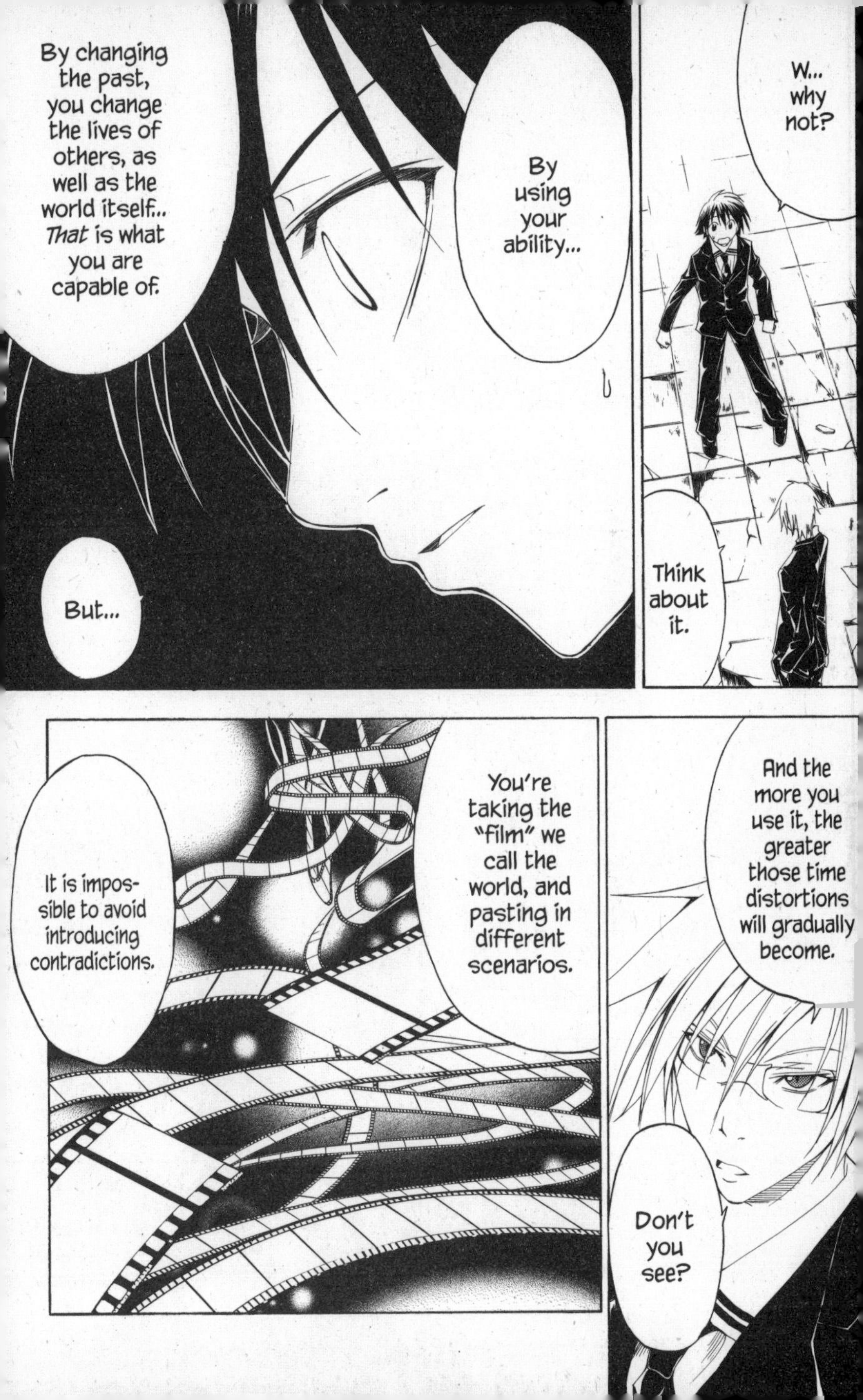

W... why not?
Think about it.
By using your ability...
By changing the past, you change the lives of others, as well as the world itself... *That* is what you are capable of.
But...
And the more you use it, the greater those time distortions will gradually become.
Don't you see?
You're taking the "film" we call the world, and pasting in different scenarios.
It is impos-sible to avoid introducing contradictions.

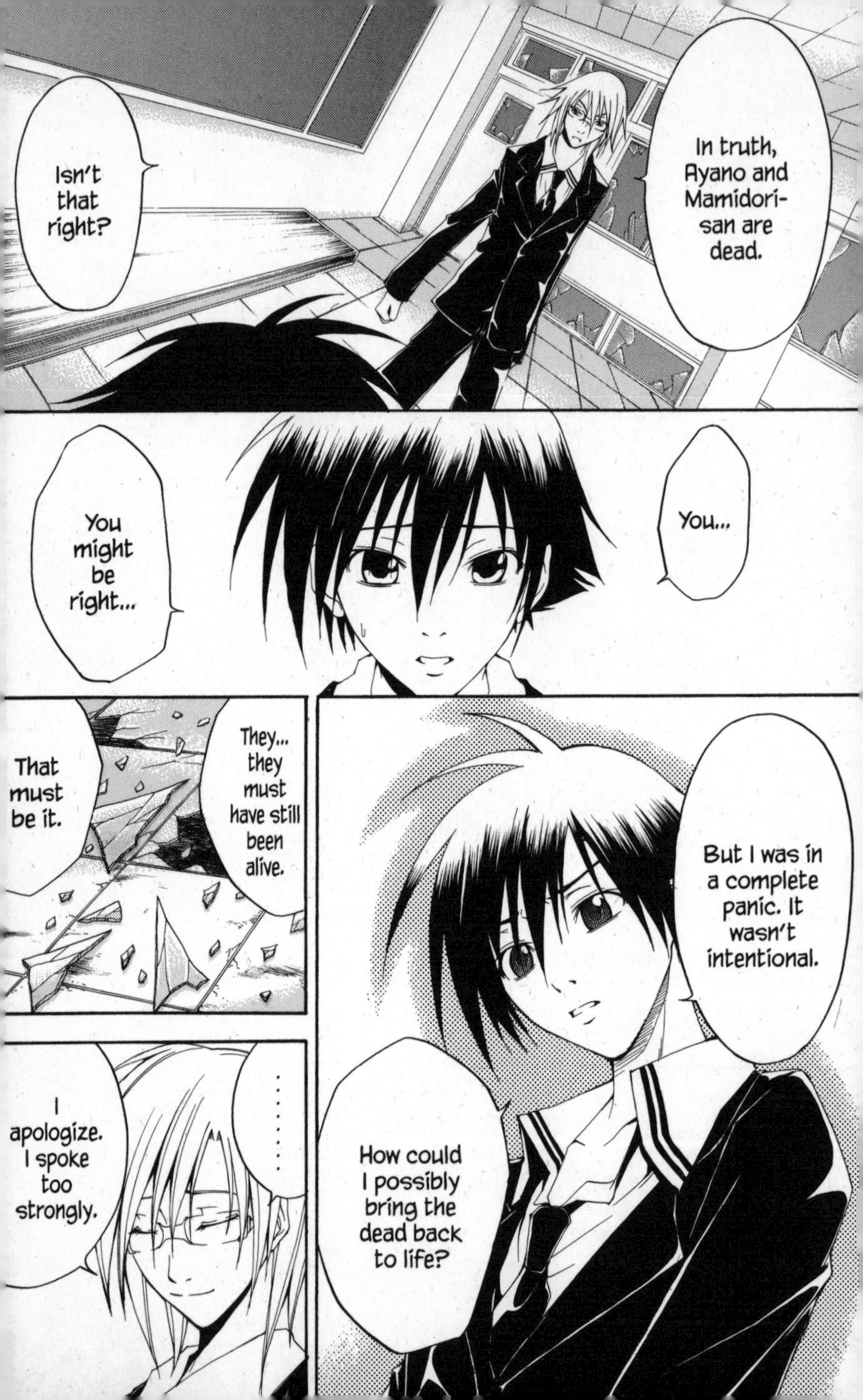
In truth, Ayano and Mamidori-san are dead.
Isn't that right?
You...
You might be right...
But I was in a complete panic. It wasn't intentional.
How could I possibly bring the dead back to life?
They... they must have still been alive.
That must be it.
......
I apologize. I spoke too strongly.

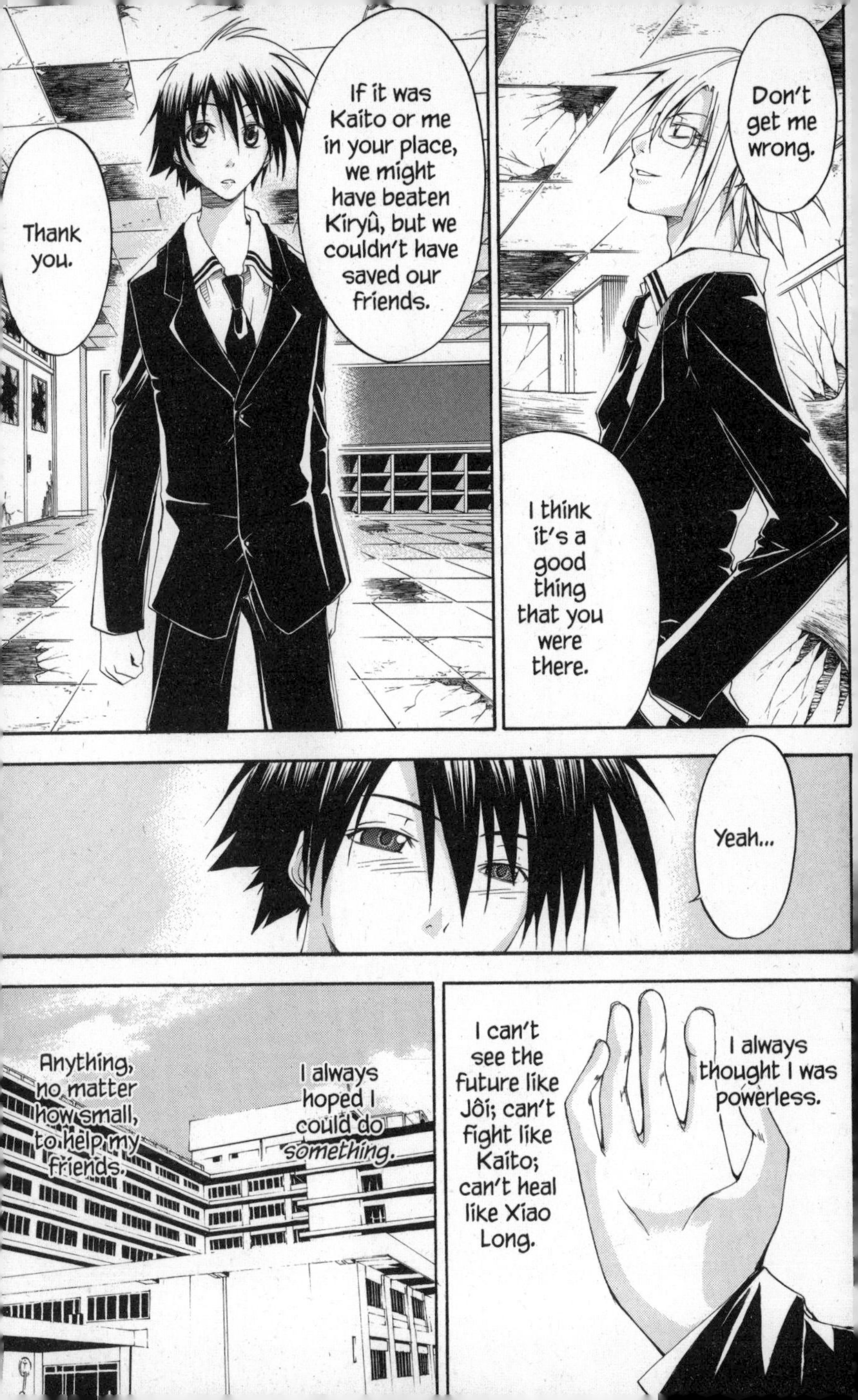
Don't get me wrong.
I think it's a good thing that you were there.
If it was Kaito or me in your place, we might have beaten Kiryû, but we couldn't have saved our friends.
Thank you.
Yeah...
I always thought I was powerless.
I can't see the future like Jôi; can't fight like Kaito; can't heal like Xiao Long.
I always hoped I could do *something*.
Anything, no matter how small, to help my friends.

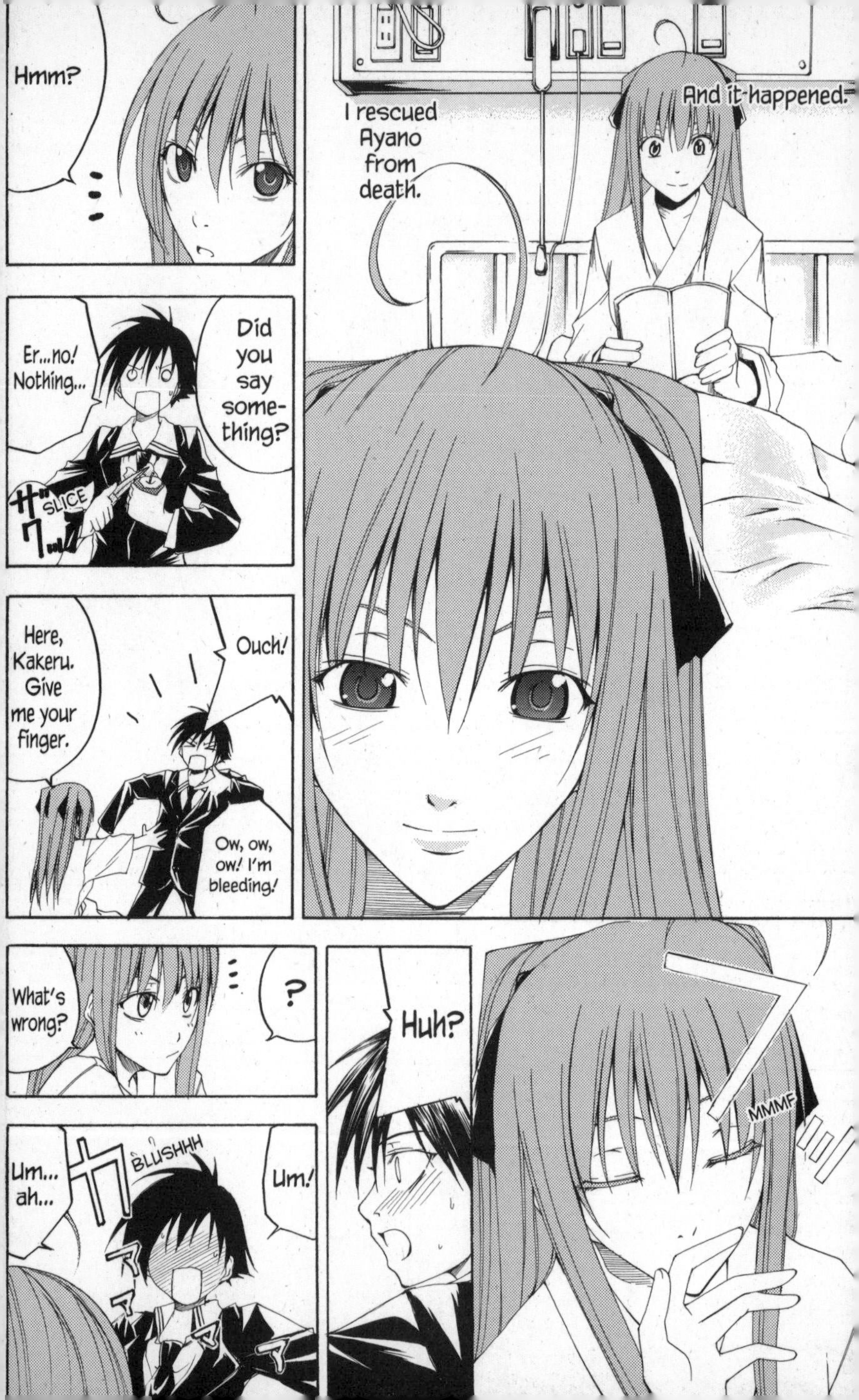
And it happened.
I rescued Ayano from death.
Hmm?
Did you say something?
Er...no! Nothing...
SLICE
Ouch!
Here, Kakeru. Give me your finger.
Ow, ow, ow! I'm bleeding!
MMMF
Huh?
?
What's wrong?
Um!
BLUSHHH
Um... ah...

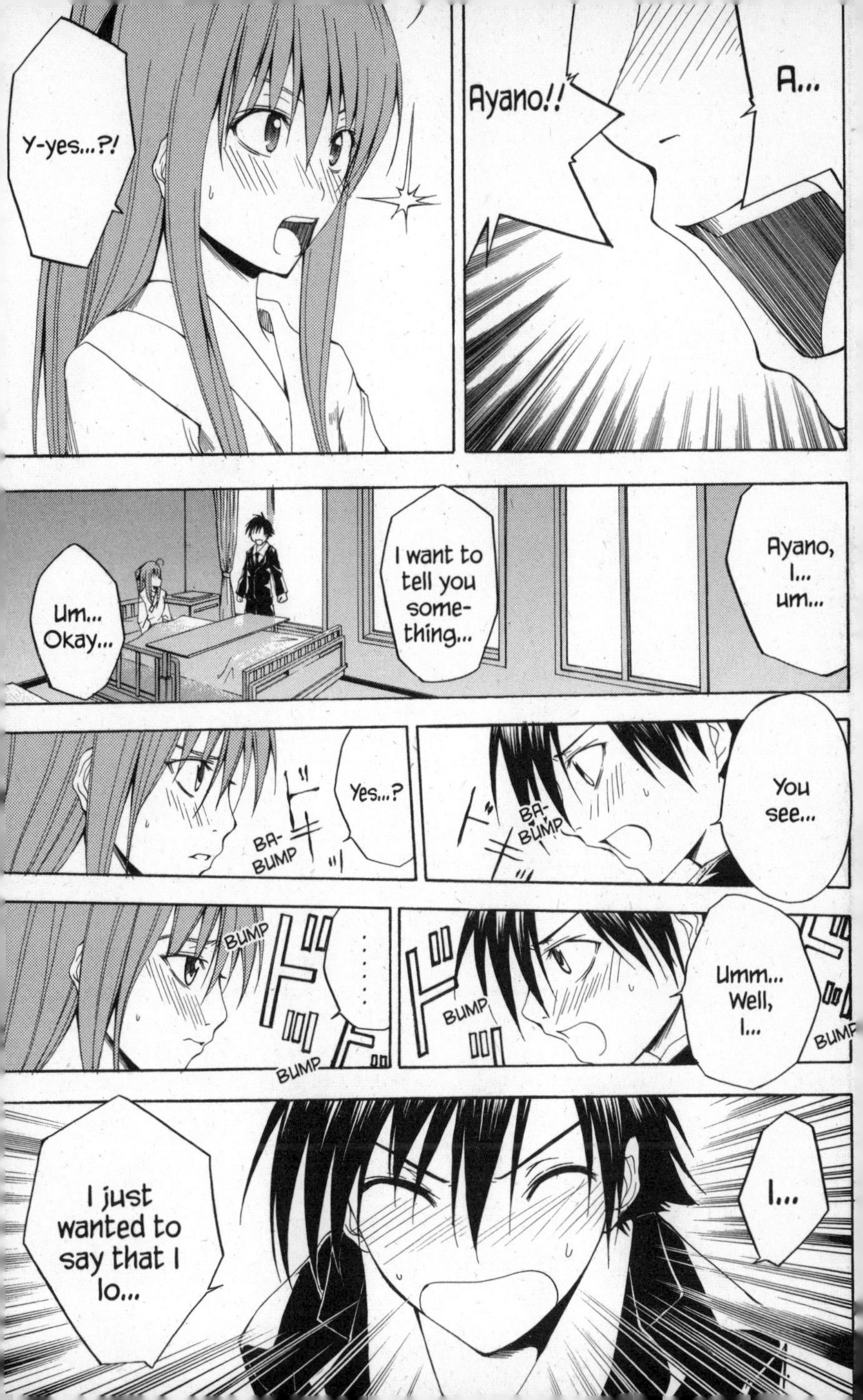
A...
Ayano!!
Y-yes...?!
Ayano, I... um...
I want to tell you something...
Um... Okay...
You see...
BA-BUMP
Yes...?
BA-BUMP
Umm... Well, I...
BUMP
BUMP
......
BUMP
BUMP
I...
I just wanted to say that I lo...

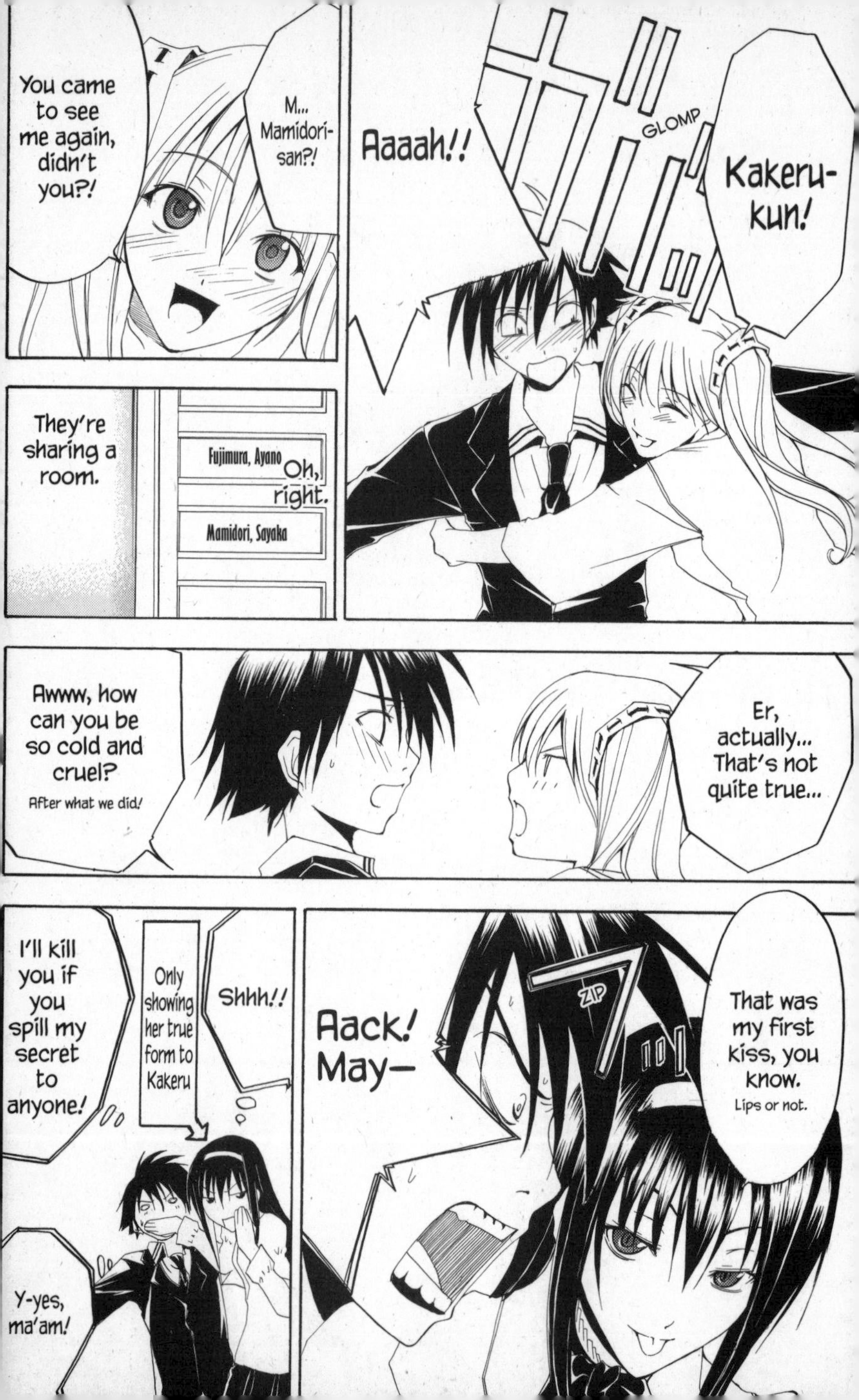
Kakeru-kun!
GLOMP
Aaaah!!
M... Mamidori-san?!
You came to see me again, didn't you?!
Oh, right.
Fujimura, Ayano
Mamidori, Sayaka
They're sharing a room.
Er, actually... That's not quite true...
Awww, how can you be so cold and cruel?
After what we did!
That was my first kiss, you know.
Lips or not.
ZIP
Aack! May—
Shhh!!
Only showing her true form to Kakeru
I'll kill you if you spill my secret to anyone!
Y-yes, ma'am!

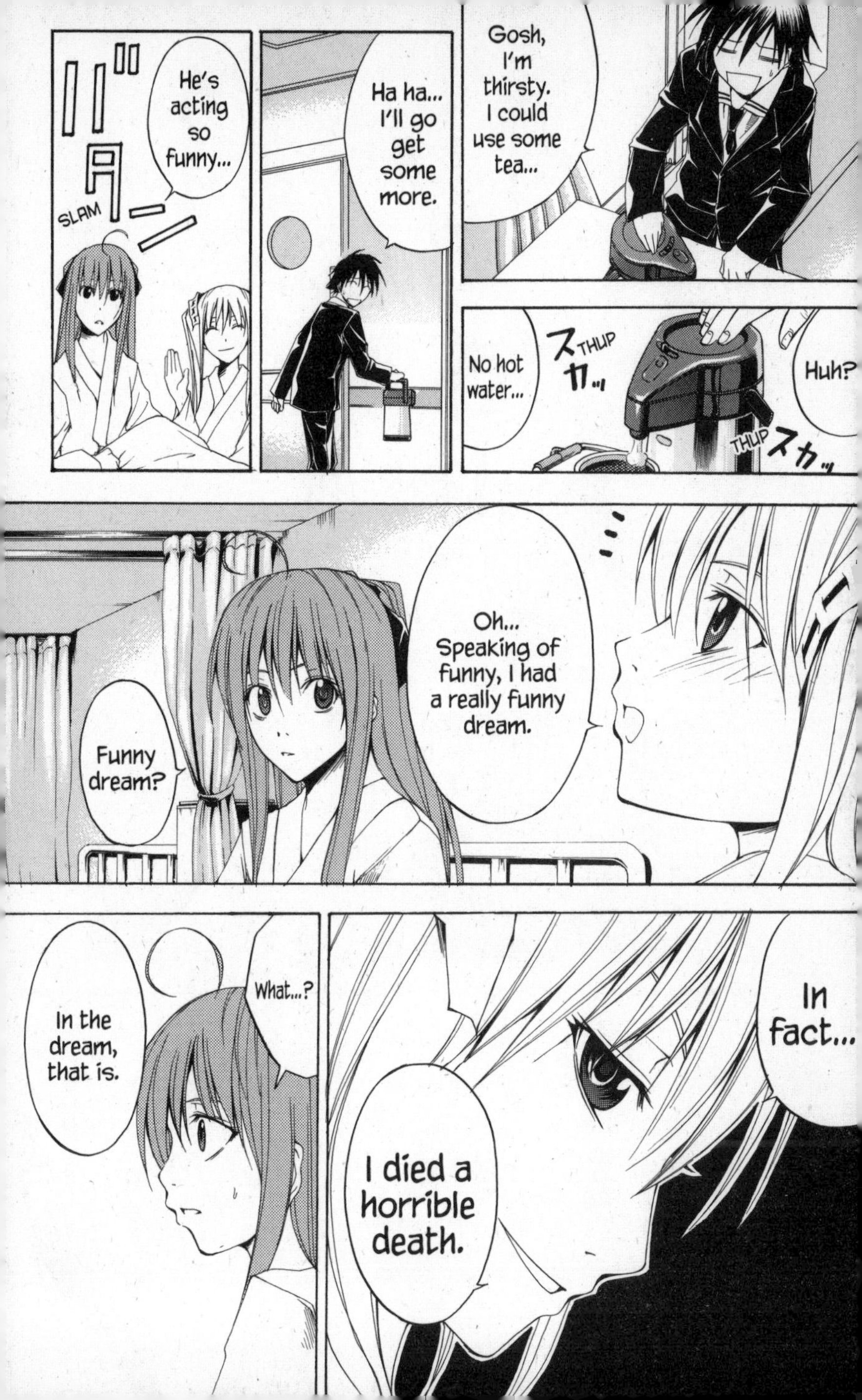
Gosh, I'm thirsty. I could use some tea...
Huh?
THUP
No hot water...
THUP
Ha ha... I'll go get some more.
He's acting so funny...
SLAM
Oh... Speaking of funny, I had a really funny dream.
Funny dream?
In fact...
I died a horrible death.
What...?
In the dream, that is.

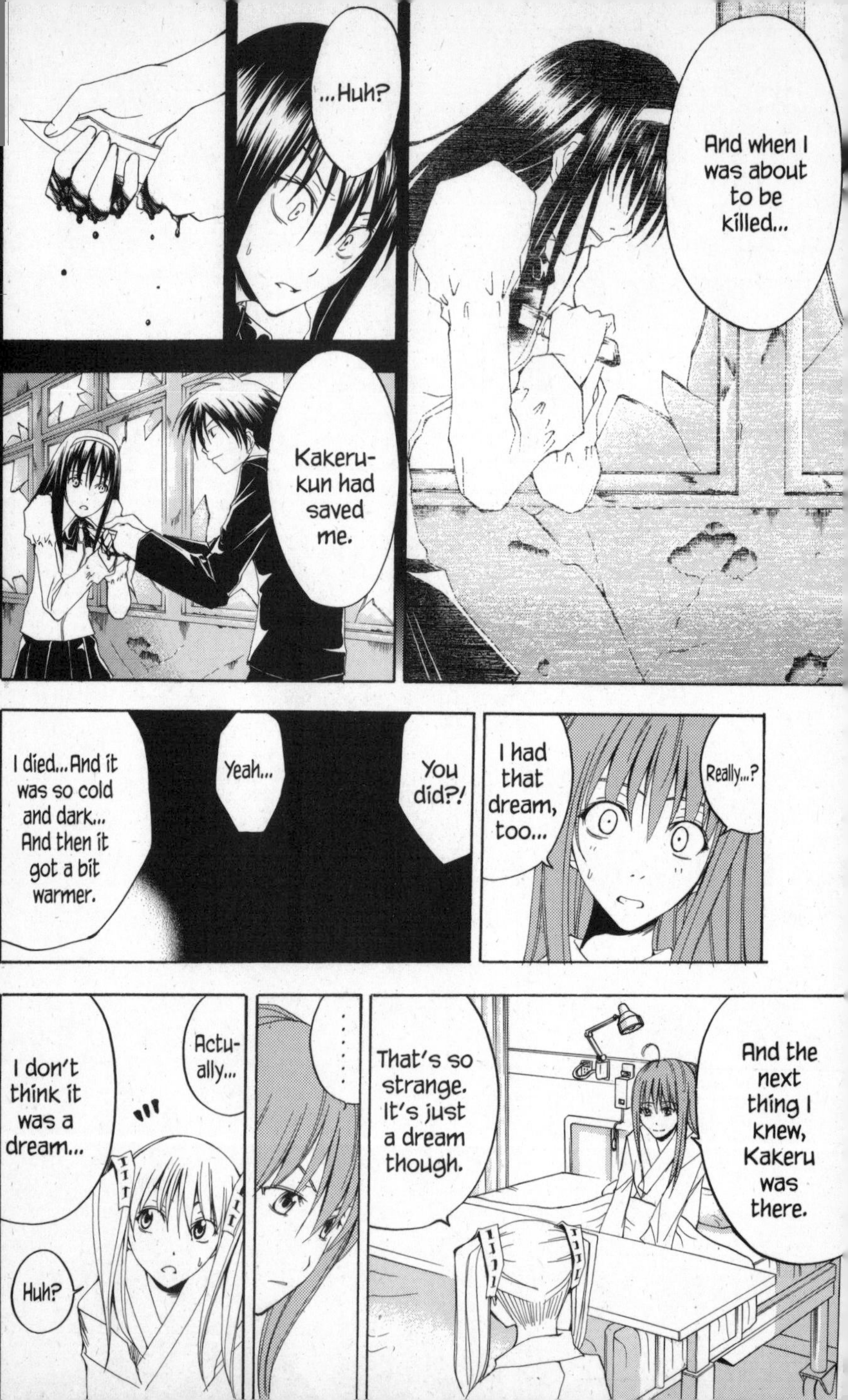
And when I was about to be killed...
...Huh?
Kakeru-kun had saved me.
Really...?
I had that dream, too...
You did?!
Yeah...
I died...And it was so cold and dark... And then it got a bit warmer.
And the next thing I knew, Kakeru was there.
That's so strange. It's just a dream though.
......
Actu-ally...
I don't think it was a dream...
Huh?

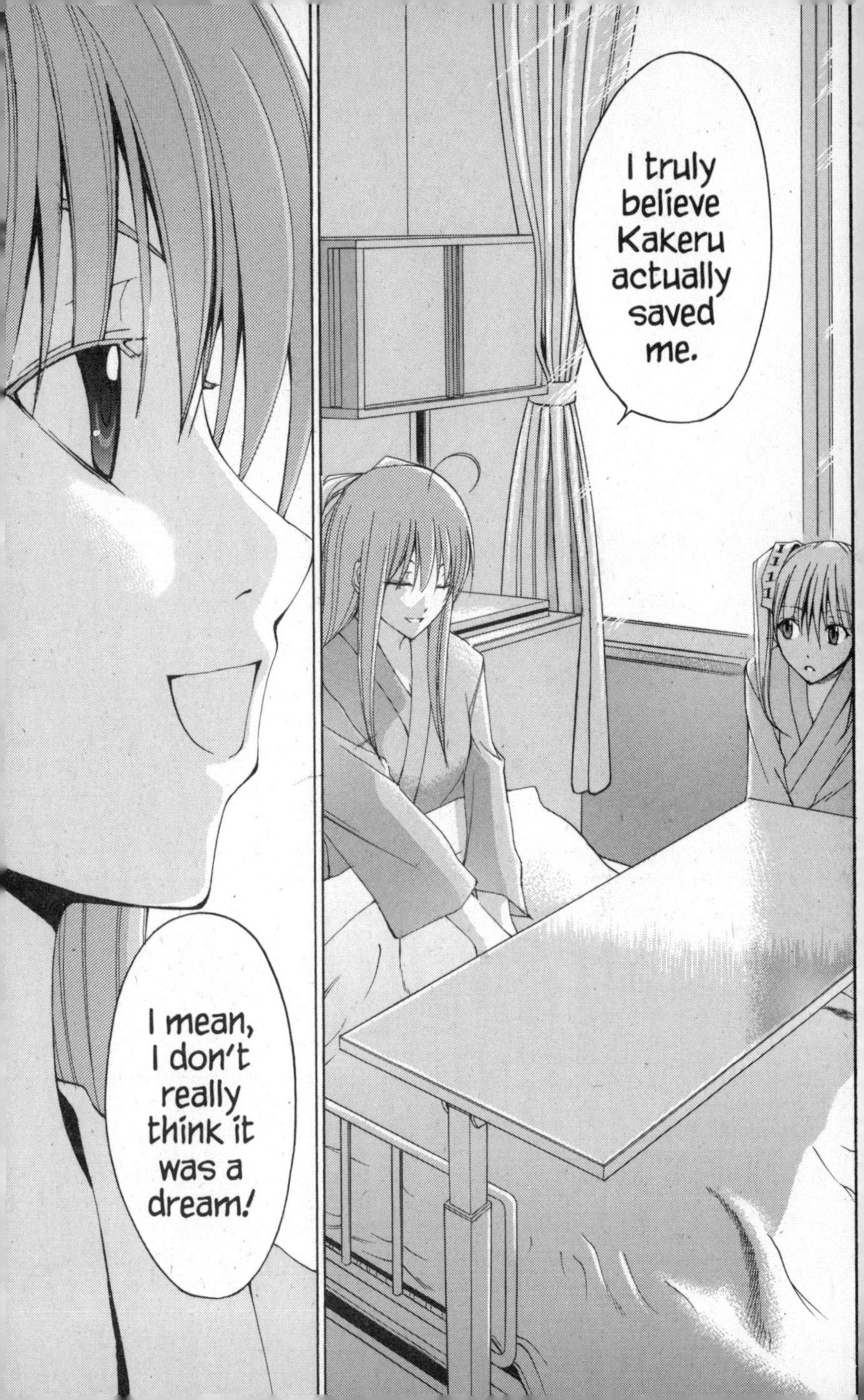
I truly believe Kakeru actually saved me.
I mean, I don't really think it was a dream!

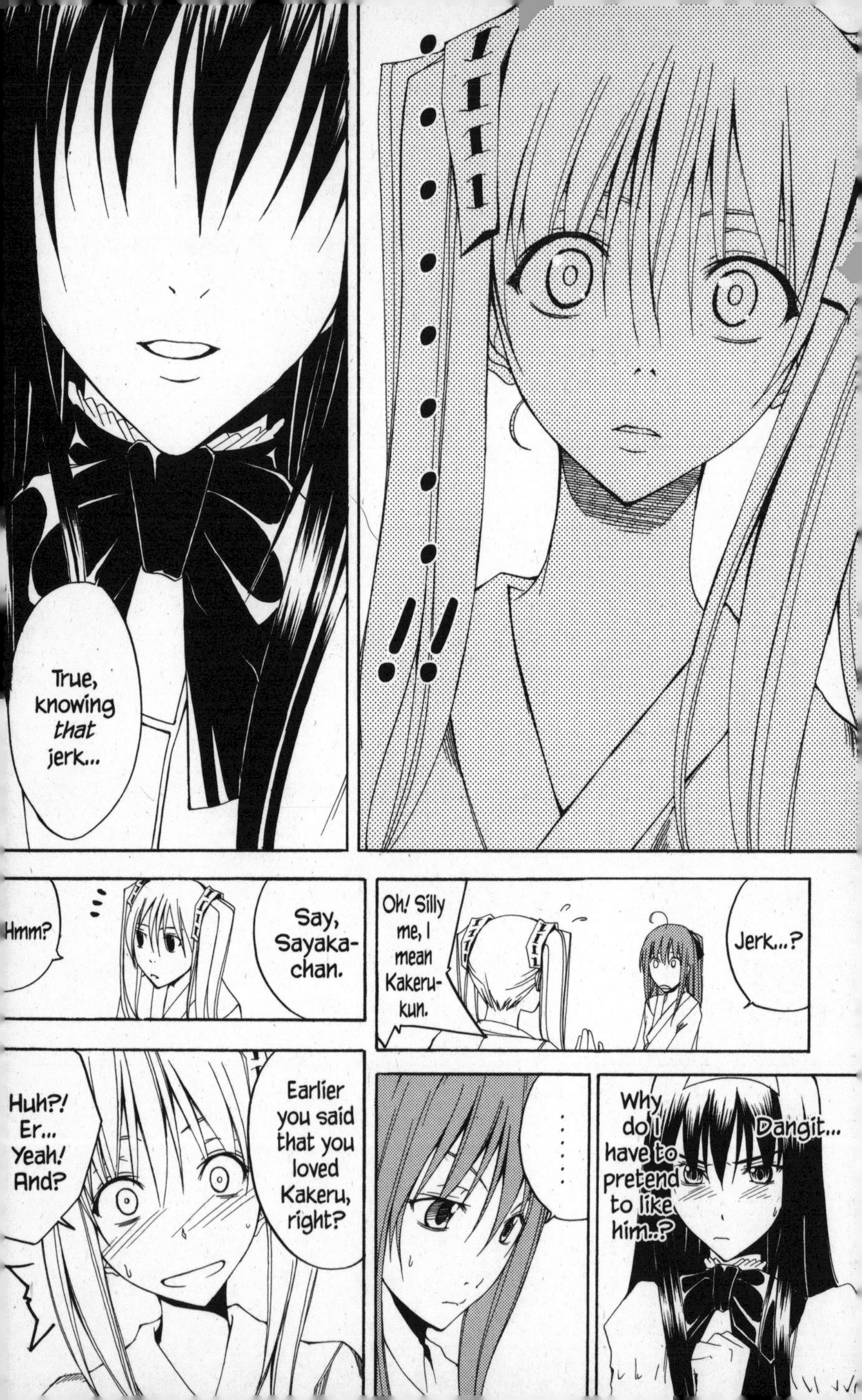
......!!
True, knowing *that* jerk...
Jerk...?
Oh! Silly me, I mean Kakeru-kun.
Say, Sayaka-chan.
Hmm?
Dangit...
Why do I have to pretend to like him..?
......
Earlier you said that you loved Kakeru, right?
Huh?! Er... Yeah! And?

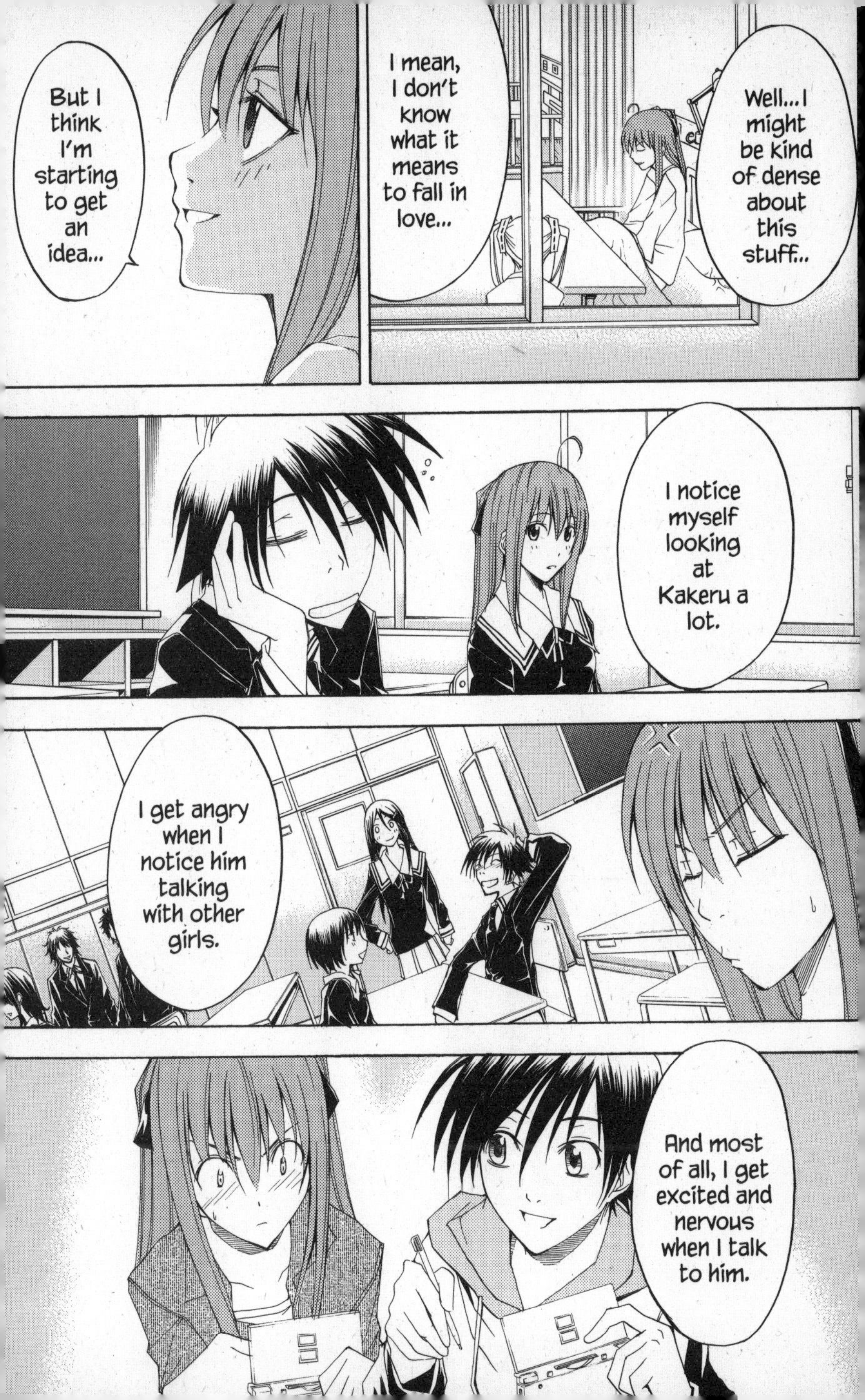
Well...I might be kind of dense about this stuff...
I mean, I don't know what it means to fall in love...
But I think I'm starting to get an idea...
I notice myself looking at Kakeru a lot.
I get angry when I notice him talking with other girls.
And most of all, I get excited and nervous when I talk to him.

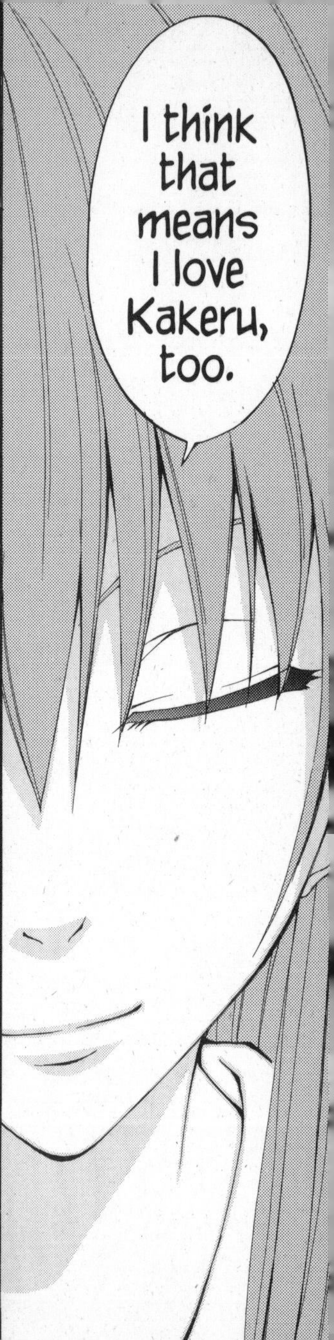
I think that means I love Kakeru, too.
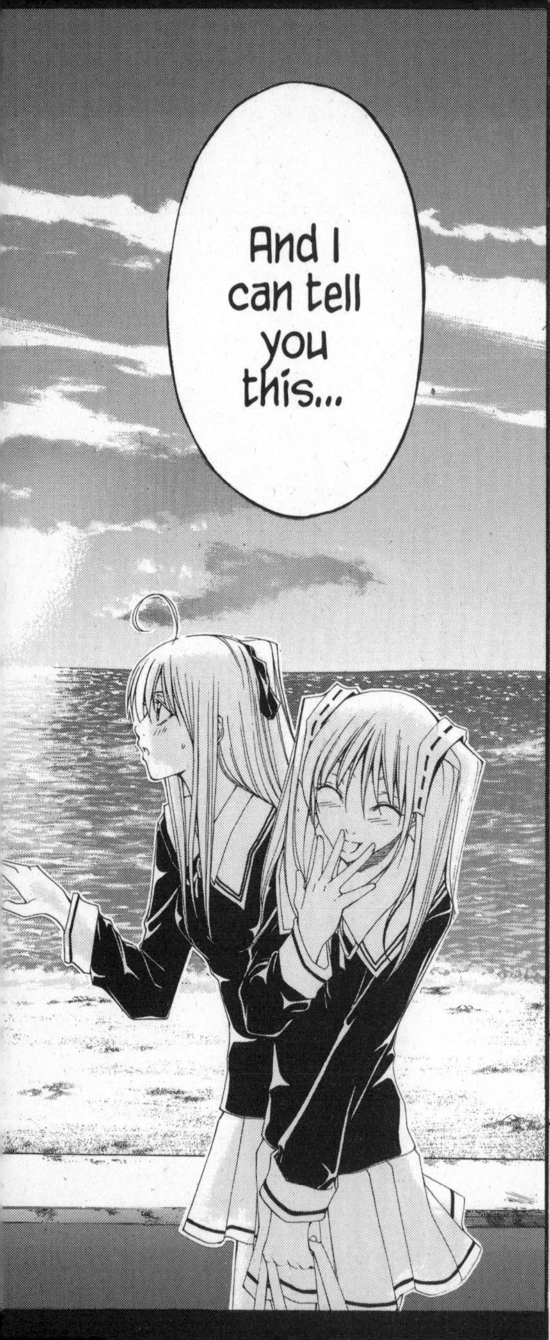
And I can tell you this...

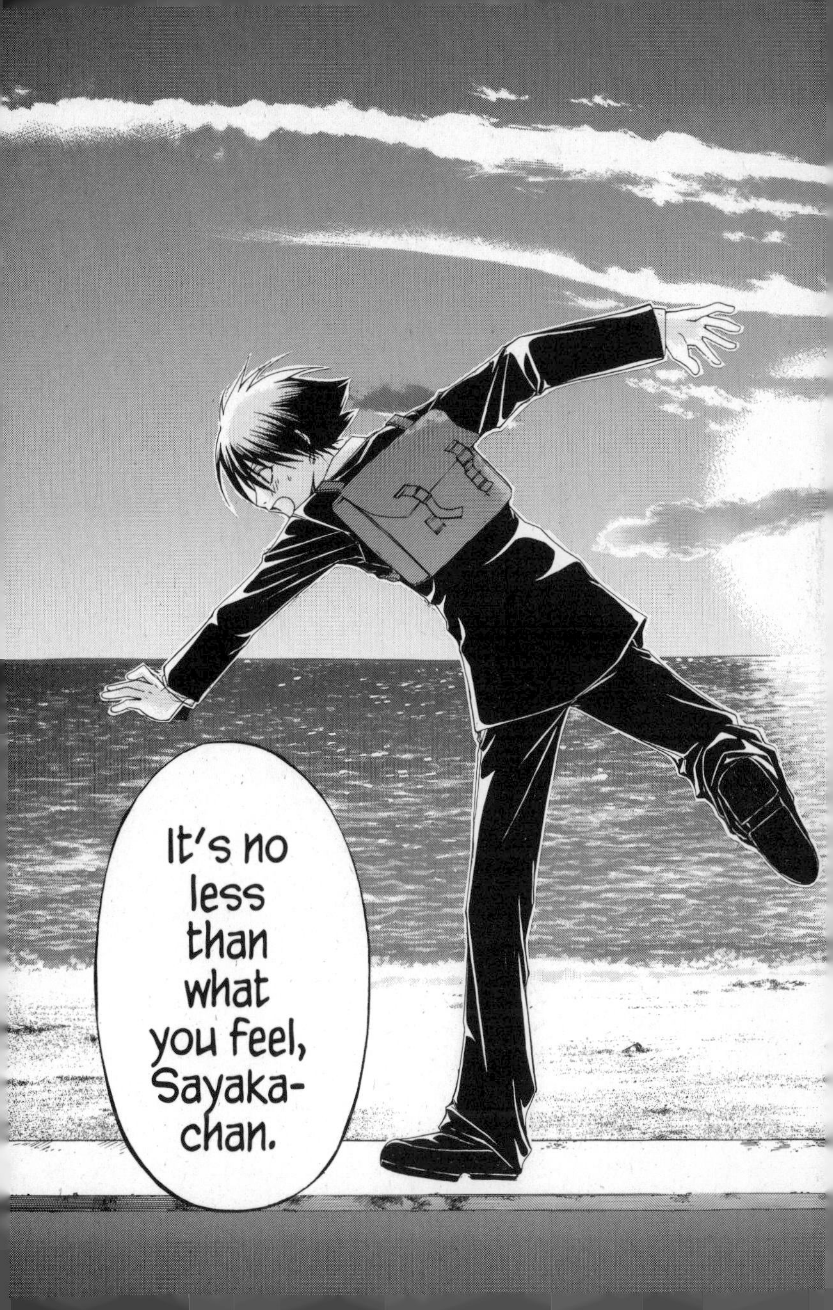
It's no less than what you feel, Sayaka-chan.

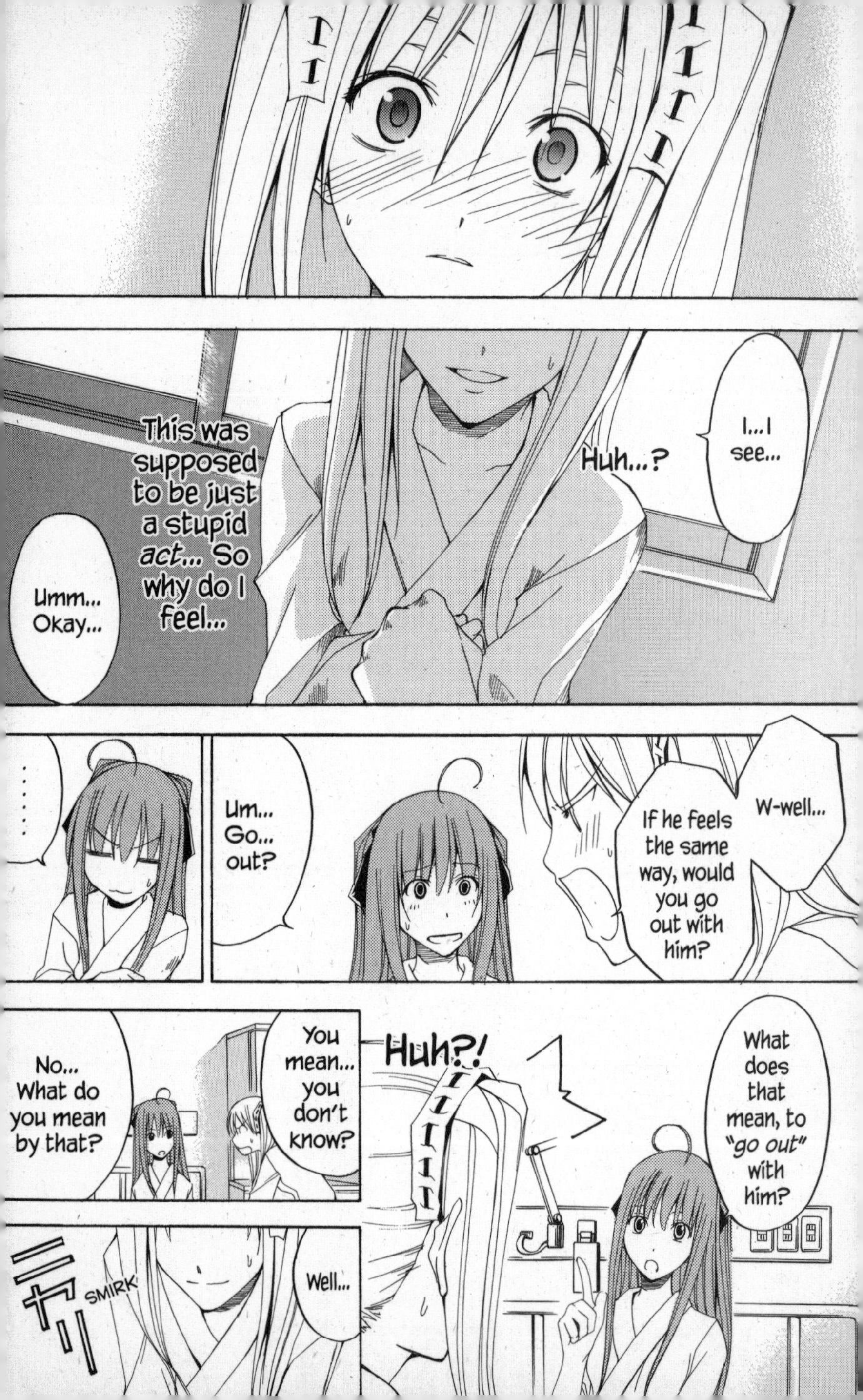
I...I see...
Huh...?
This was supposed to be just a stupid *act*... So why do I feel...
Umm... Okay...
W-well...
If he feels the same way, would you go out with him?
Um... Go... out?
......
What does that mean, to *"go out"* with him?
Huh?!
You mean... you don't know?
No... What do you mean by that?
Well...
SMIRK

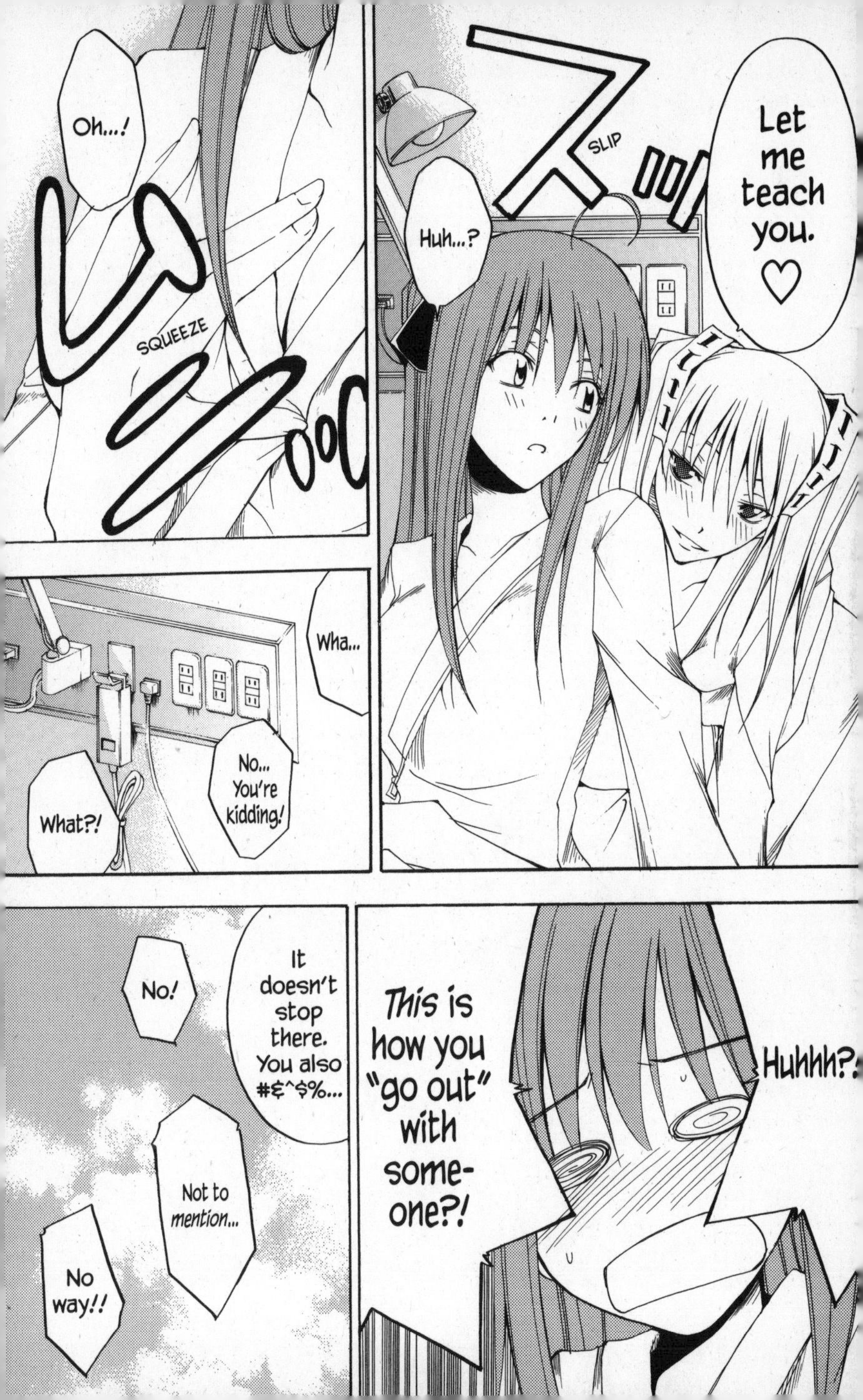
Let me teach you. ♡
SLIP
Huh...?
Oh...!
SQUEEZE
Wha...
No... You're kidding!
What?!
Huhhh?!
This is how you "go out" with some-one?!
It doesn't stop there. You also #&^$%...
No!
Not to mention...
No way!!

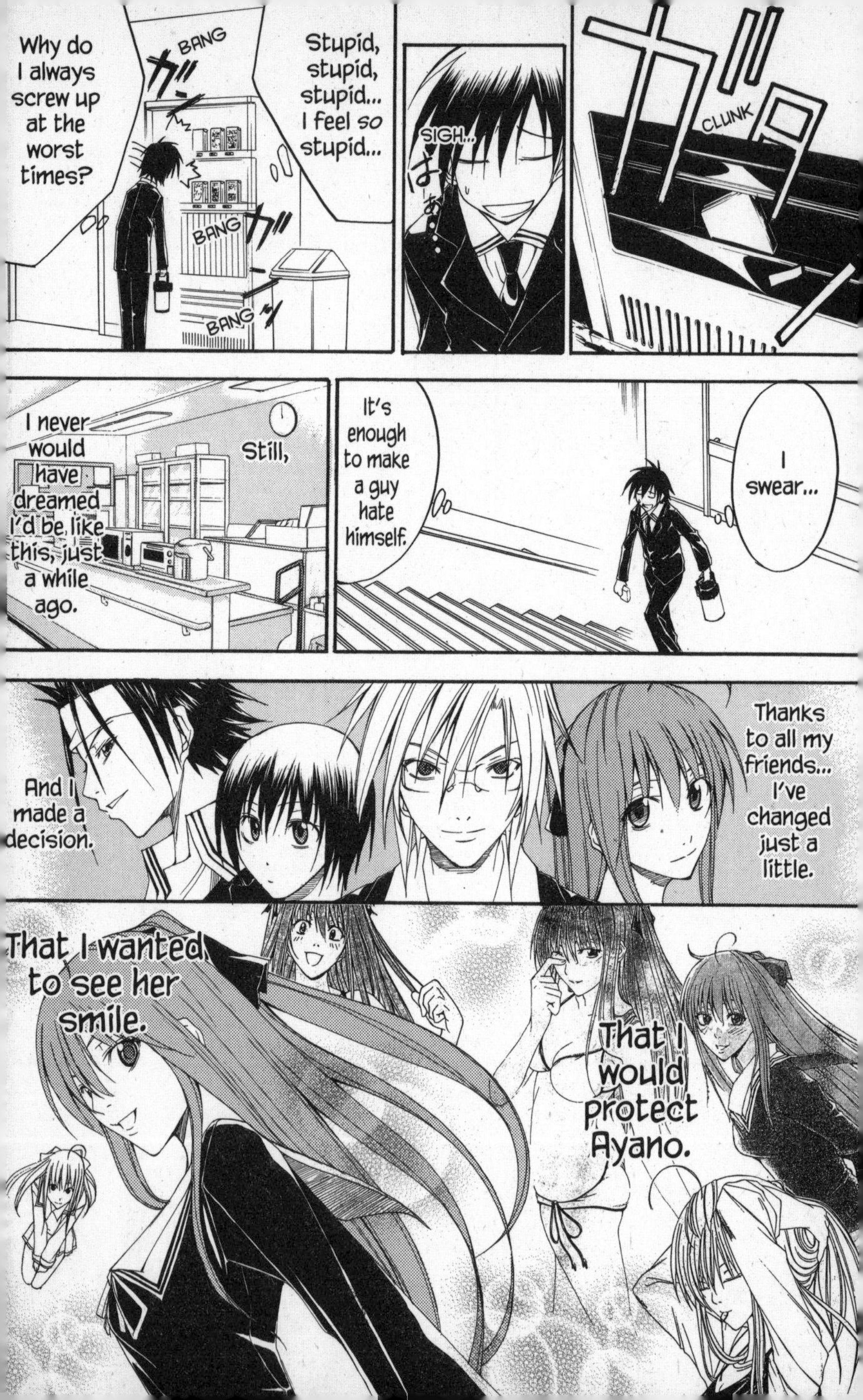

CLUNK
SIGH...
Stupid, stupid, stupid... I feel so stupid...
BANG
BANG
BANG
Why do I always screw up at the worst times?
I swear...
It's enough to make a guy hate himself.
Still,
I never would have dreamed I'd be like this, just a while ago.
Thanks to all my friends... I've changed just a little.
And I made a decision.
That I wanted to see her smile.
That I would protect Ayano.

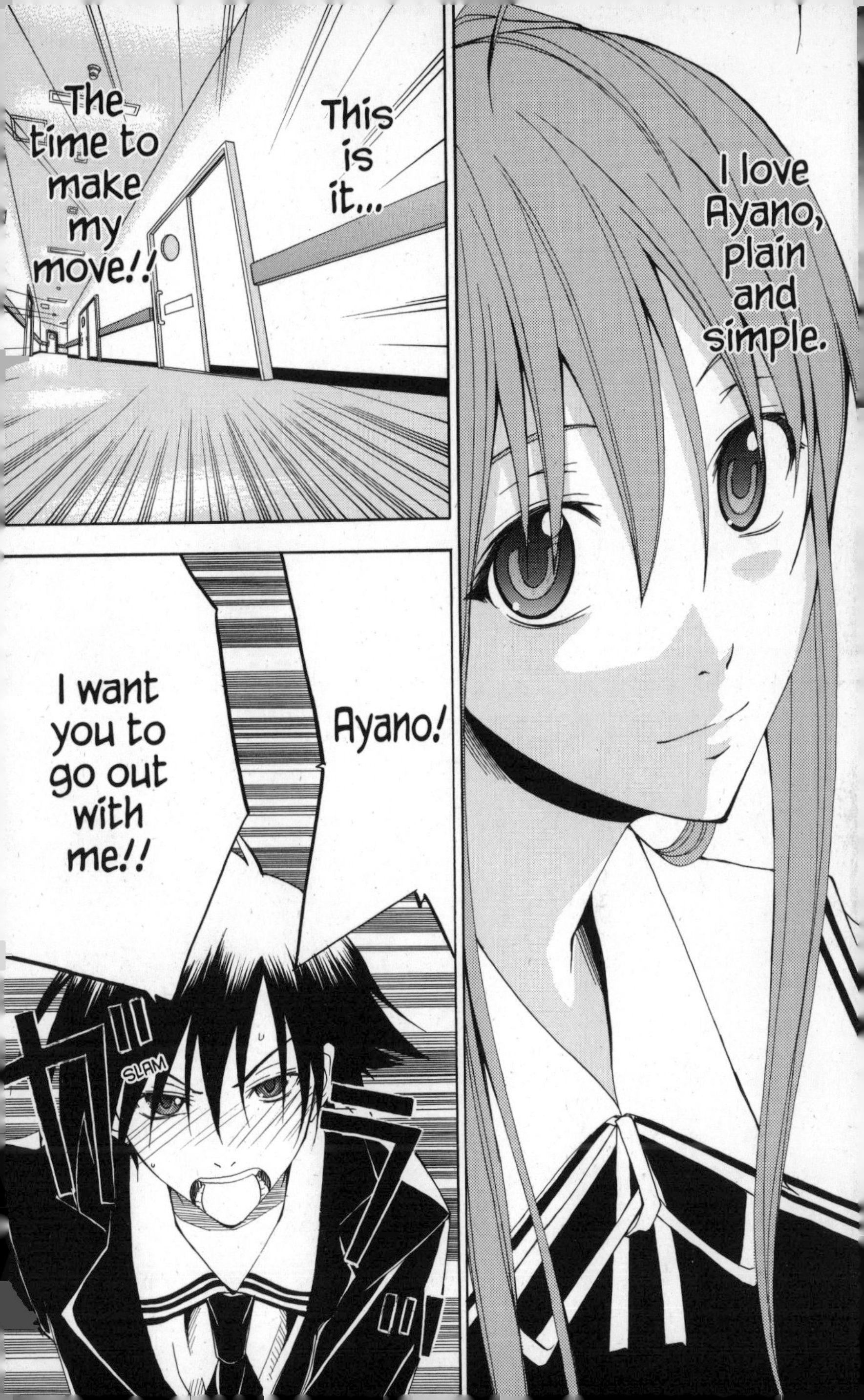
I love Ayano, plain and simple.
This is it...
The time to make my move!!
Ayano!
I want you to go out with me!!
SLAM

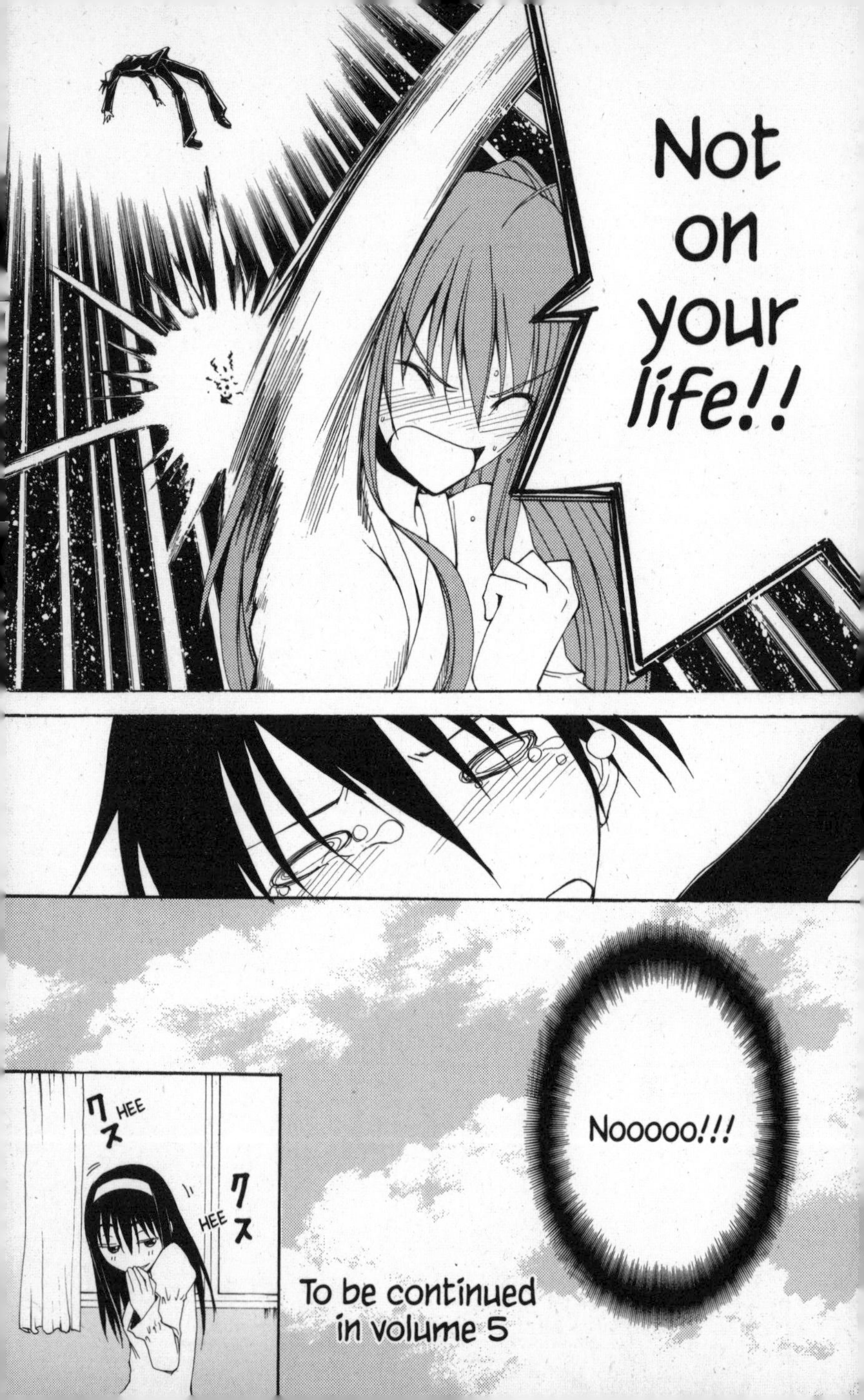
Not on your life!!
Nooooo!!!
クス HEE
クス HEE
To be continued in volume 5

STAFF: Yûya Aoki
Akinari Nao
Tatsu Nakajima
Naoto Shinoda
Kiyomizu
Subaru Matsuyama

SPECIAL THANKS:
Keitarô Yanagibashi

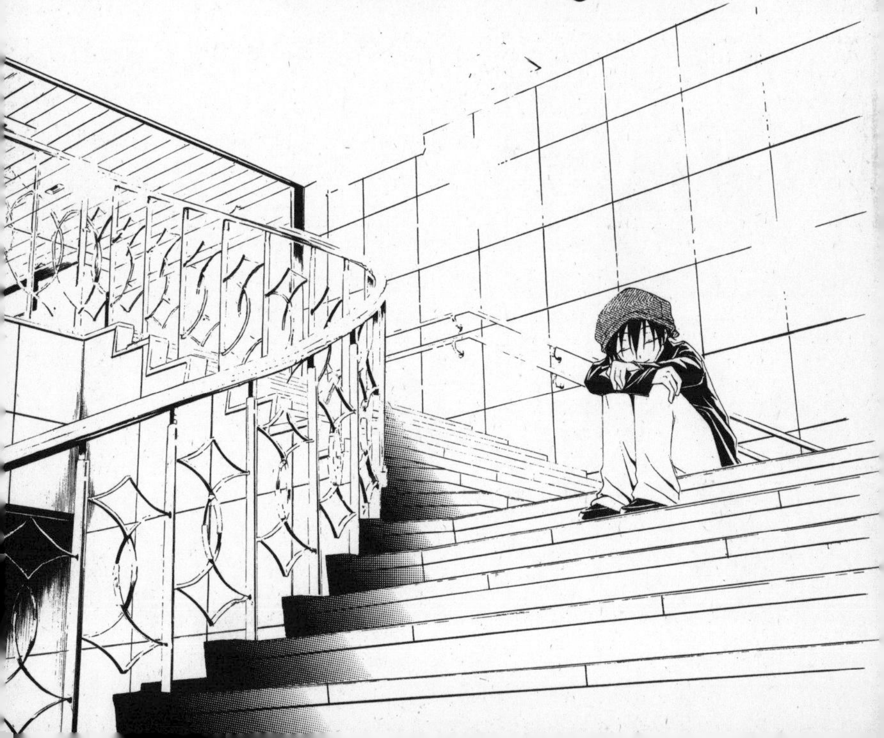

Omake 4-Panel Manga

Daily Psycho Busters

Kaito's Powers

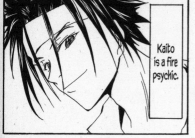

Kaito is a fire psychic.
I'll burn you to a crisp!
That means he can shoot fire from his body. He's one tough dude!
FWOOOM
I wonder sometimes. Doesn't it get hot, shooting fire from his hands?
Nah, being a fire psychic must make him impervious to heat.
Oh, no thanks. My tongue is sensitive to hot liquids.

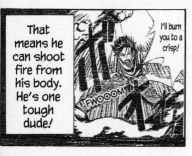

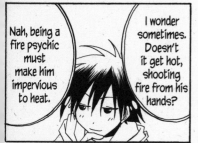

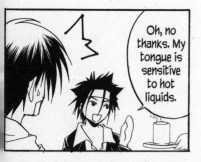

Cooking Class

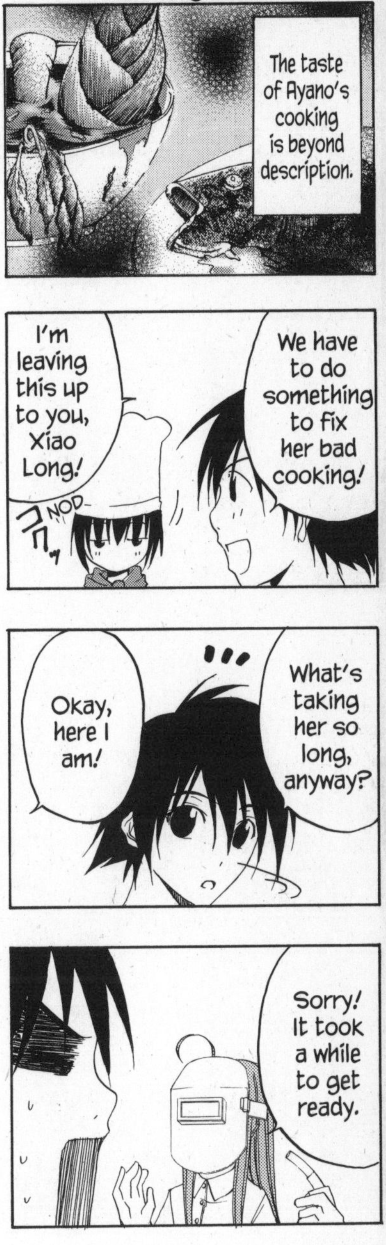
The taste of Ayano's cooking is beyond description.
We have to do something to fix her bad cooking!
I'm leaving this up to you, Xiao Long!
NOD
What's taking her so long, anyway?
...
Okay, here I am!
Sorry! It took a while to get ready.

Extreme Gourmet

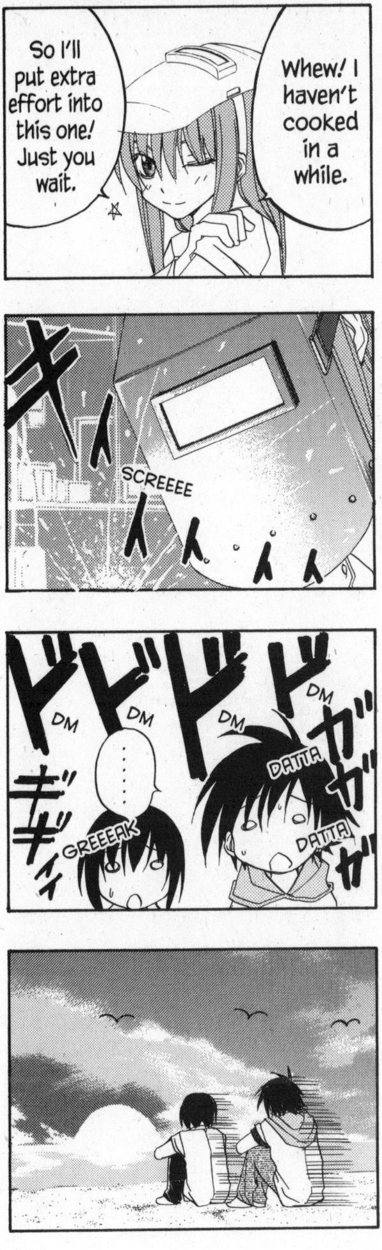
Whew! I haven't cooked in a while.
So I'll put extra effort into this one! Just you wait.
SCREEEE
DM
DM
DM
DM
DATTA
DATTA
......
GREEEAK

Puberty

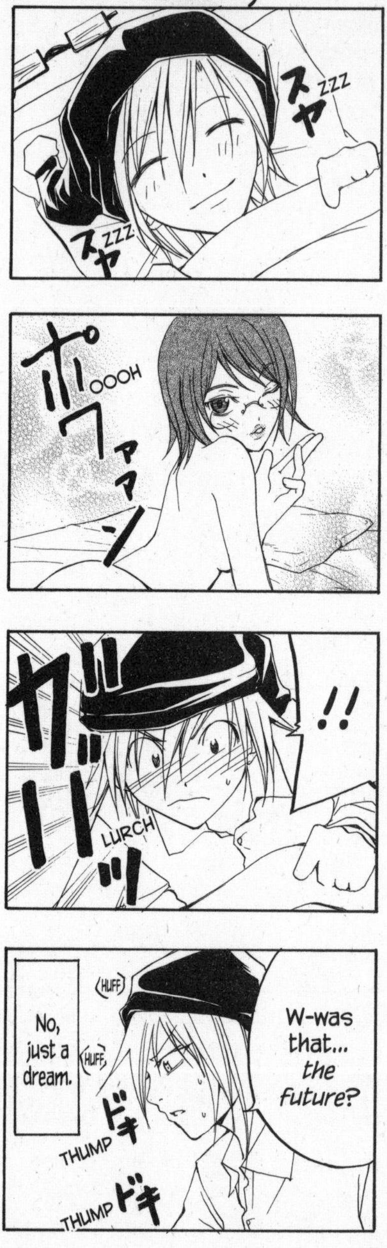
スヤ ZZZ
スヤ ZZZ
ポワァァン OOOH
!!
ガバーッ LURCH
W-was that... *the future?*
(HUFF)
(HUFF)
No, just a dream.
ドキ THUMP
ドキ THUMP

Puberty 2

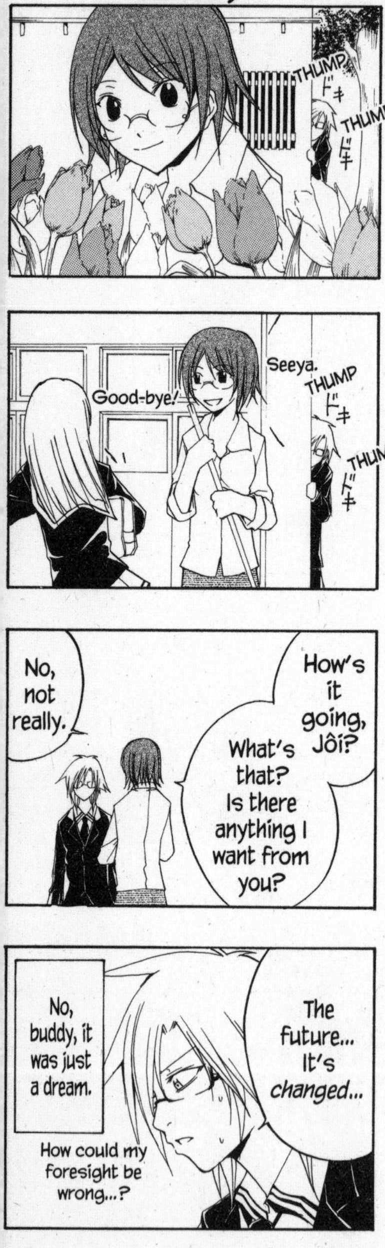
THUMP ドキ
THUMP ドキ
Seeya.
THUMP ドキ
THUMP ドキ
Good-bye!
How's it going, Jôi?
What's that? Is there anything I want from you?
No, not really.
The future... It's *changed...*
No, buddy, it was just a dream.
How could my foresight be wrong...?

Translation Notes

Japanese is a tricky language for most Westerners, and translation is often more an art than a science. For your edification and reading pleasure, here are notes on some of the places where we could have gone in a different direction, or where a Japanese cultural reference is used.

Onibi, page 9

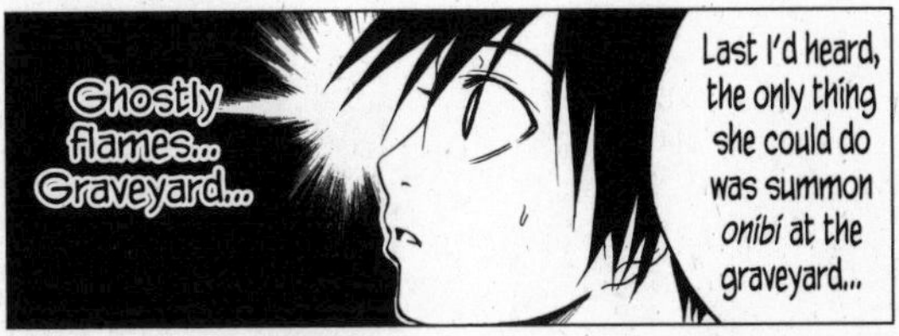
Last I'd heard, the only thing she could do was summon *onibi* at the graveyard...
Ghostly flames... Graveyard...

Onibi, which literally means "ogre flame," is a phenomenon described in much Japanese folklore. The term refers to ghostly, floating flames, much like a will-o'-the-wisp. In some ways it is a synonym for the *hitodama* that appeared in volume 2 of *Psycho Busters* but not in all cases.

Kakeru-kyun, page 104

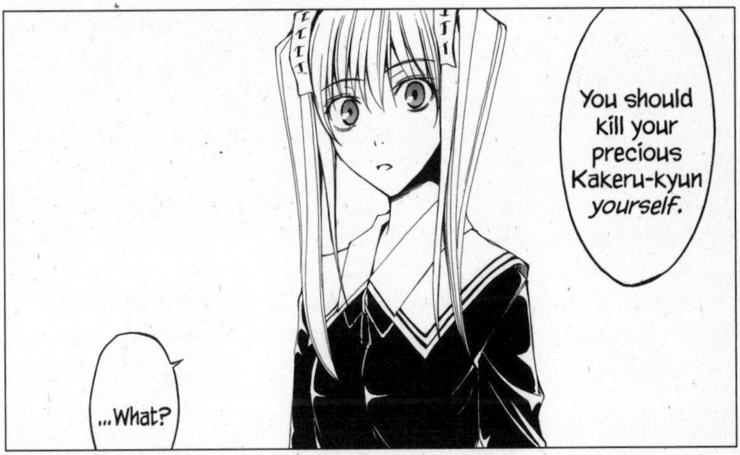
You should kill your precious Kakeru-kyun *yourself.*
...What?

Here Masato Kiryû is teasing Mamidori by twisting Kakeru's name into an embarrassing nickname that sounds like something sweethearts would use on each other, like "Sweetie Poo."

STORY BY KIO SHIMOKU
ART BY KOUME KEITO

FROM THE PAGES OF *GENSHIKEN*!

The Genshiken gang have long obsessed over a manga called *Kujibiki Unbalance*, the story of an average boy who becomes class president at a ritzy academy. Now *Kujibiki Unbalance* is a real-life manga for every fan's enjoyment!

• The eagerly awaited spin-off to the bestselling *Genshiken* series!

Special extras in each volume! Read them all!

VISIT WWW.DELREYMANGA.COM TO:
• Read sample pages
• View release date calendars for upcoming volumes
• Sign up for Del Rey's free manga e-newsletter
• Find out the latest about new Del Rey Manga series

RATING   OT AGES 16+

DEL REY MANGA

The Otaku's Choice™

TOMARE!

[STOP!]

You're going the wrong way!

Manga is a completely different type of reading experience.

To start at the *beginning,* go to the *end*!

That's right! Authentic manga is read the traditional Japanese way—from right to left, exactly the *opposite* of how American books are read. It's easy to follow: Just go to the other end of the book, and read each page—and each panel—from right side to left side, starting at the top right. Now you're experiencing manga as it was meant to be!